Torture, Humiliate, Kill

ETHNIC CONFLICT: STUDIES IN NATIONALITY, RACE, AND CULTURE

Series Editors: Daniel Rothbart and Karina V. Korostelina

TITLES IN THE SERIES

Torture, Humiliate, Kill: Inside the Bosnian Serb Camp System
Hikmet Karčić

Torture, Humiliate, Kill

INSIDE THE BOSNIAN SERB CAMP SYSTEM

Hikmet Karčić

UNIVERSITY OF MICHIGAN PRESS

ANN ARBOR

Copyright © 2022 by Hikmet Karčić
Some rights reserved

This work is licensed under a Creative Commons Attribution-NonCommercial-NoDerivatives 4.0 International License. *Note to users:* A Creative Commons license is only valid when it is applied by the person or entity that holds rights to the licensed work. Works may contain components (e.g., photographs, illustrations, or quotations) to which the rightsholder in the work cannot apply the license. It is ultimately your responsibility to independently evaluate the copyright status of any work or component part of a work you use, in light of your intended use. To view a copy of this license, visit http://creativecommons.org/licenses/by-nc-nd/4.0/

For questions or permissions, please contact um.press.perms@umich.edu

Published in the United States of America by the
University of Michigan Press
Manufactured in the United States of America
Printed on acid-free paper
First published March 2022

A CIP catalog record for this book is available from the British Library.

Library of Congress Cataloging-in-Publication data has been applied for.

ISBN 978-0-472-13296-6 (hardcover : alk. paper)
ISBN 978-0-472-03904-3 (paper: alk. paper)
ISBN 978-0-472-90271-2 (OA)

DOI: https://doi.org/10.3998/mpub.12079875

Library of Congress Control Number: 2021951351

The University of Michigan Press's open access publishing program is made possible thanks to additional funding from the University of Michigan Office of the Provost and the generous support of contributing libraries.

To Zeid,
Forever in our hearts.

Contents

List of Abbreviations	ix
List of Figures	xi
Acknowledgments	xiii
Introduction: Echoes of the Holocaust	1
Chapter 1. History of Ethnic Relations in Bosnia and Herzegovina	10
Chapter 2. Collective Traumatization	30
Chapter 3. Višegrad	75
Chapter 4. Prijedor	107
Chapter 5. Bijeljina	148
Chapter 6. Bileća	170
Chapter 7. Conclusions	191
References	217
Name Index	239
Trial Judgments Index	247
Subject Index	249

Digital materials related to this title can be found on the Fulcrum platform via the following citable URL: https://doi.org/10.3998/mpub.12079875

Abbreviations

1KK	1. Krajiški korpus (1. Krajina Corps)
ARBiH	Armija Republike Bosne i Hercegovine (Army of the Republic of B&H)
ARK	Autonomna Regija Krajina (Autonomous Region Krajina)
B&H	Bosnia and Herzegovina
CSB	Centar službe bezbjednosti (Security Services Center)
CSCE	Conference on Security and Co-operation in Europe
ECMM	European Commission Monitoring Mission
FNU	First Name Unknown
HVO	Hrvatsko vijeće obrane (Croatian Defense Council)
HDZ	Hrvatska demokratska zajednica (Croatian Democratic Union)
ICMP	International Commission on Missing Persons
ICTY	International Criminal Tribunal for the former Yugoslavia
ICRC	International Committee of the Red Cross
JNA	Jugoslovenska narodna armija (Yugoslav People's Army)
MUP	Ministarstvo unutarnjih poslova (Ministry of Interior)
RS	Republika Srpska
SAO	Srpska autonomna oblast (Serbian Autonomous Region)
SDA	Stranka demokratske akcije (Party of Democratic Action)
SDB	Služba državne bezbjednosti (State Security Service)
SDS	Srpska demokratska stranka (Serb Democratic Party)
SJB	Služba javne bezbjednosti (Public Security Station)
SNG	Srpska nacionalna garda (Serbian National Guard)
SPB	Special Police Brigade

X   ABBREVIATIONS

SRS	Srpska radikalna stranka (Serbian Radical Party)
SUP	Sekreterijat unutrašnjih poslova (Secretariat for Internal Affairs)
TO	Teritorijalna odbrana (Territorial Defense)
UN	United Nations
UNHCR	United Nations High Commissioner for Refugees
VRS	Vojska Republike Srpske (Army of Republika Srpska)
WWII	World War Two
ZOBK	Zajednica Opština Bosanske Krajine (Community [Association] of Bosanska Krajina Municipalities)

Figures

Figure 1. A map of Bosnia and Herzegovina in 1992, showing the territories controlled by the Bosnian government, the Bosnian-Croat forces, and the Bosnian Serb forces   xv

Figure 2. Ethnic composition in Višegrad 1991–2013   195

Figure 3. Ethnic Composition in Prijedor 1991–2013   195

Figure 4. Ethnic Composition in Bijeljina 1991–2013   196

Figure 5. Ethnic composition of Bileća in 1991–2013   196

Figure 6. The playground and school building in Trnopolje near Prijedor, used as a camp in 1992   211

Figure 7. The ceramic tile factory Keraterm near Prijedor, used as a camp in 1992   211

Figure 8. The main building and the infamous white house at Omarska mine near Prijedor, used as a camp in 1992   212

Figure 9. The Vilina Vlas spa in Višegrad, used as a rape camp for Bosniak women and girls by Serb forces in 1992   212

Figure 10. The police station in Višegrad, used as a detention facility for Bosniak civilians in 1992.   213

Figure 11. The fire station in Višegrad, used as a detention facility for Bosniak civilians in 1992   213

Figure 12. The Hasan Veletovac School in Višegrad, used as a detention facility for Bosniak civilians in 1992   214

Figure 13. The Batković farm near Bijeljina, site of the concentration camp for Bosniaks and Bosnian Croats by Serb authorities during the entire 1992–95 war   214

xii   FIGURES

Figure 14. The police station in Bileća, used as a detention facility
for Bosniak civilians in 1992   215

Figure 15. The student dormitory in Bileća used as a detention facility
for Bosniak civilians in 1992   215

Figure 16. The Moše Pijada Military Barracks, used as a detention camp
for Bosniak civilians in 1992   216

Figure 17. The old prison in Bileća used as a detention camp for
Bosniak civilians in 1992   216

Acknowledgments

There are so many people who helped make this book possible. I am profoundly grateful to my editors Karina Korostelina and Daniel Rothbart, who accepted and believed in this project from day one. I am especially grateful to Karina, to whom I pitched the idea while on a bus ride from Sarajevo to Srebrenica in 2018.

I would like to thank Elizabeth Sherbun Demers, editorial director, and Haley Winkle, editorial assistant, at the University of Michigan Press for their guidance and support in making the final product possible.

I am especially thankful to my longtime friend and ally Richard Newell, for his careful reading of the manuscript. His valuable comments, suggestions and criticism with a good dose of British cynicism has enriched this book. My thanks also to Nina Newell for all her help and understanding.

I am thankful to Admir Mulaosmanović for his support in overcoming several obstacles in the earlier stages of my writing. This project was part of my work as a researcher of genocide studies at the Institute for Islamic Tradition of Bosniaks in Sarajevo. I am thankful for their support and patience.

I spent several months at the Holocaust and Genocide Studies Department at Keene State College in fall 2017 as the inaugural Auschwitz Institute for the Prevention of Genocide and Mass Atrocities (AIPG)—Keene State College Global Fellow. The lectures and profound discussions with my mentor James Waller were life-changing and broadened my horizons. Professor Paul Vincent let me share an office with him and also selflessly shared knowledge about the Holocaust. Judge Patricia Whalen read segments of the book and gave precious comments. Tom White, John Sturtz, and Celia Rabinowitz helped out with resources and were the best coffee companions. I also extend my thanks to Jan and Rick Cohen for their hospitality and friendship.

While writing this book I benefited from discussions and conversations with friends and colleagues: Amor Mašović, Hariz Halilovich, Marko Attila Hoare, Jasmin Medić, Satko Mujagić, Sudbin Musić, David Pettigrew, Peter Lippman, Emir Suljagić, Avdo Huseinović, Muhamed Mujkić, Samir Šabanija, Suvad Halilović, and many others.

This topic is a deeply personal one. There is no Bosniak family in Bosnia and Herzegovina that has not been affected by the genocide. As a child in the 1990s in Kuala Lumpur, I played with children of concentration camp survivors and remember the narrations of imam Sakib, Samir, Šerif, Seid, and others. Later on, I would meet others whose testimonies inspired me. This book is just one small piece in the large mosaic of literature on the Bosnian genocide.

Special thanks go to those without whom this topic would have been lesser known: the Western journalists who uncovered the camps in the summer of 1992. Their accounts left a lasting impact on me. Books by Roy Gutman, Ed Vulliamy, Peter Maass, and David Rohde as part of my father's library were read and shared by Bosnian expats and refugees.

Throughout my research, my family were a fundamental source of support and advice. My mother, Hamida, and my father, Fikret, always supported me in researching these heavy topics. My brothers Hamza and Harun shared their knowledge and thoughts. I am eternally grateful and indebted for their advice, support, and suggestions.

Last but not least, my wife Amra was my greatest supporter. I thank her for continuous support, inspiration, and patience in the long sleepless nights while I was researching and writing this book. Finally, I would like to thank our son Zeid, born in August 2020, who brought joy into our lives. I held him on my chest while writing responses to the external reviewers. He suddenly passed away at just two months old. This book is dedicated to him. Thank you for letting us be your parents even for this short time.

Figure 1. A map of Bosnia and Herzegovina in 1992, showing the territories controlled by the Bosnian government, the Bosnian-Croat forces, and the Bosnian Serb forces. (Courtesy of Alija Gušić.)

Introduction

Echoes of the Holocaust

During the night of June 28, 1992, in the eastern Bosnian town of Višegrad, hundreds of Bosniak Muslim civilians—mainly women and children along with some elderly males—were incarcerated in the Hasan Veletovac Elementary School, where the sports hall along with other school facilities had been converted into a temporary detention camp for the town's Bosnian Muslim (Bosniak) population. That night, their captors, local Bosnian Serbs, were celebrating Vidovdan (St. Vitus Day), a Serb Orthodox holiday, as well as the 603rd anniversary of the 1389 Kosovo battle in which the invading Ottoman army defeated and subsequently invaded the then Serbian kingdom.

That night, Milan Lukić, an already infamous member of the Bosnian Serb Army, entered the sports hall with his fellow soldiers and took out an elderly man, Ibro Šabanović. His screams were cut short as Milan Lukić and another soldier slit his throat and threw his severed head among the other imprisoned civilians, saying, "Balijas, tonight is Vidovdan, you will all end up like this" and "This is your Kurban."[1,2]

Brutal, personalized, public, and ceremonial executions such as that visited upon Ibro Šabanović were common throughout the Bosnian Serb–run camp system in Bosnia and Herzegovina between 1992 and 1995. Milan Lukić's rhetoric and behavior, laden with ethnoreligious hatred, were echoed by other per-

---

1. *Balija* is a derogative term for Bosniak Muslims.
2. *Kurban* is animal sacrifice Muslims practice on Eid.

petrators throughout the Bosnian Serb camp system, and events that took place in the camps were calculated to inflict deep and indelible trauma on the now unwanted non-Serb population of the fledgling Republika Srpska. Initially kept a secret, their existence became known to the world only after the publication of the disturbing images of detainees at the Omarska and Trnopolje camps in August 1992. The pictures of the emaciated, terrified men trapped behind barbed wire shocked everyone.

In July 1995, in the Buchenwald concentration camp near Weimar in Germany, protestors, gathering in support of Bosnia and Herzegovina and its citizens, carried a banner that read: "Europe learned nothing from the Holocaust—Bosnia is a posthumous victory for Hitler."[3] This provocative statement came a few days after the UN Safe Area Srebrenica was overrun by the Republika Srpska army and details of the genocide were beginning to filter out. The policies of the Republika Srpska authorities during the entire war often resembled those of the Nazis. That is not to say that these two events can be compared, but rather that similarities exist, behaviors were repeated. Journalist Ed Vulliamy, who along with Penny Marshall discovered the camps, has perhaps found the best way to place Serb and Bosnian Serb aggression toward Bosniaks in the context of the Holocaust by writing that the former has *echoes* of the latter.

These echoes became more distinct with the reintroduction of concentration camps into modern Europe. This phenomenon demands research and wider understanding. The camps that existed in the Republika Srpska remain important, since thousands of people who survived them are still affected by the traumas they endured therein. There are many constraints, however, to carrying out such research; first, in the case of the camps formed and run by civilian authorities, there is little or no paper trail, as in most cases the perpetrators did not keep records of a plan to incarcerate or lists of people who were incarcerated. Second and sadly, proper professional research with survivors was not conducted. Testimonies from survivors should have been recorded immediately after their being released, while their memory was still fresh. This book is an attempt to take the first steps in filling a gap that exists in both local and international understanding, and it is regrettably necessary in the face of continued denial by the perpetrators, politicians, press, and academia in both Serbia and the Bosnian Serb entity of Bosnia and Herzegovina, Republika Srpska.

The Serbian attack on Bosnia and Herzegovina in spring 1992 was followed

---

3. "dpa: Bosnier demonstrieren in Gedenkstätte Buchenwald," in FR, 28.7.1995, 5, cited in Margit V. Wunsch Gaarman, *The War in Our Background: The Bosnia and Kosovo War Through the Lenses of the German Print Media* (Berlin: Neofelis Verlag 2015), 117–18.

INTRODUCTION 3

by massive unlawful detentions over the whole territory of the self-proclaimed Republika Srpska, the name the Bosnian Serbs gave to the territory they occupied in Bosnia and Herzegovina. The Yugoslav People's Army, along with local Serb separatists, special forces, and militias had a specific pattern when it came to "cleansing" territories. They started with bombardments, the execution of elites, deportations of women, children, and elderly civilians, and the detention of mostly male civilians. In some cases, entire villages were destroyed and their inhabitants massacred. Throughout the country, dozens of detention/concentration camps were set up for Bosniaks and Croats. Several locations of detention were created exclusively for women as a strategy of organized rape-warfare. These patterns were similar, almost identical, across towns and villages from the Krajina region in Bosnia and Herzegovina's northwest, the Posavina to the north northeast, Gornje and Donje Podrinje to the east, and the Herzegovina regions in the southeast.

These unlawful detentions started in May 1992 and lasted until April 1996, when the last prisoners were finally exchanged. The functioning length of camps and detention facilities differed; some existed either for a short time, such as the Hasan Veletovac School in Višegrad (three months), or, like the camp in Batković near Bijeljina, they lasted for longer periods (three and a half years). Most of these detention facilities and concentration camps, however, existed from May until December 1992. After the media coverage of the Omarska and Trnopolje camps in August 1992, the international community, under public pressure, forced the Bosnian Serbs to close the most well-known camps and either exchange the detainees or set them free to third countries. Other lesser-known locations, those unregistered by the International Committee of the Red Cross and by other international observers, lasted much longer.

It has been, at the time of writing, twenty-six years since the war ended and as yet no concrete research has been done on camps, and neither is there any will to do any since it is a sensitive issue. The survivors, as well as the perpetrators, are still alive and mostly live in the same country, sometimes even the same town, even the same street. The political and academic climate in Republika Srpska vis-à-vis such lines of inquiry is probably best described as hostile. Thus the only research that has been conducted so far is the "Mapping of detention camps in Bosnia and Herzegovina 1992–95," which gathers the raw facts on each and every location.[4] No categorization of the camps or wider context,

---

4. For more information on the project, visit Association TPOS website at http://www.tranzicijska-pravda.org/.

however, is given in the project. Other publications are either too generalized or are personal testimonies. Thus this is the first book that draws the raw data together, placing the camps in both their local historical context and their global context.

The research relies on two sources of primary documentation, court judgments, reports, documents, accepted evidence, and perpetrator documentation. This is supplemented by a range of secondary publications. Court judgments are an important primary source since they provide verified information about the crimes committed and the perpetrators. Thus, a total of fifty-seven judgments, brought by four different types of judicial institutions, are used, including rulings from the International Criminal Tribunal for the Former Yugoslavia (ICTY); the Court of Bosnia and Herzegovina; cantonal courts in the Federation of Bosnia and Herzegovina or regional courts in RS; and one judgment from the Vancouver Federal Court in Canada and another from the Dubrovnik Municipal Court.

The judgments were selected on two bases: first, their territorial connection to the towns presented in this book: Prijedor, Bijeljina, Višegrad, and Bileća, and second, according to political, police, or military responsibility, that is, high-ranking officials and officers whose criminal span of responsibility covered a larger area than the case studied itself.

In pursuing the above, this book relies upon a methodology known as historical comparative research, an approach that studies data on events and conditions in the historical past and/or different societies and from the conclusions generated builds and develops connections and explanations that endure beyond their contemporary context. In this work that means performing a qualitative case-study-based analysis of Bosnia and Herzegovina's concentration camps, as part of a continuum of the overall history of concentration camps, and from this generating a series of conclusions as to what made these particular camps different and what made them the same as those that preceded and followed them. Historical comparative research methods are particularly useful in that they allow us to perform a meso-level analysis,[5] walking the line between the particular (Bosnia and Herzegovina's camps) and the general (the rest of the world's camps) of a meso-level phenomenon, that of genocide's middle managers, the men who created and ran Republika Srpska's camps.

---

5. Matthew Lange, *Comparative Historical Methods* (e-book version) (Newbury Park, CA: Sage Publications, 2013), (printed version, 1–10).

As well as contributing to the emerging literature on concentration camps as a distinct phenomenon, this book is valuable to a wider audience than just the researcher interested in camps themselves. It serves to introduce into the discourse events and facts about places that have thus far remained hidden. While the general reader might (hopefully) have heard of Srebrenica, and just possibly Omarska, who outside of the survivors and a specific circle of academics, journalists, and of course perpetrators has heard of Višegrad, Batković, or Bileća?

So beyond a historical comparative exercise in concentration camp history, this book is a simple statement of facts, shining a light into some of Bosnia and Herzegovina's darkest corners. The names of those killed that fill the following pages were supposed to be erased forever—that is the point of genocide—but here their tragic stories are shared, and the memory of what happened to them, and who did it, are preserved.

Collective Traumatization

The establishment of camps differed from municipality to municipality. These were brutal torture and humiliation camps. In most cases, the men were kept separate from women, whether in parts of the camp or even in different camps. This was the initial shock intended by the perpetrator, the division of families. Those who were executed were considered and identified by the perpetrator as extremists of the highest category. The educated and other elites belonged in this category. Other men were beaten, tortured, sexually abused, and starved. Women and children were kept together in separate camps, where they usually spent a shorter amount of time than the men. The women and girls were raped and sexually abused. Occasionally public ritual executions would take place. Children were threatened in front of their mothers and family members.

The Bosnian Serb perpetrators invented a new purpose for concentration camps: collective traumatization. The primary aspects of the collective traumatization in these camps were torture, sexual abuse, humiliation, and killings. These were the key elements needed in order to inflict pain on a large mass of people. Camps should not be looked at outside of the entire ethnoreligious cleansing project. They were just a tool for a quick and efficient operation in order to establish the Serb *Lebensraum*. The perpetrators were able to, in a short period of time, collectively traumatize large populations of Bosniaks and Croats to such an extent that they would never have the will to return to their homes. Since the crimes were organized and committed by local members of the community, the victims knew the perpetrators. Thus this made the crimes much more personal. The women and children were kept in camps for a few days to a few weeks, depending on the municipality. In this period, women and girls would usually be taken out of the room where the civilians were kept, raped and sexually abused, then returned back to the room after some time. This is visible in the cases of Višegrad (Hasan Veletovac School camp) and Foča (Partisan camp). Other women inside the camp knew that those women had been raped, and they feared for their lives. In most cases, they would also witness public executions and humiliation of fellow detainees.

The main argument of this work is that in the case of Bosnia and Herzegovina, a new motivation or purpose was found for establishing camps: collective traumatization. This is an important argument when one takes into consideration the current academic or public opinion about camps in Bosnia and Herzegovina. On one hand, camps are considered "death camps" (*logori smrti*), but on the other hand they are totally discarded, as with Robert Hayden, whose only remark about Omarska was that it "operated only from late May to late August 1992, and that about 3,000 detainees passed through it during this time." For Hayden, four months and three thousand detainees were nothing remarkable in comparison to the Nazi camps. These theories and opinions are widespread among Western leftist academics who view the Omarska and Trnopolje camp coverage from August 1992 as a Western media conspiracy or a wag-the-dog scenario. Thus I aim to lay down a new theory in which murder was a part of but not the primary aim in the RS camp system.

So what was the intended impact of the detention camps in Serb-held territories? The main position here is that collective traumatization of non-Serbs was the primary aim and intended outcome of the camps. The camps were organized with the sole purpose of severely traumatizing non-Serbs, to the extent they would never return to their prewar homes. The Bosnian Serb authorities could have killed each and every one of the camp detainees if they had wanted to. But instead the perpetrators opted for torture and humiliation with a low-scale mortality rate. It is difficult to get into the mind of the perpetrator and especially gain insight into the plan of the masterminds of the ethnoreligious-cleansing campaign. A pattern of almost identical behavior, however, can be established by looking at the towns discussed in later chapters. The psychological warfare, which the collective traumatization is part of, is an area that needs to be researched in depth. It is certain that the psychological element was a crucial part of the entire Serb cleansing project. One of the first orders given by VRS general Ratko Mladić in the first days of the war, while he was ordering the bombardment of Sarajevo, was "Don't let them sleep at all. Make them go insane."

Meso- and Micro-Level Perpetrators

The cleansing process was conducted on a municipal level, and in the majority of cases the perpetrators knew their victims. The rapists knew who they were raping. The murderers knew who they were killing. This was a very personalized crime. This can be easily concluded through eyewitness testimony and by identifying the status of the perpetrators. These were, to borrow Browning's term, "ordinary men," mostly members of the active or reserve Republika Srpska Police Force.[6] The meso-level involvement in the cleansing process is demonstrated through the role of the Crisis Committees (Krizni štab). The Crisis Committees were the meso-level organizational units that coordinated, instructed, and enforced the cleansing policy that came from the top down. Formed by the Serb Democratic Party, they served as a parallel local governing body on the municipality level.

As it will be later explained in detail, the Crisis Committees were preceded by the establishment of parallel regional institutions called Serbian Autonomous Regions (Srpska autonomna oblast). In order to show the meso-level involvement, the four towns chosen according to these autonomous regions will be discussed in detail: Prijedor (Autonomous Region of Krajina); Bijeljina (Autonomous Region Romanija-Birač); Bileća (Autonomous Region Herzegovina) and Višegrad, which formally was not part of AR Herzegovina. These towns also represent the geographical regions in Bosnia and Herzegovina: Krajina, Semberija, Upper Podrinje, and eastern Herzegovina. Thus the towns were chosen on two bases: geographical position and according to the Serb Autonomous Regions formed prior to the war. By using this political and geographical distribution, a systematic and widespread policy of the detention of non-Serb civilians throughout the Republika Srpska will be shown.

---

6. Christopher Browning, *Ordinary Men: Reserve Police Battalion 101 and the Final Solution in Poland* (New York: Harper Perennial, 1998).

Structure of the Book

Chapter 1: The "History of Ethnic Relations in Bosnia and Herzegovina" gives a brief overview of the rise of nationalist politics in the last years of Yugoslavia. The chapter shows how the Serb elites used events in Kosovo as a catalyst to mobilize their masses in both Serbia and Bosnia and Herzegovina. The emotive symbolism of (a supposedly under threat) Kosovo, in combination with grievances related to the genocide of Serbs in the Second World War at the hands of the primarily Croatian Nazi allies, the Ustaša, were a perfect match for the rebirth of the new Serbian nationalist movement. The chapter shows how the resurgent nationalism helped fuel the creation of parallel state institutions in Bosnia and Herzegovina—the Serb Autonomous Regions—which were set up as a basis for a future "Greater Serbian state." The foundation of the project was the Six Strategic Goals of the Serbian People, promulgated on May 12, 1992, a moment on a local level similar to the Wannsee Conference, which laid down the aims of the Serb people in wartime.

Chapter 2: "Collective Traumatization." Drawing from Raphael Lemkin and wide range of other authorities on genocide and camps, this chapter lays the theoretical groundwork for our assertions that the Bosnian Serb ethnic cleansing was genocidal; that the camps were an integral and evidential part of this; that along with violence and murder, the primary function that the camps served within the process of genocidal ethnic cleansing was to collectively traumatize the Bosniak detainees; and that this campaign of traumatization is in and of itself genocidal. The second part of the chapter gives a brief overview of the global history of concentration camps.

Chapter 3: "Višegrad" deals with the eastern Bosnian town of Višegrad and gives an overview of the town and the military and political events that happened there in 1992. Seven camps and detention facilities are presented: Hasan Veletovac School, the Višegrad Spa, Vilina Vlas Hotel, the fire station, the police station, the Dobrun Community Center, and the Orahovci Elementary School. The conditions and events in the camps are explained in detail and are placed within the context of the events that were taking place around them, such as deportations, massacres, the destruction of religious buildings, and filling of mass graves. An analysis of perpetrators who took part in operating the camps is also given.

Chapter 4: "Prijedor" offers a detailed insight into the most infamous camps of the war—Omarska, Keraterm, Trnopolje, and Manjača—whose existence became known due to their discovery by Western journalists in the summer of

1992. The images of the "man behind the wire" caused outrage throughout the world. The case of Prijedor is unique because the role of the Crisis Committee—a temporary governing body in the municipality—is well-documented, unlike the rest of the cases examined here. This chapter also discusses the profile of the perpetrators as well as events that took place before the camp's creation, including the massacres, cultural destruction, and, again, the construction of mass graves.

Chapter 5: "Bijeljina" is a town located on the Drina River and the border with Serbia. The chapter describes how it was the first town to be attacked, from across the border in Serbia, before the war officially started. Unlike other towns, Bijeljina had one large camp—Batković—which existed during the entire period of the war and served as a regional and transit camp. This chapter also deals with the issue of a specific case of "voluntary removal" in which Bosniaks who lived in ghettoized communities were forced to pay for their own deportations.

Chapter 6: "Bileća" describes the events in a small eastern Herzegovinian town with a small Bosniak minority. The chapter provides, in detail, the conditions and events inside the Bileća police station, the Stari zatvor (Old Jail), the Moše Pijade Military Barracks and Đački dom (Student Dormitory). It also shows how detainees from various other neighboring towns were transported back and forth throughout the region as part of a coordinated regional effort. Another specific element is the description of the main perpetrators, who were members of a special police unit.

Chapter 7: "Conclusions" gives an analysis of the main elements the camps had in common, and the similarities between the overall cleansing process in the towns presented in the previous chapters. An explanation of the collective traumatization strategy along with its constitutive components are explored town by town. The perpetrators are profiled, and it is shown that a majority of the perpetrators were members of the Bosnian Serb regular or reserve police force. In addition to this, the long-term effects of this collective traumatization is presented by showing the drastic demographic changes in the municipalities by presenting the prewar and postwar population census. Lastly, the main conclusions about the specifics of the Republika Srpska camp system as well as its ethnoreligious cleansing process are provided and placed in a larger historical perspective showing that each genocide is unique, but that perpetrators learn from each other.

CHAPTER 1

History of Ethnic Relations in Bosnia and Herzegovina

Background

Several years after the death of Josip Broz Tito, in 1986 the Serbian Academy of Arts and Sciences (SANU) drafted a memorandum that claimed that Serbs in Yugoslavia were victims of discrimination in other republics; Serbs living in Croatia and Bosnia were the victims of economic and political oppression, while in Kosovo they were at risk of genocide at the hands of the Kosovar Albanians. The draft of this memorandum was published by *Večernje Novosti*. Its raw nationalism and the sheer scale of its fabrications stunned the people of Yugoslavia. It was, as Kemal Kurspahić clearly states, "the first document to challenge the foundations of the Yugoslav federation with the unofficial approval of a prominent national institution such as the Serbian Academy of Arts and Sciences."[1] Kurspahić identifies the memorandum's four key claims: (a) that within Yugoslavia there was a disturbed balance between the principle of unity and the principle of autonomy, thus denying the Serbian nation their right to have their own state. Naturally, this lead to the call for "All Serbs in one state"; (b) there was consistent discrimination against Serb economy "in the context of the political and economic dominance of Slovenia and Croatia" in Yugoslavia; (c) these vindictive policies have grown even stronger, to the point of genocide, and (d) that the (alleged) physical, political, legal, and cultural genocide of the Serbian population currently underway in Kosovo and Meto-

---

1. Kemal Kurspahić, *Prime Time Crime* (Washington: United States Institute of Peace Press, 2003), 31.

hija was a worse defeat than any experienced in the wars waged by Serbia since the First Serbian Uprising against the Ottoman Turks in 1804.

SANU knew that these allegations, about Kosovo in particular, would be a powerful catalyst for mobilizing Serb masses. SANU did not forget, however, to mention Bosnia and Herzegovina as well: "The leaders of the artificially created Muslim nation have done everything in their power to turn Bosnia and Herzegovina into a republic under the domination of the Muslim population."[2] The timing was right for low-level Communist Party member Slobodan Milošević to come to power. Using propaganda and media as his main tools, Milošević rose to the position of president of the Central Committee of the League of Communists of Serbia.

In April 1987, a group of Serb and Montenegrin activists gathered at Kosovo Polje to protest the alleged mistreatment of Serbs in Kosovo and to tell Milošević firsthand the terror they were enduring under (again, alleged) Albanian oppression.[3] The crowds chanted, "They are beating us" and "murderers, murderers," referring to the Albanian-majority police. Milošević at that moment appears heroically and states to the crowd, in front of the TV cameras, "Nobody is allowed to beat you." The hero-like image of Milošević, a young politician defending the rights of Serb minority in Kosovo, was repeated on TV and in newspapers ad infinitum, primarily to help Milošević with popular support and allow him to seize the position of president from his long-time mentor, Ivan Stambolić.

The right moment to deal with the Kosovo question came in September 1987 when a mentally disturbed Albanian JNA army conscript, Aziz Keljmendi, ran amok and killed four soldiers in his barracks and injured four others. Milošević's media saw this as a great opportunity and used this killing to portray the Serbs as victims of Albanian terrorists. Milošević and his allies eventually secured the removal of Stambolić and all other potential opponents and he was finally elected as president of the Socialist Republic of Yugoslavia. The next major event that helped pave the road to Milošević's final success was the six hundredth anniversary of the Battle of Kosovo on June 28, 1989, at Kosovo Polje. The event was a public relations triumph, as almost a million supporters gathered to hear him.

The 1389 Battle of Kosovo saw the Serbian kingdom, led by Prince Lazar, fall

---

2. Kemal Kurspahić, *Prime Time Crime*, 33.
3. The BBC documentary *Yugoslavia: Death of a Nation* (1995) clearly shows that this was a staged event.

to the ever-encroaching might of the Ottoman Empire. Although insignificant for the Ottomans, this battle and defeat was crucial in the construction of the victimhood myth of Serbdom, and Prince Lazar became a heroic icon in Serb nationalist mythology. Milošević skillfully used the anniversary of the battle to warn Yugoslav's Serbs that Kosovo and its Serbs were once again under threat and the enemies were still Muslims, but this time around they were Albanian. On live TV and in front of the vast crowd, bussed in from all over Yugoslavia, he stated, "The Kosovo heroism has been inspiring our creativity for six centuries, and has been feeding our pride and does not allow us to forget that at one time we were an army great, brave, and proud, one of the few that remained undefeated when losing."[4] He then went on to state, "Six centuries later, now, we are being again engaged in battles and are facing battles. They are not armed battles, although such things cannot be excluded yet. However, regardless of what kind of battles they are, they cannot be won without resolve, bravery, and sacrifice, without the noble qualities that were present here in the field of Kosovo in the days past."[5] Lastly, he portrays the Serbs as defenders of Europe from the *eastern occupiers*: "Six centuries ago, Serbia heroically defended itself in the field of Kosovo, but it also defended Europe. Serbia was at that time the bastion that defended the European culture, religion, and European society in general."[6] With this, the ideological ground was prepared for all that was to come, and one year later, through constitutional changes, the autonomy of Vojvodina and Kosovo was abolished. Both were absorbed into Milošević's Greater Serbia.

Tensions between Serbia and Croatia grew as their competing nationalisms fed off each other. Talk of secession from Yugoslavia was common in both Slovenia and Croatia, while in return Milošević spoke of the need to ensure that Serbs living in Croatia and Bosnia and Herzegovina would remain in a Serbian state. Naturally, these tensions began to make themselves felt in Bosnia and Herzegovina too. Bosnian Croats formed the HDZ BiH, which primarily served as the Bosnian wing of its parent, the HDZ, Croatia's largest political party, led by Franjo Tuđman. In 1990, Serbs in Croatia, under Jovan Rašković, formed the Serbian Democratic Party, while Radovan Karadžic also formed a Serbian Democratic Party (SDS) in Bosnia and Herzegovina. Milošević regarded both

---

4. Slobodan Milošević, St. Vitus Day Speech, Gazimestan, June 28, 1989, https://bit.ly/SlobMilStVDay.
5. Slobodan Milošević, St. Vitus Day Speech.
6. Slobodan Milošević, St. Vitus Day Speech.

parties as natural extensions of his own party, the SPS, and indeed this is how the relationship functioned for most of the war.

In 1990, elections were held in Bosnia and Herzegovina. All three main parties had been formed on an ethnic basis, and they relied heavily on memory politics to mobilize the masses. The Bosnian Croats (HDZ) commemorated victims of the Bleiburg massacre and murders of Franciscan priests at the end of World War II.[7] The Bosniak party (SDA) commemorated the World War II genocide of Bosniaks from eastern Bosnia, committed by Serb nationalists (Četniks). The Serbs (across Yugoslavia) were by far the most creative, however. In the runup to the Milošević's Kosovo Polje speech, the Serb Orthodox Church had sent the remains of Prince Lazar on tour through all Serb areas of the region, provoking deeply emotional responses. Subsequently, the Serb Democratic Party (SDS) organized the exhumations of Serb genocide victims from World War II. The exhumed victims were reburied in a huge mass funeral attended by political and religious dignitaries. Velibor Ostojić, a high-ranking Serb politician, would later explain the importance of reburials: "We began with excavation of the remains of the Serbian people who were brutally killed during World War II. It was a warning regarding all the misconceptions that the Serbian people accepted about the shared life with the enemies. All of a sudden, the Serbian people felt that they had been deceived."[8] Accompanied by this, there was what Michael Sells calls "a pornography of victimhood,"[9] as Serb-owned magazines, newspapers, and TV stations poured out a constant stream of images showing the dismembered bodies of Serbs murdered by the Ustaša during World War II.

Democracy and Division in Bosnia and Herzegovina

With the fall of the communism throughout Eastern Europe, the citizens of Yugoslavia sought democratic elections. In November 1990, the first demo-

---

7. David B. MacDonald, *Balkan Holocausts? Serbian and Croatian Victim-Centred Propaganda and the War in Yugoslavia* (Manchester: Manchester University Press, 2002), 145.

8. Adis Makšić, "Priming the Nation for War: An Analysis of Organizational Origins and Discursive Machinations of the Serb Democratic Party in Pre-war Bosnia-Herzegovina, 1990–1992," *Journal of Muslim Minority Affairs* 35, no. 3 (August 2015): 338, https://doi.org/10.1080/13602004.2015.1073959.

9. Michael Sells, "Crosses of Blood: Sacred Space, Religion, and Violence in Bosnia-Hercegovina," *Sociology of Religion* 64, no. 3, Special Issue (Autumn 2003): 313, https://doi.org/10.2307/3712487.

cratic elections were held in Bosnia and Herzegovina, in which the three (SDA, HDZ, and SDS) main ethnic-based political parties (two of them with strong links to Belgrade or Zagreb) gained a majority of the votes.

By February 1991, the SDS already started to plan in case the federal republic of Yugoslavia ceased to function. On February 23, 1991, a confidential SDS position paper was drafted: "Modus Operandi of Municipalities in the Conditions that Republican Organs Cease to Function," which stated that "power would devolve to municipal agencies which would co-operate with federal agencies if republican organs ceased to function." The same document also foresaw the use of the Yugoslav People's Army (JNA) and security forces in this situation.[10]

In 1991, the Ministry of Information of the Republic of Serbia published a small booklet titled "The Creation and Changes of the Internal Borders of Yugoslavia." This booklet contained several academic pieces by Serb intellectuals regarding the borders and disintegration of Yugoslavia. This was state propaganda aimed at a foreign, English-speaking, diplomatic, and academic audience. In an interview section of the booklet titled "Possible Borders of New Yugoslavia," Dr. Jovan Ilić, a geographer and professor at the Natural Science and Mathematics Faculty in Belgrade gave answers and predictions on several questions related to the dissolution of Yugoslavia. Replying to the question "What would happen in the event of a dissociation with Bosnia and Herzegovina?" Ilić replied that "the population of Bosnia and Herzegovina is extremely inter-mixed. The degree of inter-mingling is even more drastic if we observe the settlements. It is, therefore, extremely difficult to delimit on a national basis." He then states that it is yet still possible to find territories where one nation is a majority. He gives the example of Serb majority regions:

Serbs are predominant in Western Bosnia, and Croats in Western Herzegovina and in a smaller part of Northern Bosnia. Territories predominantly inhabited by Serbs are inter-linked. Both territories, along with the commune of Prijedor where the Serbs are in the relative majority, cover an area of 20,300 sq. meters. This in fact means that, if viewed individually, they are vaster than Slovenia, Montenegro and Kosovo and Metohija.[11]

---

10. Christian Axboe Nielsen, "The Bosnian Serb Ministry of Internal Affairs: Genesis, Performance and Command and Control, 1990–1992," United Nations International Criminal Tribunal for the Former Yugoslavia, research report prepared for the case of Krajišnik (IT-00-39), updated for Mićo Stanišić (IT-04-79). Corrected version May 19, 2011, 19.

11. Stanoje Ivanović, ed., *The Creation and Changes of the Internal Borders of Yugoslavia* (Belgrade: Ministry of Information of the Republic of Serbia, 1991), 99.

HISTORY OF ETHNIC RELATIONS IN BOSNIA AND HERZEGOVINA   15

Ilić's recommendation, in the case of Croatia's secession, was to divide Bosnia and Herzegovina. Western Herzegovina and parts of Posavina (i.e., territories with Croat majorities) would be given to Croatia. Eastern Herzegovina would be annexed to Montenegro. The Serbian Autonomous Region of Krajina would be annexed to Bosnia and thus a new federal unit would be formed. It would be part of a new Federal Yugoslavia. Ilić ends his answer by stating that "Serbs and Muslims can live together. As regards mentality, ethno-psychic construction, Muslims and Serbs are much closer to each other than Muslims and Croats."

Clearly there were not many homogeneous areas for the ethnic groups in Bosnia and Herzegovina. Drawing any new borders would clearly not be easy, nor could it be done without bloodshed or forced migration.

At beginning of 1991, as Yugoslavia began to separate, both Croatia and Serbia saw a historical opportunity to carve up Bosnia and Herzegovina between them for their *greater state* projects. This was a chance for the presidents of the republics of Serbia and Croatia to leave a triumphant and victorious legacy. Their nationalistic ideologies both found historical sources to their claims on Bosnia and Herzegovina. The Serbs cited Jovan Cvijić's 1908 publication "The Annexation of Bosnia-Herzegovina and the Serb Issue," while the Croats referred to Stjepan Radić's study "The Live Croatian Rights to Bosnia-Herzegovina." As David B. MacDonald states,

> For Croatia, the addition of Bosnian and Hercegovinian lands would have substantially reduced its eastern border with Serbia, creating an important buffer zone between Dalmatia and Serbia proper. The Serbs likewise saw the merits of incorporating this geo-strategic region into their smaller rump-Yugoslavia, giving them a much larger common border with Croatia. Each regime thus had political and military objectives in mind, which made the annexation of Bosnian territory paramount.[12]

Things became more complicated for Bosnia and Herzegovina in March 1991. A population census showed that a plurality of its population (43.7 percent) was Muslim (Bosniaks), while Serbs comprised 31.1 percent and Croats 17.3 percent.[13] Although many Serb intellectuals had already been issuing dire

---

12. MacDonald, *Balkan Holocausts?*, 220–21.
13. Federalni zavod za statistiku (Yugoslav Federal Bureau of Statistics), "Popis stanovništva 1991," 1991 Census of Bosnia and Herzegovina, now available at Bosna i Hercegovina Federalni zavod

16   TORTURE, HUMILIATE, KILL

warnings about the growing Muslim populations in both Kosovo and Bosnia and Herzegovina, the new results provided Serb nationalists a powerful weapon to pursue their goals.

On March 25, 1991, a meeting was held between Franjo Tuđman and Slobodan Milošević in Karađorđevo, Serbia. Although details from this meeting are not available, there is significant evidence that suggests that it was at this meeting the division of Bosnia and Herzegovina was agreed upon by the two leaders. Bosnia and Herzegovina was to be divided along the lines proposed in the 1939 Cvetković-Maček agreement. Never fully implemented due to the outbreak of World War II and Nazi Germany's subsequent invasion of Yugoslavia in 1941, the plan allocated large parts of Bosnia and Herzegovina contiguous to Croatia to Zagreb, while the rest of central and eastern Bosnia and Herzegovina was to be allocated to Belgrade. No independent space was envisaged for Bosniaks.

The 1939 plan to divide Bosnia and Herzegovina was never implemented. However, 1991 seemed like a good time to both Tuđman and Milošević to correct this historical *mistake*.[14] Although Milošević cunningly always denied this, Tuđman on the other hand bragged about it on multiple occasions. In order to split the inevitable resistance of the Bosniaks, Milošević attempted to strike a deal (the Belgrade Initiative) with prominent Bosniak businessman and political pretender Adil Zulfikarpašić. This rapidly failed however and soon new, increasingly radical forms of intimidation of Bosniaks began. With Bosniaks a plurality in the country and with signals from the major Bosniak political establishment that they would not be willing to let their country be divided, Serb and Croat separatists opted for the establishment of parallel semiautonomous regions as a first step to splitting away from Bosnia and Herzegovina.

Parallel State Institutions

In February 1991, once it had become clear that neither Bosniaks or Bosnian Croats were willing to live in a Serb-dominated rump Yugoslavia, the Banja Luka branch of the SDS announced a plan to establish the Community of Municipalities of Bosanska Krajina (Zajednica Opstina Bosanske Krajine—

---

za statistiku—The Bosnian and Herzegovinan Federal Bureau of Statistics, https://bit.ly/PopisStan1991.

14. See testimonies by Ante Marković, Stjepan Mesić, and Herbert Okun available at https://bit.ly/ICTYAnteMTest, https://bit.ly/ICTYStipeMTest, https://bit.ly/ICTYHerbOTest.

ZOBK). The ZOBK was formed in April and initially was represented as an economic and cultural region.[15] This was an imitation of the breakaway Croatian Serb autonomous regions formed just across the border in Croatia. The ZOBK, subsequently renamed Autonomous Region of Krajina (Autonomna Regija Krajina—ARK), was formed on September 16, 1991. In central Bosnia, in the environs surrounding Sarajevo to the south and east, the Autonomous Region of Romanija was formed on September 17, 1991. In northeastern Bosnia, the Serb Autonomous Region of Birač-Semberija was formed on September 19, 1991. All these regions had a mini-state-like structure. Their leadership comprised mainly SDS members, most of whom had already held positions in the preseparation municipal and state governments.

Ten days after the Bosnian parliament voted for secession from Yugoslavia on October 24, 1991, the Bosnian Serb political establishment formed an illegal and unconstitutional Serbian assembly, which again was composed predominantly of Bosnian Serb SDS members from municipalities throughout Bosnia and Herzegovina. At the assembly, SDS cofounder and leader Radovan Karadžić told the Serb delegates, "This is a historic step, a step the Serbian people take to shatter the last illusions, to discern between its friends and enemies, and to round our entity in such a way that [one word redacted] it would never again find itself endangered from within."[16] This was the moment when the autonomous regions were to be amalgamated into one state-like structure. The Bosnian Serb assembly organized a plebiscite in November 1991, which was to determine if Serbs in Bosnia and Herzegovina wished to remain in Yugoslavia or not. Just before the plebiscite, Karadžić stated, "I am asking you to be energetic and strict; to get ready and establish authority in your territories; in municipalities, regions, local communities, and to prepare yourselves for restructuring and regionalizing the municipalities."[17]

On December 20, 1991, during an SDS meeting at the Holiday Inn in Sarajevo, a secret document was given to the SDS municipality leaders. This document was the "Instruction for Organization and Activity of Organs for the Serb People in Bosnia and Herzegovina in Extraordinary Circumstances." This instruction had two variants. As historian Patrick Treanor explained, "Variant

---

15. Adis Makšić, *Ethnic Mobilization, Violence, and the Politics of Affect: The Serb Democratic Party and the Bosnian War* (London: Palgrave Macmillan, 2017), 139.

16. Prosecutor v. Radovan Karadžić ("Prosecution's Submission Pursuant to Rule 65 ter (E)(i)-(iii)"), IT-95-5/18-PT (International Criminal Tribunal for the former Yugoslavia (ICTY)), May 18, 2009, 11, https://bit.ly/ICTYKaradzic090518.

17. Prosecutor v. Radovan Karadžić, 12.

A implied the total takeover of power in municipalities where Serbs were the majority, and its implementation started immediately after it was adopted. Variant B was only announced as the next phase, and it was actually adopted on February 14, 1992 after an independence referendum for Bosnia-Hercegovina had been called by the Bosnian government."[18] The instructions contained two important points for each municipality: the establishment of an Assembly of Serb People and the establishment of a Crisis Committee. In variant A, the Crisis Committee would be headed by the president of the assembly. In variant B, the Crisis Committee would be headed by the president of the SDS. The function of the Crisis Committee was to act as an ad hoc municipal government with a small number of members, making expeditious decisions and coordinating activities with the army, police and other higher institutions. These Crisis Committees played a central role in the *cleansing* process. The establishment of camps and detention facilities, lists of "extremists," and deportations were operated and coordinated by the Crisis Committee.

During one of the SDS meetings in December 1991, senior Bosnian Serb official Momčilo Krajišnik instructed delegates to authorize local party officials to "form municipal assemblies of the Serb people in existing municipalities where the SDS does not have a majority of the seats."[19] The main idea was to establish parallel institutions, draw new municipal borders, and thus isolate Bosniaks. Vojo Kuprešanin, president of ARK, stated, "I personally think that our living space and the territory where we live and work is threatened, and we must avert that danger. In fact we must prevent Muslims from moving into our territories and space."[20] On January 9, 1992, the Serb Republic of Bosnia and Herzegovina was declared. At the same time, the official gazette was formed and published and other formal, informal, and ad hoc organs were established. The aim of this declaration was to undermine the referendum for independence that was planned for February 29 and March 1, 1992. Karadžić realized that if the Serb minority raised its voice and concern before Bosnia and Herzegovina officially proclaimed independence, it would simplify the takeover of municipalities.[21] Only after the Bosnian parliament voted to hold a referendum

---

18. Velma Šarić, "Bosnian Serb Power Grab Was Pre-Planned," *Institute for War and Peace Reporting* (*IWPR*), June 3, 2011, https://iwpr.net/global-voices/bosnian-serb-power-grab-was-pre-planned.
19. Robert Donia, *Radovan Karadžić: Architect of the Bosnian Genocide* (Cambridge: Cambridge University Press, 2014), 129.
20. Donia, *Radovan Karadžić*, 130–31.
21. Karadžić made an interesting statement at the SDS Deputies Club in February 1992: "[U]ntil two or three months ago we were hoping to be able to play the 'Yugoslav card' [. . .]. This is slipping out of

HISTORY OF ETHNIC RELATIONS IN BOSNIA AND HERZEGOVINA   19

on independence did the Bosnian Serbs' plans change and the idea of establishing a Serb state within Bosnia and Herzegovina rapidly became a reality. On January 9, 1992, the Bosnian Serb municipalities were consolidated to form "Republika Srpska." Later on, the Bosnian Serbs' plans would radicalize further as they launched the twin tasks of claiming territory and "cleansing" it.[22] At around the same time, during the SDS's formation of its autonomous regions, HDZ BiH also declared the establishment of Herceg-Bosna in November 1991.[23] This para-state within Bosnia and Herzegovina was to be composed of municipalities with a Croat majority. During the next couple of years, Herceg-Bosna enjoyed the full support of the Croatian state, including its president, Franjo Tuđman.[24]

Genocidal Intent

In September 1991, the Bosnian parliament held a debate on Bosnia and Herzegovina's future in Yugoslavia. SDA and HDZ proposed secession. This angered the Bosnian Serb political establishment, most visibly Radovan Karadžić. In intercepted telephone calls, Karadžić, while talking to his friends and colleagues, made it very clear what was to happen to the Bosniak people if they opted for secession and independence. In September 1991, while debates in parliament were still being held, Karadžić told Krajišnik to tell the Bosniaks, "Can you see where this leads?" and "Do you realize that you will disappear in this? . . . Man, you will disappear. Many of us will disappear, but you will be

---

our grasp. That's why we started on another track: a Serbian Bosnia and Herzegovina. Our sovereign right, our army. We are preparing the constitutional framework to be able to have immediately [. . .] to have a national guard, to have our own police force, to have a government, to turn the Yugoslav army into the army of the Serbian Bosnia and Herzegovina." See Prosecutor v. Radovan Karadžić (Judgment), IT-95-5/18-T (ICTY), March 24, 2016, 1079–80, https://bit.ly/ICTYKaradzic160324.

22. Benjamin Valentino argues that genocide is a solution after other plans fail, while Michael Mann argues that "organic nationalism" is the initiator of genocide. I would argue that in the case of the Bosnian Serbs, it was a combination of both these theories. See Scott Straus, "The Promise and Limits of Comparison: The Holocaust and the 1994 Genocide in Rwanda," in *Is the Holocaust Unique? Perspectives on Comparative Genocide*, ed. Alan S. Rosenbaum (Boulder, CO: Westview Press, 1997), 251.

23. Richard Caplan, *Europe and the Recognition of New States in Yugoslavia* (Cambridge: Cambridge University Press, 2005), 129.

24. Six high-ranking Herceg-Bosna officials were sentenced for Joint Criminal Enterprise for cleansing of Bosniaks in Herzegovina. See Prosecutor v. Jadranko Prlić, Bruno Stojić, Slobodan Praljak, Milivoj Petković, Valentin Ćorić, Berislav Pušić (Prosecutor v. Prlić et al.) (Judgment, Volume III), IT-04-74-A (ICTY), November 29, 2017, 1400–1409, https://bit.ly/ICTYPrlic171129.

annihilated!"[25] On October 12, 1991, just two days before the parliamentary vote on the future of Bosnia and Herzegovina, Karadžić spoke to his Belgrade friend and poet Gojko Đogo: "I think that they should be beaten if they start the war. . . . They will disappear, that people will disappear from the face of the earth if they, if they insist now."[26] A few days later, he talked to his brother Luka Karadžić, where he repeated his threat that there "would be a war until their obliteration. . . . First of all, none of their leaders would stay alive. They would all be killed in three or four hours. They couldn't stand a chance."[27]

On September 14, 1991, during the parliamentary debates and the vote on secession, Karadžić publicly threatened the Bosniak people: "Do not think you will not lead Bosnia and Herzegovina into hell and the Muslim people into possible annihilation, as the Muslim people cannot defend themselves in case of war here."[28] In July 1992, during a Bosnian Serb assembly meeting, Karadžić stated that "this conflict was roused in order to eliminate the Muslims. [. . .] They think they are being nationally established, but in fact they are vanishing."[29] The threats given by Karadžić in public were mirrored by other SDS officials. Sveto Veselinović, SDS president in Rogatica, told Muslims that "all the Muslims will disappear" and that "everything's going to be the way it should be: A third of the Muslims will be killed, a third become Orthodox, and a third will escape."[30]

Dehumanization/ Portraying the Other

In order to give moral legitimacy to their political aims and to prepare themselves and their voters for a seemingly inevitable conflict, the Bosnian Serb leadership, in concert with the leadership in Belgrade, stepped up their rhetorical attacks on Bosnia's Muslims. Media channels and political speeches were filled with poisonous rhetoric, designed to terrify Serbs and convince them of the need to separate, and in doing to to defend or take what was "rightfully" theirs.

Three main ideas were promulgated that portrayed Bosniaks as an existen-

---

25. Prosecutor vs. Radovan Karadžić (Judgment), IT-95-5/18-T (ICTY), 1032.
26. Prosecutor vs. Radovan Karadžić, 1032.
27. Prosecutor vs. Radovan Karadžić, 1032.
28. Prosecutor vs. Radovan Karadžić, 1032.
29. Prosecutor vs. Radovan Karadžić, 1032.
30. Prosecutor vs. Radovan Karadžić, 1032.

tial threat: (1) Bosniaks as subhuman, (2) Islamophobia (stoking fears of return of Muslim rule to the Balkans), and (3) portraying Bosniaks as descendants of Ustaša, war criminals upon whom revenge must be taken.

Bosniaks as subhuman. Amidst many, two notable examples of discussions of Bosniaks as being subhuman spring to mind. First, Biljana Plavšić, a professor of biology at the University of Sarajevo and later a high-ranking Bosnian Serb politician, stated, "It was genetically deformed material that embraced Islam. And now, of course, with each successive generation it simply becomes concentrated. It gets worse and worse. It simply expresses itself and dictates their style of thinking, which is rooted in their genes. And through the centuries, the genes degraded further."[31] Second, a quote from former assistant commander for morale, religion and legal affairs in the Sarajevo-Romanija Corps, Luka Dragičević, stated in his guidelines on lifting the moral of soldiers: "We are genetically stronger, better, handsomer and smarter. . . . Remember how many Muslims there were among the ten best pupils, students, soldiers? Precious few. Why? Because they are *poturice*[32] and only the weakest among the Serbs became *poturice*."[33]

Islamophobia. Bosniaks in Bosnia and Herzegovina were portrayed as wanting to establish a Muslim state, implement Shariah law and rule over non-Muslims as second-class citizens.[34] Myths of a "Green Transversal," or "Islamic Arc" were promoted. *New York Times* journalist Roger Cohen wrote about how, in an interview with the Bosnian Serb general staff they eagerly "display[ed] maps in which they pencil in what they call 'the green transversal'—an alleged Islamic plan of sinister scope to establish power from Bihac, south of Zagreb, all the way eastward to Albania and so, they claim, cut the Christian world in half." In an interview, a soldier told Cohen, "If we don't stop Islam now, fundamentalism will dominate Europe in 10 to 20 years."[35]

---

31. Maya Shatzmiller, ed., *Islam and Bosnia: Conflict Resolution and Foreign Policy in Multi-Ethnic States* (Montreal: McGill-Queen's University Press, 2002), 58.
32. *Poturice* is a derogative term, used to insult someone who had supposedly betrayed their ethnicity by converting to Islam. Many Serb nationalists simply viewed Bosniaks as treacherous Serbs who long ago had broken faith with orthodoxy out of moral weakness in return for personal gain and comfort.
33. "Mladic's Witness: Serbs are Genetically Stronger, Better, Handsomer and Smarter," *Sense Agency*, August 9, 2014, http://archive.sensecentar.org/vijesti.php?aid=15996.
34. A good overview of the origins of this bigotry can be found in Admir Mulaosmanović, "Islam and Muslims in Greater Serbian Ideology: The Origins of an Antagonism and the Misuse of the Past," *Journal of Muslim Minority Affairs* 39, no. 3 (September 2019): 300–316, DOI: 10.1080/13602004.2019.1652408.
35. Roger Cohen, "Cross vs. Crescent; The Battle Lines Are Being Redrawn in Bosnia along Old Religious Scars," *New York Times*, September 17, 1992, https://bit.ly/NYTCrossvCrescent.

In July 1991, after Izetbegović asked to join the Organization of Islamic Countries, Karadžić reacted by stating that "even our gloomiest forecasts, which say that Izetbegović wants Bosnia-Herzegovina to become an Islamic Republic, are being fulfilled."[36]

In a further bid to link contemporary Bosniaks to their historic Ottoman rulers, Bosnian Serb academics and the political and military leadership constantly referred to Bosniaks as Turks in both private and public communications, which can be seen in Interior Ministry and army documents. In painting Bosniaks as the heirs of the Ottoman imperial power, intent on reimposing their dhimmitude upon them, the Serbs were trying to persuade themselves that their Bosniak neighbors presented an existential threat. By expelling and killing "the Turks," the perpetrators convinced themselves they were partaking in a worthy and sacred ritual.[37]

In 1994, Momčilo Krajišnik attended a celebration in Foča, and that day the town was renamed Srbinje: "Today you are not as you were before. Now I see a true Serbian town. And you proudly bear your Serbian name. You are the example to every Serb. All that was coming from this town you've managed to eliminate, you prevented it from happening. [. . .] Izetbegović said that this town would be another Mecca. But you did not let them. And for that, in the name of all Serbs, I thank you."[38]

Bosniaks as descendants of Ustaša (Revenge for World War II). Serb nationalists seemingly derived a sense of morality, and moral justification for their project, from the fate suffered by Serbs especially in World War II. Milorad Ekmečić, the *eminence grise* behind Serbia's nationalist politics, stated in a speech at the Congress of Serb Intellectuals: "In the history of the world only the Jews have paid a higher price for their freedom than the Serbs. Because of their losses in the war, and because of massacres, the most numerous people in Yugoslavia, the Serbs, have, in Bosnia Hercegovina, fallen to second place, and today our policy and our general behavior carry within themselves the invisible stamp of a struggle for biological survival."[39]

The Serb and Bosnian Serb establishment drew upon this sense of grievance, telling their voters that an Ustaša return was imminent and that they were

---

36. Laura Silber and Allan Little, *Yugoslavia: Death of a Nation* (London: BBC/Penguin Books, 1995), 213.
37. Michael A. Sells, *The Bridge Betrayed: Religion and Genocide in Bosnia* (Berkeley: University of California Press, 1998), 43.
38. Prosecutor v. Radovan Karadžić (Judgment), IT-95-5/18-T (ICTY), 1077.
39. MacDonald, *Balkan Holocausts?*, 237.

HISTORY OF ETHNIC RELATIONS IN BOSNIA AND HERZEGOVINA   23

protecting their people, preventing "1941 from repeating," and ensuring that such acts did not occur again.[40]

In Bosnia and Herzegovina, the World War II crimes narrative was highly instrumentalized by the Bosnian Serb political establishment. This can be seen in the constitution of the Serb Republic of Bosnia and Herzegovina, which was proclaimed on February 28, 1992. Article 2 stated, "The territory of the Republic consists of autonomous regions, municipalities and other Serbian ethnic entities, including territory on which genocide was committed against Serbs in the Second World War."[41] Implicit in this is the idea that this territory once belonged to Serbs, and to Serbs it would be returned.

As it will be seen in the following chapters, all the above themes emerge in the treatment of camp detainees and their ceremonial ritual executions and massacres.

Attack on Bosnia and Herzegovina

Soon after Bosnia and Herzegovina's referendum on independence was held and the results were proclaimed, Serb militias set up barricades throughout the country. The institutional and physical division of the country had begun, and the Bosnian Serb parallel institutions sprang into life. At the barricades, armed local Serb men stopped traffic, verified the identities of legitimized citizens, and clashed with the regular police force. These militia were composed of SDS members, although many other paramilitary units appeared, most of which had Yugoslav state funding and support.[42]

---

40. This was visible in Prijedor. The elitocide and the subsequent mass concentration of all Bosniaks and Croats was justified by claiming that their ancestors took part in Ustaša crimes against the partisans at Mount Kozara during World War II. This does not add up, however, since in Prijedor, even the children of famous partisan fighters, such as Esad Sadiković and Ahmet Melkić, were killed in Serb concentration camps. The perpetrators used the Serb victims from Mount Kozara as justification for the slaughter of Bosniaks in and around Prijedor. The local Partisan Veterans Association (SUB-NOR) in Prijedor supported the newly established Serb authorities in the town. They expelled non-Serb members and their former comrades and pledged loyalty to the new Serb state. On June 11, 1992, SUBNOR then held a meeting and expressed their "full support to the new government in their efforts to stabilize the situation in the municipality" and stated that "even besides old age and great exhaustion, the fighters have joined the ranks of the defense forces with the aim of defending our village and our town from the attacks of the Muslim-Croat formations." See Darko Karačić, "Od promoviranja zajedništva do kreiranja podjela," in Darko Karačić, Tamara Banjeglav, and Nataša Govedarica, Re:vizija prošlosti: politike sjećanja u Bosni i Hercegovini, Hrvatskoj i Srbiji od 1990. godine (Sarajevo: ACIPS/ Fondacije Friedrich Ebert, 2012), 55.
41. Prosecutor v. Radovan Karadžić (Judgment), IT-95-5/18-T (ICTY), 21.
42. Iva Vukušić, "Serbian Paramilitaries in the Breakup of Yugoslavia" (PhD diss., Utrecht University, 2020), 52, 75.

During February and March, in a last-minute bid to avoid a repeat of the war already raging in Croatia, an international peace delegation led by José Cutileiro and Lord Carrington proposed a deal known as the Lisbon Agreement. By March 28, however, this deal collapsed and a few days later, on April 1, 1992, in what was labeled as a *general rehearsal* for the rest of the country,[43] Bijeljina in eastern Bosnia was attacked by a combination of forces from Serbia, who overtook the town without any major resistance. None was expected, however, as Bijeljina was the center of the recently established SAO Birač-Semberija and Serbs were a majority in the municipality. Though not militarily necessary, the attack on Bijeljina was intended as a statement, a public, televised terror campaign aimed at frightening Bosniaks and Croats. Alongside the JNA, now subservient to Milošević, were several militia units, most notably, the Tigers, led by Serbian gangster Željko Ražnatović (Arkan). Over the next few years, Arkan and his men would go on to massacre several dozen Bosniaks and Albanians, and in 1999 he was indicted by the ICTY on twenty-four charges of crimes against humanity.

At the same time as Bijeljina, several strategic towns were taken over by a combination of JNA/MUP/paramilitary: Bosanski Brod (March 27); Kupres (April 4); Foča (April 8); Zvornik (April 8); Višegrad (April 13); Vlasenica (April 21); Brčko (April 30); and Prijedor (April 30).[44] This secured the Drina Valley (the border with Serbia) and territories bordering Republic of Serbia Krajina (seized from Croatia).

Sarajevo was next. Street clashes, shootings, and bombardment had been flaring up intermittently in the city since April 6. The Serb political leadership had not expected any resistance. They realized that more forceful and drastic measures were needed if the city were to be taken, and they launched a full on attack against the city, trying to sever it between its east and west and seize the centers of power. They failed, but they nevertheless managed to occupy a large part of the city. The areas that were under Serb occupation were the scenes of incredible brutality. Grbavica, a quarter of the city of Sarajevo, was taken over by Serb forces in mid-May 1992. It basically became a ghetto for Bosniaks and Croats, whose path to freedom was just to cross over the Miljacka River. The trapped civilians were subjected to terror, forced into hard labor, and under

---

43. A Bosniak survivor and author from Bijeljina, Jusuf Trbić is most probably the first person to use this saying.
44. Charles W. Ingrao, *Confronting the Yugoslav Controversies: A Scholars' Initiative* (West Layafette, IN: Purdue University Press, 2013), 125.

constant fear of being killed. The most infamous perpetrator, Veselin "Batko" Vlahović, roamed the streets of Grbavica in search of his victims, raping and killing dozens.[45]

May 2 and 3, 1992, were the war's most decisive days. This was the Serbs' last chance to overtake the country in a coup. The Serb leadership realized that one of their main targets—the capital Sarajevo—would not be taken so easily. The situation in the rest of the country was not that clear for them either. Bosniaks, Croats, and a few notable Serbs loyal to Bosnia and Herzegovina were putting up a greater resistance than had been imagined. On May 6, 1992, a semi-secret meeting was held in Graz, Austria, in a bid to find a quick fix, between a Bosnian Serb delegation consisting of Radovan Karadžić, Momčilo Krajišnik, and Branko Simić, and a Bosnian Croat delegation represented by Mate Boban and Franjo Boras, among others. A joint statement was released stating that a "peace agreement" had been reached to divide Bosnia and Herzegovina along the 1939 Cvetković-Maček Agreement,[46] as (it is alleged) that Tuđman and Miloševic had done a little earlier. In the end, no agreement was officially signed.

Bosnian Serb Police Force (MUP RS)

While the Bosnian Serbs searched for ways to make progress militarily, behind the front lines the police and the civil authorities turned their attentions to the Bosniaks and Bosnian Croats living in the newly conquered areas. The Bosnian Serb leadership placed high hopes in their police force (MUP RS) as the main implementers of their plans for these "ethnic minorities." An important segment of the new MUP RS that is often unnoticed was the reserve police force, who were the main force behind the cleansing policy. The reserve police force was made up of "civilians who were not in the regular police force but were part of a defense organization, which was separate from that of the TO."[47] They were activated and armed by the MUP RS "upon the instruction of the Presidency and could be deployed by the CSB [State Security Services] or SJB [Public Security Station] chiefs."[48] As stated in the Stanišić judgment, "After the multi-party

---

45. Irena Antic, "Law and Justice: Ghosts of Grbavica's War Time Past," *Helsinki Charter No. 149–150* (March, April 2011), https://www.helsinki.org.rs/hcharter_t35a03.html.
46. Prosecutor v. Prlić et al, IT-04-74, vol. 4, 4. https://www.icty.org/x/cases/prlic/tjug/en/130529-4.pdf.
47. Prosecutor v. Mićo Stanišić and Stojan Župljanin (Judgment, vol. 2), IT-08-91-T (ICTY), March 27, 2013, 8, https://www.icty.org/x/cases/zupljanin_stanisicm/tjug/en/130327-2.pdf.
48. Prosecutor v. Mićo Stanišić and Stojan Župljanin, 204.

elections, the SDS, SDA, and HDZ began filling positions with their own people, resulting in a sudden increase in the number of reserve police" (. . .) "it was possible that reserve police positions were filled by people who could not meet even the minimum set of requirements for such a position, including those with criminal records." According to a September 1991 Socialist Republic of Bosnia and Herzegovina State Security Service (SRBiH MUP SDB) position paper, it proposed four steps on how to secure municipalities in which Serbs were a minority. One of the steps suggested was "The active engagement of Serbs in both the SRBiH Government and Assembly regarding the passage of a new Socialist Republic of Bosnia and Herzegovina Ministry of Interior (SRBiH MUP) Rulebook on Wartime Organization, with the emphasis on an increase of reserve police officers in police stations in areas with a Serbian majority."[49]

A few days before the attack on eastern Bosnian towns, the Bosnian Serb assembly was held on March 24, 1992. At the assembly, Karadžić stressed the importance of the reserve police force. Emphasizing that no international agreement limited the size of a regular and reserve police force,[50] he further informed the delegates that "we have a legal basis in the Law on Internal Affairs, we also have badges and in that moment to come—and this will be very soon—we can form what we wish to. There are reasons why this will come in two to three days, such are the estimates, I cannot give you the reasons now. At that moment, all the Serbian municipalities, both the old ones and the newly established ones, would literally assume control over the entire territory of the municipality concerned."[51]

Republika Srpska (RS) had passed its own Law on Internal Affairs. According to this law, five Security Services Centers (Centri službi bezbjednosti—CSBs) were formed that corresponded to the existing Serb regions: Banja Luka, Autonomous Region of Krajina; Trebinje, Serbian Autonomous District of Herzegovina; Doboj, Serbian Autonomous District of Northern Bosnia; Sarajevo, Serbian Autonomous District of Romanija-Birač; and Bijeljina, Serbian Autonomous District of Semberija. These CSBs would go on to become key bodies in the cleansing and creation of camps. Each municipality within the RS had an SJB (Stanica javne bezbjednosti, Public Security Station), which served primarily as a police station but also as the police force's local administrative center, which issued documentation (fines, drivers licenses, etc).[52] The SJBs in the RS were

---

49. Nielsen, *The Bosnian Serb Ministry of Internal Affairs*, 20.
50. Nielsen, *The Bosnian Serb Ministry of Internal Affairs*, 32.
51. Nielsen, *The Bosnian Serb Ministry of Internal Affairs*, 32.
52. Nielsen, *The Bosnian Serb Ministry of Internal Affairs*, 41.

subsequently used as detention facilities in which hundreds of non-Serbs were detained for various periods of time. As will be seen in the following chapters, the MUP RS played a large and important role in the detention, interrogation, and all-around aggression toward non-Serb civilians in Republika Srpska.

Six Strategic Goals of the Serbian People

Furious with the failure of the blitzkrieg on Sarajevo and with the success of the resistance in other parts of the country, the Bosnian Serb establishment organized the "Assembly of the Serb People" in Banja Luka on May 12, 1992. At the assembly, several important organizational, strategic, and political decisions were made. The most important document they adopted was the Six Strategic Goals of the Serbian People. Karadžić addressed the assembly and read them aloud:

1. Establish state borders separating the Serbian people from the other two ethnic communities;
2. Set up a corridor between Semberija and Krajina;
3. Establish a corridor in the Drina River valley, that is, eliminate the Drina as a border separating Serbian states;
4. Establish a border on the Una and Neretva Rivers;
5. Divide the city of Sarajevo into Serbian and Muslim parts and establish effective state authorities in both parts;
6. Ensure access to the sea for Republika Srpska.[53]

These goals had been drawn up by the Bosnian Serb political and academic leadership. As a continuation of their previous policies of separatism and parallelism, their goal was now to divide the Serb population along ethnic lines in each and every municipality. Karadžić emphasized that Serbs needed to separate from their "enemy."[54] The second goal was to establish a Serb-controlled territory that would link Republic of Serbian Krajina in Croatia, the Serb territories in northern Bosnia, with Yugoslavia (which by then comprised Serbia,

---

53. Prosecutor v. Radovan Karadžić (Judgment), IT-95-5/18-T (ICTY), 1091.
54. Prosecutor v. Radovan Karadžić, 1092: In 1994, while addressing the RS Assembly, Karadžić stated that "our primary strategic aim, which is to get rid of the enemies in our house, the Croats and Muslims, and not to be in the same state with them anymore. Every divorce has a price, we have to give something up, but we are the winners, we have a majority of the territory now, not only under our control, but also in our ownership." Cited in Prosecutor v. Radovan Karadžić (Judgment), IT-95-5/18-T, 1064.

Macedonia, Montenegro, and Kosovo). The third goal was eliminating the Drina River as the border between Serb people. Karadžić stated, "We are on both sides of the Drina and our strategic interest and our living space are there. We now see a possibility for some Muslim municipalities to be set up along the Drina as enclaves, in order for them to achieve their rights, but that belt along the Drina must basically belong to Serbian Bosnia and Herzegovina."[55] The Drina River valley, however, was home to a large number of Bosniaks, who could not simply be placed in enclaves.

It can be argued, in fact, that the capturing and cleansing of the Drina River valley, which has a special place in Serb extremist ideology,[56] was the most important goal of all. In Foča, a local politician echoed this sentiment, noting that "the Drina would never become a border but a windpipe between two lungs."[57]

The strategic goals should not, however, be simply interpreted as a political manifesto. These were, at the same time, a comprehensive set of military goals that constituted de facto ethnoreligious cleansing, a fact that General Ratko Mladić was more than aware of. After the strategic goals were read and explained, General Mladić took the stand.[58] He spoke to the assembled delegates regarding the six strategic goals: "We cannot cleanse, nor can we have a sieve to sift so that only Serbs would stay, or that the Serbs would fall through and the rest leave. I do not know how Mr. Krajisnik and Mr. Karadzic would explain this to the world. People, that would be genocide."[59]

Speaking of Bosniaks and Croats, Mladić said that it needed to be determined whether to "throw both of them out, employing political and other moves, or to organize ourselves and throw out one by force of arms, and we will be able to deal somehow with the other."[60] He went on further to stress the

---

55. Hikmet Karčić, "Blueprint for Genocide: The Destruction of Muslims in Eastern Bosnia," *Open Democracy*, May 11, 2015, https://bit.ly/BlueprintGenKarcic.
56. A famous Serb patriotic song from the First World War was called "March on the Drina." One Serb nationalist called the river the "backbone of the Serbian nation." One Bosnian Serb delegate in the RS Assembly stated that the Serb state is impossible "without Podrinje [. . .] from Foča to Bijeljina." See Prosecutor v. Radovan Karadžić (Judgment), IT-95-5/18-T, 1073. In 1993 one delegate recalled, "the Drina has become a noble border, not a hostile one. We have become united with Serbia and Montenegro along our border. . . . This, gentlemen, is how wisely and cleverly the Republic of Srpska, a Serb state within former Bosnia, is being established." See Hikmet Karčić, "Uncovering the Truth: The Lake Perućac Exhumations in Eastern Bosnia," *Journal of Muslim Minority Studies* 37, no. 1 (March 2017): 4, https://doi.org/10.1080/13602004.2017.1294374.
57. Prosecutor v. Radovan Karadžić (Judgment), IT-95-5/18-T (ICTY), 1093.
58. According to Mladić's diary, he, Karadžić, Krajišnik, and others discussed and developed the Six Strategic Goals a few weeks before the assembly. See Prosecutor v. Radovan Karadžić (Judgment), IT-95-5/18-T, 1095.
59. Prosecutor v. Ratko Mladić (Judgment, vol. 4), IT-09-92-T (ICTY), November 22, 2017, 1883, https://www.icty.org/x/cases/mladic/tjug/en/171122-4of5_1.pdf.
60. Prosecutor v. Radovan Karadžić (Judgment), IT-95-5/18-T (ICTY), 1093. This shows that just like in

HISTORY OF ETHNIC RELATIONS IN BOSNIA AND HERZEGOVINA   29

importance of identifying the enemies, and then "we must make our move and eliminate them, either temporarily or permanently."[61]

Members of the assembly supported the strategic goals but also had a lot of questions regarding certain issues. Some asked in cases of municipalities where Serbs were a majority "whether they should injure the Muslims, whether they can hold certain posts, whether loyal Muslims and loyal Croats exist."[62] Radislav Brđanin, a former civil engineer and then-president of SAO Bosanska Krajina, stated that he did not know why Muslims were pickling cabbages for winter, since they will not be there to eat them.[63] RS health minister Dragan Kalinić emphasized that the enemy "cannot be trusted until they are physically, militarily destroyed and crushed, which, of course, implies eliminating and liquidating their key people."[64] This policy of targeting elites—eliticide—would prove to be a central element of Bosnian Serbs' strategy to cleanse the region. Kalinić also suggested the destruction of radio and television facilities and medical facilities "so that the enemy has nowhere to go for medical help."[65] After the assembly was over, the Bosnian Serb leadership came out onto a balcony to a cheering crowd of Banja Luka Serbs and then watched a parade of the MUP RS.[66] That same day, the Vojska Republike Srpske (VRS) was formed and Mladić was named its "Commander of the Main Staff." In the weeks preceding this, however, Mladić had held a high-ranking position in the JNA Second Military District headquarters.[67] He gained a reputation during the war in Croatia, where he served in Knin. As the war in Bosnia and Herzegovina began, he was transferred to manage the JNA's failing efforts in and around Sarajevo.

What followed were months of unlawful mass detention, massacres, rapes, destruction, and carnage that left thousands of people traumatized.

---

the cases of other genocides, there was a lot of improvisation among the leadership of the perpetrators.

61. Prosecutor v. Radovan Karadžić, 1093.
62. Prosecutor v. Radovan Karadžić, 1094.
63. Prosecutor v. Radovan Karadžić, 1094.
64. Prosecutor v. Radovan Karadžić, 1095.
65. Prosecutor v. Radovan Karadžić, 1095.
66. Prosecutor v. Mićo Stanišić and Stojan Župljanin (Judgment, vol. 2), IT-08-91-T (ICTY), March 27, 2013, Exhibit P1393, 128, https://www.icty.org/x/cases/zupljanin_stanisicm/tjug/en/130327-2.pdf. Video footage of police parade held in Banja Luka, May 12, 1992.
67. Prosecutor v. Ratko Mladić (Amended Indictment), IT-95-5/18-I (ICTY), October 10, 2002, 1, http://www.icty.org/x/cases/mladic/ind/en/mla-ai021010e.pdf.

CHAPTER 2

Collective Traumatization

Camps as Trauma: Trauma as Genocide

The following chapter gives an overview of the theory from which this work proceeds, and thus also establishes its theoretical foundations. The fundamental idea is that the Bosnian Serb camps, established in what is known today as Republika Srpska, were *not* prima facie death camps, despite the extremely high rate of murders within the camps. They were primarily sites of a collective traumatization intended to destroy the humanity of the detainees, both at an individual and collective level. Many survived the camps, many were murdered; none passed through without being deeply traumatized.

Does making this statement mean that the Bosnian Serb leadership, with the help of the Serbian state, was not genocidal and that what happened to Bosniaks (and to lesser extent, Bosnian Croats) in Bosnian Serb areas was not genocide? Certainly not. Rather than undermining the Bosniak claim that events that spanned the country across these four hellish years were genocide, this argument strengthens the claim, as by returning to Raphael Lemkin and drawing from the literature on other genocides, it highlights that genocide is much more than just mass murder of individuals. Murder is the very last step, the destruction of the body. In many cases, the psychological destruction is, if not complete, already certainly well-advanced.

The debt that genocide studies owes to Raphael Lemkin is incalculable, not purely because of his work in establishing the 1948 Genocide Convention, but his deep and wide-ranging academic output around it. It is to Lemkin, then, that we return, at the foundation of this chain of argumentation.

COLLECTIVE TRAUMATIZATION   31

While an often flawed and deeply imperfect institution, the International Criminal Tribunal for the Former Yugoslavia (ICTY) has had some noteworthy successes, notably the genocide convictions of both Rakto Mladić and Radovan Karadžić for their action regarding Srebrenica. Article 4 of the ICTY's founding statute draws from the 1948 Convention on Genocide, drafted by Lemkin. . It has become clear, however, that legal definitions are often unfortunately "too narrowly focused, rooted in specific historical contexts, and difficult to modify. Law requires unambiguous categories as well as clear and convincing evidence in order to reach a judgment of guilty or not guilty."[1] Genocide is better understood as a *social practice*, as *societal reorganization*. Such terminology might sound abstract, bland, and ineffectual. Its meaning, however, is not. Alexander Hinton suggests that understanding genocide as societal reorganization "tells us, [that genocide] may centrally involve not just the mass destruction of a group of marginalized 'others,' as conventional understandings hold, but a profound internal reorganization of society amidst fear and terror."[2]

Concentration camps lie at the very heart of this endeavor. In Daniel Feierstein's work on the similarities between the Third Reich and the junta's dictatorship in Argentina, he highlights how the construction of hegemony (in both locations), demonstrated by the exercise of the "technology of power,"[3] made itself manifest in genocide, which he defines also as the destruction and reorganization of social relations.[4] "The tool chosen to carry out this reorganization of society was the concentration camp."[5]

Feierstein advances Lemkin's observations still further. He notes also that the purposes of the camps in both places and times were to break down personality: "The guards' systematic brutality was intended to break the inmates as social beings, destroying their capacity for self-determination. . . . Breakdown [. . .] was both individual and social."[6] Alongside this, he also observes the value terror and trauma have to the perpetrator: "For genocide to be effective

---

1. Daniel Feierstein, *Genocide as Social Practice: Reorganizing Society under the Nazis and Argentina's Military Juntas*, trans. Douglas Andrew Town (New Brunswick, NJ: Rutgers University Press, 2014), 52.
2. Feierstein, *Genocide as Social Practice*, 52.
3. A phrase Feierstein defines as meaning "a power system with a specific set of practices . . . [which] act together as a 'technology of power' to construct hegemony—in other words, to establish the dominance of one social group over another. They can be used not only to control populations but to reconstruct their very identity." Feierstein, *Genocide as Social Practice*, 52.
4. Feierstein, *Genocide as Social Practice*, 48.
5. Feierstein, *Genocide as Social Practice*, 50.
6. Feierstein, *Genocide as Social Practice*, 191.

while the perpetrators are in power it is not enough for the perpetrators to kill and materially eliminate those who . . . the perpetrators wish to destroy. They need to spread the terror caused by genocide throughout society."[7]

Two of Feierstein's further contributions to this work, however, are the following. First, his idea that what makes reorganizational genocide different from other forms of societal reorganization (revolutions, etc.), is again that it goes beyond physical annihilation: "It does not end with the death of the enemy but attempts to capitalize on death through mechanisms of 'symbolic enactment.'"[8] Second is his observation that in both the Third Reich and in Argentina, the fact that concentration camps were set up in each province, city, town, and village was intended to involve the whole society as either victims or collaborators.[9]

Much of the Bosnian Serb campaign against the Bosniaks involved both symbolic acts of destruction, either in ritualized murder and rape, or the destruction of everything physically symbolic of Bosniak identity. Regarding the involvement of the wider society, research shows this indeed to be true, but not fully. Setting up camps in villages around the Republika Srpska allowed the involvement of wider society, encouraging everyone involved to become perpetrators. Indeed, the events described over the subsequent pages show us how blurred the lines between perpetrator and bystander often are.

Irvin-Erickson's work on Raphael Lemkin and his wider concept of genocide is useful as we build on Feierstein's analysis. Irvin-Erickson shows that although complete extinction was the Nazis' ultimate aim for the Jews, an *Endlösung der Judenfrage*, death itself was only part of genocide, a final step. Thomas Butcher states that Lemkin understood genocide as consisting of "multiple interacting techniques, which he expressed through the metaphor of a 'a synchronized attack on different aspects of life' of the victim nation."[10]

Irvin-Erickson notes that Lemkin saw in all the steps leading up to death the Nazis' desire to shatter the Jewish communities they were in the process of annihilating, not only as communities but as humans also. Every aspect of the Nazi program was geared not simply toward death only, but to utter destruction via traumatization of the individual and the community. Lemkin's argument is

---

7. Feierstein, *Genocide as Social Practice*, 121.
8. Feierstein, *Genocide as Social Practice*, 205.
9. Feierstein, *Genocide as Social Practice*, 133.
10. Thomas M. Butcher, "A 'synchronized attack': On Raphael Lemkin's Holistic Conception of Genocide," *Journal of Genocide Research* 15, no. 3 (September 2013): 254, https://www.doi.org/10.1080/14 623528.2013.821221.

that the genocidal process was well underway by the time the Jews reached the ramp at Auschwitz, beginning even before the terror, disease, and starvation of the ghettos, but with the promulgation of the anti-Jewish laws all throughout the Reich:

> [G]enocide is a gradual process and may begin with political disenfranchisement, economic displacement, cultural undermining and control, the destruction of leadership, the breakup of families and the prevention of propagation. Each of these methods is a more or less effective means of destroying a group. Actual physical destruction is the last and most effective phase of genocide.[11]

For Lemkin, the legal system was set up to completely separate and isolate the Jews from society and to remove every single right. Following the legal exclusions came the physical exclusion. The ghettoes via the constant fear of the *aktion*, the isolation, the overcrowding, the disease, and the starvation were designed to break down the Jewish "family of mind."[12] The creation of institutions like the *judenrat* were designed get the Jewish community's leaders to break their own communities apart,[13] breaking down the society still further.

If the ghetto brought about the destruction of the Jewish family of mind (and in many instances, it failed), then for Lemkin the Nazi labor camps and death camps were at the apex of the Nazis' "synchronised attack" on the Jews. They were "the most devastating technique of the Nazi German genocide because they brought together the social, cultural, economic, and physical techniques of genocide."[14]

Lemkin understood the destructive power of trauma infliction as a weapon of genocide. Writing about the Algerian genocide, he noted that the psychological trauma inflicted by the French through torture and state terror was designed to shatter the bonds of social solidarity among the Algerian nation. Irvin-Erickson observes how Lemkin understood that trauma produces a "loss of social aspirations, controls, and emotions such as altruism and resistance." The terror of genocide inflicts "'permanent psychological injury" and contrib-

---

11. Douglas Irvin-Erickson, *Raphael Lemkin and the Concept of Genocide* (Pittsburgh: University of Pennsylvania Press, 2016), 84.
12. A phrase Lemkin used to define a culture. See Douglas Irvin-Erickson, "Genocide, the 'Family of Mind' and the Romantic Signature of Raphael Lemkin," *Journal of Genocide Research* 15, no. 3 (2013): 273–96, https://doi.org/10.1080/14623528.2013.821222.
13. Irvin-Erickson, *Raphael Lemkin and the Concept of Genocide*, 122–23.
14. Erickson, *Raphael Lemkin*, 123.

utes to the perpetrator's attempt to liquidate the social group of the victims." Lemkin wrote that the *terror* alone that the French inflicted on the Algerians would constitute genocide according to the strictest interpretation of the UN Genocide Convention.[15]

The idea of camps as places of trauma and terror, as sites of individual and group breakage and destruction, is not limited solely to the Holocaust. The use of terror and trauma to ontologically destroy individuals and groups was perfected in the Gulag, as witnessed so powerfully by Solzhenitsyn. Central to the communist project,[16] the Gulag was a place wherein communists saw themselves as engineers engaged in the reforging of corrupted human raw material.[17] According to Steven Barnes, "the revolutionary re-shaping [of Soviet societies] depended on the Gulag," the purpose of which was "epistemic transformation . . . to engineer a new socialist soul." This however was not to be achieved by mere legislative measures and controls, rather, "they expected—and even sought—struggle, merciless class struggle" against "internal enemies—a contamination of the body politic. Instead of negotiation accommodation and bargaining with societal filth, violent purification of the body politic was the appropriate mode of operation"[18]

The Soviets specialized in the use of psychological terror and trauma to break the individual, such as sleep deprivation, enforced silence, etc., and physical methods: using heavy, prolonged beatings during interrogation, which broke the victim physically (and mentally), the Soviets managed to "install" a desperate servitude into their victims, who eventually would do anything to avoid prolonging the torture.[19] From the moment of arrest through the entire process of interrogation, the transport, the arrival in the Gulag, and however long the detainees lived after that, there was a slow process of breaking down the bonds between humans, until, as Solzhenitsyn observed, prisoners tortured prisoners.[20]

The Gulag and the Bosnian Serb camp system are obviously hugely different. One of the key differences lay in the intended outcome. Those running the

---

15. Erickson, *Raphael Lemkin*, 123, 218
16. Steven A. Barnes, *Death and Redemption: The Gulag and the Shaping of Soviet Society* (e-book) (Princeton NJ: Princeton University Press, 2011), 28.
17. Barnes, *Death and Redemption*, 37.
18. Barnes, *Death and Redemption*, 35–36.
19. Yochai Ataria, "Becoming Nonhuman: The Case Study of the Gulag," *Genealogy* 3, no 2 (2019): 4–6, https://doi.org/10.3390/genealogy3020027.
20. Aleksandr Solzhenitsyn, *The Gulag Archipelago 1918–1956*, vol. 1, trans. Thomas P. Whitney (New York: Harper & Row, 1975), 124–25.

COLLECTIVE TRAUMATIZATION   35

Gulag system aimed to break down the inmates completely and rebuild them, re-educate them as good communists. The Bosnian Serbs, however, showed little interest in re-educating Bosniaks in a bid to reabsorb them into their body politic as good Serbs. Yet two commonalities do emerge. First, the usage of trauma, both psychological and physical, and second, the threat of and subsequent reality of permanent exile.[21] Those who survived the Gulag or the Bosnian Serb camps were often forced out of their homes, either to other parts of the country (in the case of the Bosniaks), or to completely different countries in the case of the Gulag victims (though Bosnian Serbs would often deport camp detainees across the border also). In both cases, there was little hope of return.

The case for camps as places of deliberate, purposeful trauma and torture as a tool used by genocidaires grows stronger when observing the literature on the Native American genocide. America's concentration camps (reservations, etc.) were also sites destructive of Native American identity, individuality, and social groupings. It is worth remembering that, as with all genocides in which camps play a central feature, the process that led to the internment of the Native Americans was destructive, brutal, and terrifying. The US military carried out what Jeffrey Ostler defines as genocidal massacres of the Shoshone at Bear River (1863), the Blackfeet on the Marias River (1870), the Lakota at Wounded Knee (1890), and the massacre of the Cheyenne at Sand Creek by the Colorado Militia (1864).[22] In his 2019 book on the Native American genocide, Ostler cites missionary Daniel Butrick's recordings of soldiers who took part in the cleansing, saying they "use[d] the same language as if driving hogs, and goad[ed] them forward with their bayonets." Many years later, a soldier who participated in the roundup said that although he had "fought through the civil war and seen men shot to pieces and slaughtered by the thousands, the Cherokee removal was the cruelest work I ever knew."[23]

Ostler goes on to detail how the forced enclosure of Native Americans in camps provided white men the opportunity to enter them to rape Native American women.[24]

Benjamin Madley recounts how the Native American tribes of California were interned within a strict system of concentration camps housed within

---

21. Barnes, *Death and Redemption*, 541.
22. Jeffrey Ostler, "Genocide and American Indian History," in *Oxford Research Encyclopedia of American History*, https://bit.ly/GenocideAmericanHist.
23. Jeffery Ostler, *Surviving Genocide: Native Nations and the United States from the American Revolution to Bleeding Kansas* (New Haven, CT: Yale University Press, 2019), 270.
24. Ostler, *Surviving Genocide*, 270.

Catholic missions. Noting that the legal exclusion of California's Native Americans from society, depriving them of any rights, legal or political, was a move that "represented a broad anti-Indian consensus among voting non-Indians," and opened a door for the "non-Indians" to treat Native Americans as "outsiders at best and nonhumans at worst." This exclusion enabled violence by eliminating their "rights and legal recourse while eroding legal and moral barriers to kidnapping, enslaving, starving, raping, murdering, and massacring California Indians. Over the coming decades, vigilantes and militias took full advantage of the state of California's anti-Indian legal system to kill thousands of California Indians."[25]

Clearly, camps have, in many places around the globe, served as places of terror and torture, designed to create deep, long-lasting traumas that not only break the individual but break the individual's "family of mind," their connections with others, their community, their culture, their memory, and their past and future. As Lemkin observed in the case of the Algerian genocide, concerted efforts to break the individual and the group through extreme levels of traumatization is itself an act of genocide.

What role does the site of the actual physical camp play in this? Physical separation, another thing Lemkin understood well (as highlighted above), is another powerful element of genocide. The forced physical separation of a group from society is deeply symbolic. Camps, as formulated by Bjørn Møller, establish separations between "the good and the bad, decent folk and deviants, valuable matter and dirt, legitimate and illegitimate targets, and sometimes even between valued and worthless lives."[26] Hannah Arendt also dealt with the concept of camps. They are locations in which everything is possible, an isolated piece of territory where laws do not exist. A space of exception, camps are "a never admitted and immediately realized attempt at total domination." They are "laboratories in the experiment of total domination, for human nature being what it is, this goal can be achieved only under the extreme circumstances of human made hell."[27]

In serving as sites of what Feierstein defines as "symbolic enactment," camps become sites of the "macabresque," a term defined by Edward Weisband as

---

25. Benjamin Madley, *An American Genocide: The United States and the California Indian Catastrophe, 1846–1873* (New Haven, CT: Yale University Press, 2016), 172.
26. Bjørn Møller, *Refugees, Prisoners and Camps: A Functional Analysis of the Phenomenon of Encampment* (Basingstoke: Palgrave Macmillan, 2015), 218.
27. Hannah Arendt, Jerome Kohn, *Essays in Understanding, 1930–1954* (London: Penguin Random House, 2005), 240.

meaning "the performative transgression, dramaturgies, and esthetics of human violence in genocide and mass atrocity."[28] The macabresque is defined by dramatic acts of sadistic cruelty. Such cruelty leads to the establishment of "theatres of horror" by perpetrators, which "often revel in the perverse or exhibitionist dramaturgies of the macabresque."[29]

Putting it simplistically, the above is directly applicable to the camps run by the Bosnian Serbs, with perhaps the only false note being the idea that Bosniaks in camps were somehow *distantly isolated*. The camps and detention sites in Bileća, three sites in Višegrad, the camps in Keraterm and Trnopolje (in Prijedor) were very much in the middle of settled areas, often visibly open and not strictly guarded for those wishing to enter.

Humiliation and Trauma in Survivor Testimony

Survivor testimony is one of the most important windows the nonsurvivor can have into trying to grasp the extent of trauma that comes as part of life in the camps. Elie Wiesel's searing account of his first night in Auschwitz, possibly one of the most famous quotes in Holocaust literature, gives us just the very faintest of insight into just how deep trauma goes:

> Never shall I forget that night, the first night in camp, which has turned my life into one long night, seven times cursed and seven times sealed. Never shall I forget that smoke. Never shall I forget the little faces of the children, whose bodies I saw turned into wreaths of smoke beneath a silent blue sky. Never shall I forget those flames which consumed my faith forever. Never shall I forget that nocturnal silence which deprived me, for all eternity, of the desire to live.[30]

There are quite literally thousands of testimonies from genocide survivors now, and each could be drawn from to show the deep and lasting impact that genocide trauma has. One such work, written by Bruno Bettelheim, a survivor of two Nazi camps, was the first groundbreaking work on theory of behavior in camps. He too identifies trauma as a key element in camp life, differentiating

---

28. Edward Weisband, *The Macabresque: Human Violation and Hate in Genocide, Mass Atrocity and Enemy-Making* (New York: Oxford University Press, 2018), 4.
29. Weisband, *The Macabresque*, 57.
30. Elie Wiesel, *Night* (London: Penguin Books Limited, 2012), 34.

two types of trauma: the initial trauma when arriving at a camp and the trauma of being subjected to extraordinary abuse.[31]

A reaction to Bettelheim's work is Terrence Des Pres's *Survivor: An Anatomy of Life in the Death Camps*, a brilliant compilation of various survivor memoir and testimonies from camp survivors from both Nazi and Soviet Gulag camps. The testimonies reveal how detainees mentally disintegrated, the breakdown of their civilization casting them into a state of stunned confusion. They felt subhuman and saw their self-image in the detainee next to them.[32]

In the Bosnian context, two books in particular stand out as testimonies of the camps in Prijedor, even the mere reading of which can prove to be traumatic. Rezak Hukanović's *The Tenth Circle of Hell* gives us an insight into the physical and mental torture. "One rainy night the name Mehmedalija Sarajlic was called out. A distinguished, gray-haired man about sixty years old, he was taken outside and forced to strip naked; then the guards brought him, still naked, back into the room with Hajra, a girl who couldn't have been older than twenty-two or twenty-three. She, too, was forced to strip, and they were ordered to make love in front of all the other prisoners, who looked on in horror and silence, deeply humiliated by the utter powerlessness of the man and woman before them."[33] Alongside Hukanović was Kemal Pervanić, whose *The Killing Days* recounts the seven months he spent trapped in concentration camps around Prijedor.[34] This too is a brutal, traumatic read.

Another important book that delves deeply into the trauma inflicted onto Bosniak camp inmates is Stevan Weine's *When History Is a Nightmare*.[35] The book also explores the impact of the camps on Bosniak society. Survivors with whom Weine talked to felt the sense of betrayal from their former neighbors who participated in atrocities. They also emphasized the eternal loss of their previous livelihood and their homeland's multiculturality.[36]

Survivor testimony lies at the very heart of this book also, though it has the added advantage of having gone through a rigorous process of verification and

---

31. Bruno Bettelheim, *The Informed Heart* (New York: Avon, 1971), 120.
32. Terrence Des Pres, *The Survivor: An Anatomy of Life in the Death Camps* (Oxford: Oxford University Press, 1980), 61.
33. Rezak Hukanović, *The Tenth Circle of Hell* (New York: Basic Books, 1996), 43.
34. Kemal Pervanić, *The Killing Days* (Blake, 1999).
35. Stevan M. Weine, *When History Is a Nightmare: Lives and Memories of Ethnic Cleansing in Bosnia-Herzegovina* (New Brunswick, NJ: Rutgers University Press, 1999).
36. Ibid., 45–46. Keith Doubt, "Scapegoating and the Simulation of Mechanical Solidarity in Former Yugoslavia: 'Ethnic Cleansing' and the Serbian Orthodox Church," *Humanity and Society* 31, no. 1 (February 2007): 65–82.

COLLECTIVE TRAUMATIZATION 39

cross-examination in the courts. Despite the dry legal setting and framing of the testimonies given, either to the ICTY or the Court of Bosnia and Herzegovina, the deeply traumatic nature of their experience in the camps stands out. We are all indebted to them for their bravery.

Ethnic Cleansing as Genocide

The phrase "ethnic cleansing"—used throughout this book—gained popularity during the Serb/Bosnian Serb attacks on Croatia and Bosnia and Herzegovina during the 1990s. Much of the early literature on ethnic cleansing emerged as a result of the phrase's popularity with the Serb/Bosnian Serb political and military elite. Nevertheless, the contemporary phrase had its antecedents much further back in Serbian history. A comprehensive, historical explanation of the idea "etničko čišćenje" among the Serbian national and political establishment was given by Vladimir Petrović. He states that the idea of ethnic cleansing was used by Vuk Karadžić when referring to Muslims of Belgrade in 1806, but more importantly he mentions the contemporary idea of this policy. He positions Bosnian Serb Vaso Ćubrilović (one of the group involved in the assassination of Archduke Franz Ferdinand) and his policies on Albanians and *Volkdeutsche* as being crucial, since it is the first time the term "ethnically clean" (*etnički čisto*) was openly used: "Može biti nikad nam se neće pružiti ovakva prilika da svoju državu napravimo etnički čisto našu." (It is possible that we will never have such an opportunity to make our state ethnically clean.)[37]

It was Milošević himself who was the first modern politician to reprise the usage of the phrase "ethnic cleansing." He used it in April 1987 to describe Kosovar Albanian commanders' violence toward Serbs, while Bosnian Serb military commanders "frequently used the terms 'etničko ciscenje' [*sic*] ('cleansing of the region') and 'čišćenje prostora'[*sic*] or 'terena' ('cleaning the territory') for leaving nobody alive."[38] These quotes alone indicate the genocidal intent behind the phrase.

The first book to be published on the policy of "ethnic cleansing" in Bosnia

---

37. Vladimir Petrović, "Etnicizacija čišćenja u reči i nedelu: Represija i njena naučna legitimizacija," *Hereticus*, no. 1 (2007): 11.
38. Rony Blum, Gregory H. Stanton, Shira Sagi, and Elihu D. Richter, "Ethnic Cleansing' Bleaches the Atrocities of Genocide," *European Journal of Public Health* 18, no. 2 (April 2008): 204, https://doi.org/10.1093/eurpub/ckm011.

and Herzegovina was written by Norman Cigar. His main argument was that "ethnic cleansing" is not a by-product of the war. Rather, it was the perpetrators' core strategy. He strongly opposed the "ancient hatred" justification for the conflict and clearly demonstrated how the Serbian ideology was formulated. Cigar identified two important categories of actors who helped shape the anti-Muslim ideology in Serbia: orientalists (experts in Islam, members of the academia) and the Serb Orthodox Church,[39] which helped create an atmosphere of fear and hate in "othering" the Bosniaks.

Bruce MacDonald states that there were two key arguments advanced by the Serbian propagandists in justifying the cleansing campaign: "that Bosnian Moslems were ethnically Serbian, and that Bosnian territory was part of ancient Serbia."[40] Three main themes were used to justify camps, torture, and rape: "1. Firstly, the idea of Moslems as either ethnic Croats or Serbs; and Moslem nationalism as invented or constructed; 2. Secondly, the notion that Bosnia-Hercegovina had historically been either Serbian or Croatian, and; 3. Thirdly that claims to Moslem national identity and autonomy concealed an Islamic conspiracy to take over Europe."[41]

Keith Doubt further highlights the role the Serbian Orthodox Church had in framing ethnic cleansing as "the dominant cultural, social, and religious paradigm for inciting psychological and physical violence against non-Serbian human beings."[42]

Clearly the term "ethnic cleansing" is well-established and has proven to be a popular substitution for the word "genocide." During the early 1990s, with genocides unfolding in Rwanda and Bosnia and Herzegovina, international politicians figured out that the phrase was a useful replacement for "genocide." Using the "g-word" obliges international preventive intervention, while "ethnic cleansing" was a useful and at the time ill-defined neologism that sound vaguely terrible but did not amount to an admission of a need to intervene.

Despite being used frequently in UNSC and UNGA resolutions, the term still lacks any formal definition, and it is not defined separately as a crime. During the war, a UN commission of experts was set up to create a definition and eventually settled on the following: "a purposeful policy designed by one

---

39. Norman Cigar, *Genocide in Bosnia: The Policy of 'Ethnic Cleansing'* (College Station: Texas A&M University Press, 1995), 30.
40. David B. MacDonald, *Balkan Holocausts? Serbian and Croatian Victim-Centred Propaganda and the War in Yugoslavia* (Manchester: Manchester University Press, 2002), 224.
41. MacDonald, *Balkan Holocausts?*, 221.
42. Doubt, "Scapegoating and the Simulation of Mechanical Solidarity."

ethnic or religious group to remove by violent and terror-inspiring means the civilian population of another ethnic or religious group from certain geographic areas."[43] The commission observed that ethnic cleansing comprised, amidst a range of other things, confinement of a civilian population, rape, murder, torture, and forcible removal of said population. Crucially, it also observed that such acts could fall within the meaning of the Genocide Convention.[44] The legal possibility exists in that "forcibly transferring an ethnic group from a region effectively destroys the ethnic group, and desiring ethnic homogeneity is equivalent to denying an ethnic group the right to exist."[45] The deliberate infliction of trauma and terror, Mikol Sirkin argues, is also a key ingredient to defining ethnic cleansing as genocide. The perpetrator must use "terror-inspiring violence to inhibit any potential return by those expelled," including, "murder, rape, torture, imprisonment, theft, and destruction of public and private property."[46]

In academia, there have been calls to open the field, taking what Hinton defines as "contextualised approaches" that are adaptive to each circumstance and broadly define genocide as "the destruction of any sort of group, as defined by the protagonists."[47] Such an approach allows the inclusion of ethnic cleansing within the broader definition of genocide. This represents a fundamental step in recognizing what Bosniaks, and all other victims who have suffered ethnic cleansing, know. It is genocidal. In response to the argument that genocide equals mass death, whereas ethnic cleansing equals displacement, the following should be kept in mind: "this distinction ignores the fact that genocidal massacres often have both intents. They intentionally destroy a substantial part of an ethnic group, the specific intent necessary to prove genocide, and also have the intent to terrorize a population into flight or forced deportation."[48] While the phrase proves to be still popular, it is proposed that the term be subsumed into the concept of genocide, and then abandoned.

The idea of the destruction of a group whose identity is defined by the per-

---

43. UN Office on Genocide Prevention and the Responsibility to Protect, *Definitions: Ethnic Cleansing*, accessed November 13, 2020, https://www.un.org/en/genocideprevention/ethnic-cleansing.shtml.

44. UN Office on Genocide Prevention and the Responsibility to Protect, *Definitions: Ethnic Cleansing*.

45. Micol Sirkin, "Expanding the Crime of Genocide to Include Ethnic Cleansing: A Return to Established Principles in Light of Contemporary Interpretations," *Seattle University Law Review* 33 (2010): 510.

46. Sirkin, "Expanding the Crime of Genocide," 524.

47. Alexander Laban Hinton, "Critical Genocide Studies," *Genocide Studies and Prevention* 7, no. 1 (2012): 9, https://scholarcommons.usf.edu/cgi/viewcontent.cgi?article=1044&context=gsp.

48. Blum, Stanton, Sagi, and Richter, "Ethnic Cleansing' Bleaches the Atrocities of Genocide," 206.

petrators is useful to maintain. Many of the Bosniaks destroyed in the Bosnian Serb camps often identified themselves in many different ways: religious, secular, Yugoslav. Much of the work done to reify the identity of the Bosniaks (or at least their warped perception of it) was done by the Serbs / Bosnian Serbs themselves.

In order for the perpetrators to justify the targeting a specific group, the group first needs to be stripped of its legitimacy, divided into extreme social categories, and then excluded from society. Daniel Bar-Tal and Phillip L. Hammack identified several ways in which this delegitimization works: dehumanization (a permanent state[49]), outcasting, trait characterization, political labels, and group comparison.

In the camps in Bosnia and Herzegovina, dehumanization served as the first form of delegitimization, and, as Albert Bandura notes: "Inflicting harm upon individuals who are regarded as subhuman or debased is less apt to arouse self-reproof than if they are seen as human beings with dignifying qualities."[50] Bar-Tal helps us still further by introducing an ethnocentric element to delegitimization, which emerges from the desire to make a total differentiation between the delegitimized group and the society.[51]

This concept of delegitimization is similar to the concept of moral exclusion introduced by Susan Opotow. She explains that moral exclusion rationalizes and justifies harm committed upon others by viewing them as undeserving, expendable, exploitable, or irrelevant. The people who are morally excluded are those who are considered to be outside the scope of justice, outside the boundary of fairness. If escalated, the moral exclusion results in human rights being violated and in genocide.[52]

Bosnian Serb perpetrators relied primarily on false, nationalist tropes to justify their dehumanization of Bosniak Muslims. As Michael Sells notes, in modern Serb nationalism—"Christoslavic" views—Slavic Muslims are betrayers of the faith, Christ killers, people who converted to Islam because they were

---

49. Daniel Bar-Tal and Phillip L. Hammack, "Conflict, Delegitimization, and Violence," in *The Oxford Handbook of Intergroup Conflict*, ed. Linda R. Tropp (Oxford: Oxford University Press, 2016), 29–52.
50. Albert Bandura, Bill Underwood, and Michael E. Fromson, "Disinhibition of Aggression through Diffusion of Responsibility and Dehumanization of Victims," *Journal of Research in Personality* 9 (1975): 253–69.
51. Bar-Tal and Hammack, "Conflict, Delegitimization, and Violence," 34.
52. Susan Opotow, Janet Gerson, and Sarah Woodside, "From Moral Exclusion to Moral Inclusion: Theory for Teaching Peace," *Theory into Practice* 44, no. 4 (2005): 303–18, https://doi.org/10.1207/s15430421tip4404_4.

COLLECTIVE TRAUMATIZATION   43

weak. Since an unforgiveable sin had been committed, these betrayers needed to be punished.[53]

Adis Makšić has also provided an excellent study on the Bosnian Serbs' "othering" of Bosniaks. Makšić states that the Bosniak Muslims were portrayed in the frame of an "Islamic threat." The "SDS began specifying the Islamic threat commonplace to amplify the associated anxieties in dual ways. First, it associated the threat with *Ustaše*, the commonplace that was already circulating the most intense sentiments of resentment and anxieties. (. . .) Second, SDS spoke of a slower progressing Muslim demographic rise as a threat of renewed Islamic subjugation similar to the five-century-long Ottoman occupation lamented in Serb folk culture. The linkage served to heighten suspicion that behind all policies of SDA was a Muslim desire for domination."[54]

Destruction of Religious and Cultural Heritage

One of the distinct elements of the Serb/Bosnian Serb attack on Bosniaks was the manner in which all physical symbols and manifestations of Bosniak culture were destroyed. Such intentional destruction of religious and cultural heritage is committed with the intent of rewriting history and destroying the foundations of a people. Caroline Fournet observed that when a group's cultural heritage is targeted for destruction, it is done so in the hope that "this group will disappear from collective memory, its whole existence will be eliminated, all traces of this group's life on Earth will be annihilated—and the genocide, the destruction, will be complete. Cultural genocide is more often than not part of the genocidal plan to destroy the group, to deny it any human life, to dehumanize it."[55]

During Kristallnacht, the Nazis burned synagogues across the Reich and destroyed all symbolic public manifestations of the Jewish religion. In Sarajevo, the Nazis destroyed the beautiful *il Kal grande*, the Sephardi synagogue, and defiled the Ashkenazi synagogue by turning it into a stable. They also sought to find the legendary ancient Sarajevo Haggadah, which was to be taken from a

---

53. Michael A. Sells, *The Bridge Betrayed* (Berkeley: University of California Press, 1999), 29–52.

54. Adis Makšić, *Ethnic Mobilization, Violence, and the Politics of Affect: The Serb Democratic Party and the Bosnian War* (London: Palgrave Macmillan, 2017), 216.

55. Caroline Fournet, *The Crime of Destruction and the Law of Genocide* (Farnham UK: Ashgate, 2007), 43.

Sarajevo museum to the site of a proposed museum to a not-quite-extinguished race in Prague, wherein Reichsminister Alfred Rosenberg was gathering items of Judaica that would be shown to the world to demonstrate the triumph of the Nazis.[56] The Haggadah was saved, however, by Derviš Korkut, a Bosniak *kustos* (curator) of the museum, and it was hidden for the duration of World War II in a mosque somewhere near Sarajevo.[57]

Helen Walasak identifies two phases of the destruction of religious and cultural property in Bosnia and Herzegovina during the attack on Bosnia and Herzegovina. The first phase was committed in 1992 by JNA and VRS and the second phase in 1993 by HVO.[58] András J. Riedlmayer, who conducted the most comprehensive research on the destruction of cultural and religious buildings in the Balkans, stated in a report that "The damage to these monuments was clearly the result of attacks directed against them, rather than incidental to the fighting," adding that it was widespread and systematic, and that "in many cases is reported to have taken place just before, or in some cases just after, a mass exodus of the local Muslim population." He also gives important information on the use of mosques as sites of concentration and detention of local Bosniaks:

> In a number of other cases, mosques were reportedly used as detention centers for Muslims (such as the Hadzi-Pasha Mosque, next to the Health Centre in Brcko), and as the scenes of killings of Muslim civilians and of Muslim clergymen. Examples of the latter include the village mosque at Hanifici (Kotor Varos), where more than 30 members of the congregation were reportedly burned alive inside the mosque (. . .), and the village of Carakovo (Prijedor), where Serb forces reportedly gathered 18 Muslim villagers in front of the mosque and killed them, wrapped the imam (clergyman) in a prayer carpet and burned him to death, then burned down the mosque and blew up the minaret.[59]

David Rieff notes that the destruction of mosques and other cultural and historical buildings was no accident:

---

56. Geraldine Brooks, "The Book of Exodus," *The New Yorker*, November 26, 2007, https://www.newyorker.com/magazine/2007/12/03/the-book-of-exodus.
57. See Hikmet Karčić, *Derviš M. Korkut: A Biography* (Sarajevo: El Kalem, 2020).
58. Helen Walasek, *Bosnia and the Destruction of Cultural Heritage* (London: Ashgate Publishing, 2015), 25.
59. András J. Riedlmayer, *Destruction of Cultural Heritage in Bosnia-Herzegovina, 1992–1996: A Postwar Survey of Selected Municipalities*, 13, https://bit.ly/DestructionCultHeritageBH.

Ethnic cleansing in Bosnia has been as much about methodically humiliating a people and destroying their culture as it has been about killing them. The Serb assault on the Ottoman and Islamic architectural legacy throughout the country was not a by-product of the fighting—collateral damage, as soldiers say—but an important war aim. For the Bosnian Serb leadership, the Serbianization of areas of Bosnia that had been ethnically mixed before the fighting started could not be accomplished simply by driving out many of the non-Serbs who lived in villages.[60]

Concentration Camps: Definitions

The United States Holocaust Museum defines the term "concentration camp" as "a camp in which people are detained or confined, usually under harsh conditions and without regard to legal norms of arrest and imprisonment that are acceptable in a constitutional democracy."[61]

According to the *Encyclopedia of Genocide and Crimes against Humanity*, detention or internment camps have the sole purpose of temporarily isolating suspected or dangerous individuals. The terms used to define these camps, such as "concentration camps," "detention camps," "internment camps," "extermination camps," "and prisoner-of-war camps," all belong to the same family, forming "a coherent and in some sense logical entity."[62]

Concentration camps were at the very heart of the totalitarian concentration camp systems, as seen in Nazi Germany, the Soviet gulag, communist Europe, or Asian camps.[63] These camps are characterized by humiliation, dehumanization, punishment, re-education and slave labor. In reality they are also places of extermination, with mortality rates of up to 50 percent.[64] They are used to depersonalize detainees so that the guards could more easily "regiment

---

60. David Rieff, *Slaughterhouse: Bosnia and the Failure of the West* (New York: Vintage, 1995), 96.
61. United States Holocaust Museum (USHMM), "Concentration Camps, 1933–1939," in *Holocaust Encyclopedia*, last edited June 27, 2019, http://www.ushmm.org/wlc/en/article.php?ModuleId=1000 5263.
62. Joël Kotek, "Concentration Camps," in *Encyclopedia of Genocide and Crimes against Humanity*, ed. Dinah L. Shelton (Detroit, MI: Thomson/Gale, 2005), 196.
63. Marshall S. Clough describes the similarities between the Soviet camps and British camps in Kenya and states, "A parallel between colonial conditions and totalitarian conditions, a parallel noted by Frantz Fanon, though colonial camps were less isolated from public opinion in the metropole and in the international community than were the Soviet camps." See Marshall S. Clough, *Mau Mau Memoirs: History, Memory, and Politics* (Boulder, CO; Lynne Rienner Publishers, 1998), 205.
64. Kotek, "Concentration Camps," 199.

and brutalize them . . . as a strategy of physical control and a way of mentally compartmentalizing the 'other.'"[65]

Concentrating and detaining people had several common factors: the notion of collectively punishing an entire group; the idea of pre-emption (with most of the interned being innocent); administrative detention (whereby no court has judged the internees); and bad health conditions (with mortality high from the start).[66]

Recently two publications appeared that deal with the issue of concentration camps. The first, written by British historian Dan Stone, is *Concentration Camps: A Short History*, which gives an analytical overview of concentration camps. It is not a comprehensive historical overview, but, as the name suggests, it a short history, a mixture of historic, sociological, and philosophical analysis. Realizing the common misunderstanding and misuse of the term "concentration camp," Stone explains:

> A concentration camp is not normally a death camp, although death camps in the context of the Holocaust obviously derived from concentration camps and the killing of asylum patients (the so-called 'Euthanasia programme') in terms of their institutional history. No one was 'concentrated' in the Nazi death camps of Chelmno (which was not a camp in any meaningful sense), Sobibor, Belzec, or Treblinka, where Jews (and a small number of Roma and Sinti) where sent to die.

An important part of Stone's work is the evidence he provides that regimes and perpetrators have learned from each other over the years in the use of camps. Stone concludes that "concentration camps constitute a world-wide phenomenon which has developed over time as different states and regimes have learned from others in other parts of the world."[67]

A more comprehensive historical overview of concentration camps was given by Andrea Pitzer in her book *One Long Night: A Global History of Concentration Camps*. The author gives a good chronological overview of the establishment of camps throughout history. Like Stone, Pitzer argues that camps throughout history are not the same but derive from the same root: "while they developed differences in tactics as well as tremendous variability in outcomes due to limits that culture and governments imposed on them, most systems arose from simi-

---

65. Clough, *Mau Mau Memoirs*, 205.
66. Kotek, "Concentration Camps," 196.
67. Dan Stone, *Concentration Camps: A Short History* (New York: Oxford University Press, 2017), 108.

lar political crises and possessed parallel early goals."[68] Another important note from Pitzer is the terminology to use for persons confined in the camp. She states that concentration camps are set up to house people who do not have trials, thus the term "detainee" can be used for a person confined in a concentration camp or detention facility.[69] The serious shortcoming in Pitzer's work is that there is almost no mention of camps in Bosnia and Herzegovina at all.

All of the above helps us establish an idea of what constitutes a concentration camp, but it is perhaps Dan Stone's formulation, made later on in his book, that guides us here: The crucial characteristic of a concentration camp is not whether it has barbed wire, fences, or watchtowers; it is, rather, the gathering of civilians, defined by a regime as de facto "enemies," in order to hold them against their will without charge in a place where the rule of law has been suspended.[70]

As the following chapters will reveal, the Bosnian Serb camps, as with the camps that preceded them, were the sites at the crux of the Bosnian Serb genocide against the Bosniak community. Their creation facilitated the genocidal ethnic cleansing that swept the region, which in turn represented what Lemkin defined as a synchronized attack on the Bosniak *lebenswelt*. Within the camps and their surrounding environs, there was a concerted, macabre campaign of traumatization, rich in symbolic violence, that had the genocidal aim of breaking the Bosniaks and their "family of mind." This violence was followed up by either permanent expulsion (again, an element of genocide) or murder. Alongside this, there was the concerted campaign of cultural destruction of all property that had Muslim symbolism.

Concentration Camps: Historical Background

The idea of concentrating civilians *en masse* was first implemented around 150 years ago and continues to be popular today. The chronology of the camps shows that over the years, regimes and perpetrators learned from one another. Historically speaking, concentration camps have been utilized in two ways, either as a counterinsurgency tactic or as a nonmilitary, genocidal tactic.

---

68. Andrea Pitzer, *One Long Night: A Global History of Concentration Camps* (Boston: Little, Brown and Company, 2017), 8.
69. Pitzer, *One Long Night*,. 5.
70. Stone, *Concentration Camps*, 122–23.

As an example of the former, in 1869 wealthy Cuban farmers rose up against the Spanish Crown in what is known as the Spanish-Cuban Ten Year's War (1868–78).[71] The rebellion was started with the proclamation of independence on October 10, 1868, by Cuban sugar mill owner Carlos Manuel de Céspedes and his followers, and ultimately the Spanish proved to be unsuccessful in quelling the rebellion. In a bid to resolve the issue, the Spanish government sent General Valeriano Wyler y Nicolau to Havana to crush the rebels. Wyler had had previous experience in antiguerrilla warfare in Santo Domingo and the Philippines and was considered the best man to finish the "dirty job."[72]

Wyler deployed a new tactic in a bid to gain control of the situation. He decided to detain large groups of people in camps, with the aim of totally separating them from the guerrillas.[73] In October 1896 and January 1897, he issued a decree ordering the concentration of the civilian population in eastern, western, and central provinces of the country. These camps, known as *(re)concentrados*, saw the large-scale concentration of civilians in towns and villages under surveillance by Spanish regular and irregular soldiers. As a result of the rebellion, the Spanish were forced to involve far more troops than they had originally deployed, although the guerrilla force was smaller in size. The Spanish concentration policy from 1896–97 was "unprecedented at the time for its scale, intensity and efficiency" as it contained at least 170,000 civilian internees, around one-tenth of the total population.[74] This system had a high mortality rate, which the United States used as a justification for a "humanitarian" intervention in April 1898, which subsequently brought Spanish colonial rule in Cuba to an end.[75]

The United States also undertook a "humanitarian" intervention in the Philippines in December 1898 in a bid to bring cultural transformation to the country. The United States considered it a "civilizing mission." War broke out two months later, in February 1899, when Emilio Aguinaldo and his Tagalog and Ilocano forces in Luzon fought back against America's altruism. He was captured in 1901 and the rebellion was brought to an end in 1902 by the presence of around seventy thousand American troops. During the rebellion, the US officers demanded tight military measures, which included "not only the

---

71. Iain R. Smith and Andreas Stucki, "The Colonial Development of Concentration Camps (1868–1902)," *Journal of Imperial and Commonwealth History* 39, no. 3 (September 2011): 417–37. https://doi.org/10.1080/03086534.2011.598746.
72. Smith and Stucki, 422.
73. Kotek, "Concentration Camps," 196.
74. Smith and Stucki, "Colonial Development," 422.
75. The US Army described Wyler's policy as "uncivilized warfare."

confiscation of property, summary executions, massacres, deportations and crop destruction but also civilian concentration in designated areas." The American officers resorted to civilian concentration after learning from the Spanish in Cuba, from the British in South Africa, and also, most importantly, from their own extensive experience of establishing "reservations" for Native Americans during the genocidal "Indian Wars" in North America in the nineteenth century. The number of deaths is difficult to establish, since it is hard to separate the deaths in "concentration zones" from the deaths caused as a result of epidemics and diseases.

The Americans decided to interfere in the Philippines because they regarded the Filipinos as an inferior race, incapable of self-rule. President Theodore Roosevelt declared that "Filipino independence" would be "like granting self-government to an Apache reservation under some local chief." As Pitzer notes, in 1899, a year after the United States and Spain went into war, a meeting of international delegates took place in The Hague, where they discussed the first convention on international laws of war and war crimes. They refused, however, to talk about the issue of concentration camps, which were proving to be a simple and efficient tool for the colonialists and were soon being used by many other countries.[76]

The South African War (1899–1902), also known as the Boer War, was fought between the Boers, descendants of the earlier Dutch settlers in South Africa, and the British Empire. It proved to be one of the most humiliating, extensive, and costly wars Britain fought in its colonial history.

The Boers were a combined force of the South African Republic and the Republic of the Orange Free State.[77] The war had three phases:[78] The early phase, from October to December 1899, when the British armies, mainly infantry, were defeated or besieged by highly mobile Boer mounted troops; the second phase, from December 1899 until September 1900, which involved a British counteroffensive that resulted in the capture of most of the major towns and cities of South Africa; and the third and longest phase, from September 1900 to May 1902, when the war was mainly a guerrilla conflict between British mounted troops and Boer irregulars.

---

76. Pitzer, *One Long Night*, 40.
77. Adam Augustyn, "South African War," in *Encyclopaedia Britannica*, last modified October 4, 2020, http://www.britannica.com/event/South-African-War.
78. Australian War Memorial, "Australia and the Boer War 1899–1902," accessed January 18, 2016, https://www.awm.gov.au/atwar/boer/.

This colonial war soon evolved into a regional war. The British were supported by volunteers from Australia, New Zealand, Canada, , and British India. By 1900, the British established the first camps, known as the "protection camps," for Boers and their families who had surrendered (*hendsoppers*).[79] Later, other families that had been displaced from their homes by the fighting joined them. The system then evolved into a combination of "protection camps" for those who surrendered and "concentration camps" for the other civilian refugees, most of whose menfolk were still waging a guerrilla war against the British. The British hoped that the camps would bring an end to the war; they announced that guerrillas who surrendered could join their families in the camps while those who did not risked having their farms burned or confiscated. The Boer guerrillas captured on the battlefield were sent to POW camps overseas.

The commander-in-chief of the British Army, first Lord Roberts and later Field Marshal Horatio Herbert Kitchener, organized the harsh and systematic "scorched earth" and "clearance" policy, which swept tens of thousands of civilians—black and white—into improvised tented camps that were established along the railway lines. These camps were established without any planning, since it was believed this would be a temporary measure. There was a clear distinction and division of the "white" and "black" camp systems. The "white" camp system was administered by the British War Office and Colonial Office, while the "black" camps were administered by the Native Refugee Department.[80] As the war continued, the camps became more sophisticated, thousands of blockhouses surrounded with barbed wire and tight security manned with fifty thousand soldiers and African auxiliaries.[81] It is estimated that there were around a hundred thousand Boer camp inmates. The camps had a high mortality rate, with total deaths amounting to around twenty-five thousand people. According to the *Dictionary of Genocide*:

> These camps were an unmitigated humanitarian disaster from the first. Unsuitable locations, huge overcrowding, a thorough inadequacy of sanitary conditions and medical personnel, and unsatisfactory supply and poor quality of

---

79. Smith and Stucki, "Colonial Development," 425.
80. The "black" camps were "farm and labor" camps set up along the railway lines on unoccupied land, and the inmates constructed for themselves temporary huts or shanties. See Smith and Stucki, "Colonial Development," 429.
81. Smith and Stucki, "Colonial Development," 426.

COLLECTIVE TRAUMATIZATION 51

foodstuffs were just a few of the problems. These institutions were an amalgam of refugee and internment camps, but in concentrating together families from widely distant farms and towns they brought people into close contact who were often devoid of the necessary immunities from disease that urban living can promote. The upshot saw an unprecedented death rate."[82]

The war ended with the Treaty of Vereeniging peace agreement in May 1902, which replaced the "unconditional surrender" the British had insisted on.

In January 1904, the Hereros, who inhabited large areas of colonial German South West Africa—today's Namibia—started a revolt against the Germans. The revolt lasted two years and ended with the Germans defeating the revolt and destroying the Hereros as a cultural entity.[83] There were several reasons for the Herero uprising, but the two primary ones were, first, a massive loss of land. With the completion of the railroad "from the coast to the capital of the colony, Windhoek, the pace of alienation accelerated rapidly, so that by the end of 1903, 3.5 million hectares out of a total of 13 million had been lost, and the day when the Hereros would not have enough land to continue their traditional way of life was fast approaching. The loss of land, frightening as it was to any Herero who looked only a few years into the future, did not yet in 1903 affect the daily life of the Hereros."[84] The second, more immediate problem was that of debt. For years, Hereros were forced to borrow money from the white traders at usurious rates of interest, and their living situations had become untenable.

The revolt was led by Samuel Maharero, who was a paramount chief of the Herero people. The initial attack started in January 1904 and was aimed at German farmer families. Every German farm, village, and fort was attacked and destroyed. Soon large groups of fresh German troops were brought in to defeat the rebellion. In August 1904, the Battle of Waterberg was fought, in which the outnumbered Hereros were quickly defeated by the mighty and well-equipped German army. General Lothar von Trotha, the commander of German forces in South West Africa, did not aim only to militarily defeat the Hereros, but to utterly destroy them. The German army killed all the Herero men, women, and children they came across.[85] On October 2, 1904, von Trotha issued an order

---

82. Samuel Totten and Paul Bartrop, *Dictionary of Genocide* (Westport, CT: Greenwood Press, 2008), 84.
83. Samuel Totten, William S. Parsons, and Israel W. Charny, *Century of Genocide: Critical Essays and Eyewitness Accounts* (London: Psychology Press, 2004), 15.
84. Totten, Parsons, and Charny, *Century of Genocide*, 15.
85. Totten, Parsons, and Charny, *Century of Genocide*, 25.

stating, "All the Hereros must leave the land. If the people do not do this, then I will force them to do it with the great guns. Any Herero found within the German borders with or without a gun, with or without cattle, will be shot. I shall no longer receive any women or children. I will drive them back to their people or I will shoot them. This is my decision for the Herero people."[86] Some Hereros decided to try to make it through the Omaheke desert. A small number survived the desert and German raids and made it to Botswana.

Soon, however, there was a change in strategy. Instead of extermination, the Germans decided to "imprison" the Hereros, adopting a concept similar to the "concentration camps" that were used during the Boer War. The German term for these camps was *Konzentrationslager*.[87] According to sources, "In the German prison labor camps there were 10,632 women and children, and 4,137 men. Subsequently, in the next year, 7,682 of the imprisoned natives died as a result of forced labor and harsh treatment."[88] Thousands were used as slave labor for German businesses.[89] The main concentration camps were based in Windhoek, Okahandja, Karibib, Swakopmund, and Omaruru.

In August 1906, the labor camps were closed and the surviving Hereros were divided into small groups and shipped off to work on the farms and ranches of the German settlers. There they were kept in smaller camps called *kraals*, a word usually used to mean enclosures for cattle, which were fenced, mostly by barbed wire or with thorn-bush fencing. The interned people of the camps were mostly used for slave labor. The most common causes of mortality, which was high, were scurvy, pneumonia, influenza, syphilis, and other STDs.[90] The living conditions and accommodations were primitive and the amount of food provided by the camp administration was poor. There were also cases of forced sexual intercourse between Herero women with soldiers and settlers: "Many of our in this way deported wives and daughters later returned either pregnant or with a child from a white man. This obligation to go and work for the white man was not a government ordinance, but white men came to the

---

86. Jon Bridgman, *The Revolt of the Hereros* (Berkeley: University of California Press, 1981), 128.
87. One officer wrote to von Trotha, "I am of the opinion that the surrendering Herero should be placed in Konzentrationlager, concentration camps, in various locations of the territory, there to be put under guard and required to work." Cited in Pitzer, *One Long Night*, 81.
88. Totten, Parsons, and Charny, *Century of Genocide*, 30.
89. See Jeremy Sarkin-Hughes, *Germany's Genocide of the Herero: Kaiser Wilhelm II, His General, His Settlers, His Soldiers* (Rochester, NY: James Currey, 2011).
90. Casper W. Erichsen, *The Angel of Death has Descended Violently among Them: Concentration Camps and Prisoners-of-War in Namibia, 1904–08* (Leiden: African Studies Centre, 2005), 50, accessed January 18, 2016, https://openaccess.leidenuniv.nl/handle/1887/4646.

kraals [Camps] and just gave the order—take your blanket and come; and we had no choice."[91]

The most notorious camp was the Shark Island (*Haifischinsel*) concentration camp in Lüderitz. The island is a little offshore, and the camp was open-air, consisting of primitive huts and tents. The first group of twenty-eight Herero prisoners arrived at the camp in 1904. The exact number of people interned in the camp during its entire existence is unknown. According to one source "as many as 59 men, 59 women and 73 children had died on Shark Island in an unspecified space of time."[92] The number of prisoners brought to Shark Island increased as the need for labor increased.[93] Another interesting point is that German medical professor Eugen Fischer conducted research and medical experiments on bones and skulls of Shark Island's deceased prisoners.[94]

The First World War saw the mass internment of people become a popular practice all over the world. Almost every country at war started arresting and incarcerating foreign citizens on their territory. Germany arrested all British, French, and Russian men of military age. France interned German and Austro-Hungarian citizens. Bulgaria arrested Serb and Croat citizens, Romania held Germans and Austro-Hungarians. As Pitzer states, the "British decision to intern enemy aliens throughout the empire triggered global reciprocity."[95] In Australia for example, the British Empire arrested and incarcerated enemy aliens working in Australia including Bosniaks, Croats, and Serbs from the Austro-Hungarian Empire.[96] Ottoman citizens who traveled to Mecca for the Hajj pilgrimage were arrested in Egypt by the British, while the Ottomans arrested British and French citizens in Jerusalem. Although the conditions inside these camps were inhumane, generally speaking, the World War I internment camps were not places of

---

91. Erichsen, *The Angel of Death*, 46.
92. Erichsen, *The Angel of Death*, 73.
93. One transport rider witnessed: "The women who are captured and not executed are set to work for the military as prisoners . . . saw numbers of them at Angra Pequena put to the hardest work, and so starved that they were nothing but skin and bones (. . .) They are given hardly anything to eat, and I have very often seen them pick up bits of refuse food thrown away by the transport riders. If they are caught doing so, they are sjamboked (whipped)." See Ibid., 78.
94. Professor Fischer's studies influenced German colonial legislation and provided scientific support for the Nuremberg laws. He was later a Nazi Party member. The skulls experimented on were returned in 2011. See "Germany Returns Namibian Skulls Taken in Colonial Era," *BBC*, September 30, 2011, http://www.bbc.com/news/world-europe-15127992. Accessed January 18, 2016.
95. Pitzer, *One Long Night*, 95–96.
96. For example, see the example of Mustafa Fetahagić in Discovering Anzacs, "Index to Album of Identification Photographs of Enemy Aliens (Civilian and Prisoner of War) Interned at Liverpool Camp, NSW during World War I—A to L," accessed January 24, 2016, 25, https://discoveringanzacs.naa.gov.au/browse/records/457761/25. I would like to thank Mr. Abdulah Drury for this information.

mass murder or torture. It was during this period, however, that a much more bureaucratic approach to camp creation and management can be observed. They had also become a global phenomenon. They no longer "had to rise out of the local chaos of warfare, but instead represented a deliberate choice to inject the framework of war into society itself."[97]

Konzentrationslager were an integral part of the Nazi regime in Germany from 1933 to 1945.[98] Detention and concentration camps were set up in an ad hoc fashion as early as 1933, the year Hitler came to power. For these first camps, existing structures were converted. The first Nazi camp was opened near the village of Nohra (Thuringia) in an old school building close to the famous town of Weimar.[99] Other camps such as the Ochstumsand camp, opened in a ship near Bremen, were used to incarcerate political opponents and "asocials."[100] Another example was the makeshift camp for Roma opened in Marzhan, where they were incarcerated in the runup to the Olympic Games in 1936.[101] The Nazi regime knew of the British and of the German camps in Africa, but they also had their own experiences of the internment camps of the First World War. Now they were about to enhance the camp system and industrialize death.[102]

The camps were a part of the Nazi project and Hitler's idea of *Lebensraum*, living space for German people. The idea was that the German people did not have enough space to live freely, thus new territory, "new land and soil," was to be seized to make room for the Germans. Hitler's justification for the removal of people in Eastern Europe drew direct inspiration from the fate of the Native Americans: "The struggle we are waging there against the partisans resembles very much the struggle in North America against the Red Indians."[103] Similar to all settler colonialism, the Nazis also had ideas of establishing reservations, this time for Jews. One such idea was to deport all Jews from Europe to the island of Madagascar. These ideas, however, were dropped due to a lack of resources, and concentration camps were seen as the best solution.

---

97. Pitzer, *One Long Night*, 103.
98. Abbreviated as KL or KZ.
99. Geoffrey P. Megargee, ed., *The United States Holocaust Memorial Museum Encyclopedia of Camps and Ghettos Vol. I* (Washington, DC: United States Holocaust Memorial Museum, 2009), 140–41.
100. See USHMM, "An Early Concentration Camp (Photograph)," in Concentration Camps: 1933–1939, accessed January 7, 2016, https://www.ushmm.org/wlc/en/media_ph.php?ModuleId=10005263&MediaId=775.
101. See USHMM, "Persecution of Roma (Gypsies) in Prewar Germany, 1933–1939," in *Holocaust Encyclopedia*, last edited June 27, 2019, https://www.ushmm.org/wlc/en/article.php?ModuleId=10005482.
102. Pitzer, *One Long Night*, 165.
103. Pitzer, *One Long Night*, 195.

COLLECTIVE TRAUMATIZATION   55

The camps were formed by a variety of organizations: The SA (*Sturmab-teilungen*, Storm Troopers), the SS (*Schutzstaffel*, the elite guard of the Nazi party), the police, and local civilian authorities. The first people to be held in the camps were political opponents, those who did not agree with the Nazi party ideology.[104] The primary enemies of the state were communists and Jews who had broken the anti-Semitic Nuremberg Race Laws of 1935, who were labeled as professional criminals. Another group targeted were the "asocials," those who did not fit into the German society: "The pursuit of social deviants was a major part of the Nazi policy of exclusion, aimed at removing all those who did not (or could not) fit into the mythical national community."[105]

In 1934, Hitler ordered SS chief Heinrich Himmler to establish a centralized system and administration of the camps, as the Nazis scaled up their activity against their enemies and gained ever more control over German society. SS Lieutenant General Theodor Eicke, camp commander in Dachau, was given the task of drafting the organizational structure and administration of the proposed camp system. This planned camp system was to have a clear hierarchy and previously established responsibilities for each member of its administration and security.

During the 1936 Olympic Games, as the Olympic torch was being lit, prisoners were clearing a vast pine forest less than twenty-five miles away near Oranienburg. They were preparing ground for a new camp—Sachsenhausen—which until 1938 held mostly political prisoners.

The German security police—namely the Gestapo and the criminal police—had the authority to arrest and send people to the camps. Their legal basis for arrest was the "protective detention" (*Schutzhaft*) order or the "preventive detention" (*Vorbeugungshaft*) order.[106] Later, however, the arrest and detention of prisoners and the work of the camps would operate outside the law. Hitler placed his full support behind Himmler, allowing him to unite all the police under his control. The number of camps increased as the number of political opponents and social deviants increased. By 1939, there were six major concentration camps in Third Reich, both in Germany and the occupied territories: Dachau (1933), Sachsenhausen (1936), Buchenwald (1937), Flossenbürg (1938),

---

104. Nikolaus Wachsmann, *KL: A History of the Nazi Concentration Camps* (New York: Farrar, Straus and Giroux, 2015), 31.
105. Wachsmann, *KL*, 140.
106. USHMM, "Concentration camps 1933–1939," accessed January 19, 2016, http://www.ushmm.org/wlc/en/article.php?ModuleId=10005263.

Mauthausen (1938), and Ravensbrück (1939).[107] Their existence was not a secret. Buchenwald was near the famous German town of Weimar, where Germany's first democratic constitution was drafted, and the town's inhabitants knew about the camp. Locals living near the Mauthausen camp near Linz in Austria interacted with the camp's guards and even played football matches with them in front of the camp.[108]

During a speech in 1939, Henrich Himmler explained the function of the camps and their importance for Germany's future: "The slogan that stands above these camps is: There is a path to freedom. Its milestones are: obedience, diligence, honesty, orderliness, cleanliness, sobriety, truthfulness, readiness to make sacrifices and love of the fatherland."[109] This and similar slogans were adopted by the SS and used in camps. The most infamous slogan was "Arbeit macht frei" ("Work Makes Free") found on the entrance of Auschwitz and other camps. Forced labor was used in all the KL and it became a daily routine for the prisoners. The idea was not to make use of the prisoners to perform useful work but rather to use the work to humiliate, harm, and eventually kill prisoners.

Things changed dramatically when on November 7, 1938, a Jewish teenager, Herschel Grynszpan, walked into the German embassy in Paris and shot and wounded a German diplomat, Ernst vom Rath, who died several days later. Prior to this assassination, Grynszpan's parents had been deported from the Third Reich to the Polish border along with thousands of other Jewish Poles. The killing of vom Rath provided the Nazis with an excuse for the "night of broken glass" (*Kristallnacht*). This pogrom against the Jews was followed with mass arrests and detention, and the KL system became too small to house the sudden influx of detained Jews.

When Nazi Germany embarked on their conquest, sparking World War II in 1939, the number of interned people increased and as a result the number of camps and subcamps increased in order to house political prisoners, resistance groups, and groups considered racially inferior, such as Jews and Roma (gypsies). Deputy Führer Rudolf Hess wrote, "War came and with it the great turn

---

107. USHMM, "Concentration camps 1939–1942," accessed January 19, 2016, http://www.ushmm.org/wlc/en/article.php?ModuleId=10005474.
108. KZ-Gedenkstätte Mauthausen, "Walking Tour of the Area Around the Mauthausen Memorial," August 29, 2017, https://www.mauthausen-memorial.org/en/News/Walking-tour-of-the-area-around-the-Mauthausen-Memorial.
109. Christian Goeschel and Nikolaus Wachsman, *The Nazi Concentration Camps, 1933–1939: A Documentary History* (Lincoln: University of Nebraska Press, 2012), 302.

COLLECTIVE TRAUMATIZATION 57

in the life of the concentration camp."[110] Jews now made up the largest number of prisoners. The new camps included Gusen (1939), Neuengamme (1940), Gross-Rosen (1940), Auschwitz (1940), Natzweiler (1940), Stutthof (1942), and Majdanek (1943). With this plethora of camps rapidly emerging, Himmler worried that a sort of privatization of camps would occur—where local Nazi officials would run their own camps—so he ordered that "concentration camps can only be established with my authorization." One of his lieutenants suggested the opening of a new KL in the east to "hold down the Polish population." The SS soon opened a site near Katowice (Kattowitz). The Germans took a symbolic step and renamed it with its old German name: Auschwitz.[111]

There were several types of camps, established for different purposes: labor camps, extermination camps, transit camps, and prisoner of war camps.[112] In camps such as Dachau and Auschwitz, medical experiments were conducted on prisoners.[113] The *Kapos* were one of the secrets to the success of the KL, a core element of the camp SS's machinery of terror. *Kapos* were prisoners engaged as surrogate guards. The word is derived from the Italian word "capo," which means head or leader. Himmler explained that a few hand-picked prisoners should be selected and given privileges, and in return they would force others to work and discipline them when they stepped out of line. In this way, only a small number of SS guards were needed to control camps using the "divide and rule" mechanism. This mechanism was also used in Jewish ghettos.[114]

In a bid to speed up the process of murdering the Jews, the Nazis set up several experimental execution sites, such as an execution chamber for Soviet POWs at Gross-Rosen and a gas chamber at Block 11 in Auschwitz, where Zyklon-B was used. These experimental sites proved to be successful, and gas chambers were set up to rapidly murder large groups of people, whose bodies were later burned in crematoria. Four of the biggest camps created were immediate extermination centers: Belzec, Chelmmo, Sobibor, and Treblinka.[115] These were not camps to intern people but rather to immediately terminate them on arrival, providing the "Final Solution of the Jewish Question" (*Die Endlösung*

---

110. Wachsmann, *KL: A History*, 192.
111. USHMM, "Auschwitz," in *Holocaust Encyclopedia*, accessed January 20, 2016, https://www.ushmm.org/wlc/en/article.php?ModuleId=10005189.
112. International School for Holocaust Studies—Yad Vashem, "Concentration Camps," accessed January 19, 2016, 1–3, http://www.yadvashem.org/odot_pdf/Microsoft%20Word%20-%205925.pdf.
113. Wachsmann, *KL: A History*, 194.
114. Wachsmann, *KL: A History*, 122.
115. Kotek, "Concentration Camps," 199.

des Judenfrage). In these camps and others, work units—*Sonderkommandos*—made up of prisoners, usually Jews, were created, whose primary job was the disposal of bodies from gas chambers.[116]

Above all, stands the name Auschwitz. The largest camp in the Nazi network, the site functioned as an unusual hybrid of labor and death camp.[117] Much has been written about Auschwitz elsewhere, and this book does not, and cannot, hope to take in the enormity of what happened there, save to recount some basic figures. Of the 1.3 million people sent to Auschwitz during the camp's existence from 1942 to 1945 (though the gas chambers and crematoria were dynamited in 1944 as it became clearer that the Nazis were losing the war), 1.1 million were murdered. This factory of death reached its peak output during the 1944 deportation of the Hungarian Jews: "the SS gassed as many as 6,000 Jews each day. By November 1944, the SS had killed more than a million Jews and tens of thousands of Roma, Poles, and Soviet prisoners of war in Auschwitz-Birkenau. At least 865,000 Jews were killed immediately upon arrival. The overwhelming majority were killed in the gas chambers."[118]

The Nazi concentration camp (*Konzentrationlager*) system definitely represented the peak in the systematic and organized industrialization of murder in modern history. The camps were used as one of the tools for destruction, but not as the primary one. It is estimated that six million European Jews were murdered in Europe: "shot in ditches and fields across Eastern Europe, or gassed in distinct death camps."[119]

Most of the camps, however, alongside their genocidal function, served other purposes for the Nazis, as Wachsmann explains: "the SS used them also to destroy the Polish resistance and to forge a closer collaboration with the industry."[120]

The Nazi camp system, as the most organized and industrialized, has been the subject of much research. Nikolaus Wachsmann, in his well-documented book *KL: A History of the Nazi Concentration Camps*, states that camps were a product of modernity, with advanced systems of bureaucracy, transport, mass communication, technology, industrially manufactured barracks, barbed wire, machine guns, and gas chambers:

---

116. Jacqueline Shields, "Concentration Camps: The Sonderkommando," Jewish Virtual Library, accessed January 19, 2016, http://www.jewishvirtuallibrary.org/the-sonderkommando.

117. Wachsmann, *KL: A History*, 6.

118. USHMM, "Killing Centres: In Depth," in *Holocaust Encyclopedia*, accessed January 5, 2020, https://encyclopedia.ushmm.org/content/en/article/introduction-to-the-holocaust.

119. Wachsmann, *KL: A History*, 288.

120. Wachsmann, *KL: A History*, 624.

The KL were products of German history; they emerged and developed under specific national political and cultural conditions, and drew inspiration from the violent practices of Weimar paramilitaries, as well as the disciplinary traditions of the German army and prison service (. . .) The KL shared some generic features with repressive camps established elsewhere during the twentieth century. That said, their development still diverged from other totalitarian camps (. . .) The specific character of individual camps owed much to the initiative of the local SS. But these officials operated within the parameters set by their superiors, and in the end, the KL acted much like seismographs, closely attuned to the general aims and ambitions of the regime's rulers. The reason they oscillated so much was that the priorities of Nazi leaders changed over time, and as the regime radicalized, so did the camps.[121]

Other camps were in operation during World War II as well. In December 1941, Japanese airplanes bombed Pearl Harbor, a US naval base in Hawaii. This marked the entrance of the United States into World War II. Soon, President Franklin D. Roosevelt signed Executive Order 9066 which led to the relocation of nearly 122,000 men, women, and children of Japanese ancestry on the west coast of the United States.[122] A government agency—the War Relocation Authority (WRA)—was set up to deal with internment, the forced relocation and detention of Japanese Americans. The WRA built several relocation centers on the west coast whose aim was to exclude all people of Japanese descent from military-designated areas. It is believed that more than 100,000 people—first- (*Issei*), second- (*Nisei*), and third- (*Sansei*) generation—of Japanese descent were interned in these camps. Armed guards were placed in the camps, and the interned Japanese Americans were treated fairly unless they broke the rules of the camps. The aim of these camps was to keep the Japanese Americans under control and to *americanize* them.[123] American government intelligence determined that the Japanese Americans did not pose any national security threat, military justification was the main reason given for the relocation project. One report stated: "There will be no armed uprising of Japanese. . . . For the most part the local Japanese are loyal to the United Stated or, at worst, hope that by remaining quiet they can avoid concentration camps or irresponsible mobs."

---

121. Wachsmann, *KL: A History*, 626.
122. Japanese American Relocation Digital Archive, "Essay: Relocation and Incarceration of Japanese Americans During World War II," Calisphere/University of California, accessed February 3, 2016, https://calisphere.org/exhibitions/essay/8/relocation/.
123. Cathy Cockrell, "How Japanese Americans Preserved Traditions behind Barbed Wire," *Berkeley News*, June 10, 2010, http://news.berkeley.edu/2010/06/10/muramoto/.

Despite such reports, the government went ahead with its proposed plan. It is reasonable to believe that the decision to relocate and intern people of Japanese descent was influenced by "anti-Japanese attitudes held by individuals in strategic decision-making positions in the U.S government." General Dwight D. Eisenhower in his memoirs defends the establishment of the camps: "We called the relocation camps 'evacuation centers' . . . Never did we think of them as concentration camps. Technically, the Japanese-Americans were not restricted to the camps, although in fact they could not return to the Pacific coast and movement without safeguards to any other location would probably have endangered their lives, at least in the beginning."[124]

The relocation camps were shut down in 1945 and the interned Japanese Americans were returned to their prewar towns. The largest relocation camp in the United States was Crystal City in Texas. It was founded in 1943 and contained several thousand internees of Japanese, German, and Italian origin. Crystal City was the only family-based camp, while the other camps divided men and women. This camp also housed internees who were deported from Latin American countries.[125]

Another interesting case occurred in Indonesia during the Second World War, where the Japanese interned Jews who were living in Indonesia. Most of the Jews were from the Middle East and had come to Indonesia to open businesses. Since Japan was an ally of Nazi Germany, however, they rounded up Jews and other European citizens living on the occupied territories.[126] One of the most brutal Japanese internment camps was Tjideng in Jakarta (then known as Batavia), where an estimated ten thousand people, mostly of Dutch origin, were interned. It is said that at least one hundred thousand people of European origin were interned in Java, Sumatra, Borneo, and Timor.[127] Later on, during President Sukarno's regime in Indonesia, thousands of suspected leftists were held in concentration camps and killed.[128]

Another camp system, again too vast to do anything other than provide the

---

124. Richard Drinnon, *Keeper of Concentration Camps: Dillon S. Myer and American Racism* (Berkeley: University of California Press, 1989), 6.
125. See Emily Brosveen, "World War II Internment Camps," in *Handbook of Texas Online*, accessed November 8, 2016, http://www.tshaonline.org/handbook/online/articles/quwby.
126. Rotem Kowner, "The Japanese Internment of Jews in Wartime Indonesia and Its Causes," *Indonesia and the Malay World* 38, no. 112 (October 2010): 349–71, https://doi.org/10.1080/13639811.2010.51 3846.
127. "The Forgotten Women of the 'War in the East," *BBC*, October 19, 2014, http://www.bbc.com/news/magazine-29665232.
128. See "Amnesty International Special Report: Indonesia 1965 Documents," Amnesty International, accessed January 20, 2016, http://www.indonesia1965.org/wordpress/.

COLLECTIVE TRAUMATIZATION 61

briefest analysis of here, was the Gulag system set up by the communist regime across the Soviet Union. They were initially set up as forced labor camps for the "ideological re-education of the bourgeoisie."[129] Inmates were selected for detention by the Soviet secret police, the NKVD, who had considerable freedom in deciding on whom to deport to often distant parts of the country.[130] Conditions in these camps were extremely harsh. Economically, the camp system made little sense, as it proved to be massively inefficient due to the high mortality rates of the prisoners. Inmates often starved or froze to death due to inadequate food and insufficient clothing, which made it difficult to endure the severe Russian winters, and the incredibly long working hours. It is estimated that between 1929 and 1953, when Stalin died, some eighteen million people had passed through this massive system, while an additional six million were sent into exile outside the USSR.[131]

Between 1952 and 1960 in British Kenya, there was a revolt by the Kikuyu— the largest ethnic group in Kenya—against the British colonizers. The Kikuyu were also called Mau Mau, so the conflict became known as the Mau Mau Uprising. There are several reasons for the uprising, but economic deprivation and land expropriation were the primary triggers. The Mau Mau attacked white settlers, the British Army, and the Kikuyu who collaborated with the British. The assassination of Senior Chief Waruhiu, a supporter of the British rule, led the Colonial Office to declare a state of emergency. In order to deal with the insurgency, the British, besides leading a counterinsurgency in the forests, also developed a detention program with the aim of intimidating and isolating the insurgents from the population. Official figures stated that at least 80,000 people were detained in detention camps and heavily patrolled villages. Recent research, however, has discovered that the numbers are more likely to have been between 160,000 and 320,000.[132] The heavily patrolled villages— "cordoned off by barbed wire, spiked trenches and watchtowers—amounted to another form of detention. In camps, villages and other outposts, the Kikuyu suffered forced labour, disease, starvation, torture, rape and murder."[133] There were around fifty detention camps throughout the country, which in practice

---

129. Anne Applebaum, *Gulag: A History* (New York: Anchor Books, 2003), 10.
130. Applebaum, *Gulag*, 423.
131. Applebaum, *Gulag*, xvii.
132. Figures stated by Caroline Elkins. See Caroline Elkins, *Imperial Reckoning: The Untold Story of Britain's Gulag in Kenya* (New York: Henry Holt and Co., 2005), xiii.
133. Marc Parry, "Uncovering the Brutal Truth About the British Empire," *The Guardian*, August 18, 2016, https://www.theguardian.com/news/2016/aug/18/uncovering-truth-british-empire-caroline -elkins-mau-mau.

resembled Soviet Gulags.[134] American scholar Caroline Elkins, researching the British campaign in Kenya, concluded that it was "a murderous campaign to eliminate Kikuyu people, a campaign that left tens of thousands, perhaps hundreds of thousands, dead."[135] Similarities between post-Holocaust camps and totalitarian camps do exist. As Marshall S. Clough, while researching the Mau Mau Uprising in Kenya, noticed, "Like inmates of German or Soviet concentration camps, Mau Mau detainees often felt victimized as *much for they who were* as *for what they might have done*, seeing themselves as condemned to imprisonment and brutalization because of their convictions, their membership in a despised group, their ethnic background (as Jews or Gikuyu)."[136]

Following an armed communist insurgency in Malaya, in 1950 the "Briggs plan" was introduced by British general Sir Harold Briggs. The aim was to speed up the fight against the communists in Malaya. In order to do so, a large resettlement of Malay peasantry was conducted. There was already an existing system of detention camps in the country.[137] The "Briggs Plan" introduced a new resettlement policy of establishing "new villages" (*Kampung Baru*), partially fortified and guarded camps. The idea of the "new villages" was to separate the local populations from the communist insurgents. There was constant police supervision and an isolation of the inhabitants. The flow of materials and information into the camps was limited. It is estimated that 450 "new villages" were established and that around 450,000 people were resettled in a matter of a few years.[138]

Between October 1959 and January 1961, the French in Algeria established the *"camps de regroupement,"* similar to the British tactic in Malaya, with the aim of isolating the villages from insurgents. An observer noted, "[P]sychically [*sic*] their condition, when it can be honestly be sounded, is often not so healthy. But beyond all else it is clear that they are never going to be quite the same villages again that they once were and the longer the *regroupement* continues the more permanently changed will the face of rural Algeria be."[139]

The French in Algeria set up at least 936 *regroupement* centers, which

---

134. Clough, *Mau Mau Memoirs*, 205.
135. Parry, "Uncovering the Brutal Truth."
136. Clough, *Mau Mau Memoirs*, 205.
137. A significant number of Chinese were deported to China and claimed that had been were tortured and abused in the detention camps. One Malay nationalist-communist, Rashid Maidan, said that the conditions in the camps were primitive but not brutal.
138. For more on this case see Karl Hack, "Detention, Deportation and Resettlement: British Counterinsurgency and Malaya's Rural Chinese, 1948–1960," *Journal of Imperial and Commonwealth History* 43, no. 4 (September 4, 2015): 611–40, https://doi.org/10.1080/03086534.2015.1083218.
139. Jeffrey James Byrne, *Mecca of Revolution: Algeria, Decolonization, and the Third World Order* (New York: Oxford University Press, 2016), 99.

COLLECTIVE TRAUMATIZATION

interned almost one-fourth of the Algerian population, 2,157,000 people. Sociologist Michel Cornaton, in his study of concentration camps in Algeria, argues that in spite of their differences, "we must have the courage to recognize that the margin between the Nazi concentration camps and some of the *centre provisoires* seemed infinitesimal."[140]

In Chile, during dictator Augusto Pinochet's rule, it is estimated that from 1974 to 1977 around eighty different kinds of detention camps, secret prisons, and torture facilities existed.[141] Political opponents of the regimes were tortured and murdered. Most of their mortal remains are buried in hidden individual and mass graves. One of the most brutal detention sites was the National Stadium in Santiago, where around five thousand people were brutally tortured and murdered.[142] According to the *Dictionary of Genocide*:

> The victims were most frequently arrested, tortured, and then "disappeared," the practice of detention without trial and murder without due visible process giving its name to the victims as *Los Desaparecidos* (the disappeared ones). Often, as documented cases show, military helicopters would take the victims far out to sea, where they would be dumped. Military officers justified such acts as necessary to stop what they referred to as acts of terrorism, but, without any form of open trial, the *desaparecidos* were more than likely to have been only political opponents or those on the political left—trade unionists, students, priests of liberal opinion, and the like.[143]

During the 1988 Anfal Campaign in Iraq, Saddam Hussein deported Kurdish civilians to camps such as the Popular Army Camp Topzawa, near Kirkuk; the Popular Army Camp at Tikrit; women's prison at Dibs; Nugra Selman; and other locations.[144]

After the 9/11 terrorist attacks in New York in 2001, the war in Afghanistan

---

140. Debarati Sanyal, *Memory and Complicity: Migrations of Holocaust Remembrance* (New York: Fordham University Press, 2015), 300.

141. See *Report of the Chilean National Commission on Truth and Reconciliation Notre Dame* (Indiana: University of Notre Dame Press, 1993), accessed on January 19, 2016, https://bit.ly/ChileanTruthandRecon.

142. For more see Peter Read and Marivic Wyndham, "Putting Site Back into Trauma Studies: A Study of Five Detention and Torture Centres in Santiago, Chile," *Life Writing* 5, no. 1 (June 6, 2008): 79–96, https://doi.org/10.1080/14484520801902365.

143. Totten and Bartrop, *Dictionary of Genocide*, 18.

144. Human Rights Watch, "Genocide in Iraq: The Anfal Campaign Against the Kurds," 1993, https://www.hrw.org/reports/1993/iraqanfal/.

and later in Iraq saw the emergence of new camp systems. The most infamous camp from this period was Guantanamo Bay, off the coast of Cuba, in which several hundred "enemy combatants" were held. Instead of using the term "prisoner of war" (POW), the US authorities used the term "person under control" (PUC). Another infamous camp was the Abu Ghraib prison in Iraq, which became grimly famous for leaked pictures of detainees being tortured and humiliated. Torture was a key element inside these camps. The aim of torture was to get information or confessions out of a PUC.[145]

More recently, in 2015 Human Rights Watch published a report titled "If the Dead Could Speak: Mass Deaths and Torture in Syria's Detention Facilities," which documented in detail the systematic and brutal torture perpetrated by the Syrian regime against its opponents.[146]

Finally, at the time of writing, the People's Republic of China is operating a vast system of concentration camps (euphemistically titled Vocational Training Internment Camps) in Xinjiang, in the far west of the country, interning therein an estimate of between one million and three million Muslim Uighurs[147] for the purposes of "re-education" (breaking them from their faith), and possibly forced labor also.

There were other cases of genocidal violence where concentration camps did not play a large role, such as in Rwanda or in Cambodia, for example. Pol Pot's Khmer Rouge opted for mass torture and execution rather than internment, and it set up special torture centers such as the most infamous S-21 torture center.[148] This dreaded prison, run by the infamous Comrade Duch, was a place where, like so many others, torture was used to break and traumatize detainees, in a bid to reform and re-educate them, just before killing them.[149]

Returning finally to the Balkan historical context, concentration camps have also been used in wars before and after the war and genocide of the Bosniaks in Bosnia and Herzegovina.

During the Second World War, shortly after the Cvetković-Maček Agree-

---

145. Pitzer, *One Long Night*, 380.

146. Human Rights Watch, "If the Dead Could Speak: Mass Deaths and Torture in Syria's Detention Facilities," December 16, 2015, accessed January 20, 2016, https://bit.ly/HRWIfdeadcouldspeak.

147. Phil Stewart, "China Putting Minority Muslims in 'Concentration Camps,' U.S. Says," *Reuters*, May 4, 2019, https://bit.ly/ChinaMuslimCamps.

148. See The Killing Fields Museum of Cambodia, "S-21 Prison and Choeung Ek Killing Fields: Facing Death," accessed on January 20, 2016, http://www.killingfieldsmuseum.com/s21-victims.html.

149. David Chandler, *Voices from S-21: Terror and History in Pol Pot's Secret Prison* (Berkeley: University of California Press, 1999), 151.

COLLECTIVE TRAUMATIZATION   65

ment of 1939, Croatia, led by the Ustaša movement under Ante Pavelić, took over control of Bosnia and Herzegovina and established a Nazi puppet government called *Nezavisna Država Hrvatska—NDH* (Independent State of Croatia).[150] This new state passed racial laws that echoed those of their Nazi allies and set up several concentration camps in Croatia, either to collect and detain their opponents or simply to kill them. The most brutal and infamous are at Jasenovac and Jadovno, which were sites were tens of thousands of Serbs (the Ustaša's primary target), Roma, and Jews were murdered. The victims also included a significant number of Bosniaks who opposed the NDH, antifascist Croatian political prisoners, and members of captured partisan units.

Two smaller concentration camps existed on the territory of Bosnia and Herzegovina, in Kruščica near Vitez in central Bosnia, and in Bosanski Petrovac, on the border with Croatia.[151] The camp in Bosanski Petrovac was a transit camp where Jews from Bihać were brought in 1941. The camp in Kruščica was established in 1941 and held more than a thousand civilians from the island of Rab and later a few hundred Jews from Sarajevo. Soon this camp was shut down and the Jewish prisoners were sent to Jasenovac and Auschwitz.[152] The NDH also imposed a policy of forced conversion from Orthodoxy to Catholicism and also deportation of Serbs toward Serbia.

The Nazis invaded Serbia in 1941 and established a puppet regime led by Milan Nedić. This regime, officially known as the *Vlada narodnog spasa* (Government of National Salvation), set out to become the first country in Europe, after Estonia, to declare itself *"judenfrei."* Camps were set up for Serbian Jews and mass executions were conducted. The most infamous camp was *Staro Sajmište*, which was located in Belgrade. An estimated twenty thousand Jews were killed at this camp between 1941 and 1944.[153] Historian Christopher Browning states that Serbia is the only country other than Poland and the Soviet Union where the victims were killed on site and not deported. Also it was the only country other than Poland and the Soviet Union where an internment camp—*Staro Sajmište*—was

---

150. Ivo Banac, *With Stalin against Tito: Cominformist Splits in Yugoslav Communism* (Ithaca, NY: Cornell University Press), 76.
151. Enver Redžić, *Bosnia and Herzegovina in the Second World War* (London: Routledge, 2005), 70.
152. See Raul Hilberg, *Destruction of European Jews* (New Haven, CT: Yale University Press, 2003), 759.
153. Jovan Byford, "The Semlin Judenlager in Belgrade: A Contested Memory," The Holocaust and United Nations Outreach Programme, accessed July 1, 2016, http://www.un.org/en/holocaustremembrance/docs/paper20.shtml.

converted into a death camp where killing was conducted by poison gas.[154] Two other camps were set up in Belgrade; Banjica and Topovske Šupe.[155]

The 1998-99 war in Kosovo was the last war waged by Serbian president Slobodan Milošević's government. The Albanian population of Kosovo had been subjected to inhumane treatment and suppression by the Yugoslav government since the unrest in Kosovo during the 1980s. During the aggressive campaign of the Serbian army, thousands of Kosovar Albanians were killed, tortured, or expelled. The Serbian authorities did not set up camps as in Bosnia and Herzegovina; they used existing detention facilities to intern Kosovars. In May 1999, Serbian prison guards opened fire on Kosovar Albanian inmates in Dubrava prison and killed at least seventy people. It is believed that at least three thousand Kosovar Albanians were held in prisons in Serbia. The Smrekovnica prison was also used for detention and torture by Serbian police officers.[156] The Kosovo Liberation Army (KLA) also ran several detention facilities where Serbs and ethnic Albanian suspected of collaboration were kept, such as the facility in Lapušnik, where at least twenty-two prisoners were killed.[157] It is believed that the KLA ran several other detention facilities in Kosovo and Albania where Serbs and Roma and Albanians suspected of collaboration with the Serbs were confined and tortured.[158]

Almost every conflict in modern history has seen the use of some type of concentration camp. Concentrating civilian masses in a certain fixed area has proven to be a cheap and efficient way of controlling large masses of people. Evidently the perpetrators have learned from each other, while the rest of the world has failed, repeatedly, to learn the lessons that might ensure that concentration camps become a thing of the past.

---

154. Christopher Browning, "Sajmiste as a European Site of Holocaust Remembrance," *Filozofija i Društvo* 23, no. 4 (2012), https://doi.org/10.2298/FID1204099B.

155. Jelena Subotić, *Yellow Star, Red Star: Holocaust Remembrance after Communism* (Ithaca, NY: Cornell University Press, 2019), 52.

156. Prosecutor v. Vlastimir Đorđević (Judgment, Volume 1), IT-05-87/1-T (ICTY), February 23, 2011, 475, https://www.icty.org/x/cases/djordjevic/tjug/en/110223_djordjevic_judgt_en.pdf.

157. Pramod Mishra, *Human Rights Reporting* (Delhi: Isha Books, 2006), 85.

158. Altin Raxhimi, Michael Montgomery, and Vladimir Karaj, "KLA Ran Torture Camps in Albania," *Balkan Insight BIRN*, April 9, 2009, http://www.balkaninsight.com/en/article/kla-ran-torture-camps-in-albania.

COLLECTIVE TRAUMATIZATION 67

Previous Research on the Camps in Bosnia and Herzegovina

After the war, hundreds of books were published on the war, in Western Europe and America, as well as in the country and throughout the diaspora. Almost entirely, these publications have either dealt with mass atrocities and genocide in general or on a specific town or village. These publications can be divided into three generic groups: foreign journalist accounts, survivor memoirs, and academic publications. Until now, there has been no detailed or comprehensive publication on camps in Bosnia and Hezegovina.

Foreign journalists were the first to report and later publish accounts of their visits to the camps. Roy Gutman was the person who first "discovered" the camps (he wrote about Manjača camp in summer 1992[159]), and he was also among the first to publish a book (*Witness to Genocide*, 1993), which remains an important source of information about the crimes committed in Bosnia and Hezegovina. Gutman's book, along with its black-and-white photos, provides firsthand accounts of camps and survivor stories. As one of the rare journalists who visited various camps and massacre sites throughout the country, he brought the existence of the camps to the world's attention. When using this source and other publications from the wartime period, however, one needs to keep in mind that certain data, like the number of victims, are in most cases inaccurate or incomplete due to the lack of information at that time. The personal testimonies Gutman noted, however, as well as his well-documented observations, are a crucial contribution to the story of camps.

Ed Vulliamy, a British journalist, was part of the group that was the first to visit the Omarska and Trnopolje camps in August 1992. Like Gutman, Vulliamy, in his book *Seasons in Hell*, gives realistic (and gruesome) details about the conditions and state of detainees in the camps in Omarsa and Trnopolje:

> Their heads newly shaven, their clothes baggy over their skeletal bodies. Some are barely able to move. . . . The men are at various stages of human decay and affliction; the bones of their elbows and wrists protrude like pieces of jagged stone from the pencil-thin stalks to which their arms have been reduced. Their skin is putrefied, the complexions . . . have corroded. [They] are alive but

---

159. See for example Roy Gutman, "Serbs Have Slain Over 1,000 in 2 Bosnia Camps, Ex-Prisoners Say," *Los Angeles Times*, August 2, 1992, https://www.latimes.com/archives/la-xpm-1992-08-02-mn-5646-story.html.

68   TORTURE, HUMILIATE, KILL

decomposed, debased, degraded, and utterly subservient, and yet they fix their huge hollow eyes on us with [what] looks like blades of knives[160, 161]

Another journalist, Peter Maass, who also visited several camps in Bosnia and Hezegovina, wrote about the personalization of the mass atrocities. In his book *Love Thy Neighbor:A Story of War*, Maass writes, among other things, about a visit to two camps in Prijedor. He brilliantly explains the differences between the camps run by Serbs and by Nazis:

> Every imaginable degradation had been played out at Omarska during the previous months. It was not a death camp on the order of Auschwitz. There were no gas chamber to which the prisoners were marched off every day. What happened at Omarska was dirtier, messier. The death toll never approached Nazi levels but the brutality was comparable or, in some cases, superior, if that word could be used. The Nazis wanted to kill as many Jews as possible, and doing it as quickly as possible. The Serbs, however, wanted to interrogate their Bosnian prisoners, have sadistic fun by torturing them in the cruelest of ways and then kill them with whatever implement was most convenient.[162]

David Rieff states that the Bosnian Serbs divided the (remaining) non-Serbs into two groups (excluding those killed off in the first sweep). The first group were those the Bosnian Serbs were "undecided" about, and they were placed in what Rieff calls "intelligence camps"; some were later killed while others were released. The second group was made up of poor people and peasants, and they were marked for release while being kept in what Bosnian Serbs called "open centers." This categorization is not entirely correct, however, which is to some extent understandable given that the book was published in 1995, when the full extent of the camps was not yet understood. The camp detainees, as it will be later shown in Prijedor, were actually divided into three categories. The third category, which Rieff calls poor people were actually "people of no interest" for the Bosnian Serb perpetrators. They were mainly women, children, and

---

160. Ed Vulliamy, *Seasons in Hell: Understanding Bosnia's War* (New York: St. Martin's Press, 1994), 102.

161. Ed Vulliamy went on to report on camps in the south of Bosnia and Herzegovina, particularly Dretelj, near Mostar, wherein the Bosnian Croatian army interned Bosniaks. For example, see Ed Vulliamy, "'Neutrality' and the Absence of Reckoning: A Journalist's Account," *Journal of International Affairs* 52, no. 2 (Spring 1999): 603–20. Accessed December 20, 2020. http://www.jstor.org/stable/24358055.

162. Peter Maass, *Love Thy Neighbor: A Story of War* (New York: Vintage, 1997), 45.

COLLECTIVE TRAUMATIZATION   69

elderly, those who posed no threat to the Bosnian Serbs. Rieff, however, correctly points out another important element of the camps' usage: destruction of the Bosniak educated elite: "The Serb leaders were not acting out of blood lust. By ordering the deaths of as many educated Muslims as possible, they wanted to ensure that, whatever else happened, any future Bosnian Muslim state would be as bereft as possible of people who could make it work efficiently."[163]

After the war, several dozen associations gathering former camp detainees were formed. The largest camp detainee association is Savez logoraša BiH, which was formed in 1996. As part of this association, a Center for Research and Documentation was created with the aim of documenting facts about war crimes. According to their research, there were at least 657 sites of detention—camps (*logora*) in Bosnia and Herzegovina during the war.[164] Through their research, they have gathered the names of fifty-six thousand former detainees, persons detained in VRS and HVO camps as well as camps organized by Zapadna Bosna, the force/militia led by Bosniak *quisling* Fikret Abdić. They also registered eighty-two types of torture used in these camps. Due to methodological issues, however, the research is flawed. For example, the definition of concentration camp is too general: "any enclosed or fenced off area where the mass detention of the population is carried out for an indeterminate period of time with the purpose of ethnic cleansing."[165] With a general definition and without a proper methodology or even categorization of sites of detention, as well as the frequent politicization of this topic, their research was not usable.

One of the best works that situates the camps within the heart of the Bosnian Serb ethnic cleansing campaign was done by Emir Suljagić. His argument is that the camps were instrumental in a cleansing campaign in which torture and killing were a systematic and widespread phenomenon. He notes that the camps had a twofold purpose:

> [O]n the one hand, the practices in camps are designed to attack on the victims on the moral front and to prevent them from renewing their moral community once ethnic cleansing is completed, while on the other its more immediate and action oriented concern is to physically remove elements of the population who

---

163. Rieff, *Slaughterhouse*, 113.

164. As stated in Šaćir Srebrenica, "Žrtve agresije na Bosnu i Hercegovinu," in *Zbornik radova: Genocid nad Bošnjacima 1992–95* (Sarajevo: Okrugli sto, 2012), 96.

165. Emir Suljagić, "Ethnic Cleansing: Politics, Policy, Violence (Serb Ethnic Cleansing Campaign in Former Yugoslavia)" (PhD thesis, Universität Hamburg, 2009), 148.

are symbolic or emblematic of it from the rest and to eliminate them. It has also dealt in detail with a number of aspects of detention operation such as a. existence of a network of camps which even if not fully integrated and operating under centralized control, still functioned across the borders of different Serb entities; b. systematic and widespread abuse and torture as part of daily operations of camps; and c. killing as integral but distinct and separate practice within the detention operation.[166]

In his work, Suljagić also highlights how the camps were part of a transstate network, which was formed by the Serbian state in Croatia, Bosnia and Herzegovina, Kosovo, and Montenegro. He gives examples of the cross-border transfer of detainees, for example arrests in Belgrade and their transfer to Foča camp in Bosnia and Herzegovina.[167]

An important element of the Bosnian Serbs' modus operandi within the camps was rape and sexual abuse, of both men and women. Alexandra Stiglmayer was first to edit a publication that dealt with the phenomenon of mass rape in camps in Bosnia and Herzegovina.[168] This publication is a compilation of various pieces giving the legal, sociological, and physiological aspects of mass rape. Most of these pieces, however, were based on a feminist theory of rape, which, as the next section shows, committed serious errors in failing to understand the precise reasons why the rapists acted precisely the way they did. A much more useful text was published two years later by Beverly Allen titled *Rape Warfare: The Hidden Genocide in Bosnia-Herzegovina and Croatia*. Allen correctly puts rape into its local context, calling it a "military policy of rape for the purpose of genocide." Impregnation was the key aim, claims Allen. She goes further to criticize previous authors and studies, emphasizing the importance of the cultural identity of the raped victim and the child born of rape:

> The Serb policy of genocidal rape aimed at pregnancy, offers the specter that making more babies with a people equals killing that people off. This illogic is possible only because the policy's authors erase all identity characteristics of the mother other than that as a sexual container. It has been surprisingly difficult

---

166. Suljagić, "Ethnic Cleansing," 145.
167. Suljagić, "Ethnic Cleansing," 157.
168. Alexandra Stiglmayer, Marion Faber, and Roy Gutman, *Mass Rape: The War Against Women in Bosnia-Herzegovina* (Lincoln: University of Nebraska Press, 1994).

for many who are concerned about this phenomenon to recognize the blatant contradiction it contains, even though it is precisely that contradiction that makes this particular atrocity restive to most international war-crime legislation. Even feminists who have experience in gender-aware analysis often fail to note the specific way in which the Serb policy erases the victim's cultural identity and treats her as nothing more than a kind of biological box. As a result of this critical blindness, such feminist analyses have, by a logic shockingly similar to the Serb one, also erased all the victims' identities but the sexual.[169]

The existence of camps was denied or dismissed by many throughout the war and even afterwards.

On August 7, 1992, the UK's *Daily Mail* ran with the symbolic headline "THE PROOF" emblazoned atop an image showing several skeletal Bosniak men standing behind barbed wire. The world was rightly outraged, but nevertheless some sought to deconstruct the image as "propaganda," most notably Thomas Deichmann, a journalist writing in 1997 for the magazine *Living Marxism*. In line with *Living Marxism*'s hard-left editorial line, which portrayed media attempts to report on events in both Rwanda and Bosnia as a covert imperialist plan designed to justify intervention under the guise of empire building (a line of argumentation similar to that of Noam Chomsky), Deichmann claimed that the image of the skeletal Fikret Alić was staged and edited by Independent Television News (ITN), a UK-based TV network whose journalist Penny Marshall, along with Ed Vulliamy, revealed Omarska and Trnopolje's existence to the world. ITN sued *Living Marxism* and Diechmann for libel and won a crushing victory in the UK courts. As *Living Marxism*'s case fell apart spectacularly, it had the positive effect of creating discussion on the Bosnian Serb concentration camps, while the high standards of proof demanded by the UK's legal system helped bring legal clarification to the nature of the camp system in the Republika Srpska.

In particular, David Campbell's analysis of the case was important since it dealt with evidence presented in court regarding imagery and terminology in ITN's report. One such argument was related to the use of the term "concentration camp":

---

169. Beverly Allen, *Rape Warfare: The Hidden Genocide in Bosnia-Herzegovina and Croatia* (Minneapolis: University of Minnesota Press, 1996), 87–88.

72   TORTURE, HUMILIATE, KILL

[W]ithout wanting to suggest that Trnopolje was in the least synonymous with Bergen-Belsen, it is worth reflecting on the fact that as camps such as Bergen-Belsen were elements in a larger system, and that their precise nature varied depending on circumstances, any variations in the conditions, nature and purpose of a place like Trnopolje do not prevent it from being legitimately understood as a concentration camp.[170]

Campbell, while giving a general overview of the Republika Srpska camp system, states that it was part of the systematic targeting of non-Serbs and that it was part of a genocidal policy, explaining how "genocide is determined by the meaning of how the foundation for life of a target group is destroyed, and not the actual carrying out of murder or the number of victims."[171]

More importantly he places the RS camp system in context in relation to the Nazi system, stating that:

If we understand the camp to be an extra-legal space integral to the constitution of political order, when that order is in crisis or its sense of self is in the process of being made through violence towards others, then the place of a network of camps in an ethnic-cleansing strategy based on an exclusive and homogenous understanding of political community is only to be expected. This means that while Auschwitz and Trnopolje might be radically different places in the context of our established collective memory of the Holocaust, they are not quite as different as they first appear if an appreciation of their historical circumstances and the logic of the systems of which they are a part are fully considered.[172]

Campbell is right to say that the Holocaust and Republika Srpska camp system were not as different as might be first assumed, since the the rationale behind both systems shared certain commonalities. The RS camp system, although with a low mortality rate, had a similar (in some cases even worse) strategy of torture and humiliation than the Nazi system.

Other academics, however, failed to grasp the centrality of the camps to the Bosnian Serbs' cleansing campaign. Robert M. Hayden, for example, compares

---

170. David Campbell, "Atrocity, Memory, Photography: Imaging the Concentration Camps of Bosnia—the Case of ITN Versus Living Marxism, Part 2," *Journal of Human Rights* 1, no. 2 (June 2002): 152, https://doi.org/10.1080/14754830210125656.
171. Campbell, "Atrocity, Memory, Photography," 157.
172. Campbell, "Atrocity, Memory, Photography," 157.

COLLECTIVE TRAUMATIZATION 73

the Holocaust references made by wartime media headlines with details from ICTY judgments, suggesting they are exaggerations:

> Considering the attention paid to "camps," one might expect them to have been major sites of extermination, as were Auschwitz and Treblinka. The ICTY, however, found that the Omarska Camp operated only from late May to late August 1992, and that about 3,000 detainees passed through it during this time. The Keraterm camp, also established in late May 1992, held up to 1500 prisoners.[173]

Hayden, although citing ICTY judgments, obviously did not read them in detail and cherry-picked details to prove his point on the equal distribution of guilt. He fails to mention, for example, any testimony, such as Rezak Hukanović's *The Tenth Circle of Hell*. And although he apparently only opted to read ICTY judgments, he missed the most important judgment relating to camps in Krajina: the Radoslav Brđanin case. Among other issues, Hayden also questions accounts of the massacres in Srebrenica and criticizes the ICTY for "extending the law" in the Krstić case.[174] Hayden downplays the mass atrocities in Bosnia and Herzegovina and compares them to other conflict sites in the world, such as Pakistan-India and Nagorno-Karabakh, which is obviously intentionally misleading and a denial of facts established in court.

Another important contribution to the research of camps in Bosnia and Herzegovina was a project titled "Mapping Detention Camps 1992–95 in Bosnia Herzegovina" led by two local NGOs: Transitional Justice, Accountability and Remembrance in B&H (TJAR in BiH) and the Center for Democracy and Transitional Justice.[175] This project was focused on fact-based research and interviewing former camp prisoners.

Finally, between 2004 and 2005, the ICTY's Outreach Department conducted a series of public conferences titled "Bridging the Gap," designed to provide a transparent and open account of the court's judgments to date and to brief the general public across Bosnia and Herzegovina on the contents of the cases and why the people had been indicted, judged, and sentenced. These sessions were held in Prijedor (RS), Foča (RS), Srebrenica (RS), and Brčko and Konjic (FB&H), and they discussed the cases from these areas, which of course

---

173. Robert M. Hayden, *From Yugoslavia to the Western Balkans: Studies of a European Disunion, 1991–2011* (Leiden: Brill, 2012), 156.
174. Hayden, *From Yugoslavia to the Western Balkans*, 167.
175. I participated in this project for several months as a project coordinator in early 2014.

touched upon the camps. The conference proceedings were produced in a book format and provide a useful introduction to the events in these regions, as documented by the court.

For such an important topic, there has been, sadly, too little research done on the Bosnian Serb camp system. It is hoped that this will change over the coming years.

CHAPTER 3

Višegrad

Introduction

Višegrad is a town in eastern Bosnia on the border with Serbia. It was always a crossroads for armies, merchants, and travelers. Its strategic geographical position, sitting on the main road between southern Serbia and Bosnia and Herzegovina, controlling one of the few bridges across the River Drina, made it a place of frequent turbulent changes over the centuries. The town is famous for its UNESCO world heritage site, the Mehmed-paša Sokolovič Bridge, and for being the location for Nobel Prize winner Ivo Andrić's[1] book *The Bridge on the River Drina*.

Mehmed-paša Sokolović, the grand vizier of the Ottoman Empire, who was born near Višegrad, had the bridge built in 1577.[2] Almost four hundred years later Ivo Andrić, drawing on Serb myths and oral history, made the bridge the central "character" of his prize-winning novel. Thee book is considered controversial by some because of its negative portrayal of Bosniaks.[3]

As Bosnian Serb leadership prepared to separate RS away from the newly forming state of Bosnia and Herzegovina, the town was set for turbulent, brutal times once again.

---

1. Ivo Andrić was a famous Yugoslav writer who authored several novels, including *Travnička hronika* (Bosnian Chronicle) and *Na Drini Ćuprija* (Bridge on the Drina), for which he received the Nobel Prize.
2. Mehmed Pasha Sokolović was the grand vizier of the Ottoman Empire from 1565 until 1574, serving under Sultan Suleyman the Magnificent and Sultan Selim II.
3. In his brilliant work *The Bridge Betrayed*, Michael Sells identifies Andrić's key ideas about "race betrayal" as presented in his doctoral thesis and later projected in his world-famous novel.

76 TORTURE, HUMILIATE, KILL

According to the census from 1991, Višegrad had a population of 21,199, of which Bosniaks were 13,471 (63.54 percent), Serbs 6,743 (31.80 percent) and Croats 32 (0.15 percent).[4] With its majority Bosniak population, surrounded by many mainly Bosniak villages, the town presented a real obstacle to the Bosnian Serb leadership's aim to establish a contiguous, enthnically cleansed Serbian territory.

The Attack from Serbia

Following the first democratic elections in Bosnia and Herzegovina, the SDA and the SDS won a majority of the seats in the Višegrad municipality.[5] Out of a total of fifty seats, the SDA took twenty-seven and SDS took thirteen, while the rest were divided among other parties.[6] Following the death of Yugoslavia's long-time leader Josip Tito after half a century of communist rule, there began a national and religious revival in Serbia, and as the situation worsened across the dying republic, the increasingly aggressive Serb propaganda caused the first ethnic tensions in Višegrad and in other parts of Bosnia and Herzegovina to surface. Bosniaks were shocked and enraged when they saw the destruction of Vukovar, and especially Dubrovnik. On one occasion in 1991, Bosniaks in Višegrad blocked Yugoslav Peoples' Army (JNA) transporters en route to Dubrovnik from crossing through Višegrad.

On April 20, 1991, local Bosnian Serbs gave an indication of their future plans in a joint statement issued by the "Stara Hercegovina" SDS Regional Council in Foča. In this statement, "representatives of the government and people" stated among other things that "this is a historical moment to, using democratic methods, fight for the unity of the Serb people."[7] The SDS representatives from Višegrad were present at this proclamation.

In early 1992, a Bosnian Muslim JNA officer, Asim Džambasović from the 216th Brigade, was the first to sound the alarm, in a report to his superiors

---

4. Federalni zavod za statistiku (Yugoslav Federal Bureau of Statistics), "Popis stanovništva 1991."
5. The SDA was the predominantly Bosniak party led by Alija Izetbegović, while the SDS was a predominantly Serb party led by Radovan Karadžić.
6. Prosecutor v. Mitar Vasiljević (Judgment), IT-98-32-T (ICTY), November 29, 2002, 15, https://www.icty.org/x/cases/vasiljevic/tjug/en/vas021129.pdf.
7. See "Regionalni odbor Stara Herzegovina. Foča, 20 aprila 1992," cited in Smail Čekić, *The Aggression against the Republic of Bosnia and Herzegovina. Sarajevo: Institute for the Research of Crimes Against Humanity and International Law, 2005*, 236.

regarding the mobilization of personnel, with the aim of securing the safe passage of Užice Corps troops from Višegrad to the Neretva Valley. Officer Džambasović noted several problems during the mobilization, including the "stealing ammunition and arms from units;—high cooperation between JNA and SDS leaders;—reading religious literature and glorifying Serbs."[8]

The first serious incident took place on on the April 4, 1992, in Dobrun, the first Bosniak village near the Serbian border, which lies on the main road between Višegrad and the border. Bosniak men working in a stone quarry were shot at, and so they hurriedly left the quarry and returned to Višegrad.[9] The next day, mortar shelling of the town and villages inhabited by Muslims began. Dozens of people were injured in these shellings, including the local imam, Suljo ef. Haljković.

Several days later, a police unit along with members of the Territorial Defense were on a routine patrol when they came across a group of twelve armed Serb men, some of whom had previously been in the police force.[10] Some of those arrested were dressed in police uniforms and the others in military fatigues.

On April 6, 1992, the Užice Corps of the Yugoslav People's' Army invaded Bosnia and Herzegovina with the aim of taking over Višegrad. They met resistance at Dobrun, however, where armed Bosniaks (members of the Bosniak Patriotic League) partially succeeded in blowing up one part of a tunnel, thus delaying the advance.

The Serbia-based JNA Užice Corps tasked with securing Višegrad was commanded by Colonel Dragoljub Ojdanić, and almost all the soldiers under his command were from Serbia and Montenegro. Many of them sported Serb nationalist gear such as flags and caps. Ian Traynor of *The Guardian* was with the JNA when they attacked Višegrad. He witnessed as paramilitaries and special forces and the JNA cooperated in the attack on Višegrad:

> I was with them as they moved toward Visegrad. They were all together and I was with them while they were firing their rockets toward the town. This wasn't the JNA. These were two different elements fighting in parallel and I was with them, (. . .) They used the same equipment, moved together in formation,

---

8. Čekić, *The Aggression against the Republic of Bosnia and Herzegovina*, 460.
9. Prosecutor v. Mitar Vasiljević (VG022 Witness Statement), IT-98-32-T (ICTY), September 10, 2001, 137, https://www.icty.org/x/cases/vasiljevic/trans/en/010910ED.htm.
10. Prosecutor v. Mitar Vasiljević, 138.

78   TORTURE, HUMILIATE, KILL

spoke to each other, and attacked what they considered to be their mutual enemy. I couldn't see anything which wouldn't suggest that they weren't cooperating,[11]

Traynor's observation was later confirmed at the ICTY by Milomir "Kole" Kovačević, a reserve officer of the JNA. His unit was under the control of Colonel Ojdanić. In his statement, he claims that along with the JNA, the attack was also joined by a Serbian Ministry of Interior unit and by local police officers from Užice, Čajetina, Prijepolje, and Priboj. Besides the official units, paramilitary forces such as Šešelj's Chetniks and White Eagles were also present.[12]

As the JNA advanced toward Višegrad, a small group of armed Bosniak men took the previously arrested Serb men up to the Višegrad dam and kept them hostage there, warning the JNA that they would blow the dam up if they entered the town. But this threat never materialized.[13] The Bosniak resistance in Višegrad was scattered and poorly organized. After holding off the JNA at Dobrun, the Bosniak fighters retreated back into the town, where the street fighting continued for several days until the JNA finally entered the town on April 15, 1992. Despite this, the Bosniaks managed to keep control of the eastern half of the town, including Pionirska street and the road leading toward Užice. The injury of Zijad Subašić, the local Patriotic League leader, was a turning point in the Bosniak resistance. He was wounded by a Serb sniper in Pionirska Street, and he and two injured civilians were quickly sent to a hospital in Foča, which at that time was still under Bosnia and Herzegovina government control. After the fall of Foča, these men went missing from the hospital. Serb soldiers from Višegrad brought Zijad back to the town and murdered him on the Mehmed-paša Sokolović Bridge.[14]

Journalist Philip Sherwell, reporting for the *The Telegraph*, recalled how he met a high-ranking JNA officer during their bloody drive toward Višegrad: "The Serbian army officer took a pre-breakfast swig of slivovitz plum brandy, stared at me coldly, and drew his finger sharply across his neck. We were on the

---

11. Velma Šarić, "UK Reporter Recalls Visegrad Offensive," *Institute for War and Peace Reporting*, May 24, 2010, https://iwpr.net/global-voices/uk-reporter-recalls-visegrad-offensive.
12. Prosecutor v. Jovica Stanišić and Franko Simatović, IT-03-69 (ICTY), witness statement by Milomir Kovačević given to the ICTY on April 29, 2003, 16.
13. This ragtag group was led by Murat Šabanović. They bluffed that they had wired the dam with explosives.
14. His remains were found during the 2010 Lake Perućac exhumations. It was later established that Zijad was briefly detained in the correctional facility in Foča.

outskirts of the eastern Bosnian town of Visegrad on a crisp spring Balkan morning. I had just asked him about his plans for the Muslim inhabitants—his response was the universal sign language for slaughter."[15]

Several days after occupying Višegrad, talks between the JNA, SDS, and SDA were scheduled to take place, but the first meetings failed because the SDS representatives failed to show up. VG-22, a witness to the negotiations, spoke of an event he witnessed before the start of one of the negotiations at Uzamnica camp:

> But then he explained to the other officers how far each of the units from Uzice got, how far they reached. And now this topic really got my—got me interested. I was looking at what he was pointing at at the map and listening to what he was saying to the other officers. He explained to them, very briefly, showing them on the map the points where the units were, the points that the units had reached, saying, "This whole area is clean." "Another unit reached this such and such point. This is all clean." And so he went through the whole of the right bank of the river, indicating the points that the units had reached and saying, "This is all clean."[16]

The deputy minister of the Bosnian Serb MUP, Momčilo Mandić, was informed on April 23, 1992, that Višegrad had been taken.[17] With the arrival of the JNA, an SDS government was installed in the municipality. An SDS Crisis Committee was formed and had full control of the town's institutions and police.[18]

Soon after, influential Bosniaks were removed from their positions and replaced with Bosnian Serbs. The chief of the police station in Višegrad, Ševal Murtić, was sacked by the new goverment and replaced by Risto Perišić, a Bosnian Serb high school professor from Višegrad.

As the JNA took control, most of Višegrad's Bosniaks escaped to Goražde. Some of them escaped to the woods and many of Višegrad's citizens sought refuge in the mental institution at Okolište, above Višegrad, which was on

---

15. Philip Sherwell, "Ratko Mladić Arrest: The Balkan Beasts Are No More," *The Telegraph*, May 26, 2011, https://bit.ly/SherwellTelegraphMladicarrest.
16. Prosecutor v. Mitar Vasiljević (VG022 Witness Statement), IT-98-32-T (ICTY), 148–49.
17. Prosecutor v. Radovan Karadžić (Judgment), IT-95-5/18-T (ICTY), 1067.
18. Crisis Committees were formed on December 19, 1991, by the decision of the SDS' Glavni Odbor (General Committee) titled "Instructions for the Organization and Activity of Organs of Serbian People in Bosnia and Herzegovina in Extraordinary Circumstances." See Prosecutor v. Radovan Karadžić (Judgment), IT-95-5/18-T (ICTY), 19.

higher, isolated ground. Another group of citizens sought refuge at the Uzamnica military barracks. At these barracks, at least two unsuccessful attempts at peace talks between Bosniak and Serb representatives were held. A week after the JNA occupied Višegrad, they issued a call to all Bosniaks telling them to return to their hometown, promising them safety and protection from "extremists." Using television and radio, the newly appointed town officials called for Bosniaks to return to work or they would lose their jobs at the factories and municipality.

The fear of being left without a job, the decades-long belief and trust in the JNA, the evident wish of Goražde's citizens to resolve the refugee issue in their town, and lastly the lack of instructions or suggestions from the government in Sarajevo or the SDA were the main reasons why many Bosniaks decided to return to Višegrad. Several Bosniak activists came to the bus station in Goražde, from where a convoy of buses back to Višegrad had been organized, and tried to persuade the men not to return. Most of them unfortunately did not listen.

Once the refugees arrived back in Višegrad, they and the rest of the town's population were gathered at the Ušće Sports Center, where the military-aged men were separated out and the crowd was searched for weapons. Throughout the town, several checkpoints were set up, where the cars driven by Bosniaks were stopped and cross-checked on a list. In the meantime, the Crisis Committee had come up with lists of "extremists" who needed to be detained and questioned. All Višegrad Bosniaks who had legal arms were arrested and their houses searched. Once their arms were seized, they received confirmation from the Višegrad police that their arms had been confiscated. In one such case on April 21, 1992, Višegrad police officer Željko Lelek confiscated a Hamerles hunting rifle and a box of ammunition. The Bosniak whose rifle was confiscated was issued a "Confirmation note of temporary seizure of items" by the Višegrad Public Security Station, signed by Željko Lelek.[19]

Those who returned to Višegrad faced a different atmosphere from that which was promised over the radio. Almost immediately, most men suspected of "extremist" activities were arrested and interrogated. Educated Bosniaks working in the municipal institutions were sacked. In the Višegrad secondary school for example, the Bosniak professors and workers were dismissed by the newly appointed Bosnian Serb school director and a JNA officer. The high school principal, Himzo Demir, was also sacked and replaced by a Serb.[20]

---

19. A copy of this document is in the possession of the author.
20. After a few days, he was abducted from his house and executed by Serb soldiers.

VIŠEGRAD   81

On May 15, 1992, thousands of kilometers away in New York, the UN Security Council passed Resolution 752, instructing all JNA and Croatian army troops to leave the territory of Bosnia and Herzegovina. The JNA officially left Bosnia and Herzegovina in late May, but most of the existing forces simply changed their insignia from the JNA to VRS. Across the country, most of the heavy artillery was handed over to the Bosnian Serb Army. JNA officer Milomir "Kole" Kovačević stated that his entire unit left all their weapons behind except for their personal firearms. The Užice Corps retreated to Serbia and kept control of the right bank of the Drina River, providing artillery support for Republika Srpska's army.[21]

Targeting Bosniak Elites

One of the wealthiest Bosniak families in Višegrad was the Zukić family. Behija and her husband Džemo had lived and worked in Germany, returning to Višegrad before the war, where they owned several shops. Džemo had bought a new red Volkswagen Passat. They were the first victims of Milan Lukić's unit.[22] On May 18, 1992, Milan and Sredoje Lukić arrived at Behija Zukić's house, and Milan murdered her with his automatic rifle. Behija was buried on May 21 at the Stražište cemetery along with two elderly victims, Medo and Sadika Smajić. During the funeral, Milan Lukić arrived in the Passat that had belonged to the Zukićs, and several other soldiers followed in a TAM truck. They rounded up fifteen men from the funeral and drove them off. Džemo and his eighteen-year-old son Faruk were also abducted by Lukić's unit and never seen again.[23]

On 28 May Himzo Demir, the head teacher at the Višegrad secondary

---

21. Prosecutor v. Jovica Stanišić and Franko Simatović, IT-03-69 (ICTY), witness statement by Milomir Kovačević given to the ICTY on April 29, 2003, Exhibit P00051.E, 17.

22. ICTY witness VG-042 testified about the seizure of Zukić's car: "One day I went to the MUP building in town to get a pass to leave town just to make sure we were safe. I was on my way back to Dusce. There were two roads. One was next to the Drina River; it was an asphalt road, surfaced. And then there was a macadam road parallel to the rail line, so we took that road in order not to meet any Chetniks on our way back. As soon as I reached the Varda furniture factory, there's a house there belonging to a man named Ševko Hodžić. Džemo Zukić and his Behija passed us, and then there was a white Fićo driving behind us and it pulled over right outside Ševko Hodžić's house. Milan Lukić got out of that Fićo vehicle and walked up to Vico [as interpreted] Zukić and his wife Behija. He seized their car. We walked on past the Varda factory to our homes. I said, 'Džemo, my dear, what was that?' And Behija told me one thing, 'Don't ask a question. Milan Lukić just took my car away.' And that was that. We talked no more." See Prosecutor v. Milan Lukić and Sredoje Lukić, IT-98-32/1 (ICTY), witness statement by witness VG-042 given to the ICTY on October 27, 2008, 2778–79, https://www.icty.org/x/cases/milan_lukic_sredoje_lukic/trans/en/081027ED.htm.

23. Their remains were exhumed from Kurtalići mass grave.

82 TORTURE, HUMILIATE, KILL

school, who had been previously sacked, was "disappeared" from his home. One of the soldiers who took Himzo away was his former pupil. He patted Himzo on the shoulder, saying, "You were the best school principal."[24] Others in the group spoke with accents that suggested that they were from Serbia.

Safet Zejnilović was a well-respected doctor in Višegrad. Originally from Bijelo Polje in Serbia, he had come to work to Višegrad.[25] Two or three hours after arriving back from a trip to Serbia, Dr. Zejnilović was abducted from his home. His house was looted and set ablaze two days later. According to some witnesses he was taken to Pale along with several other prominent Višegrad Bosniaks. His partial remains were found there after the war.[26]

For almost everyone, simply fleeing the town was no longer an option, with MUP RS checkpoints set up along every road. All those who wished to exit the town first had to receive a travel permit from the SDS authorities or police. Most of these permist were issued by Risto Perišić, head of Public Security Station in Višegrad.

Bloody Trail

The Bosniaks of Višegrad became, to paraphrase Martin Shaw, *the civilian enemy*, and a one-sided war was waged against them because of the social identities previously ascribed to them by their oppressors.[27]

From mid-May to approximately the end of July, the entire Bosniak

---

24. Amnesty International, "Bosnia-Herzegovina: The 'Disappeared.' Himzo Demir—head-teacher: 'disappeared' from Višegrad," December 3, 2001, http://www.amnesty.org/en/library/info/EUR63/016 /2001/en.

25. ICTY witness VG-32 testified about Dr. Zejnilović's fate: "Dr. Safet Zejnilović was in the town of Višegrad before the war, and before the Užice Corps came to town he went to Goražde together with the head of the health center across Čajniče and Pljevlja. He went on to his native birthplace Bijelo Polje and doctor—the other doctor, the head of the center, he went on to Tara, Dr. Uljarević. He stayed there until the Užice Corps came to town. At the initiative of the then war commander of the wartime hospital managed to persuade his wife, also a doctor, medical doctor, and they even provided them with a driver to go and collect Dr. Safet and provide him with all the guarantees for his safety but that his services were needed in the town. They did so, managed to persuade him to come back to town. As he returned home an hour or two later, a group of armed individuals came and took him away. She told him that they manhandled him at the time." See Prosecutor v. Milan Lukić and Sredoje Lukić, IT-98-32/1, witness statement by witness VG-32 given to the ICTY on September 4, 2008, 1148, https://www.icty.org/x/cases/milan_lukic_sredoje_lukic/trans/ en/080904ED.htm.

26. Partial skeletal remains of Dr. Zejnilović were found near Pale. The remains of the rest of the group have still not been found.

27. Martin Shaw, *What Is Genocide?* (Cambridge: Polity Press, 2015), 16.

population—almost 6,500 people—were either expelled or murdered. The only Bosniaks left at that time were those confined in concentration camps or in private prisons. Throughout the summer, hundreds of Bosniaks were dragged through the streets and executed on the Mehmed-paša Sokolović Bridge; a public and ceremonial execution of *Turks* on a *Turkish* bridge. Victims were rarely shot; the perpatrators preferred using knives. The victims were brought to the center of the bridge to a stone balcony called the *sofa*, where the slaughters took place. Their throats were slit and their bodies were dropped into the cloudy Drina. Sometimes, victims were brought in groups to the banks of the Drina and shot.

On two occasions, Bosniak civilians—women and children—were barricaded into houses and burned to death. The first massacre was committed on June 14, 1992, in the house of Adem Omeragić on Pionirska Street.[28] The second massacre was committed on June 28, 1992, in the house of Meho Aljić on Bikavac hill.[29] Collectively, a total of 140 civilians were killed. In August 1992, a mixed force of VRS soldiers and policemen attacked the village of Barimo on the outskirts of Višegrad. Barimo is a village downstream, which was in a sort of no-man's-land at the time. The village was populated by the elderly and children. At least 26 Bosniak civilians, the oldest victim being ninety-two-year-old Hanka Halilović, were massacred and the entire village burned down.[30]

Hasan Veletovac Elementary School

The Hasan Veletovac Elementary School in Višegrad is in the city center between the neighborhood of Nova Mahala and the Muslim graveyard Stražište. It was turned into a detention center where mostly elderly Bosniaks, women, and children were held. These were mostly civilians from the now overrun villages around Višegrad. On June 18, the village of Kuka was attacked and occupied by the VRS and MUP RS, who killed several civilians in the village and took the rest to the school, where they were interned.[31] On July 25, the village of

---

28. Prosecutor v. Milan Lukić and Sredoje Lukić (Judgment), IT-98-32/1-T (ICTY), July 20, 2009, 115–38, https://www.icty.org/x/cases/milan_lukic_sredoje_lukic/tjug/en/090720_j.pdf.
29. Prosecutor v. Milan Lukić and Sredoje Lukić, 209–18.
30. BIRN Balkans, "TV Justice Magazine I Episode 24: Crimes on the River Drina Bank," February 18, 2013, https://www.youtube.com/watch?v=a631z7x2Elw.
31. Tužilaštvo BiH v. Boban Šimšić (First Instance Verdict), X-KR-04/05 (Sud Bosne i Hercegovine) July 11, 2006, 3, http://www.sudbih.gov.ba/predmet/2417/show.

84 TORTURE, HUMILIATE, KILL

Velji Lug was attacked and several Bosniak female civilians were killed and the rest taken to the school.[32] The other civilians incarcerated in the school were from villages of Vlahovići, Gostilja, Žlijeb, and Omeragići.

It is estimated that at least five hundred civilians were kept at the school during 1992.[33] It was surrounded with barbed wire and the people inside the school were not able to move freely. Serb soldiers and police guarded the school and regularly entered and mistreated the civilians.

One of the tactics used by the VRS soldiers at the school to terrorize the internees was the "repurchase-your-child" tactic. Children would be taken from the school and their mothers would be told to gather money or else their children would be killed. This would cause chaos, and the women would start gathering money from each other in order to save their child's life.[34] Azmir Šabanović was a fourteen-year-old when Milan Lukić took him from the school and told him that he would be killed on the Mehmed-paša Sokolović Bridge if his mother did not gather money to "buy" him. Lukić told him, "We'll slaughter you and throw your body into the Drina and have you float to Žepa. We'll let Žepa see what we in Višegrad can do."[35] Lukić told Azmir's younger brother to tell his mother to give him two thousand deutschmarks for Azmir's life. Azmir's mother did not have the money and she started crying and pulling her hair out. Quickly a woman from the crowd called her and gave her the money. This is how Azmir survived.

In mid-June 1992, Boban Šimšić assisted Milan Lukić and other members of the Serb army, police, and paramilitary formations in taking away imprisoned Bosniak civilians Ismet Bulatović, Šemso Poljo, and Eniz Smajić from the school, after which they were executed.[36]

In second half of June 1992, during the nights, Boban Šimšić singled out girls and young women who were held captive in the school and took them away, "procuring" them for members of the VRS, who carried out multiple rapes, beatings, and humiliations of several women, including Latifa Hodžić,

---

32. See Tužilaštvo BiH v. Boban Šimšić, 3. In the attack, nine-month old Amela Ahmetspahić was killed along with the rest of her family. Their remains were found in the village of Velji Lug in the municipality of Višegrad.

33. Prosecutor v. Lukić and Lukić, IT-98-32/1-T (ICTY), 269.

34. Witnesses Fatima Poljo and Naila Ahmetagić both gave money for their children. See Avdo Huseinović, *Bloody Višegrad on the Drina*, Pravda Bosna, May 21, 2015, [46], https://www.youtube.com/watch?v=-oJW0HGwNXg&ab_channel=PravdaBosna.

35. Huseinović, *Bloody Višegrad on the Drina*, [47].

36. The remains of some of these victims were found in the Drina River i.e., Lake Perućac. See Tužilaštvo BiH v. Boban Šimšić (First Instance Verdict), X-KRŽ-04/05 (Sud BiH), 1–2.

VIŠEGRAD 85

Fata Šabanović, Naila Ahmetagić, FNU Ramić, Amira Nuhanović aka Dada, Razija Hurem, Senada Hurem, Zineta Murtić, Mula Užičanin, and Alma Hafizović.[37] Most of the rapes and sexual abuse were conducted in the biology classroom. One witness recalled how the class was full of ripped women's clothes and torn underwear.[38] Witness VG063 was raped several times by Milan Lukić and other soldiers at the school:

> In the classroom, he ordered VG063 to take off her clothes, and when VG063 backed away in a corner, he ripped her skirt and leggings with a knife. Milan put the barrel of a rifle in her mouth and threatened to blow her head off. He bit her lips, neck and breasts, placed her on a desk and raped VG063, penetrating her mouth, vagina and anus, causing her great pain. While raping her, Milan Lukić made constant threats to VG063. Milan Lukić said to VG063 that he "could make a little Milan to each and everyone of us."[39]

On June 21, 1992, a large group of civilians was brought to the school. S.H. was called by Serb soldiers to make a list of the men, women, and children. There were around fifty men on the list who were called out and taken to another room, where they were subsequently beaten and murdered.[40] In the night of June 28, 1992, St. Vitus Day (Vidovdan), an elderly man, Ibro Šabanović, was taken out of the school hall. Milan Lukić and another soldier slit his throat and threw his severed head among the other imprisoned civilians, saying "Balijas, tonight is Vidovdan, you will all end up like this"[41] and "This is your Kurban."[42] This event, clearly remembered by every person detained, had an important symbolism.

---

37. Tužilaštvo BiH v. Boban Šimšić, 3.

38. For witness statement see: Huseinović, *Bloody Višegrad on the Drina* [48.30].

39. Prosecutor v. Lukić and Lukić (Judgment), IT-98-32/1-T (ICTY), 229.

40. Hasena Bajramović testified about the brutal death of her husband Mehmed Bajramović: "After they had been taken out into the other room from which loud weeping, screaming and crying could have been heard, which lasted for 10 to 15 minutes, they came back beaten black and blue, being in a very poor condition, some walking in with great difficulty. When they had brought them back, they turned the light off. Her stepdaughter Medina was crying, begging him to release her father and to stop beating him, but Boban said to her to get back to her place and sit down. When the people came in, her husband was blue, red, he did not have his teeth at all, and his blood was oozing out; her stepdaughter said to her that her father's tongue had been cut off. Then, they were taking men out again, and it was her husband's turn, he left, and there remained some elderly women and children. Thereafter, she never saw her husband again." In Tužilaštvo BiH v. Boban Šimšić (Appeals Chamber Verdict), X-KRŽ-05/04, August 7, 2007, 29, http://www.sudbih.gov.ba/predmet/2417/show.

41. Tužilaštvo BiH v. Boban Šimšić, 35–36.

42. Prosecutor v. Lukić and Lukić (Judgment), IT-98-32/1-T (ICTY), 228–29.

86 TORTURE, HUMILIATE, KILL

First, Vidovdan is an important day in the Serb Orthodox calender, marking the anniversary of the date in 1389 when the Kingdom of Serbia was defeated by the Ottomans and subsequently absorbed into the Ottoman Empire. The defeat passed into Serbian myth and was weaponized by Serb politicans, academics, and church leaders in the run-up to the war. Steven Mock notes that "at each commemoration, priests and politicians would exhort the people to avenge Kosovo by unifying the divided territory of Serbia."[43]

Secondly, as per Foucault, the spectacularly brutal, ceremonial, theatrical, and public nature of the executions and rapes had the simple aim of communicating two things to the Bosniak detainees: their Bosnian Serb captors had the power to do with them as they wished, and submission was the only option. In this case, the public decapitation of Ibro Šabanović not only had the aim of demonstrating power, but also to collectively traumatize the Bosniak detainees. This trauma was intended to break its audience's grasp on reality and to terrify them into submission.

An interesting event, one of the rare known cases of a successful escape from the school was managed by a young girl, Senada Hurem. She was taken by Boban Šimšić and another soldier out of the big room where the civilians were interned, and she managed to escape. Her mother Razija "Šuhra" Hurem was then beaten and threatened by the perpetrators. Pointing at red-hot plates of an electric stove, they told Razija and the women with her, "Now we're going to rip your hearts out and fry them on these plates." A laughing Šimšić told them, "You'll eat now until you're stuffed."[44]

One day, several elderly men were called out of the school and forced by Milan Lukić, Sredoje Lukić, Boban Šimšić, and others to sing Četnik songs and beat each other on the head with sticks.[45] On another occasion, Lukić forced the elderly men "to show him their penises because he wanted to know how big Muslim penises were."[46] On June 17, a group of civilians from the Župa region who had been incarcerated in the school were deported toward Skopje, Macedonia.[47]

---

43. Steven Mock, *Symbols of Defeat in the Construction of National Identity* (Cambridge: Cambridge University Press, 2012), 119.
44. Tužilaštvo BiH v. Boban Šimšić (Appeals Chamber Verdict), X-KRŽ-05/04, 3. In one version of the judgment, the names of the witnesses are revealed, while in another version, only the initials are written. Both versions are available on the Court of Bosnia and Herzegovina website.
45. Prosecutor v. Lukić and Lukić (Judgment), IT-98-32/1-T (ICTY), 270.
46. Prosecutor v. Lukić and Lukić, 271.
47. The convoy was supposed to go to Olovo but one of the buses broke down and they returned to Višegrad, after which they were deported to Skopje.

VIŠEGRAD   87

Sometime around June 20, the VRS organized trucks that gathered the few remaining Bosniak civilians from villages on the right side of the Drina River, including the village of Drinsko. The trucks were taken to the school, where the civilians were told to hand over all money and gold, after which there were deported to Knežina, territory controlled by the Bosnia and Herzegovina government.[48] On June 30, VRS 3rd Company commander Momir Savić, who commanded a large group of soldiers, captured around thirty Bosniak civilians on "Lim Bridge" near Međeđa, after which they were transported by trucks to the school. At the time there were already fifty people inside the school.[49] They were kept in inhumane conditions and exchanged after four days.[50] According to one source, the school ceased to be active on July 5, 1992. There are statements, however, that claimed that the school was used as a detention camp again in October 1992 after a group of Bosniak civilians were captured in the locale and taken to the school.[51]

It is not clear who had effective control over the detention camp. Boban Šimšić, as one of the guards, was a member of the Reserve Police Forces of the Republika Srpska Ministry of the Interior, based at Višegrad police station. Sredoje Lukić was also a member of the Višegrad police, but he is better known as a member of the Avengers, a paramilitary group headed by his cousin Milan Lukić, while the Avengers were a part of the VRS Višegrad Brigade. Other guards at the school were members of the VRS and they wore the old Yugoslav People's Army uniform. During the trial of Momir Savić, the commander of the VRS 3rd Company Višegrad Brigade, he claimed that the school was the command post of his unit.[52] The camp had no concrete commander or command structure but instead was under mixed army-police control. There is also no clear information on the number of people killed in the school, but by comparing the witness statements and judgments, the number is at least several dozen. Most of the remains of these victims were found in Lake Perućac, part of the Drina River.[53]

---

48. Ibrahim Kljun, *Hronika genocida nad Bošnjacima Višegrada* (Zenica: Centar za istraživanje zločina i zločina nad Bošnjacima, 1996), 281.
49. Tužilaštvo BiH v. Momir Savić (First Instance Judgment), X-KR-07/478 (Sud Bosne i Hercegovine), July 3, 2009, 94–95, http://www.sudbih.gov.ba/predmet/2528/show.
50. Tužilaštvo BiH v. Momir Savić, 3.
51. According to Islam Kustura from Zlatnik village. See Prosecutor v. Lukić and Lukić (Judgment), IT-98-32/1-T (ICTY), 249.
52. Tužilaštvo BiH v. Momir Savić (First Instance Judgment), X-KR-07/478, 80.
53. During the 2010 Lake Perućac exhumations.

Višegrad Spa

On June 1, Rade Saponjić arrived in Menzilovići village with a group of Serb soldiers. They told their neighbors Bajro Murtić, Ibro Murtić, Mehmed Menzilović, and Ismet Menzilović that they had to come to Prelovo for an "agreement." In Prelovo, Lukić's unit arrived and took them to the Višegrad Spa, a building northeast of the town. They were kept there for several days, beaten and mistreated by Serb soldiers. Besides them, the two Bosno brothers from Mušići village were also brought to the spa, but they were soon let go after their family paid a ransom. A former municipality employee, Esad Ibišević, was brought one day and severely beaten. While they were held at the spa they heard women's screams coming from the nearby Vilina Vlas hotel, where Bosniak women and girls were being raped. One night the men decided to try and escape. After breaking down the door, they split into three groups and ran toward the woods. After a few days they managed to arrive in safe territory.[54]

Vilina Vlas Hotel

The Vilina Vlas Hotel is a spa center seven kilometers northwest of Višegrad. In early 1992, the spa was frequently visited by Serb nationalists. In the days following the occupation of Višegrad, it became the command center for Milan Lukić's "Avengers," a paramilitary unit composed of members of the Republika Srpska army and police as well as volunteers from Serbia. Vilina Vlas soon became infamous as a rape center, where Bosniak women and girls were brought from the town and surrounding villages to be raped by Republika Srpska army soldiers and police officers. It is not known exactly how many Bosniak women and girls were interned in Vilina Vlas but it is estimated that the number is at least two hundred. A majority of those kept in the hotel rooms were usually chained to radiators. There were also many cases where women and girls who were raped in Vilina Vlas woulb be returned either to the town or to their homes, or to other concentration camps. On May 29, Milan Lukić took witness VG094 from her home and drove her to Vilina Vlas, where he later raped her, and then she was later raped by his cousin Sredoje Lukić.[55] On June

---

54. Kljun, *Hronika*, 268.
55. Prosecutor v. Lukić and Lukić (Judgment), IT-98-32/1-T (ICTY), 221.

VIŠEGRAD 89

9, Milan Lukić and another soldier entered the apartment of witness VG131 where they told her, her sister, and friend that they had to come with them to the police station to identify some individuals. Instead they were taken to the Vilina Vlas spa hotel where VG131 was raped by Milan Lukić. Her friend was taken by Sredoje Lukić for "interrogation" and never seen again.[56] American journalist Peter Maass spoke to one survivor, Mersiha, and published her testimony in the *Washington Post* in December 1992:

> Then he ordered me to take off my clothes. I didn't want to do that. He said I must, that it would be better to take my clothes off myself, or else he would do it and he would be violent. . . . I started to cry. He said I was lucky to be with him. He said I could have been thrown into the river with rocks tied around my ankles. But I didn't want to do it. He got angry and cursed and said, "I'm going to bring in 10 soldiers."[57]

Emina S. was one of the rare survivors of Vilina Vlas. She was raped on a daily basis by Milan Lukić, who would take her to Vilina Vlas and and then return her to her home. Emina was raped in the rooms as well as by the hotel pool.[58] During the trial of Oliver Krsmanović, Radovan Milosavljević, prosecution witness and former member of the VRS who was a guard at a checkpoint near Vilina Vlas, stated, "Oliver Krsmanovic, the Milosavljevic brothers and Zeljko Lelek were among them. I did not know what was happening inside the hotel." It is hard to believe that a person regularly stationed only fifty meters away from a rape camp did not know what was going on.

Nevertheless, one of his statements is important since it provides us with an insider account. He spoke about one victim—Igbala Bećirević—who was brought to the hotel by Lukić and other soldiers: "They took her clothes off and pushed Slobodan Vuković, who was deaf and dumb, towards her. The team was there . . . Oliver was there too,"[59] Željko Lelek was tried by the Court of Bosnia and Herzegovina and found guilty of rapes in Vilina Vlas. Specifically he was

---

56. Prosecutor v. Lukić and Lukić, 266.
57. Peter Maass, "The Rapes in Bosnia: A Muslim Schoolgirl's Account," *The Washington Post*, December 27, 1992, https://bit.ly/MaassWaPoRapesinBosnia.
58. Merima Husejnović, "A Month in the Hands of Milan Lukic," *BIRN*, November 6, 2009, http://www.justice-report.com/en/articles/for-the-record-a-month-in-the-hands-of-milan-lukic. See also Fergal Keane, "Grim History of Bosnia's 'Rape Hotel,'" *BBC*, April 8, 2016, https://www.bbc.com/news/av/world-europe-35992642.
59. Mirna Buljugić, "Indictee in 'Vilina Vlas' with Lukic's Team," *Detektor*, May 28, 2013, https://detektor.ba/2013/05/28/indictee-in-%C2%93vilina-vlas%C2%94-with-lukic%C2%92s-team/?lang=en.

found guilty of raping witness M.H.[60] Several witnesses, such as A, C, D, M.H., and Zineta Kulelija, testified at Lelek's trial and confirmed that Vilina Vlas was a site where Bosniak women and girls were brought, kept, and raped by Serb soldiers and policemen.[61]

Vilina Vlas was also used as a detention center in the "Sjeverin" case. On October 22, 1992, sixteen Bosniaks from Sjeverin, a village in Serbia, all of whom were citizens of Serbia, were abducted from a bus in the village of Mioča in Bosnia and Herzegovina. The bus was stopped by a group of armed men led by Milan Lukić. The Bosniaks were taken from the bus to Vilina Vlas, where they were tortured and beaten. Members of the "Avengers" took photographs of the men during their abuse.[62] After a unknown period of time, they were executed. The remains of one of the abducted civilians was exhumed from the Drina River in 2010. With regard to the control of Vilina Vlas, it is not clear who was in charge. It is certain that Milan Lukić and the "Avengers" used it as their base. Some reports mention that Duško Andrić, the prewar director of Vilina Vlas, was also present. Milivoje Šušnjar, a prewar employee, remained in the hotel as a guard during the war.[63] Some fifty meters from the hotel was a checkpoint manned by VRS soliders.

---

60. Tužilaštvo BiH v. Željko Lelek (First Instance Verdict), X-KR/06/202 (Sud Bosne i Hercegovine), May 23, 2008, 2, http://www.sudbih.gov.ba/predmet/2445/show.

61. The rapes and sexual abuse were conducted by the Bosnian Serb soldiers and policemen solely because the women and girls were Bosniaks: "The very fact that non-Serb women and girls were forcibly brought to the Vilina Vlas spa, by armed men, under physical threat against them and their families, and that they were imprisoned precisely to be sexually and physically abused surely causes terrible suffering and the feeling of helplessness with the victim who is placed there, completely helpless and without any possibility to protect herself or avoid sexual abuse. As the witness stated, she was brought to the Vilina Vlas spa and was raped for the exclusive purpose of the perpetrator's sadistic abuse because of her ethnic affiliation and for purposes of illicit discrimination." See Tužilaštvo BiH v. Željko Lelek, 42–43.

62. These photographs were published in 2002 in the documentary "Otmica u Sjeverinu." See Ivan Markov, "Otmica u Sjeverinu," B92, 2002. Photos available at (trigger warning): https://www.b92.net/specijal/sjeverin/foto.php.

63. This was confirmed by convicted war criminal Mitar Vasiljević during his trial in front of the ICTY. See Fond za humanitarno parvo, "Transkripcija i redaktura transkripta—Tužilac protiv Mitra Vasiljevića (Predmet IT-98-32-A)," December 15, 2005, https://bit.ly/TranscriptMitVasiljevic. At the end of 1992, an American journalist visited Vilina Vlas, but found it empty except for an armed Šušnjar, who was in an SMB uniform at the reception.

VIŠEGRAD 91

Fire Station

The *Vatrogasni dom* (fire station), is located in the center of Višegrad.[64] It became a detention center in mid-June 1992, after a VRS attack on the villages of Žlijeb, Odžak, and Kragujevac.[65] A group of at least 150 Bosniak civilians were brought from these villages to the fire station in VRS military trucks. Several women from the group were taken to an adjoining room, where they were first beaten and then raped by VRS soldiers.[66] On June 18, a group of men were taken out of the fire station and executed, most probably on the bridge or near the river bank.[67] The remains of some of the men were later exhumed from the Drina River. After being kept in the fire station for a few days, they were called out by one Serb soldier to gather on the town's square for deportation to Olovo, in Bosniak territory. In the town's square they noticed a lot of civilians, including those held in Hasan Veletovac School.[68] More than a thousand of them, mostly women and children, were loaded on buses and trucks and sent west. Near the Bosnian Serb village of Gornja Lijeska, the buses drove past a group of Bosnian Serb soldiers sitting around a bonfire, drinking alcohol. Next to them was a skinned man on a skewer, being roasted.[69]

The reason a detention center was established at the fire station is probably because the Hasan Veletovac School was already overcrowded with incarcerated civilians. Thus this facility existed as a concentration camp only for a short time.

---

64. This building was the first synagogue in Višegrad, built in 1905.
65. The Court of Bosnia and Herzegovina in the case of Boban Šimšić stated the following regarding the attack on Žlijeb: "[T]he attack was directed against civilian population, in this case against Bosniak population, that criminal actions were taken against them as a collective protected value identifiable by their ethnic, cultural and religious affiliation out of discriminatory intentions, which characterize them as persecution." See: Tužilaštvo BiH v. Boban Šimšić (First Instance Verdict), X-KR-04/05 (Sud Bosne i Hercegovine), July 11, 2006, 27, http://www.sudbih.gov.ba/predmet/2417/show.
66. Tužilaštvo BiH v. Boban Šimšić, 3.
67. The victims are Mujo Gluščević, Hasan Gluščević, Hasib Gluščević, Meho Agić, Emin Agić, Meho Softić, Samir Softić, Mustafa Šabanović, Avdija Nuhanović, Sead Hodžić, Adem Kozić, Dželal Hodžić, Dževad Hodžić, Salko Sućeska, Huso Bulatović, Husein Vilić, Hamed Kešmer, Ibrahim Kešmer. Tužilaštvo BiH v. Boban Šimšić, 3.
68. Witness statement by A. H., found in Kljun, *Hronika*, 282–83.
69. This scene was confirmed to me by several of the deported civilians, those who dared to look.

Police Station

The police station is in the center of town, near the new bridge, and was used as a temporary detention facility. It was the first place Bosniak civilians were unlawfully detained at the start of the killings. The first victims to be brought to the police station were Bosniak men who were arrested in their homes or at checkpoints manned by the VRS or JNA. The first to be arrested and interrogated at the police station were the military-aged men and elites, educated Bosniaks, basically all who "posed a threat." Almost all who were arrested and interrogated were later executed or sent to Uzamnica camp. In April 1992, several dozen Bosniak men were arrested and brought to the police station for interrogation and torture. Some of whom were raped..[70]

In May 1992, several Bosniak civilians, among them Suvad Subašić, Enver Džaferović, Safet Tvrtković, Nezir Žunić, Osman Kurspahić, Abid Murtić, Suvad Dolovac and his brother, and a young man aka Salko were detained in the police station.[71] Some survived by pure luck or by paying ransom for their freedom.[72] Also in May, one Serb soldier interrogated and beat Zijad Kustura in the basement of a house, after which he took him to the police station, where the abuse continued.[73] Two men from Rodić-brdo—Rešad Mučovski and Fadil Zukić—were taken from their houses into the police station. Fatma Zukić saw her husband at the police ptation: "After they had taken him away, I searched for him. I saw him in the police building. He was beaten up, covered in bruises, blood was pouring from his ear. . . . He just told me to leave the town with our children."[74] Nenad Tanasković, a reserve policeman of the Višegrad Public Security Station, participated in an attack in May 1992 on a village in the Višegrad municipality along with Nenad Mirković and an unknown soldier of the Užice Corps. There they took Junuz Tufekčić and a

---

70. Nidžara Ahmetašević, Nerma Jelačić, and Selma Boračić, "Visegrad Rape Victims Say Their Cries Go Unheard," *Balkan Insight.* December 10, 2007, https://balkaninsight.com/2007/12/10/visegrad-rape-victims-say-their-cries-go-unheard/.
71. Tužilaštvo BiH v. Željko Lelek (First Instance Judgment), X-KR/06/202, 2.
72. Some were freed after giving information about the hiding places of wanted men or arms possession.
73. As stated in the November 18, 2011, indictment for Oliver Krsmanović. See Tužilaštvo BiH v. Oliver Krsmanović (First Instance Judgment), S 1 1 K 006028 11 Kri (Sud Bosne i Herzegovine), August 31, 2015, 5, http://sudbih.gov.ba/predmet/2867/show. See also Marija Taušan, "Prosecution Calls for Long-Term Imprisonment for Krsmanovic," *Detektor*, May 19, 2015, https://detektor.ba/2015/05/19/prosecution-calls-for-long-term-imprisonment-for-krsmanovic/?lang=en.
74. "Krsmanovic: Covered in Bruises Due to Beating," *Detektor*, September 19, 2012, https://detektor.ba/2012/09/19/krsmanovic-covered-in-bruises-due-to-beating/?lang=en.

female civilian (witness A) and drove them to the police station where witness A was interrogated by Drago Samardžić and later raped by two unknown soldiers in the police station.[75]

In early May 1992, after an attack on the Bosniak villages of Crni Vrh and Donja Lijeska, the Bosnian Serb perpetrators detained a group of Bosniak civilians. Safet Tvrtković and Muhamed Čukojević were taken out of this group to the police station by Novo Rajak, a reserve policeman of the Visegrad Public Security Station, where they were beaten and tortured. Čukojević testified that the walls of the cell they were in were covered in blood and that all the men who were there had visible scars. He noted that most of them were taken out of the cell late at night and beaten for several hours. Another witness, a Bosniak woman who arrived at the Police Station one day heard beatings and screams while Muslim religious songs—nasheeds—were being played.[76] After some time, Safet Tvrtković was taken out of the police station by Novo Rajak.[77] His remains were later found in a mass grave. Čukojević was released after several days, but was obliged to report to the police station every day and also was obliged to find out and reveal where several Bosniaks were hiding.[78]

On May 23, 1992, Nenad Tanaković, Novo Rajak, Miloš Pantelić, and Slavko Trifković participated in an attack on the Osojnica neighborhood, where they arrested Suvad and Kemal Dolovac, who were then taken to the community office in Donja Lijeska for interrogation. After a short interrogation, they were moved to the police station, where they were kept for four days. Suvad Dolovac was released after four days while Kemal was then moved to Uzamnica camp.[79] In late May 1992, Fadil Jelačić and Nezir Žunić were unlawfully detained in the police station, where they were beaten for days. Žunić was taken out of the police station after a few days and never seen again.[80]

Bosniak men who were of interest or considered as a potential threat were told to report themselves on a daily basis to the police station. They would be made to report in the morning and released back home at night, being beaten and tortured during the day. Since the town was sealed off by Serb forces, there

---

75. Tužilaštvo BiH v. Nenad Tanasković (First Instance Judgment), X-KR/06/165 (Sud Bosne i Hercegovine), August 24, 2007, 2, http://www.sudbih.gov.ba/predmet/2443/show.
76. Witness Mirsada Tabaković. See Tužilaštvo KS v. Novo Rajak (Trial Judgment), K-53/04 (Kantonalni sud u Sarajevu), November 27, 2006, 15.
77. Tužilaštvo KS v. Novo Rajak, 3.
78. The Serb policemen requested he find out where some members of the Bosniak resistance were hiding. See Tužilaštvo KS v. Novo Rajak, 4.
79. Tužilaštvo KS v. Novo Rajak, 3.
80. Tužilaštvo KS v. Novo Rajak, 4.

was little chance of escaping to free territories. Many of the men who were brought to the police station and who have been missing ever since were executed by the Serb soldiers or policemen. There are, however, no eyewitnesses or survivors to testify. For example, Zajko Džafić visited the police station on June 1 to seek information about his son and he has been missing ever since.[81]

Several women and girls were raped inside the police station. New evidence presented in the courts has also revealed that male prisoners were subjected to sexual abuse. In the Milisavljević et al trial at the Court of Bosnia and Herzegovina, Ahmo Zulanović testified about sexual abuse at the police station. He was arrested along with witness M-1 on May 8, 1992, in the village of Kabernik by two unknown soldiers. They were taken to the police station where they were put in a room which already had twenty civilians incarcerated. He recalled, "They were all civilians in there. Men. There was only one woman, who was tied to the radiator by the door. A lot of them were bruised and beaten, but no one was saying anything." He and M-1 were later taken out by two soldiers who sexually abused them in the police station: "They immediately made us take our underwear off in order to make sure we were circumcised. When we did it, they took their underwear off. One soldier took me, the other took the other prisoner. The soldier who was holding me asked me whether I had ever given a blow job, and if I had not, now was my chance to do it, and ordered me: Suck!"[82] M-1, who was fifteen years old in 1992, testified about his abuse: "I cried and pleaded, I was telling him I am only a child and nothing's my fault. I was sitting, he approached me, took off his underwear and put his sex organ into my mouth. . . . In the beginning I could not do it, but he pushed and beat the back of my head . . . Then he told me to take off my pants. He told me it won't hurt and it would be over quickly . . . He bended me over the table, stood behind me and I waited for him to do what he intended."[83] Another witness, J.T., stated, "We were beaten, humiliated. . . . Some of them urinated on my hands and told me: 'Balija, do your ablutions now.' When they were beating us, one was questioning, the other one hitting."[84]

The police station was again used as a detention facility in July 1995. Its last prisoners were a group of Bosniak men who, after the fall of UN Enclave Žepa

---

81. See Hikmet Karčić, *An Appeal for Truth* (Sarajevo: Fondacija Konrad Adenauer e. V., 2013), 41.
82. Dragana Erjavec, "Policeman 'Raped Male Prisoners,'" *Detektor*, April 3, 2013, https://detektor.ba/2013/04/03/policeman-raped-male-prisoners/?lang=en.
83. Erjavec, "Policeman 'Raped Male Prisoners.'"
84. Albina Sorguč, "Prisoner Recalls Visegrad Police Station Abuse," *Detektor*, April 9, 2013, http://detektor.ba/en/prisoner-recalls-visegrad-police-station-abuse/.

in July 1995, were arrested near Višegrad after attempting to cross over to Serbia. In early August 1995, the men were caught near Dobrun, some ten kilometers east of Višegrad, and handcuffed by Serb soldiers. Said Kešmer and Sead Pjevo were taken to the police station for interrogation. There they saw Mustafa Sibalo, another Bosniak from the enclave, who was arrested by Yugoslav border police near Uvac and handed over to the Višegrad police. There were around ten other Bosniaks in the police station at that time. All of them were interrogated, beaten, and tortured.[85] Afterwards, the same men were taken to Uzamnica camp where they later saw Kemal Smajić, another Bosniak from Žepa enclave who was caught in the woods. Smajić was severely beaten by one guard. He lay unable to move for several days and was then taken out and never seen again. His remains were later found in the Drina River. After Uzamnica, Kešmer, Sibalo, and Pjevo were taken to KPD Foča—a concentration camp in the town of Foča—and were exchanged in June 1996.[86] Another man, Enes Starhonić, was captured by the VRS in Rogatica in June 1995 and moved to the police station in Višegrad, where he was beaten and tortured. He was later moved to the military base in Okolište near Višegrad and then to KPD Foča.[87]

In 2012, the US magazine *The Atlantic* published a number of photographs to commemorate the twentieth anniversary of the war.[88] One photograph—and the only one publicly available—shows the beating of a Bosniak civilian in the police station on June 8, 1992. The photo was taken by Serb photojournalist Milan Timotić for Associated Press. Family members and friends recognized the victim in the photo as Jasmin (Hamdija) Hodžić.

Uzamnica Camp

Uzamnica was a JNA military barracks on the left side of the Višegrad hydroelectric dam. At the start of the attack on the town by the Užice Corps, a number of Bosniaks and Serbs, afraid of being caught in crossfire, sought refuge at the barracks. After the situation calmed down, people returned to their homes. But Uzamnica soon changed its purpose: it went from being a civilian refuge to

---

85. Tužilaštvo KS v. Novo Rajak (Trial Judgment), K-53/04, 6.
86. In KPD Foča, they saw twenty to thirty Bosniaks from Višegrad. See i Tužilaštvo KS v. Novo Rajak, 22.
87. Tužilaštvo KS v. Novo Rajak, 5.
88. Alan Taylor, "20 Years Since the Bosnian War," *The Atlantic*, April 13, 2012, http://www.theatlantic.com/photo/2012/04/20-years-since-the-bosnian-war/100278/#img14.

an infamous concentration camp. In May and June 1992, several dozen Bosniak civilians were brought to Uzamnica, where they were interrogated, beaten, and tortured. They were kept in the camp until October 1994, when they were exchanged in Sarajevo. Half a year later, Uzamnica was reopened to serve as a detention center for Bosniak men who, after the fall of UN enclave Žepa, were caught near Višegrad trying to get to Serbia. Almost all those incarcerated were civilians, except for a few Bosniak soldiers, who were captured and also kept in the camp.

The exact number of people held in Uzamnica is unknown, as people were constantly being brought in and taken out. The conditions in the camp were bad. The incarcerated civilians were not given enough food. There were no sanitary facilities or medical care. There was no heating or electricity in the warehouse.[89] According to one survivor, Mirsad Selimbegović, the civilians were chained in pairs, one to another.[90]

Uzamnica was a military-run camp, and of all the other detention camps in Višegrad, it had the clearest structure. From June 1992 to beginning of 1993, Đure Đurišić served as camp commander.[91] On May 25, after the VRS attack on the Bosniak village of Kabernik, two civilians, M.M and his father H.M, were taken to Uzamnica, where they were beaten.[92] On May 31, the VRS attacked the Bosniak villages of Osojnica, Holijaci, and Orahovci, and the men were interned in the elementary school in Orahovci, where some of them were severely beaten and then moved to Uzamnica.[93]

At least three Bosniak civilians—Meho Bečirević, Čamil Bečirević, and Bekto Salić—died in Uzamnica as a result of beatings. Mustafa Ćuprija developed diabetes and died due to lack of medical care. The ninety-two-year-old mother of Islam Kustura broke her leg and died due to lack of medical attention. The beatings were conducted mostly by soldiers and policemen who arrived at Uzamnica on a regular basis.

One of the men interned in Uzamnica was Adem Berberović, who was caught in the woods near Hamzići while escorting Bosniak women and children toward Goražde (which was under the control of the Bosnian army). He

---

89. Prosecutor v. Lukić and Lukić (Judgment), IT-98-32/1-T (ICTY), 244.
90. Albina Sorguč, "Brutal Beating in Uzamnica," *Detektor*, January 14, 2015, https://detektor. ba/2015/01/14/brutal-beating-in-uzamnica/?lang=en.
91. Prosecutor v. Lukić and Lukić (Judgment), IT-98-32/1-T (ICTY), 245.
92. Tužilaštvo BiH v. Nenad Tanasković (First Instance Verdict), X-KR/06/165 (Sud Bosne i Hercegovine), August 24, 2007, 2 http://www.sudbih.gov.ba/predmet/2443/show.
93. Tužilaštvo BiH v. Nenad Tanasković, 3.

VIŠEGRAD 97

was wounded and brought to Uzamnica, where he was beaten by Milan Lukić and others. Lukić while beating him said: "Fuck your Ustaša mother. You have green eyes like a true Ustaša."[94] Later, Berberović was subjected to electric shocks by Lukić. Islam Kustura, who was sixty-two years old in 1992, was caught in the woods near Zlatnik and first taken to Hasan Veletovac School in October 1992 and then moved to Uzamnica. He was severely beaten by the guards. Nurko Dervišević was arrested in Kupalište, near Višegrad in June 1992 by Bosnian Serb soldiers Nebojša Todorović and Goran Popović. They took him to the police station, where he was asked to hand over his identity card, after which Milan Lukić took him to Uzamnica. Nurko Dervišević was beaten on a regular basis by Serb soldiers and policemen because he was the father of two famous ABiH fighters.[95]

One of the characteristics of Uzamnica that was not the case in other detention camps was the Bosnian Serbs' use of forced labor. Incarcerated civilians from Uzamnica were sent to work on a farm near the Župa River, in Okolište, and on a farm in Dobrun. They were also used as human shields, a practice introduced by the VRS during the war while fighting the ABiH. Usually, the civilians would be tied together and pushed forward while the Serb soldiers would place their rifles on their shoulders and shoot at the ABiH soldiers. The civilians from Uzamnica were used as human shields on at least one occasion in August 1992.[96] Three women from Dobrun—S-1, her mother, and Fatima Isić—were brought to Uzamnica on August 28, 1992, after being interned in the community center in Dobrun for a few weeks.[97] VG025 was captured as a member of the ABiH and brought to Uzamnica.[98]

Uzamnica probably had the highest mortality rate among all the Višegrad camps. In July 1992, Milan Lukić took out Pero Gacić, a Serb from Goražde and a member of ABiH. He was never seen again. Also in July 1992, Milan Lukić and a group of Serb soldiers entered Uzamnica and removed Enes Džaferović, his brother Dževad Džaferović-Cipa, Muharem Imamagić, and

---

94. Prosecutor v. Lukić and Lukić (Judgment), IT-98-32/1-T (ICTY), 246–47.
95. He is the father of prominent Bosnian army officers.
96. Prosecutor v. Lukić and Lukić (Judgment), IT-98-32/1-T (ICTY), 245.
97. Tužilaštvo BiH v. Petar Kovačević (First Instance Verdict), S 1 1 K 014093 14 Kri (Sud Bosne i Hercegovine), November 2, 2015, 6, http://www.sudbih.gov.ba/predmet/3286/show.
98. Prosecutor v. Lukić and Lukić (Judgment), IT-98-32/1-T (ICTY), 252–53. "One day, Milan Lukić, Dragan Šekarić and Boban Inđić made him and other detainees lie down one by one on a wooden table in the warehouse. They had brought a wooden board, approximately 1.5 metres long, ten centimetres thick and ten centimetres wide, and started to beat the detainees on their naked backs with this board until they fainted."

Mirsad Mameledžija. He told them that they were going out for "a holiday in Bajina Bašta."[99] Later, Juso and Rasim Avdić were also taken out by Serb soldiers and never seen again. In late July, at night, Milan Lukić came to the Uzamnica camp in a green TAM truck and took away more than twenty of the younger detainees.[100] Lukić said he was taking them to Pale but none of them have been seen since. Most of their remains were found in the Drina River.[101] In June 1992, Nezir and Sumbula Smajić were captured by the VRS and taken to Uzamnica and never seen again.[102]

One of the female prisoners in Uzamnica camp was Fahrija Sejdić, who was deaf. She was also the sister of Ahmet Sejdić, a commander of the ABiH Višegrad Brigade. One day in September, she and another prisoner, Muharem Bajraktarević, were taken out of the camp by Milan Lukić. Both of their remains were found in the Drina River. In November, Bajro Šišić was taken out of the camp and never seen again. In July 1993, seventeen-year old Mirza Bajić from Gostilja village was also taken out from Uzamnica and never seen again.

The female section of Uzamnica consisted of an unknown number of female civilians, including elderly women and children. These women were most probably sexually abused by the guards and other soldiers who regularly came to the camp. The soldiers also forced the internees to sexually abuse each other.[103] The aforementioned Šaban Muratagić was brought to Uzamnica in June 1992.

Initially, he was mistreated and beaten by the Serb soldiers, but he later started collaborating with the guards and taking part in beating against fellow Bosniaks. He became a *kapo*. Adem Berberović and Nurko Derviševič testified about this several times.[104] Muratagić was exchanged together with the rest of the prisoners

---

99. This meant that they were going to be thrown into the Drina River and float up to the hydroelectric dam in Bajina Bašta, Serbia.

100. Prosecutor v. Lukić and Lukić (Judgment), IT-98-32/1-T (ICTY), 254.

101. During the Slap exhumations in 2001 and Perućac Lake exhumations in 2010.

102. Sadija Smajić appealed to the Human Rights Chamber regarding their disappearance. See Karčić, *An Appeal for Truth*, 46.

103. Prosecutor v. Lukić and Lukić (Judgment), IT-98-32/1-T (ICTY), 255. "At the beginning of February 1993, Mićo Spasojević ordered Adem Berberović and Duda Dizdarević to go behind the warehouse. After forcing the woman to undress, he ordered Adem Berberović to have sexual intercourse with her. Five days later, Spasojević tried to force Anes Čuprija to have sexual intercourse with Duda Dizdarević, but he was unable to do so. On another occasion, Spasojević tried to force Adem Berberović to have sexual intercourse with Sena Muharemović, but he was unable to do so. When Muharemović struggled, Spasojević hit her with a rifle butt. He then took a nail and repeatedly struck her on the head with it. The guards also allowed Šaban Muratagić to have sexual intercourse with the detained women."

104. Marija Taušan, "Defence Witnesses Speak about Abusers in Uzamnica," *Detektor*, August 20, 2013, https://detektor.ba/2013/08/20/defence-witnesses-speak-about-abusers-in-uzamnica/?lang=en.

in late 1994.[105] He later denied his collaboration and claimed that he was forced to do it. Several witnesses, however, claim differently, stating that he voluntarily took part in beatings and sexual abuse. He was also a source of information to the guards about the prisoners, giving them names and information.[106]

Community Center Dobrun

Dobrun is twelve kilometers east of Višegrad and several kilometers from the Serbian border. It had a mixed Bosniak and Serb population and was in the Višegrad municipality. The community center (*Mjesni ured*) in Dobrun is an old two-story building situated on the main road between Višegrad and the Serbian border. The VRS unit in Dobrun had its base on the lower floor. From May until August 1992, the community center and other locations were used as temporary detention facilities by the VRS. Although there is not enough information about these locations, and most of the interned civilians were moved to other detention camps in the town, I will try to give an overview of the events at these locations. With regard to the community center, at one point there were around fifty men inside.[107] It is estimated that at least five women were interned at the community center, where they were subjected to sexual abuse and forced to cook and clean for the VRS.[108] Three women from Dobrun—S-1, her mother, and Fatima Isić—were brought to Uzamnica on August 28, 1992, after being interned in the community center in Dobrun for a few weeks.[109]

In September 1992, an American journalist, Nina Bernstein, visited Višegrad and uncovered a story of six Bosniak civilians doing slave labor on a farm near Dobrun.[110] The civilians included two girls aged nine and seven.[111] The journal-

---

105. The prisoners were exchanged in October 1994. A total of seventeen Bosniak civilians from Uzamnica were exchanged in Sarajevo. The oldest prisoner was born in 1906 while the youngest was in 1985. See Prosecutor v. Lukić and Lukić (Judgment), IT-98-32/1-T (ICTY), 246.
106. Prosecutor v. Lukić and Lukić, 245. He was described as a kind of "watchman" in the camp.
107. According to the witness Eniz Mutapčić. See Tužilaštvo BiH v. Petar Kovačević (First Instance Verdict), S 1 1 K 014093 14 Kri, 47. The witness was previously detained in the garage of Avdo Hajdarević.
108. Interview with E, January 19, 2017. See Tužilaštvo BiH v. Petar Kovačević (First Instance Verdict), S 1 1 K 014093 14 Kri, 50, 73–74.
109. Tužilaštvo BiH v. Petar Kovačević, 6.
110. Nina Bernstein, "Private Prisoners: Small-Group Detention Believed Common in Bosnia," *Newsday*, September 7, 1992, 5 and 11.
111. They were Nermina and Nusreta, the daughters of Hasena Muharemović. The rest of the group included Fatima Isić, Behija Dizdarević, and Mustafa Dragović. See Bernstein, "Private Prisoners," 5 and 11.

ist saw several armed men keeping guard, including the Višegrad police chief Risto Perišić, while the manager of the farm was Brano Marković. The Serb hosts tried to convince the journalist that the civilians had no problems and were treated well.[112] It is not known how long they were kept here but some of them were later sent to Uzamnica.

Orahovci Elementary School

On May 31, the VRS attacked the villages of Kabernik and Holijaci, where they burned several Bosniak houses and captured several Bosniak male civilians and detained them in the elementary school in Orahovci, which was a good example of a temporary detention center. At night, several Bosnian Serb soldiers beat up three Bosniak men: Salko Šabanović, Esad Džananović, and Ramo Mlinarević.[113] After being detained in the school, the men were moved to Uzamnica camp. During their movement, however, Ramo Mlinarević and Esad Džananović were taken toward Donja Lijeska, where a VRS command center was located.[114] They have not been seen since. Džananović's body was thrown into the Drina River.[115]

False Testimonies and Enforced Disapearances

It is believed that at least two Bosniak detainees—Abdullah "Dule" Kahriman, captured as a prisoner of war, and Izet Husović, a civilian who got lost in the mountains from Grebak to Goražde—were forced to give false testimony about war crimes committed by Bosniaks, after which they were executed. They were both captured in 1993 and interned in the police station and then in Uzamnica camp. There are various versions about their fate, but it is certain that both gave statements to the police in Višegrad. These statements were later used by for-

---

112. At one point, Marković, "[s]itting down on a stool, he took hold of little Nusreta's arm and pulled her close. 'Tell them,' he instructed, 'Nobody touches us,' She repeated the words after him; 'They give us good food.' He coached her, 'They give us good food,' she repeated." See: Bernstein, "Private Prisoners," 11.

113. Tužilaštvo BiH v. Vitomir Racković (First Instance Verdict), S1 1 K 014365 14 Kri (Sud Bosne i Hercegovine), May 11, 2015, 6, http://www.sudbih.gov.ba/predmet/3175/show.

114. Tužilaštvo BiH v. Vitomir Racković, 85.

115. His remains were found in Slap, Žepa. See Tužilaštvo BiH v. Vitomir Racković, 85.

mer Yugoslav president Slobodan Milošević's defense counsel at the ICTY. The Committee for Collecting Data on Crimes Committed Against Humanity and International Law was a body set up by the RS government to try and exonerate itself and place blame for the crimes on the Bosniaks and the Bosnian Croats. In October 1996, they published a report titled "The Situation in the Municipality of Višegrad Prior to the Outbreak of War and Crimes Committed against Serbs During the War." The statements given by Kahriman and Husović are cited in this report.[116] The remains of Izet Husović were found in the Drina River, while Kahriman's remains are still unaccounted for.[117]

Deportations

Deportations of Bosniak civilians was organized by the Red Cross in Višegrad.[118] Lists of people were sent to the police and to the municipality.[119] The meeting point for deportations was organized at the town's square near the old Mehmed-paša Sokolović Bridge. The office of the Red Cross was in the square.[120] Before the deportations, Bosnian Serb soldiers roamed around the town in cars with megaphones, announcing that Bosniaks were not safe anymore and that they had to leave. On or around June 20, trucks gathered Bosniak civilians from villages on the east side of the Drina River, including the village of Drinsko. The trucks were taken to the Hasan Veletovac School, were the civilians were told to hand over all their money and gold, after which there were deported to Bosnia and Herzegovina government–controlled areas. The deportations were either toward Macedonia or Bosnia and Herzegovina government–controlled areas such as Olovo or Kladanj. Interestingly, many local Serbs had information about whether certain convoys were safe or not. Some of them would advise their Bosniak friends on which convoy to take or not to take.[121]

---

116. See http://www.slobodan-milosevic.org/documents/reports/8-a.htm.

117. The remains of Izet Husović were exhumed in 2010 during the Lake Perućac exhumations.

118. Amer Jahić, "Tasic Was Not Responsible for Convoy," *Detektor*, October 22, 2013, https://detektor.ba/2013/10/22/tasic-was-not-responsible-for-convoy/?lang=en.

119. As witness Fahrija Hošo stated, it was done in order to know "who was leaving, and who wasn't." See Amer Jahić, "Witnesses Recall Visegrad Bosniak Convoys," *Detektor*, March 11, 2014, http://detektor.ba/en/witnesses-recall-visegrad-bosniak-convoys/.

120. One might notice that the role of the Red Cross in Republika Srpska, with local staff, is quite problematic. This is a virtually unresearched topic. To make matters more interesting, the first president of the Republika Srpska Red Cross was Ljiljana Karadžić-Zelen, the wife of Radovan Karadžić.

121. For example, an influential Serb doctor in Užice, Serbia, told his former colleague to tell his family which convoy his mother needed to take.

Massacres during Deportations

On at least two occassions, convoys of deported Bosniak civilians were stopped and men were taken off and executed. These executions are similar to the infamous *Korićanske stijene* massacre (described in more detail later on). On May 26, 1992, a convoy of buses transporting around two hundred Bosniaks from Višegrad was returned from the Serbian border at Mokra Gora. On the way back to the town, at Bosanska Jagodina, an unidentified armed group stopped the bus and took out seventeen Bosniak men. The remains of these victims were found in a mass grave in Crncici near Bosanska Jagodina.[122] The rest of the civilians were deported to the Bosnia and Herzegovina government–controlled town of Olovo. On June 14 1992, a convoy was organized for five hundred Bosniaks from Bosanska Jagodina and surrounding villages: Gornji and Donji Dubovik, Velatovo, Žagre, Smrijeće, Župa, and Dobrun. They embarked on buses on the town's square and left toward Olovo. The convoy stopped at Išerić brdo, where forty-nine men were taken off the bus and taken to a pit called Paklenik, where they were executed.[123]

Perpetrators

In mid-April 1992, Višegrad was under the control of the JNA Užice Corps. As explained earlier this chapter, the JNA retreated in late May. Physical control of the municipality was handed over to the VRS. The VRS Višegrad Brigade (Višegradska brigada Vojske Republike Srpske) was formed on May 12, 1992. Its first commander was Drago Gavrilović.[124] In June, Vinko Pandurević took up the position and was also the commander of the Višegrad Tactical Group (Taktička grupa Višegrad). In December 1992, he was appointed commander of the VRS Zvornik Brigade (Zvornička brigada Vojske Republike Srpske), and, finally, Luka Dragičević took the position of commander of the Višegrad Bri-

---

122. "First Report on the War Crimes in the Former Yugoslavia: Submission of Information to the United Nations Security Council in Accordance With Paragraph 5 of Resolution 771 (1992)," September 22, 1992, accessed March 3, 2016, https://www.phdn.org/archives/www.ess.uwe.ac.uk/documents/sdrpt1.htm.

123. Only one man—Ferid Spahić—survived the execution. See Tužilaštvo BiH v. Predrag Milisavljević et al. (First Instance Verdict), S1 1 K 0011128 12 Krl (Sud Bosne i Hercegovine), October 28, 2014, 51–52, http://www.sudbih.gov.ba/predmet/3013/show.

124. "Višegradska brigada branila i odbranila srpski narod," *Glas Srpske*, May 26, 2012, https://www.glass-rpske.com/lat/drustvo/panorama/visegradska-brigada-branila-i-odbranila-srpski-narod/80241.

VIŠEGRAD 103

gade. The Višegrad Brigade was officially named the Second Podrinje Light Infantry Brigade. Certain members of this brigade belonged to the Interventions Company (Interventna četa) or the First Company (Prva četa) of the First Battalion of the Second Podrinjska Light Infantry Brigade (Prvi Bataljon Druge podrinjske lahke brigade).[125] The VRS took an active role in the incarceration and deportations of Bosniak civilians from Višegrad. Camps such as Uzamnica were under military control for the entire war. Members of the Višegrad Brigade based there, such as Momir Savić, commander of the VRS 3rd Company of the Višegrad Brigade; Vitomir Racković, a member of the VRS 4th Company of the Višegrad Brigade, and Dragan Šekarić, a member of the VRS Goražde Brigade, took part in torture and murder of the detainees and were convicted by local courts for atrocities.

The Bosnian Serb police were the key authority in executing the SDS Crisis Committee's orders regarding the cleansing of Višegrad's Bosniak population. After the JNA handed over the political and administrative power to SDS, Risto Perišić became the chief of police. The station commander was Dragan Tomić. Mićo Maksimović was the officer for defensive preparations. Dobro Tomić was the crimes inspector. There were seven other police officers, among whom was Sredoje Lukić. As can be seen from the court cases mentioned in this chapter, however, the majority of the crimes were committed by members of the MUP RS Reserve Police Force: Boban Šimšić, Nenad Tanasković, Željko Lelek, and Novo Rajak.[126] The question of paramilitaries may be one of the hardest to answer.

Since Milan Lukić and his group definitely committed most of the crimes, it would be important to try and define his role. His group had different names: the Avengers (Osvetnici), the White Eagles (Beli orlovi) and Garavi Sokak (Sooty Alley). But there is little evidence to prove their existence, and most of the information is hearsay. The White Eagles were present in Višegrad but for a very short time; they entered along with the JNA in April and left quickly. The

---

125. Soldiers such as Luka Dragičević, Boban Inđić, Obrad and Novak Poluga, Dragan Šekarić, Oliver Krsmanović, Petko Inđić, Radojica Ristić, Vuk Ratković, and Mico Jovičić. See more at "Strpci Victims' Relatives 'Heard about Abductions via Media," BIRN BiH, May 16, 2016, http://www.justice-report.com/en/articles/strpci-victims-relatives-heard-about-abductions-via-media#sthash.PdWBMsxb.dpuf.

126. An important document is the one issued by the RS Ministry of Interior Srbinje Public Security Centre titled "List of participation in war of all v/o conscripts who had wartime assignments in the SJB/Public Security Station in the period from 4 August 1991 to 30 June 1996," dated June 7, 1999, number 15-5/-010239/99, ICTY no.: 06345001, Exhibit 2D00060.E, https://bit.ly/RSMUPListConscripts1991-96.

104　TORTURE, HUMILIATE, KILL

Garavi Sokak were supposedly headed by Lukić during the Strpci kidnapping case in 1993. The Avengers did not formally exist. They were composed of members of the VRS and MUP RS and the reserve police force. It is obvious that they were acting on instructions from higher authorities; when they carried out pre-planned executions of Bosniak elites, they had lists of the names addresses of the people they were looking for, which had been given to them beforehand. These units are usually referred to as paramilitaries.[127] The ICTY, in its trial, noted the following regarding Lukić and his membership in the Avengers:

> There has been no convincing evidence presented to the Trial Chamber as to Milan Lukić's and Sredoje Lukić's membership of the White Eagles or Avengers, or any linkage between the White Eagles or Avengers and any of the crimes with which Milan Lukić and Sredoje Lukić are charged. The Trial Chamber notes in particular that no inference as to membership of the White Eagles can be drawn from the clothes, hats or insignia worn by Milan Lukić and Sredoje Lukić. Further, the Trial Chamber does not place much weight on the police interviews in which Milan Lukić is reported to have stated that he was the leader of the "Avengers."[128]

Interestingly, after Milan Lukić was arrested in Serbia in late October 1992 for illegal possession of arms right after the Sjeverin abduction, he was interviewed by the police in Užice. He stated in his interview that he was a member of the "Obrenovac Detachment, and that is a special unit within the Višegrad Police." He also stated that later, his unit was transferred to the Višegrad Territorial Defense as the "Avengers," a volunteer unit.[129] In the Stanišić and Župljanin case, it was found that Lukić was a member of the reserve police

---

127. Edina Bećirević, *The Genocide on the Drina River* (New Haven, CT: Yale University Press, 2014), 75. Bosnian scholar Edina Bećirević explained the problems in using this term: "In public, these units were referred to as paramilitary in order to create the illusion that the state had no control over them. In this way, special forces can be used to realize the most malicious of goals, including mass murder, assassination of political opponents, expulsion of people, and the like. Orders are communicated directly, so there are rarely outside witnesses, and there is no need for a 'paper trail.' To have this kind of power is essential for political manipulation, but also for the perpetration of mass crimes such as genocide."

128. Prosecutor v. Lukić and Lukić (Judgment), IT-98-32/1-T (ICTY), 31.

129. Record of Interview with the Accused Milan Lukić, Kio. no. 118/92, dated October 30, 1992. The document was used as evidence at the ICTY, no. 0644-6149-0644-6154-ET/Translation. SeeAnother useful document is a certificate issued by the Command of the 1st Višegrad Light Infantry Brigade signed by Chief of Staff, Lieutenant Colonel Luka Dragićević stating that Milan Lukić is a soldier of the VRS since May 19, 1992. ICTY no. 0422–4603-EDT/Draft translation. See: https://bit.ly/LukaDragicevicCert1992.

force who headed a paramilitary group.[130] Despite having different members, the aim of the VRS and RS police was the same. They cooperated and jointly conducted crimes against humanity. Višegrad, like the rest of the Drina Valley, was an important part in the establishment of the Serb republic. Karadžić stated in August 1995, "To tell the truth, there are towns that we've grabbed for ourselves, and there were only 30 percent of us. I can name as many of those as you want, but we cannot give up the towns where we made up 70 percent. Don't let this get around, but remember how many of us were in Bratunac, how many in Srebrenica, how many in Višegrad, how many in Rogatica, how many in Vlasenica, in Zvornik, etc. Due to strategic importance they had to become ours, and no one is practically questioning it any more."[131]

Destruction of Religious Buildings

The first mosque to be burned down in Višegrad was the emperor's mosque (Careva džamija), in the first days of June 1992. Within a few months, all the mosques in the Višegrad municipality were looted and dynamited: The Gazanferbegova mosque in the town was blown up and turned into a park. The Drinsko, Orahovci, Žlijeb, and Dobrun mosques were also destroyed. Two *maktabs* (religious schools) in Holijaci and Barimo were also destroyed as well as the Sijerčić Tomb in the center of Višegrad. All elements of Islamic architecture were cleansed from the town.

Concentration Camps and Mass Graves

Since the detention and concentration camps in Višegrad were temporary, it is difficult to establish who was in which camp or facility. Also, in the case of Višegrad, no journalists or International Committee of the Red Cross (ICRC) visited the town and the camps in the months while it was being *cleansed*. In other locations, such as Prijedor or Srebrenica, mass gaves have been found, which have allowed families to rebury victims and evidence to be gathered. The perpetrators in Višegrad, however, opted to use the Drina River as a way to

---

130. Prosecutor v. Stanišić and Župljanin (Judgment, Volume 2), IT-08-91-T (ICTY), 286–87.
131. Prosecutor v. Radovan Karadžić (Judgment), IT-95-5/18-T (ICTY), 1079.

conceal their crimes rather than digging mass graves, and so for fifteen years it was not possible for investigations and exhumations to take place. In 2010, though, work on the hydroelectric dam spanning the Drina in Bajina Bašta, a town roughly fifty kilometers downstream, required that the stretch of river between the Višegrad Dam and the Bajina Bašta Dam be drained. As the river level dropped significantly, draining the (artificial) Lake Perućac, Višegrad's largest mass grave was revealed, as well as smaller sites in Slap, Kurtalići, Kameničko točilo, and Barimo.[132] Subsequently, in the brief window of time available, the remains of some 250 people were recovered, including most of the men who were taken out of Uzamnica in July 1992. The remains of Jasmin Hodzić, photographed at the police station, were also found in the Drina, as well as those of Jasmina Ahmetspahić. After being taken to Vilina Vlas at at some point during 1992 by Milan Lukić and raped there, Jasmina escaped her tormentors by jumping to her death from one of the spa's windows.[133]

Though welcome, the chance to excavate the Drina River bed was a rare one that is unlikely to be repeated for some time, and the remaining families of the victims may never get the chance to see their loved ones exhumed.

---

132. Hikmet Karčić, "Uncovering the Truth: The Lake Perućac Exhumations in Eastern Bosnia," *Journal of Muslim Minority Studies* 37, no. 1 (March 2017): 114–28, https://doi.org/10.1080/13602004.2017.1294374.

133. See Tužilaštvo BiH v. Željko Lelek (Second Instance Judgment), X-KRŽ-06/202 (Sud Bosne i Hercegovine), January 12, 2009, 14, http://www.sudbih.gov.ba/predmet/2445/show.

CHAPTER 4

Prijedor

Introduction

The town of Prijedor (and its surrounding municipality) is in the northwestern part of Bosnia and Herzegovina, roughly thirty-two kilometers from the Croatian border.

According to the 1991 census, it had a total of 112,543 inhabitants, of which, 49,351 (43.85 percent) were Muslims, 47,581(42.27 percent) were Serbs, 6,459 (5.73 percent) identified as Yugoslav, 6,316 (5.61 percent) were Croats, with 2,836 others.[1]

Between 1992 and 1995, it was the scene of some of the worst atrocities committed by Bosnian Serbs on Bosniaks during the genocide. These crimes, committed in and around Prijedor, represent the most sophisticated, well-organized, and systematic effort to cleanse the region of its non-Serb population.

In 1990, when the first democratic general elections were held in Bosnia and Herzegovina, the two main parties in Prijedor, SDA and SDS, won a majority of the seats in the assembly. The parties agreed that the mayor of Prijedor should be Prof. Muhamed Ćehajić from the SDA, while his deputy would be Dr. Milomir Stakić from the SDS.[2] As in Višegrad, the elections were marked by a spike in nationalist rhetoric, which spilled over from the breakaway Croatian

---

1. Državni zavod za statistiku Republike Bosne i Hercegovine, "Popis stanovništva, domaćinstava, stanova i poljoprivrednih gazdinstava 1991, Nacionalni sastav stanovništva—Rezultati za Republiku po opštinama i naseljenim mjestima 1991," December, 1993, 234, https://bit.ly/ResultsBiHPopSurv 1991.
2. Jasmin Medić, *Genocid u Prijedoru* (Cazin: Grafis d.o.o., 2013), 20.

108   TORTURE, HUMILIATE, KILL

Serb areas nearby. Due to its closeness to Croatia, many Serb politicians rallied throughout Krajina, giving speeches and supporting their counterparts in Bosnia and Herzegovina.

On August 17, 1990, for example, the founding assembly of the Serb Democratic Party was held in Benkovac, near Prijedor, where a Serb nationalist leader from Croatia, Dr. Jovan Rašković, gave a speech as the crowds chanted, "Ubit ćemo Tuđmana. Ubit ćemo ustaše" (We will kill Tuđman. We will kill Ustašas), referring to Croatian president Franjo Tuđman and the World War II Croat fascists.[3]

In April 1991, the local Bosnian Serb political leadership in the northwest of Bosnia and Herzegovina decided to establish a community of Serb-dominated municipalities in order to cherish cultural, educational, and other ties. The Association of Bosanska Krajina Municipalities (Zajednica opština bosanske Krajine, or ZOBK), was made up of representatives from municipalities with a predominantly Serbian population. In September 1991, the ZOBK was transformed into a more organized Autonomous Region of Krajina (Autonomna regija Krajina, or ARK). The aim and goals of the Bosnian Serb leadership were clear: to establish a separate Bosnian Serb state from which non-Serbs would be removed.[4]

The ARK functioned as an intermediate level of government, established to coordinate municipal implementation of the strategic plan.[5] On January 17, 1992, the Assembly of the Bosnian Serb People of Prijedor Municipality decided unanimously to join the ARK.[6] In August 1991, a Bosnian Serb paramilitary group "Wolves of Vučjak" (*Vukovi s Vučjaka*), took over the TV transmitter on Mount Kozara near Prijedor. The unit was led by Veljko Milanković and was

---

3.   A copy of the video of this speech, titled "Buković kod Benkovca, govor dr. Jovana Raškovića 17.8.1990," is held in the author's archive.
4.   As stated during the trial: "During the second half of 1991, it already appeared increasingly unlikely that the SRBH would remain within the SFRY. The Trial Chamber is satisfied beyond reasonable doubt that during this period, the Bosnian Serb leadership, including the members of the Main Board of the SDS, as well as Bosnian Serb representatives of the armed forces, formed a plan to link Serb-populated areas in BiH together, to gain control over these areas and to create a separate Bosnian Serb state, from which most non-Serbs would be permanently removed (as part of the 'Strategic Plan'). The Bosnian Serb leadership knew that the Strategic Plan could only be implemented by the use of force and fear." See Prosecutor v. Radoslav Brđanin (Judgment), IT-99-36-T (ICTY), September 1, 2004, 28–29, http://www.icty.org/x/cases/brdanin/tjug/en/brd-tj040901e.pdf.
5.   It was composed of the following municipalities: Banja Luka, Bosanski Petrovac, Bosansko Grahovo, Čelinac, Glamoč, Ključ, Kotor Varoš, Kupres, Laktaši, Mrkonjić Grad, Prijedor, Prnjavor, Sanski Most, Skender Vakuf, Srbac, Šipovo, Titov Drvar, Bosanska Krupa, and Donji Vakuf.
6.   Prosecutor v. Radoslav Brđanin (Judgment), IT-99-36-T (ICTY), 73–75.

composed of mainly Serbs from Prnjavor.[7] From then on, most of the Bosanska Krajina municipalities could not receive TV and radio programs from Sarajevo; they were only able to receive information and news from Belgrade. Soon most of the Bosniak and Bosnian Croat employees of the TV and radio stations in Bosanska Krajina were dismissed.[8] Then the Assembly of the Serbian People in Bosnia and Herzegovina requested local SDS boards to organize a plebiscite of the Serbian people in the municipality on whether they wanted to remain in Yugoslavia or in the proposed new state of Bosnia and Herzegovina.[9] The participants in the plebiscite voted with different ballot papers depending on whether they were Serbs or non-Serbs. "Kozarski vijesnik" reported that "45,003 registered Serbs in the Municipality of Prijedor participated in the plebiscite, as did 2,035 people categorized as non-Serbs. 99.9% of the Serbs and 98.8% of the non-Serbs voted in favor of Bosnia and Herzegovina remaining in a joint state of Yugoslavia."[10]

Within the ARK, a Crisis Staff was formed with the aim of implementing the strategic plan by ensuring the cooperation between the political authorities, the army, and the police at the regional level.[11] At the meeting of the Prijedor SDS Municipal Board on December 2, 1991, Simo Mišković, the board's president, read the results of the plebiscite and, in summary, posed two choices for the future: "The plebiscite vote has shown that 60% of the electorate are Serbs. This indicates two options: (1) repeat the municipal elections, or (2) take over and establish independent organs. It will be decided later which of the two options will be chosen."[12] On December 27, 1991, during the meeting of the Prijedor Municipal Board of the SDS, the second option was adopted. The Assembly of the Serb People of the Municipality of Prijedor was formed on January 7, 1992. It had sixty-nine members, and Milomir Stakić was elected as president. Two days later, the Republic of Serb People of Bosnia and Herze-

---

7. Milanković completed his military training in 1991 in Knin, Croatia, under the command of Captain Dragan Vasiljković.

8. Prosecutor v. Radoslav Brđanin (Judgment), IT-99-36-T (ICTY), 35.

9. The Assembly of Bosnia and Herzegovina adopted a "Memorandum" on the sovereignty of Bosnia and Herzegovina, paving the way for a referendum on the republic's independence on October 14, 1991. A couple of days later, on October 24, 1991, a separate "Assembly of the Serb People" was proclaimed by the Serb deputies, which called for a plebiscite of the Serb people in Bosnia and Herzegovina on the question of whether or not they wanted to remain in the federal Yugoslav state. See Prosecutor v. Milomir Stakić (Judgment), IT-97-24-T (ICTY), July 31, 2003, 6, https://www.icty.org/x/cases/stakic/tjug/en/stak-tj030731e.pdf.

10. Prosecutor v. Milomir Stakić, 12.

11. Prosecutor v. Radoslav Brđanin (Judgment), IT-99-36-T (ICTY), 84.

12. Prosecutor v. Stakić (Judgment), IT-97-24-T (ICTY), 12.

govina was proclaimed. On January 17, the Assembly of the Serb People of the Municipality of Prijedor voted unanimously to join the ARK.[13]

In March 1992, the Territorial Defense arms cache was overtaken by local Serbs. The (in)equality of arms was seen in the weeks to come.[14] Public segregation and discrimination against non-Serbs was already visible on the streets of Prijedor; when purchasing flour, for example, two separate lines were formed by the Serb authorities, one for the Serbs and one for non-Serbs.[15] On April 16, 1992, the Assembly of the Serbian People of the Municipality of Prijedor elected a government for Prijedor.[16] On April 23, 1992, the Prijedor Municipal Board of the SDS decided to "reinforce the Crisis Staff and to subordinate to the Crisis Staff all units and staff in management posts" and "to immediately start working on the takeover, the coordination with JNA notwithstanding."[17] By late April 1992, the SDS had taken over almost all police stations in Prijedor. *Kozarski vijesnik* published an article in April 1993 stating that it was Simo Drljača who had masterminded the operation: "He executed his task so well that after six months [on the night of 29th to 30th May 1992] of illegal work, a force of 1,775 well armed men in thirteen police stations was ready to carry out the difficult tasks in the time ahead."[18]

Coup d'etat

In the night of the April 29–30, 1992, the coup d'etat began. Serb members of the Public Security Station and Reserve Police divided themselves into five groups of around twenty people each. Each group was responsible for the takeover of certain important buildings: the Municipal Assembly building, one for the SUP

---

13. Prosecutor v. Stakić, 13.
14. Medić, *Genocid u Prijedoru*, 22.
15. See witness K.B.'s statement in Helsinki Watch/HRW, *War Crimes in Bosnia and Herzegovina, Volume II* (New York: Human Rights Watch, 1993), 43,
16. The municipality government was made up of president of the Assembly of the Serbian People of the Municipality of Prijedor, Dr. Milomir Stakić; chairman of the Executive Committee of the Prijedor Serbian Municipality, Dr. Milan Kovačević; deputy chairman of the Executive Committee, Boško Mandić; secretary for economic affairs, Ranko Travar; secretary for national defense, Slavko Budimir; director of the Public Utilities Company, Milovan Dragić; commander of the Public Security Station (SJB), Simo Drljača; and commander of the TO Municipal Staff, Slobodan Kuruzović. See Prosecutor v. Stakić (Judgment), IT-97-24-T (ICTY), 13–14.
17. Prosecutor v. Stakić, 14.
18. Prosecutor v. Stakić, 13–14.

building, one for the courts, one for the bank, and the last for the post office.[19] The operation was finished quickly "without a bullet fired" and with no casualties. After the operation was completed successfully, Milomir Stakić arrived at Radio Prijedor and read out an announcement in which he stated the reasons why they had taken over power in the town:

> Due to the fact that the Party of Democratic Action [SDA], all this time did not wish to share power, either with the winning parties or with the opposition parties, the work of the Municipal Assembly has been blocked, and the work of all other organs of government has been blocked. Because of this, the citizens and peoples of the municipality of Prijedor are living in a state of anarchy, insecurity, poverty and great fear, and this is not all.[20]

In his announcement he states one interesting fact that gives an answer as to why the coup d'etat was executed on the April 29–30:

> The last straw was on 29 April 1992 when the so-called Ministry of Defense of the Ministry of the Interior of the so-called sovereign Bosnia and Herzegovina, when a dispatch arrived with an order to the municipal Secretariat for the Interior and the secretariat for People's Defense, as well as the Territorial Defense staff, to the effect that in Prijedor municipality they should immediately block communications, military barracks, and military facilities to mount attacks on the JNA, to take away from them weapons and technology, all of which would mean war, death, destruction, and arson in our municipality. On several occasions, Nijaz Duraković, the president of the Socialist Democratic Party, has called on its members, the members of his party, to wage a war against Yugoslavia, the regular JNA, and thus, the Serbian people, which is unacceptable for all citizens of good will.[21]

This shows that although the coup d'etat was conducted the same day as the dispatch from the Ministry of Interior of Bosnia and Herzegovina from Sarajevo, it was almost certainly planned and organized in advance of that day, as its

---

19. Prosecutor v. Stakić, 16.
20. Prosecutor v. Stakić, 27.
21. Prosecutor v. Stakić, 27.

112   TORTURE, HUMILIATE, KILL

the execution was pre-emptive.[22] Drljača and Kovačević also issued announcements for the population to be calm and to hand over their weapons. Besides members of the SDS, several high-ranking SDA officials, including Dr. Sadiković, Muhamed Čehajić, and Dedo Crnalić called for calm.[23] This was quite a naive move considering that in the days to come, all were arrested and taken to Omarska, where they were murdered.

Prijedor Crisis Committee

In late 1991, the Prijedor Crisis Committee was formed within the SDS. The aim of the Prijedor Crisis Committee was, among other things, "to co-ordinate government, for the defense of the territory of the municipality."[24] The Crisis Committee became the core institution for the implementation of the ethnoreligious cleansing of Bosniaks and Croats and other non-Serbs in the Prijedor municipality. One of their first activities was enforcing the dismissals of non-Serbs from municipal institutions. These decisions were made before the ARK had even issued such orders. The Prijedor Municipal Assembly adopted the "Decision on the Organization and Work of the Prijedor Municipal Crisis Staff" on May 20, 1992. The president of the Crisis Committee was Dr. Milomir Stakić and its vice president was Dragan Savanović.[25] Military liaison was provided by

---

22. The Trial Chamber in the Karadžić case provided five pieces of evidence to show that the takeover was planned ahead of the supposed fax on April 29.

23. Prosecutor v. Stakić (Judgment), IT-97-24-T (ICTY), 28. Also Jasmin Medić calls Čehajić's reaction to the coup as "Gandhi-style resistance." See Jasmin Medić, "'Kozarski vjesnik' u službi zločina," *Godišnjak Bošnjačke zajednice kulture: Preporod* 1 (2016): 4.

24. Republika Srpska prime minister Branko Đerić issued the "Instruction for the work of the municipal Crisis Staffs of the Serbian People," which stated the tasks of the Crisis Committees: "1. in a state of war, the Crisis Staff shall assume all prerogatives and functions of the municipal assemblies, when they are unable to convene (. . .). 3. The Crisis Staff coordinates the functions of authorities in order to ensure the defense of the territories, the safety of the population and property, the establishment of government and the organization of all other areas of life and work. In so doing, the Crisis Staff provides the conditions for the Municipal Executive Committee to exercise legal executive authority, run the economy and other areas of life (. . .). 4. The command of the TO and police forces is under the exclusive authority of the professional staff, and therefore any interference regarding the command of the TO and/or the use of the police forces must be prevented (. . .). 8. The Crisis Staff has the obligation to provide working and living conditions for JNA members (. . .)." See Prosecutor v. Radoslav Brđanin (Judgment), IT-99-36-T (ICTY), 84.

25. According to the Decision on the Organization and Work of the Crisis Staff, there were nine members of the Crisis Committee: the president of the Municipality Executive Committee, commander of the Municipal Territorial Defense Staff, commander of the Municipal People's Defense Staff, chief of the Public Security Station, secretary of the Municipal Secretariat for Trade, Industry and Public Services, secretary of the Municipal Secretariat for Town Planning, Housing, Utilities, and Legal

PRIJEDOR 113

Colonel Arsić and Major Zeljaja, who were regularly present at Crisis Committee meetings. Soon after the Prijedor Crisis Committee was formed, it decided to form several local crisis committees within the municipality, almost entirely in Serb-majority areas.[26]

By late June 1992, the Prijedor Crisis Committee had been renamed the "War Presidency." This was done after "a decision from the government and the presidency of the Serbian Republic of Bosnia and Herzegovina."[27]

Immediately after the Bosnian Serbs established control over the town, the Crisis Committee decided to get rid of all non-Serbs from the local administration. Similar decisions were being made all over the newly established Serbian state. The Crisis Committee of the ARK issued a decision on June 22, 1992, stating that "All executive posts, posts involving a likely flow of information, posts involving the protection of public property, that is all posts important for the functioning of the economy, may only be held by personnel of Serbian nationality."[28] The Prijedor Crisis Committee had by April 30, 1992, however, already dismissed non-Serbs from their workplaces.[29] They were refused entry to their workplaces and were dismissed from governing and management positions. Nusreta Sivac tried to enter the court where she worked but was denied access by Serb soldiers who had surrounded the building. In the Prijedor Medical Center, Dr. Ibrahim Beglerbegović was handed a decision stating that he was no longer head of his department. Serbs who were not loyal to the SDS were removed from governing positions. Non-Serb employees at Radio Prijedor were fired by a decision of the ARK Crisis Committee.[30] At the same time, plans regarding setting up concentration camps were being put into practice. For the Bosnian Serb officials, the establishment of concentration camps was a completely normal process and they found justification for it in history. In late August 1992, Radislav Brđanin stated on television: "Those who are not loyal are free to go and the few loyal Croats and Muslims can stay (. . .) If Hitler,

---

Property Affairs, the health and security officer at the Municipal Secretariat for the Economy and Social Affairs, and the information officer at the Municipal Secretariat for the Economy and Social Affairs. See Prosecutor v. Stakić (Judgment), IT-97-24-T (ICTY), 22.

26. They were formed in Ljubija, Prijedor Center, Lamovita, Omarska, Tukovi, Orlovača, Brezičani, Rakelići, Božići, and Palančište. See Prosecutor v. Stakić, 25.

27. As stated in the Stakić judgment, "The change of name from Crisis Staff to War Presidency was purely cosmetic. There was no change in the duties and functions of the Crisis Staff and no change in the membership of that body as a result of the change in name. In other words, de facto it remained the same body." Prosecutor v. Stakić, 26.

28. Prosecutor v. Stakić, 35.

29. Prosecutor v. Radovan Karadžić (Judgment), IT-95-5/18-T (ICTY), 651–52.

30. See Prosecutor v. Radovan Karadžić, 653, for more examples of dismissals from positions.

114   TORTURE, HUMILIATE, KILL

Stalin, and Churchill could have working camps so can we. Oh come on, we are in a war after all."[31]

Media

In Banja Luka, the largest Bosnian Serb city, Banja Luka TV ran a series of special reports from Prijedor called the *Prijedor Chronicles* (*Prijedorska hronika*), which broadcast video footage of SDS's initial victories and subsequent attacks on villages around Prijedor, as well as other propaganda material. It was two local media outlets, however, Radio Prijedor and *Kozarski vijesnik* that played a major role in the process of polarizing the communities and dehumanizing the local Bosniaks in the days before and especially after the coup d'etat.

Radio Prijedor played Serb nationalist music and hysterically portrayed non-Serb leaders as extremists. Derogatory terms, such as *ustasha* and *mujahedin*, were used when referring to non-Serbs. Non-Serb doctors were especially targeted. Dr. Mirsad Mujadžić was accused of making Serb women incapable of giving birth to male children by injecting them with certain drugs. Dr. Mujadžić, who was also president of SDA Prijedor, explained that the intent of such propaganda was "to stifle non-Serb resistance by undermining the credibility of prominent and respected non-Serb citizens of Prijedor."[32] Mujadžić's colleague Dr. Željko Sikora, a Bosnian Croat, was referred to as the "Monster Doctor." He was accused of "making Serb women abort if they were pregnant with male children and of castrating the male babies of Serbian parents."[33] Mile Mutić and Rade Mutić, journalists of Radio Prijedor and *Kozarski vijesnik*, intermittently attended the Crisis Committee meetings, so they had firsthand information regarding the war-related activities in and around Prijedor.[34] In an article published on June 10, 1992, Dr. Sikora was accused of "for years, using monstrous methods, in a planned fashion worked on the decrease of birthrate of Serb people" and also stating that "his Church would forgive this crime, it is enough

---

31. Prosecutor v. Radoslav Brđanin (Judgment), IT-99-36-T (ICTY), 201.
32. Dr. Mujadžić did not end up in one of the camps. After the shelling of Hambarine he escaped on foot to Kurevo forest and then to Bihać. His survival has been something of a controversy. See "Radoslav Brdjanin's Off-Color Jokes," *Sense Agency*, October 31, 2011, http://archive.sensecentar.org/vijesti.php?aid=13325.
33. Prosecutor v. Stakić (Judgment), IT-97-24-T (ICTY), 28–29.
34. Prosecutor v. Stakić, 29.

PRIJEDOR 115

for him to kneel down before the confessional."[35] Dr. Osman Mahmuljin was accused of intentionally giving his colleague, Živko Dukić, wrong medicine for his heart condition. *Kozarski vijesnik* published an article about them titled "Surviving All Therapies" ("Preživio sve terapije").[36] Dr. Mahmuljin was arrested and taken to Prijedor police station where he was beaten and tortured. He was then moved to Omarska, where he was soon murdered.

The capture of Bećir Medunjanin and his wife Sadeta was celebrated triumphantly by *Kozarski vijesnik*. Medunjanin was the secretary for national defense in Prijedor municipality. After the coup in Prijedor and the later attacks on Kozarac and surrounding villages, Bećir, his wife Sadeta, and his twenty-year-old son hid on Mt. Kozara. They were captured in the beginning of June. *Kozarski vijesnik* published a piece titled titled "Bećir Medunjanin Arrested and a picture of Bećir, his wife Sadeta, son Anes, and Fehim and Suad Trnjanin kneeling on the ground with their hands tied. They were all taken to Omarska camp.[37] As violence toward Bosniaks increased, *Kozarski vijesnik* published an article on July 31, 1992, suggesting that it was the Bosniaks who were killing each other: "The followers of jihad are clashing now with their compatriots, so because of that, late last week, at the hands of religious fanatics, several dozens of their brethen were killed in a cruel manner. This all shows, to what extent are ready the blinded followers of Allah, but it is also a proof of their weakness and defeat that has led to mutual recriminations and friction."[38]

The Killing Days

Bosniaks and Croats in and around Prijedor were initially subjected to discrimination, movement restriction, and intimidation. This steadily grew worse and culminated in a bloody wave of ethnic cleansing, which saw thousands of Bosniaks and a small number of Bosnian Croats murdered and their property looted. The few thousand who remained in the Prijedor municiliaty were herded off to concentration camps Keraterm, Omarska, and Trnopolje. Keraterm was a former factory converted into a concentration camp. Omarska is a

---

35. Medić, "Kozarski vjesnik," 4.
36. Published on July 10, 1992. See Medić, "Kozarski vjesnik," 4.
37. "Bećir Medunjanin arrested," *Kozarski vijesnik*, June 12, 1992. Prosecutor v. Stakić, IT-97-24 (ICTY), Exhibit S162/5A.
38. "Ubijali se međusobno," *Kozarski vijesnik*, July 31, 1992, in Medić, "Kozarski vijesnik," 480.

mine located several kilometers from Prijedor, and Trnopolje is a small village where an open-air concentration camp was established in and around the village school. Trnopolje interned the largest number of people and mainly women and children. Those who remained in the town of Prijedor were forced to wear white armbands on the streets of Prijedor so as to identify themselves as non-Serbs.

In May 1992, the old town in Prijedor, Stari Grad, which was predominantly inhabited by Bosniaks, was destroyed. Non-Serb houses in the town were also marked for destruction. One member of the group who marked these houses claimed to be acting pursuant to the orders of the Crisis Committee.[39] The Republika Srpska army and police attacked Bosniak and Croat villages around the town in an organized fashion. Those who were not killed on the spot were forced to sign over their property to either the ARK or Republika Srpska.[40]

The ARK implemented the policies of ethnoreligious cleansing in a bureaucratic fashion. On June 12, 1992, the ARK established the Agency for Population Movement and Exchange of Material Wealth (Agencija za preseljenje stanovništva i razmjenu materijalnih dobara), based in Banja Luka. The decision to form this agency was published in the *ARK Official Gazette*. The decision stated, among other things, that "An agency shall be established to work on the problem of population resettlement."[41] Professor Miloš Vojinović from Glamoč was appointed its chief. The Banja Luka–based daily newspaper *Glas* stated on July 18, 1992, that the agency was "successfully conducting the relocation of citizens of all three nationalities, i.e. the exchange of their material goods" and that "In this agency there are about five hundred registered Muslim, Croat and Albanian persons who want to leave Krajina."[42]

Later on that year, in August 1992, Stojan Župljanin, the head of the CSB (Security Service Center) and member of the ARK Crisis Staff, set up a commission to inspect the resettlement of Bosniaks and Croats in Prijedor, Sanski Most, and Bosanski Novi. On August 18, the commission filed a report titled "Reports from Prijedor, Bosanski Novi, and Sanski Most SJBs regarding the current situation of detainees, detention centers and refugees and the role of SJBs in relation to these."[43] According to this report, the resettlement of Bos-

---

39. Prosecutor v. Radoslav Brđanin (Judgment), IT-99-36-T (ICTY), 228.
40. Prosecutor v. Radoslav Brđanin, 230.
41. Prosecutor v. Radoslav Brđanin, 52.
42. A. Anušić, "Migrants—With the State's Mediation," *Glas*, July 18, 1992. See Prosecutor v. Radovan Karadžić, IT-95-5/18 (ICTY), Exhibit D04048.E.
43. Report submitted by the commission for the inspection of the municipalities and the Prijedor, Bosanski Novi, and Sanski Most SJB/Public Security Stations, titled "Report concerning the situation

PRIJEDOR 117

niaks and Bosnian Croats from the Bosnian Krajina, as stated in the Brđanin judgment, "occurred in furtherance of both the ARK Crisis Staff decisions on resettlement and the subsequent municipal decisions implementing this policy. The report explained that the Prijedor, Bosanski Novi, and Sanski Most SJBs implemented these decisions by issuing certificates for departure and by canceling the residency of those leaving the territory of the Bosnian Krajina."[44]

On May 22, 1992, a car with six Bosnian Serb soldiers was stopped at a checkpoint in the village of Hambarine. Shooting broke out between the Bosniak TO soldiers and the Serbs in the car, resulting in several deaths on both sides. The Republika Srpska army used this incident to give an ultimatum to the residents of Hambarine to surrender the Bosniak TO members. The next day, after the Bosniak TO members did not surrender, the VRS began indiscriminately shelling the village, followed by an all-out attack which left resident killed.[45] The next day the town of Kozarac, after being given an ultimatum to surrender, was surrounded, shelled for two days, and attacked and then occupied by the Republika Srpska army.[46] As a result of the attack, at least eighty Bosniaks were killed. During the shelling of Kozarac, a doctor from the medical center in Kozarac contacted the Republika Srpska army to negotiate the evacuation of two injured children. The doctor was told over the radio, "Die, *balijas*, we're going to kill you anyway."[47] After the shelling stopped, the Bosniaks of Kozarac surrendered. Most of the men were sent to Omarska while the rest were transferred to Trnopolje by buses.

By May 28, Kozarac was entirely destroyed and its entire population removed. The local newspaper in Prijedor, *Kozarski vjesnik*, wrote about the "conquer of Kozarac and defeat of Muslim extremist forces which started a jihad by following their heroes and martyrs."[48]

---

as found and questions relating to prisoners, collection centres, resettlement and the role of the SJB in connection with these activities," dated August 14, 1992, ICTY No. B0032527, Prosecutor v. Stakić, IT-97-24-T (ICTY), Exhibit S407A. The commission consisted of Vojin Bera, Vaso Škondrić, Ranko Mijić, and Jugoslav Rodić.

44. Prosecutor v. Radoslav Brđanin (Judgment), IT-99-36-T (ICTY), 109. Ex. P717: "Report concerning the situation as found and questions relating to prisoners, collection centers, resettlement and the role of the SJB in connection with these activities to the CSB."

45. Prosecutor v. Radoslav Brđanin, 161.

46. The small town of Kozarac had a population of twenty-four thousand people. Almost all the members of the police station in Kozarac, including the commander Osman Didović, were killed. See Medić, *Genocid u Prijedoru*, 38. Radmilo Zeljaja delivered an ultimatum on Radio Prijedor threatening to raze Kozarac to the ground if they did not hand in their weapons. See Prosecutor v. Stakić (Judgment), IT-97-24-T (ICTY), 40.

47. Prosecutor v. Radoslav Brđanin (Judgment), IT-99-36-T (ICTY), 162.

48. Medić, *Genocid u Prijedoru*, 39. The author of the article deliberately and cynically used Turkish words *gazije* (heroes) and *šehiti* (martyrs).

118   TORTURE, HUMILIATE, KILL

Soon after the destruction of Kozarac, it was renamed Radmilovo by Radmilo Zeljaja, the JNA officer who conducted the operation.[49] On May 24, 1992, Major General Momir Talić signed a 1st Krajina Corps Command regular combat report, which was sent to the Serbian Republic/BH Army Main Staff. It stated, "The mopping up of the extremist Muslim units in the area of Hambarine village near Prijedor has been completed and Kozarac village is sealed off. A group of 35 experienced soldiers from the 5th Infantry Brigade was sent to Prijedor."[50] During the attack on Kozarac and Hambarine, a group of around one hundred Bosniaks and Croats from the Kevljani area tried to escape through the Kozara mountain range, but they were captured the next day by the Republika Srpska army. One man was shot and killed on site while the rest were taken to Benkovac, a JNA military camp near Prijedor that was turned into a detention camp. After they were brought to Benkovac, four Bosniak men were singled out and shot dead. During the day around sixty of these men were taken to the nearby woods and executed.[51] The rest were put on buses and taken to Omarska camp.[52]

On June 28, 1992 (Vidovdan), a review of the VRS Prijedor brigade was conducted in Brežičani village. Colonel Vladimir Arsić, commander of the 343 Brigade, Dragan Savanović, deputy mayor of Prijedor, and Ranko Maletić, a priest from the Serb Orthodox Church, addressed the soldiers. Savanović stated, "On this day in 1389, Serbian heroes fought in the Kosovo field against the Turk army. And they then, as Serb soldiers today, were forced into battle because freedom to this people, just like 603 years ago, and today, has the greatest meaning. It means not to allow killings, expulsion, and killings of children."[53]

Starting on July 20, 1992, the Bosniak villages on the left bank of the Sana River, to the east southeast of Prijedor, were attacked by the VRS. The left bank, also known as the Ljubija region, had a population of around eleven thousand people[54] and included the villages in the Mataruško Brdo area: Bišćani,[55]

---

49. "Defense Counsel Karadzic Defends His Client Karadzic," *Sense Agency*, January 11, 2011, http://archive.sensecentar.org/vijesti.php?aid=13331.
50. Prosecutor v. Stakić (Judgment), IT-97-24-T (ICTY), 39.
51. Prosecutor v. Radovan Karadžić (Judgment), IT-95-5/18-T (ICTY), 664.
52. Prosecutor v. Radoslav Brđanin (Judgment), IT-99-36-T (ICTY), 162.
53. The video of the review can be found here: GENOCID U PRIJEDORU—Brezicani -pravoslavna crkva i genocid, https://www.youtube.com/watch?v=777wlJsV498. Savanović uses the term *nejač*, which in translation means child or infant, those who cannot defend themselves.
54. "The Wailing Wall in Prijedor," *Sense Agency*, August 28, 2011, http://archive.sensecentar.org/vijesti.php?aid=13231.
55. Bišćani is composed of a number of hamlets, namely Mrkalji, Hegići, Ravine, Sredići, Duratovići, and Kadići.

Čarakovo,[56] Hambarine, Zecovi,[57] Rakovćani, and Rizvanovići. Within a few days, several hundred Bosniak civilians from the area had been massacred.[58] Those who survived were bused to the Keraterm and Trnopolje concentration camps.[59] In total, at least 1,800 Bosniak and Croat civilians from these six villages were massacred in their homes or later in the camps. This massacre remains one of the most unknown and often ignored episodes of the Prijedor genocide.[60]

On July 27, 1992, the village of Briševo—an exclusively Croat village—was attacked by the Sixth Krajina and Fifth Kozara Brigades of the VRS. In a blitzkrieg attack, at least sixty-eight Bosnian Croat civilians were massacred.[61] Several soldiers surrounded a sixty-five-year old man, Pero Dimač, threw him to the ground, and started beating him with a Bible they found in his house, saying "let the Catholic Jesus help him now" and asking him "why Tudjman wasn't helping him."[62]

On May 31, 1992, the newly established Serb authorities in Prijedor made an announcement that all non-Serbs had to place white flags or sheets on their windows and that all non-Serbs had to wear white armbands to distinguish themselves from the others. Nusret Sivac stated, "When the town was set on fire, the old town began to burn when the Serb soldiers and police entered it. And I watched from my flat long columns of elderly people, women, children, and men with white armbands moving down the streets led by a person called

---

56. See Tužilaštvo Bosne i Hercegovine v. Dragomir Soldat i dr., (Dragomir Soldat et al.), S1 1 K 011967 14 Krž (Sud Bosne i Hercegovine, 2015), http://www.sudbih.gov.ba/predmet/3048/show.

57. During the attack on Zecovi, at least 150 civilians were massacred. See Tužilaštvo Bosne i Hercegovine v. Dušan Milunić i dr. (Dušan Milunić et al.), S1 1 K 017538 15 KrI (Sud Bosne i Hercegovine, 2018), http://www.sudbih.gov.ba/predmet/3403/show.

58. James Gow, *The Serbian Project and Its Adversaries: A Strategy of War Crimes* (London: Hurst Publishers, 2003), 133; Bradley Campbell, *The Geometry of Genocide: A Study in Pure Sociology* (Charlottesville: University of Virginia Press, 2005).

59. The Serb authorities had made a list of "extremists" they were seeking. See List of Persons from the Brdo Area Who Participated in Procuring Weapons and Preparing the Genocide Against the Serbian People, dated June 2, 1992, no. 00635454. See Prosecutor v. Miroslav Kvočka et al. (Judgment), IT-98-30/1-T (ICTY), November 2, 2001, Exhibit P2/3.13, https://www.icty.org/x/cases/kvocka/tjug/en/kvo-tj011002e.pdf.

60. Only a few perpetrators have been prosecuted. For the massacre of nine people in front of the Čarakovo mosque, three VRS solders were convicted. See Amer Jahić, "Bosnia Upholds Convictions for Prijedor Mosque Killings," *Detektor*, February 16, 2015, https://detektor.ba/2015/02/16/bosnia-upholds-convictions-for-prijedor-mosque-killings/?lang=en.

61. "Mladic: Big Crimes in Small Village," *Detektor/BIRN*, September 6, 2012, https://detektor.ba/2012/09/06/mladic-big-crimes-in-small-village/?lang=en.

62. Prosecutor v. Radovan Karadžić (Judgment), IT-95-5/18-T (ICTY), 690.

120   TORTURE, HUMILIATE, KILL

Adem Music carrying a white flag."[63] Charles McLeod and Barnabas Mayhew, from the European Commission Monitoring Mission (ECMM), visited Prijedor municipality in late August 1992 and testified that while visiting a mixed Serb/Muslim village he saw that the Muslim houses were identified by a white flag on the roof and that they were marked thus in order to distinguish them from the Serb houses.[64]

On July 27, 1992, around 110 Bosniaks were captured in the village of Miska glava. The Crisis Committee in Ljubija and the VRS 6th Ljubija Battalion of the 43rd Brigade held the men in a temporary detention facility in the cultural center in Miska glava. At least 11 Bosniak men were executed, while the survivors were transferred to the Ljubija football stadium,[65] which for a time served as a temporary detention camp were Bosniak civilians were brought and beaten. A number of them were killed by Serb soldiers belonging to a Serb special forces unit.[66] One bus of detainees was brought to Ljubija, where they were executed and dumped into a mass grave.[67] In a document dated August 18, 1992, and titled "Report concerning the situation as found and questions relating to prisoners, collection centers, resettlement and the role of the SJB in connection with these activities" was compiled by the Security Services in Banja Luka. It stated the following:

[T]he Crisis Staff of the municipality of Prijedor assessed that it would be advisable for security reasons as well to transfer the prisoners to another place and decided on the facilities of the administrative building and workshops of the Omarska RZR. The same decision determined that the Keraterm facilities in Prijedor should be used exclusively for transit, that people who had been brought in should be received there solely for transportation to the facilities in

---

63. Nusret Sivac testifying in the Stakić case on July 31, 2002. See Prosecutor v. Stakić (Transcript) IT-97-24-T (ICTY), 6703–74, http://www.icty.org/x/cases/stakic/trans/en/020731ED.htm.

64. Prosecutor v. Stakić (Judgment), IT-97-24-T (ICTY), 36.

65. See: Tužilaštvo BiH v. Slobodan Taranjac et al., S1 1 K 024175 17 Kri (Sud Bosne i Hercegovine). The trial began on April 10, 2017, and is still in progress, http://www.sudbih.gov.ba/predmet/3625/show; Rachel Irwin, "Survivor Tells of Bosniak 'Volunteers' Selected for Death," *Institute for War and Peace Reporting*, February 22, 2013, https://iwpr.net/global-voices/survivor-tells-bosniak-volunteers-selected-death. I would like to thank Sudbin Music for providing information about this case.

66. See Prosecutor v. Stakić (Transcript) IT-97-24-T (ICTY), 78–79. Nermin Karagić is the only survivor of these two massacres. His testimony can be found here: http://www.icty.org/x/cases/stakic/trans/en/020626ED.htm.

67. Two mass graves, Redak and Redak I, contained a total of eighty-nine bodies. See Mujo Begić, "Genocid u Prijedoru—Svjedočenja," in *Hrvatski memorijalno-dokumentacijski centar Domovinskog rata u Zagrebu* (HMDCDR) (Sarajevo/Zagreb: Institut za istraživanje zločina protiv čovječnosti i međunarodnog prava Univerziteta u Sarajevu, 2015), 112.

Omarska and Trnopolje. This could not be done in Prijedor SJB because of the lack of space.[68]

The Prijedor Crisis Committee established several detention and concentration camps with the aim of concentrating the non-Serb population, either temporarily or long-term. These camps can be divided into two groups: temporary detention facilities and concentration camps. The temporary detention camps were the Prijedor SJB building[69]; Miška Glava Dom; Ljubija football stadium, and the Prijedor JNA barracks.[70] The aim of these detention facilities was to temporarily detain non-Serbs; to separate the "persons of security interest," that is, the intellectuals and elites, out from society; and to collectively traumatize the population. The detention in these facilities did not last for a long time, from a few days to several weeks. After detention in these more temporary facilities, however, one part of the detained group would be transferred to concentration camps, while others would be executed on site.[71]

Apart from these detention facilities, the Crisis Committees established three concentration camps: Omarska, Keraterm, and Trnopolje. The establishment of these three camps in the Prijedor municipality had the primary aim of concentrating, isolating, and filtering out the non-Serb population.[72] Omarska and Keraterm were for the most "extreme" non-Serbs and mainly included men, while Trnopolje was a camp for women and children and the men who were not of interest to the Serb authorities. The filtering was done mainly through interrogation. Everybody was interrogated at least once, and the victims were placed into one of three categories of detainees: "the first contained those determined to pose the greatest threat to the Serb regime, defined as 'people who had directly organized and taken part in the armed

---

68. See: Prosecutor v. Stakić (Judgment), IT-97-24-T (ICTY), 47.

69. The SJB was used as a detention facility from May 26 to June 24 and "the detainees were held in a small cell for up to two days in poor conditions before being transferred to Omarska or Keraterm camps." See Prosecutor v. Radovan Karadžić (Judgment), IT-95-5/18-T (ICTY), 699.

70. This was officially known as the Žarko Zgonjanin barracks. It was a temporary transit and detention facility. See Prosecutor v. Radovan Karadžić, 754.

71. In this chapter, the case of Miska Glava and Ljubija Stadium is briefly explained. These are perfect examples of temporary detention facilities.

72. There were several other temporary detention facilities where civilians were initially brought and then transferred to the three main camps. One such location was the Ljubija football stadium. One day in July 1992, at the Ljubija football stadium, a Bosnian Serb police officer known as "Stiven" fired a pistol at Irfan Nasić and killed him in front of the group of civilians. Another Bosnian Serb police officer then severed Irfan Nasić's head from his body with an automatic rifle and stated, "Look at this. The man even didn't have any brains." See Prosecutor v. Stanišić and Župljanin, IT-08-91 (ICTY), 181.

rebellion'; the second consisted of 'persons suspected of organizing, abetting, financing and illegally supplying arms' to the resistance group; and the third category was limited to those who were, in the words of Simo Drljača, 'of no security interest.'"[73]

Alongside these three concentration camps, the Manjača concentration camp will also be included, because although Manjača camp is not in Prijedor municipality, it was used to detain non-Serbs from Prijedor after the camps there were forced to close in September 1992.[74]

As the camps were created and rapidly filled, Bosniaks and Croats were completely deprived of their rights and prerogatives, and they lived and died at the whim of their Bosnian Serb captors without property or possessions.[75] Crimes committed against them were no longer crimes. The *actual* political, religious, or any other affiliation of the Bosniaks and Croats did not matter; as long as they were deemed as belonging to these ethnoreligious cultural groups, they were targeted. Communists, religious Muslims, or even agnostics for that matter, all needed to be cleansed. The victims entered the camp as a result of their blood, their biological being, and not because of the choices they had made.

Omarska Camp

The Omarska camp was in an iron mine adjacent to the dominantly Serb village of Omarska. People from all over the municipality worked in this mine. The location itself consisted of a large compound with a huge hangar and several smaller buildings. Soon after the Serbs took control of the region, work in the Omarska mine stopped and it was converted into a concentration camp for non-Serbs. The camp was created and controlled by the police. On May 31, 1992, Simo Drljača, the chief of the Prijedor SJB, ordered its formation.[76] The first people to be arrested and taken to Omarska were members of SDA and HDZ,

---

73. Prosecutor v. Kvočka et al. (Judgment), IT-98-30/1-T (ICTY), 7.
74. Manjača camp was a regional camp and held detainees from all over Bosanska Krajina, but in September 1992, a majority of the detainees were from Prijedor.
75. For example, cattle that belonged to Bosniak villages Kozarac and Kamičani were sold at a public sale in DP "Stočara" in Banja Luka in late August 1992. See letter by Simo Drljača dated August 28, 1992, II-98-30/1-T, ICTY no. 00633314. See Prosecutor v. Kvočka et al. (Judgment), IT-98-30/1-T (ICTY), Exhibit P2/3.40.
76. See Prosecutor v. Stakić (Judgment), IT-97-24-T (ICTY), 46.

PRIJEDOR   123

intellectuals, religious figures, and other community leaders.[77] This was done with the systematic aim of dividing elites from the targeted group. Rezak Hukanović, a prewar journalist in Prijedor, recalled the arrival to Omarska:

> The bus stopped outside the administration building of the iron-ore mine at Omarska, only a few kilometers from the village of the same name. On one side looted cattle grazed in the mowed fields while, across from them, the mining embankments—only days ago they had been busy with workers—lay remote and isolated, seared by the unbearable heat. Two huge buildings stood in the center, separated by a wide asphalt lot with two smaller buildings. The prisoners were ordered to get off the bus with their arms raised over their heads, holding up three fingers on each hand. Two rows of fully armed soldiers opened a path through which they had to walk.[78]

People were killed and tortured in Omarska on a daily basis. One witness stated that the first large massacre occurred on May 28, 1992. He saw a guard, Mlađo Radić, lining up prisoners who were later killed.[79] One of the first victims in Omarska was Ahil Dedić from Kozarac. One witness testified that a camp guard, Cigo Mamuzo, killed him: "A.V. saw Mamuzo kill Ahil Dedic on May 28 on a bus outside the camp gate when he was first brought to Omarska. Mamuzo beat Ahil on the head with the wooden butt of a rifle until his skull broke."[80] Detainees were often killed upon arrival, an act by the guards to show power and control. The 28th of May can be considered as the date of the official opening of the Omarska camp. The chief of security and de facto Omarska camp commander was Željko Mejakić. He was a twenty-eight-year-old police officer, born in a village near Prijedor called Petrov Gaj. Until 1992 he lived in Omarska village. Omarska was now not only to be his hometown but also his place of work. He "supervised and was responsible for all three shifts of guards

---

77. The Serbs were interested in capturing those who organized and participated in the failed attack to retake Prijedor on May 30, 1992. A list of suspected combatants was made. See Grupa koja je učestvovala u napadu na Prijedor May 30, 1992, II-98-35/1-T, No. 2657. Another list was made of those who supposedly possessed arms; see II-98-30/1-T, No. 2643.

78. Rezak Hukanović, "The Evil of Omarska," *New Republic*, February 12, 1996, 28. The three-finger salute represents a Serb nationalistic symbol.

79. Medić, *Genocid u Prijedoru*, 52.

80. "Cygool: Human Rights Abuses in Bosnia—Hercegovina [*sic*]—Cases of X., F. B., and A. V.;—The Personnel Structure at Omarska Camp," *Wikileaks* (October 16, 1992), accessed May 6, 2017, https://wikileaks.org/plusd/cables/92ZAGREB2038_a.html. For a detailed description of Dedić's murder see Prosecutor v. Kvočka et al. (Judgment), IT-98-30/1-T (ICTY), 25.

in the camp and had effective control over the work and conduct of all Omarska camp guards and other persons working within the camp, as well as most camp visitors."[81] The Omarska camp consisted of two large buildings; the hangar;[82] the administrative building; and two smaller buildings: the white house (*bijela kuća*) and the red house (*crvena kuća*). In the hangar was a "cloakroom," also known as *Mujina soba*, Mujo's room.[83] It was named after a detainee, Mujo, who was chosen as the orderly of the room. This had some of the worst conditions in the camp. It was overcrowded and too hot, and since there was no toilet facility, waste and feces poured out of the room. This small room held almost 625 prisoners, most of whom were soon lice-infested. North of the hangar was an open concrete area known as the *pista* (runway). On the other end of the *pista* was the administration building, which comprised a canteen where prisoners ate and office rooms upstairs where the inmates were interrogated. In this part of the building, the women prisoners were also kept. West of the hangar was a grassy area in the middle of which laid the "white house," a small house with three rooms. A small distance away from the "white house" was the "red house," also on the grassy area.

The "white house" became one of the most feared places in the camp, as it was where the detainees were tortured, often to death. Among the detainees it was said that "whoever enters the 'white house' never leaves it." There were, however, several survivors, from whose testimony, given to the ICTY, we can get insight into what happened. According to witness Asmir Baltić, the room in which he was kept in was 2.5 by 2.5 meters, while sixty-four detainees were held there.[84] The walls were stained with blood while the detainees stank of sweat and blood. In the corner of the room was a bucket where they could conduct their bodily needs. Easily visible for all to see were the bodies of the detainees who were killed inside and dumped out the window and onto the grass, after which they would be loaded onto trucks and taken away.

---

81. Tužilaštvo Bosne i Hercegovine v. Željko Mejakić i dr. (Mejakić et al.), (Verdict), X-KR/06/200 (Sud Bosne i Hercegovine), May 30, 2008, 2, https://bit.ly/ProsvMejakicVerdict.

82. "The hangar was a large oblong structure, running north-south, along the eastern side of which were a number of roller doors leading into a large area extending the length of the building with the ground floor designed for the maintenance of heavy trucks and machinery used in the iron-ore mine. The western side of the hangar consisted of two floors of rooms, over 40 in all, extending over the whole north-south length of the building and occupying rather less than one half of the entire width of the hangar. Access to these rooms could be gained either from a door on the western side or, internally, from the large truck maintenance area described above. The bulk of the prisoners were housed in this building." Prosecutor v. Duško Tadić, IT-94-1-T (ICTY), May 7, 1997, 57, cited in Prosecutor v. Duško Tadić, 48.

83. Prosecutor v. Duško Tadić, 81.

84. Prosecutor v. Duško Tadić, 81.

A security ring was formed around the camp some five to six hundred meters from the mine complex, with a guard post every two hundred meters that was manned by members of the Omarska Territorial Defense.[85]

On July 17, 1992, Radislav Brđanin, president of the ARK Crisis Staff and a prominent SDS member, visited the Omarska camp and the rest of the Prijedor region. He was heading a delegation of prominent Serb politicians including Kuprešanin, Župljanin, Stakić, Radoslav Vujić, Predrag Radić, and Talić.[86] A choir of detainees welcomed them, being forced to sing Serb nationalist songs and show the three-finger salute. He publicly stated that "what we have seen in Prijedor is an example of a job well done." He also added that "it is a pity that many in Banja Luka are not aware of it yet, just as they are not aware of what might happen in Banja Luka in the very near future."[87]

Several prominent members of the Bosniak and Bosnian Croat local communities were confined in the Omarska camp. The mayor of Prijedor, Professor Muhamed Čehajić, was the highest-ranking Bosniak official in the camp. On July 27, 1992, he was called out from the room and taken out of the camp, never to be seen again.[88] His remains were exhumed from the Kevljani mass grave in 2004. The president of the local HDZ political party, Silvije Sarić, and his deputy Jozo Maručić were also held in the camp. Faruk Burazerović and Zdenka Rajković witnessed that Silvije Sarić was taken by guards at least three times to the room next to theirs. They heard screams and beating every time. On the last time, he was returned in a semiconscious state, and after ten days he died.[89] Another influential Bosniak member of the community was Dr. Esad Sadiković, a physician who had previously worked for the UNHCR. One night, a guard called out his name. Everybody in the room knew he would not return, so they all stood up and bid him farewell. His remains were exhumed from the Hrastova glavica mass grave in 1998.[90]

On July 28, a list of 174 persons who were identified as belonging to the first category of detainees (i.e., the most "extreme") was drawn up by the camp

---

85. Prosecutor v. Kvočka et al. (Judgment), IT-98-30/1-T (ICTY), 14.

86. Prosecutor v. Radovan Karadžić (Judgment), IT-95-5/18-T (ICTY), 713.

87. Exhibit P284, "Representatives of the Krajina in Prijedor: It Is Not Easy for Anyone," *Kozarski vjesnik*, July 17, 1992. See Prosecutor v. Radoslav Brđanin (Judgment), IT-99-36-T (ICTY), 140.

88. Čehajić was arrested on May 23, 1992, and taken to Prijedor police station, then to Keraterm camp, Banja Luka prison, and finally back to the Omarska camp. See Prosecutor v. Stakić, IT-97-24-T (ICTY), statement by Minka Čehajić given to the ICTY on May 14, 15, and 16, 2002, 3037–71, https://www.icty.org/x/cases/stakic/trans/en/020514IT.htm.

89. "Cygool: Human Rights Abuses in Bosnia," accessed June 5, 2017.

90. Prosecutor v. Radoslav Brđanin (Judgment), IT-99-36-T (ICTY), 176.

126 TORTURE, HUMILIATE, KILL

authorities. This list included the names of three women. All on the list were taken away and executed.[91]

The conditions in Omarska were inhumane. The prisoners were confined in the hangar, sleeping on concrete floors. Personal hygiene and showers were out of the question. Food was only provided once a day and it mainly consisted of a watery soup and a piece of bread.[92] Although in some cases, sixty hours passed between meals.[93] Almost everybody was suffering from dysentery or diarrhea, and everybody stank, which made the air inside the camp foul.[94] According to survivors, they were able to take a bath only once during the whole time. On that occasion, they were stripped naked and washed with a fire hose, a humiliating and dehumanizing experience.[95] In June and July 1992, inside the premises of the Omarska camp, several dozen civilians were murdered or beaten to death.[96] Several witnesses testified about the murder of Riza Hadžalić in Omarska: "Riza had received his daily slice of bread and was walking away, when a guard said '*dobar tek*' (good appetite). Riza replied spontaneously '*bujrum*' the Muslim dialect equivalent. Several guards immediately set upon Riza and beat him senseless. Afterwards Riza lay on his back and vomited. No one was allowed to turn him over. Riza suffocated on his vomit in front of the others."[97]

On June 26, 1992, several guards at Omarska camp beat Mehmedalija Sarajlić, an elderly Bosniak man, to death after he refused to rape a female detainee.[98]

The bodies of victims were dumped in a pile near the white house, and early in the morning a yellow *tamić*[99] would arrive. The detainees were forced to load the bodies onto the truck and it would leave for a mass grave.[100]

---

91. See: Prosecutor v. Kvočka et al. (Judgment), IT-98-30/1-T (ICTY), 7. The document ICTY no. is P0002164, Exhibit P 3/204. These names are Edina Dautović, Sadeta Medunjanin, and Hajra Hadžić.

92. "[T]he Court undoubtedly concluded that the food in the camp was not appropriate, that is, that it was of bad quality and in insufficient quantities." See Tužilaštvo BiH v. Mejakić et al., X-KR/06/200, 85.

93. Testimony of Šerif Velić in: "Cygool: Human Rights Abuses in Bosnia," accessed June 5, 2017.

94. See Hasiba Harambašić's testimony in Documentary by Mandy Jacobson and Karmen Jelincic, *Calling the Ghosts* (Croatia/USA: Bowery Productions, 1996), [14:10–14:20], https://www.imdb.com/title/tt0115805/.

95. Tužilaštvo BiH v. Mejakić et al., X-KR/06/200, 84.

96. Tužilaštvo BiH v. Mejakić et al., X-KR/06/200, 197.

97. "Cygool: Human Rights Abuses in Bosnia," accessed June 5, 2017.

98. It is stated that "[h]e begged them 'Don't make me do it. She could be my daughter. I am a man in advanced age.' The guards laughed and said, 'Well, try to use the finger.' A scream and the sound of beatings could be heard, and then everything was silent. The guards had killed the man." See Prosecutor v. Radoslav Brđanin (Judgment), IT-99-36-T (ICTY), 196.

99. A *tamić* is a popular Yugoslav truck company from Slovenia called TAM (*Tovarna avtomobilov Maribor*).

100. Tužilaštvo BiH v. Mejakić et al., X-KR/06/200, 92.

PRIJEDOR 127

In the beginning of June, Bećir Medunjanin, the secretary for national defense of Prijedor municipality, his wife Sadeta, son Anes, and Fehim and Suad Trnjanin were captured on Mt. Kozara, where they had been hiding in the woods. They were then brought to the Omarska camp. Bećir was murdered within the camp. His remains were exhumed from Kevljani mass grave. Sadeta was one of forty-three camp prisoners who were taken out of the camp and driven toward Bosanska Krupa, where they were executed. Her remains were exhumed from Lisac pit.[101]

In the Serb Orthodox Christian tradition and belief, St. Peter's Day (Petrovdan) is marked on July 12. On the eve of this traditional orthodox Christian celebration, which is dedicated to St. Peter and St. Paul, Serbs light bonfires. This feast day is known as *petrodavnsko lilanje* and is most likely a pagan custom in which dry birch or cherry trees are burned at sunset. It is believed that with fire and cries, demons will be chased away.[102] On July 12, 1992, a huge bonfire, composed mostly of tires, was set ablaze in front of the white house. On this occasion, the guards selected a number of detainees and beat them with sticks, knives, and batons while forcing them to walk around the burning fire. One detainee, a former football player named Smail Duratović, and at least nine others were "forced into the fire or smoldering cinders" and were burned to death.[103] Detainee Hase Icić witnessed this event:

At the time, the Serbs, on the eve of Petrovdan, had a real, all-out sort of manifestation rally of civilians and guards. . . . As night began to fall, they started to take the people out of the first rooms . . .

Q. What did you hear after some detainees were taken out?

A. I remember that, and I'll remember it for the rest of my life, the cries of women who were outside or in the first room. I'll never forget their cries and screams. Then I smelt the stench of burning meat. You know when meat begins to burn, it has a specific smell, and this smell of burning flesh was mixed with the smell of the burning rubber from the tires.[104]

---

101. Prosecutor v. Karadžić (Judgment), IT-95-5/18-T (ICTY), 709.
102. Špiro Kulišić and Petar Ž. Petrović, *Srpski mitološki rečnik* (Belgrade: Etnografski institut SANU, 1998), 291–92; Petar Ž. Petrović: "Lila, olalija i srodni običaji," *Bulletin of the Ethnographic Museum* 2 (Belgrade: Ethnographic Museum, 1927), 4, https://etnografskimuzej.rs/en/o-muzeju/izdavastvo/periodika/gem-2/.
103. Tužilaštvo BiH v. Mejakić et al., X-KR/06/200, 125; Prosecutor v. Radovan Karadžić (Judgment), IT-95-5/18-T (ICTY), 707.
104. Tužilaštvo BiH v. Mejakić et al., X-KR/06/200, 30.

128 TORTURE, HUMILIATE, KILL

The brutal, ceremonial, and public nature of the murder of these detainees is, once again, important to underline. This ceremony had three actors: the perpetrators (the Serb guards); the victims, and, most importantly, the audience. Again, as in Višegrad, it was the effect on the audience that mattered.

The victims and individual murders described here represent only a slight glimpse of what occurred in Omarska. The beatings, murders, and rapes were conducted by guards while even more were committed by so-called visitors: individuals, members of police and military units who entered Omarska to only sadistically beat or kill.[105] This freedom of civilians to enter and kill or administer their own beatings makes Omarska fairly unique. There were cases of revenge, settling scores from before the war. Mevludin Sejmenović, an MP of the SDA from Prijedor, was incarcerated in Trnopolje and Omarska camps. He mentioned the visit of high-ranking Serb politician Vojo Kuprešanin: "In Omarska it was all death, death, and only death, and then suddenly Kuprešanin showed up and started talking high politics. . . . I kept silent, thinking it was another thing I had to endure before I die. Kuprešanin talked on the phone with Karadzic, who told him to buy me a suit, feed me, and bring me to Banja Luka," where he was to be shown off for publicity.[106]

In the summer of 1992, Omarska was the heart of evil. Nowhere in the Bosanska Krajina was rape and sexual abuse committed more than in Omarska. Sexual abuse of male prisoners was common. One of the most horrific acts was committed in July 1992 by a group of Serb guards, among whom was a civilian, Dušan Tadić:

Witness H was ordered to lick his naked bottom and G to suck his penis and then to bite his testicles. Meanwhile a group of men in uniform stood around the inspection pit watching and shouting to bite harder. All three were then made to get out of the pit onto the hangar floor and Witness H was threatened with a knife that both his eyes would be cut out if he did not hold Fikret Harambašić's mouth closed to prevent him from screaming; G was then made to lie between the naked Fikret Harambašić's legs and, while the latter strug-

---

105. For example Milorad Tadić, member of reserve police forces from Prijedor, came to the Omarska camp and told the guards to bring him Sejad Sivac, whom he then murdered behind the white house. See Goran Obradović, "Tadic Sentenced to Five Years for Killing a Detainee," *Detektor/BIRN*, July 5, 2013, https://detektor.ba/2013/07/05/tadic-sentenced-to-five-years-for-killing-a-detained/?lang=en.

106. "Mladic: Bosniak ex MP Talks About Omarska Camp," *Detektor/BIRN*, October 2, 2012, http://www.justice-report.com/en/articles/mladic-bosniak-ex-mp-talks-about-omarska-camp.

gled, hit and bite his genitals. G then bit off one of Fikret Harambašić's testicles and spat it out and was told he was free to leave. Witness H was ordered to drag Fikret Harambašić to a nearby table, where he then stood beside him and was then ordered to return to his room, which he did.[107]

Dušan Tadić is an interesting figure. He was the first person to be tried at the ICTY. A citizen of Kozarac, he lived happily and peacefully among his Bosniak neighbors, even operating his cafe and a karate club in the center of Kozarac. Then, in 1992, he suddenly brutally mutilated and murdered his former friends.[108] Duško Tadić was, sadly, not an isolated case either; many others behaved like this.[109]

The camp itself did not hold a lot of women. There were around forty of them, and they were kept in a separate area, in the former business offices of Omarska mine. These offices were used as sleeping areas for the women prisoners at night, and during the day they were used as interrogation rooms for the male prisoners. The women prisoners held in Omarska were specifically handpicked from Prijedor, mainly Bosniak and Croat intellectuals. The two most prominent women prisoners of Omarska were Nusreta Sivac, a former judge, and Jadranka Cigelj, a former lawyer from Prijedor. Both appear in a 1996 documentary *Calling the Ghosts*, where they described the conditions in the camp. They were awakened and brought to the camp restaurant at 7 a.m., where they helped prepare the food for the men, who came at 9 a.m. They were forced to run from the hangar to the restaurant. Nusreta Sivac mentions how she and the other women initially could not believe what was happening around them; "I thought that camps were part of the past. Something which I saw in the movies." For Nusreta, there was no doubt why she was targeted: "I am an intellectual and I am a Muslim. That is the only reason."[110] Women from these quarters were raped and sexually abused on multiple occasions.[111] At the trial of camp

---

107. Prosecutor v. Duško Tadić, aka "Dule" (Opinion and Judgment), IT-94-1-T (ICTY), May 7, 1997, 73, https://www.icty.org/x/cases/tadic/tjug/en/tad-tsj70507JT2-e.pdf.

108. See: Prosecutor v. Tadić, IT-94-1-T, Case Summary at: http://www.icty.org/x/cases/tadic/tjug/en/970507_Tadic_summar_en.pdf.

109. Duško Tadić was also the SDS president in Kozarac, where he remained living among the ruins of the blown-up houses of his former neighbors. See Prosecutor v. Duško Tadić, aka "Dule" (Opinion and Judgment), IT-94-1-T (ICTY), 66.

110. Once she was brought to the camp, she was interrogated by police inspectors about her involvement in implementing the referendum for a sovereign BiH. See Prosecutor v. Radovan Karadžić (Judgment), IT-95-5/18-T (ICTY), 705.

111. For a report on a Croat rape victim and the policy of rape, see Ann Leslie, "Rape as an Instrument of War?" *Daily Mail*, January 25, 1993, 6.

130   TORTURE, HUMILIATE, KILL

commander Željko Mejakić, several witnesses testified about rape and sexual abuse in Omarska. K019 was sexually abused on numerous occasions by camp guards; witness K027 was sexually abused by the shift commander, Mlađo "Krkan" Radić, and on another occasion in July 1992 by Nedeljko Grabovac; while witness K040 was sexually assaulted twice by camp guard Lugar.[112] KO19 was arrested and brought to Omarska camp on July 14, 1992:

> After she was brought to the Omarska Camp, a guard would often take her out and he would rape her every time, and she noted that it took place approximately seven times during the night and two times during daytime. While she was describing her being taken out, witness K019 noted that she would be taken to the room at the end of the corridor on the first floor of the administration building and that, along with the guard who would regularly take her out, other men would come too, according to her estimation two or three or more of them, who would, as she stated: "come in one by one, do their thing and leave."[113]

Of the three dozen women confined in the offices inside the Omarska administrative building, at least five did not see freedom. The remains of Edna Dautović, Sadeta Medunjanin, Mugbila Beširević, Velida Mahmuljin, and Hajra Hadžić were found in mass graves along with other camp detainees.[114]

In the morning of August 5, 1992, Radovan Vokić, Simo Drljača's driver, came to the guards with a list, signed by Drljača, of detainees who had to be transported to Kozarac. But Bosniak and Croat detainees from the Keraterm and Omarska camps were put on buses and instead driven toward Sanski Most. They never reached their destination. At least 124 persons were taken from the buses and executed at a site called Hrastova Glavica, from where their remains were later exhumed.[115]

The same day as the executions were taking place, Simo Drljača informed his superiors in Banja Luka about the results of the interrogations that had been taking place at the camp over the past months:

> [T]he Prijedor Public Security Station, in co-operation with the competent security services of the Banja Luka CSB [security service center] and the army of the

---

112. Tužilaštvo BiH v. Mejakić et al., X-KR/06/200, 5.
113. Tužilaštvo BiH v. Mejakić et al., X-KR/06/200, 128–29.
114. Begić, "Genocid u Prijedoru," 115.
115. Prosecutor v. Radoslav Brđanin (Judgment), IT-99-36-T (ICTY), 179.

Serbian Republic of Bosnia and Herzegovina, has completed the processing of the prisoners of war. The investigation has found elements of criminal liability in 1,466 cases, for which valid documentation exists, which we shall transfer under guard, along with the persons it pertains to, to the Manjača military camp on 6 August 1992. The remaining persons are of no security interest and will be transferred to the reception camp in Trnopolje on the same day. . . . Further operation of the investigation center in Omarska is therefore no longer required.[116]

When the camp was closed in on August 18, it held 179 detainees, who were then transported to Manjača camp near Banja Luka and then either freed in late 1992 or moved to Batkovići camp near Bijeljina.

Similarly, like in most other camps in Bosnia and Herzegovina, Omarska had several detainees who decided to collaborate with the guards and camp authorities.[117] A US report on the camp, based on survivor testimonies, identified one such collaborator: "Several witnesses identified Hakija Pidić as an informer. Pidić was a Muslim from the Prijedor area. He visited all the camps regularly and identified people whom he claimed were involved in anti-Serb activity. Most of these people were led away and never seen again. At first he came every two or three days, but towards the end of the summer he came about once a week."[118]

The camp's closure was prompted by the visit of American journalist Roy Gutman in June 1992. He had heard stories from refugees about camps in the Prijedor area and had initially thought they were an exaggeration. After some time, however, the stories became more and more frequent. Finally in July, he and freelance photographer Andree Kaiser visited both the Omarska and Manjača camps, after which he published two articles on July 19, 1992, in *Newsday* along with the first photos of the camps.[119] Only after the publication of these articles did the UN start to take the issue of war crimes in Bosnia and Herzegovina seriously. Gutman's visit proved to be a turning point. The UN quickly appointed former Polish president Tadeusz Mazowiecki as a special rapporteur to investigate human rights abuses in the former Yugoslavia.

---

116. Prosecutor v. Kvočka et al. (Judgment), IT-98-30/1-T (ICTY), 7.
117. In his book *Kolika je u Prijedoru čaršija: zapisi za nezaborav* (Sarajevo: Bonik, 1995), Nusret Sivac mentions a number of Bosniaks who cooperated with or were members of the VRS.
118. "Cygool: Human Rights Abuses in Bosnia," accessed June 5, 2017.
119. They most probably visited Manjača on July 6, 1992. See the photograph, Andree Kaiser, "Prisoners in the Manjaca Camp, Bosnia and Herzegovina," *Agencja Fotograficzna Caro / Alamy Stock Photo* (Manjaca, Republika Srpska, Bosnia and Herzegovina, July 6, 1992), https://bit.ly/AlamyManjaca-Camp. See Eric Stover, *Medicine under Siege in the Former Yugoslavia 1991–1995* (Boston: Physicians for Human Rights, 1996), 24.

132   TORTURE, HUMILIATE, KILL

As a result of media coverage, public outrage, and international pressure, Radovan Karadžić confidently denied the existence of the camps and stated, "I invite any foreign correspondent to come to the Serbian part of Bosnia and Herzegovina and to point out which town or city they would like to search for a concentration camp."[120]

Taking Karadžić up on his offer, journalists Ed Vulliamy from *The Observer* and Penny Marshall from ITN entered the Omarska and Trnopolje camp on August 5. The camp authorities had managed to prepare for the visit and brought out the *"best-looking"* detainees they had.[121] The journalists were not allowed to freely walk and explore the camp by themselves. The rest of the detainees, including the women, were hidden from the cameras. The images of skinny, terrified men running from one building to the other, waiting in line for food, shocked the entire world. As with Gutman's visit, Marshall and Vulliamy's shocking reportage marked the final days of Bosnian Serb camps in Bosnia and Herzegovina, though, as will be seen, some camps managed to last for a good while longer. Nusreta Sivac stated, "That surprise visit saved us. That was our destiny. Otherwise there was no way that anyone could live through the camp that we could ever get out of."[122]

Trnopolje Camp

Trnopolje was a concentration camp in a mainly Bosniak village of the same name. Situated near Kozarac, Prijedor, and Omarska, it served mainly as a transit facility. After Bosniak and Croat villages in the area were attacked, the men were taken to Omarska and Keraterm, while the women and children were transferred to Trnopolje. Trnopolje also had a number of male detainees, those who were not of "security interest." Others arrived on their own initiative after seeing the carnage in other villages. Detainees were forced to sign documents handing over their property to Republika Srpska.

---

120. This statement can be found in Jacobson and Jelincic, *Calling the Ghosts* [22:42–22:58].

121. On August 3, 1992, the 1st Krajina Corps sent out a memo signed by Momir Talić to the 43rd Brigade, Command of Manjača Camp, CSB Prijedor and Security Section of 1. KrK/PKM stating that in the next two days journalists will be visiting Manjača, Trnopolje, Omarska, and Prijedor and that everything must be done to make the conditions "satisfactory." This included "order, cleanliness, functional medical care." See Approval for visit of the International Committee to the detention camps at Manjača, Trnopolje, Omarska and Prijedor, dated August 3, 1992, see ICTY no. 01029866, Prosecutor v. Radoslav Brđanin (Judgment), IT-99-36-T (ICTY), Exhibit P405.

122. As stated in Jacobson and Jelincic, *Calling the Ghosts* [22:38–25:49].

PRIJEDOR 133

After a certain period, groups of interned civilians from Trnopolje were expelled out of Republika Srpska territory on a convoy of buses.

Trnopolje camp comprised a number of buildings in the center of the village, which included a former school, a theater, and the municipal center. Detainees were placed inside these buildings, but the number was larger than the buildings could accommodate, so on the grounds outside the school, a makeshift camp was formed in tents.[123] The Bosnian Serb authorities officially named Trnopolje as Reception Center (Prihvatni centar) Trnopolje. Their aim was to present Trnopolje as a safe zone for non-Serb civilians who wanted to escape the *"fighting"*. The conditions in the camp were so evidently appalling, however, that no one believed this claim.[124] That it served as a transit camp also does not mean it was any less horrible than the other two camps.

The commander of Trnopolje camp was Slobodan Kuruzović, while the guards were Republika Srpska soldiers. Just like with the other camps, many "visitors" and members of other units entered the camp freely to abuse, torture, and rape detainees. Several dozens Bosniak and Croat civilians were killed inside in the camp, and a number of women and girls were raped.[125] One woman, Witness Q, was raped a number of times by the camp commander Kuruzović himself, who told her, "I want to see how Muslim women fuck." After she screamed, he threatened her by saying, "It is better that you stay quiet or all the soldiers outside will take their turn."[126] The witness knew the perpetrator as he was her brother's schoolteacher. On August 21, 1992, several buses were driven from Trnopolje camp by the Bosnian Serb authorities.[127] The civilians were told they would be deported to Travnik, which was under Bosnian government control. The convoy was joined by several buses of prisoners from Tukovi. The special police unit of the Prijedor SJB—the Intervention Squad

---

123. At least two Bosniak civilians from Trnopolje village were killed by Serb soldiers. See Goran Obradović, "Bosnian Serb Soldiers Jailed for Prijedor Murders," *Detektor/BIRN*, December 8, 2014, https://detektor.ba/2014/12/08/bosnian-serb-soldiers-jailed-for-prijedor-murders/?lang=en.

124. Na "Mozganje" kod Karadžića," *Sense Agency*, March 31, 2016, http://arhiva.sensecentar.org/vijesti.php?aid=163.

125. Prosecutor v. Radoslav Brđanin (Judgment), IT-99-36-T (ICTY), 177. See also Maggie O'Kane, "UN Condemns Serb 'Policy' of Rape," *Guardian Weekly*, December, 27, 1992, 8.

126. See: Prosecutor v. Stakić (Judgment), IT-97-24-T (ICTY), 219.

127. One day earlier, a number of detainees were transferred from Manjača camp to Trnopolje camp. See Dispatch No. 11-12-2213 of the Public Security Station Prijedor Reporting on Completion of the Selection of Prisoners in the Manjaca Camp on 20 August 1992 and the transfer of Detainees from Manjaca Camp to Trnopolje on 21 August 1992 signed by Simo Drljača to CSB Banja Luka on 22 August 1992, ICTY No. 00633308, Prosecutor v. Radovan Karadžić, IT-95-5/18 (ICTY), Exhibit D01865.E.

134   TORTURE, HUMILIATE, KILL

(Interventni vod)—accompanied the convoy.[128] Two of these buses, each with around one hundred Bosniak men, were driven through Banja Luka and Skender Vakuf toward Travnik. Near the front lines on Mt. Vlašić, at a place called Korićanske stijene, the convoy stopped and the men were forced out of the buses. One side of the road is a "deep gorge and on the other side a steep face of rock."[129] The men were forced to line up on the edge of the cliff and ordered to kneel down. The Serb officer in charge proclaimed, "Here we exchange the dead for the dead and the living for the living."[130] Shootings followed and the bodies fell down into the abyss. A few men survived the fall either by jumping before the shooting started or after being severely wounded.[131] Witness KO18 testified:

"Three men dressed in blue uniforms (policemen) were standing in front of us. We were turned toward them at first. I watched the man who was going to shoot me in his face. They cursed us and said: 'We do not want to look at your faces. Turn around.' When we turned to the other side, they shot me on my shoulder. I fell down on my back on some fir tree. I stayed on it."[132]

One man who jumped and survived stated how he saw a number of bodies around him, some of which were already black, swollen, and rotting, which showed that this location had been used previously as an execution site by the perpetrators.

It remains unknown as to who the mentioned victims were, since all the bodies from Korićanske stijene were later removed to a mass grave, and in some cases acid was used to destroy them on site. There had, however, been reports of executions at the same site of Bosniak victims from Kotor Varoš and also Bosnian Croat POWs on another occasion.[133]

---

128. Prosecutor v. Darko Mrđa (Sentencing Judgment), IT-02-59-S (ICTY), March 31, 2004, 3, https://www.icty.org/x/cases/mrda/tjug/en/sj-040331.pdf.

129. Prosecutor v. Radoslav Brđanin (Judgment), IT-99-36-T (ICTY), 180.

130. Prosecutor v. Radoslav Brđanin, 180.

131. For more information on the Korićanske stijene massacre, see Tužilaštvo BiH v. Babić Zoran i dr., S1-1-K-003472-12 Kžk (Sud Bosne i Hercegovine, 2009), http://www.sudbih.gov.ba/predmet/2574/show, and Tužilaštvo BiH v. Čivčić Petar i dr., X-KR-09/772 (Sud Bosne i Hercegovine, 2009), http://www.sudbih.gov.ba/predmet/2621/show; Stojan Župljanin even confirmed to the *Washington Post* that the several dozen Muslim men were killed. See Mary Battiata, "Slayings in Bosnia Confirmed; Detainees in Convoy Killed, Police Say," *Washington Post Foreign Service*, September 27, 1992, A1.

132. "Koricanske stijene: Standing in Line for Shooting," *Justice Report*, December 24, 2010, http://www.justice-report.com/en/articles/koricanske-stijene-standing-in-line-for-shooting.

133. Helsinki Watch/HRW, *War Crimes*, 40.

Keraterm Camp

Keraterm camp was formed around May 23–24, 1992.[134] It was based in a ceramic factory on the outskirts of Prijedor. The camp had two floors and was composed of four rooms. Room 2 was the largest, while room 3 was the smallest. Room 2 was twelve meters long by seven or eight meters wide, and it contained between 200 and 500 detainees.[135] There were machine-gun emplacements in front of the rooms. Searchlights were also placed in the camp.[136] The number of prisoners inside the camp increased daily throughout the early months. It is estimated that by late June 1992, there were about 1,200 people in the camp, almost entirely Bosniaks and Croats.[137] All four of the rooms were overcrowded. Most of the detainees were Bosniak men, although there were a smaller number of women as well. The Keraterm security commander was Duško Sikirica. There were three shifts and each would last for twelve hours. Each shift had a shift leader and about ten guards. The shift leaders were Dušan Fustar, Damir Došen, and Dragan Kolundžija.[138]

When the detainees were brought to Keraterm camp, they were searched, and identity cards and other official documents were taken.[139] Personal belongings, money, watches, and jewelry were taken along the way to Keraterm camp. New arrivals were beaten systematically with rifle butts, metal rods, and wooden sticks. The living conditions inside Keraterm camp were awful. Prisoners slept on wooden pallets or on bare concrete. The rooms were so cramped that people had to sleep on top of each other.[140] Each room had a "room leader" who served as a link between the guards and the detainees, and he had to keep a list of detainees in his room. The food was inadequate, and as a result detainees suffered from malnutrition and starvation as they were given only one meal a day, which usually consisted of two small slices of bread and some sort of stew. The hygiene situation was similar to Omarska. There were only a few toilets and detainees were allowed to go only once a day, otherwise they had to relieve

---

134. See Prosecutor v. Stakić (Judgment), IT-97-24-T (ICTY), 47.

135. Prosecutor v. Kvočka et al. (Judgment), IT-98-30/1-T (ICTY), 34.

136. Prosecutor v. Duško Sikirica, Damir Došen, Dragan Kolundžija (Sentencing Judgment), IT-95-8-S (ICTY), November 13, 2001, 15 https://www.icty.org/x/cases/sikirica/tjug/en/sik-tsj011113e.pdf.

137. See Prosecutor v. Stakić (Transcript), IT-97-24-T (ICTY), 47.

138. There were more shift commanders but these two along with Sikirica pleaded guilty at the ICTY for crimes committed in Keraterm. See Prosecutor v. Sikirica et al. (Sentencing Judgment), IT-95-8-S (ICTY), 10, 16.

139. Prosecutor v. Sikirica et al., 16.

140. For a more detailed description of each room see Prosecutor v. Sikirica et al., 17–19.

136 TORTURE, HUMILIATE, KILL

themselves in barrels or bags. They could not bathe and there was no soap or toothpaste.[141] Beatings, torture, and humiliation quickly became the norm in Keraterm. Detainees were forced to sing Serb nationalist songs on a daily basis.[142]

On July 20 or 21, 1992, prisoners from room 3 at Keraterm were moved to other rooms in the camp. Prisoners from the Brdo area (Hambarine, Bišćani, and Rakovčani) were brought into room 3. The Brdo area had been attacked and *"cleansed"* by the Republika Srpska army the previous day. An estimated two hundred Bosniak prisoners were crammed into each room. The next day, after dark, a machine gun was brought by the guards in front of the room and they started shooting through the window. Some kind of tear gas or poisonous gas was thrown inside, and detainees began behaving strangely, pushing against one another, forcing themselves through the metal door.[143] Serb soldiers standing in front of the building started shooting with the machine gun, and other guards joined in with light arms. The shooting lasted for half an hour. The next day, bodies were taken out of the room and piled onto a truck, which dumped the bodies into a mass grave. Soon after, a fire engine arrived and cleaned room 3, which was covered in blood.[144] Witness N managed to survive the massacre: "[T]hese bullets—they [the people in front of him] were absorbing these bullets that were being fired from outside. They were bouncing from the bullets that were hitting them. It was horrible. It was like being in hell, a night in hell."[145]

Just like the Omarska camp, Keraterm was used a filtering facility, a separation/isolation institution to divide the non-Serbs into those who were of "security interest" and those who weren't. Every new detainee was "interrogated" for eight to twelve days upon their arrival.[146] Similarly to Omarska, "visitors" regularly came to Keraterm to beat and terrorize detainees. One such man, nicknamed "Duća," arrived and ordered all men from Kamičani village to get out of room 3 and line up. He then hit each and every one with a metal baton that had

---

141. Prosecutor v. Sikirica et al., 20.
142. "The evidence is overwhelming that abusive treatment and inhumane conditions in the camps were standard operating procedure. Camp personnel and participants in the camp's operation rarely attempted to alleviate the suffering of detainees. Indeed, most often those who participated in and contributed to the camp's operation made extensive efforts to ensure that the detainees were tormented relentlessly." In Prosecutor v. Kvočka et al. (Judgment), IT-98-30/1-T (ICTY), 35.
143. Prosecutor v. Radovan Karadžić (Judgment), IT-95-5/18-T (ICTY), 725.
144. Prosecutor v. Radoslav Brđanin (Judgment), IT-99-36-T (ICTY), 177.
145. Prosecutor v. Sikirica et al (Sentencing Judgment), IT-95-8-S (ICTY), 30.
146. Prosecutor v. Sikirica et al., 24.

a metal ball on the end.[147] Simo Drljača wrote a report on August 16, 1992, explaining the formation of the camps:

> The Crisis Staff of Prijedor municipality decided that all detainees from Keraterm in Prijedor be transferred to the premises of the administration building and workshop of the iron ore mine in Omarska, where mixed teams of operative personnel would continue the initiated processing, which is the reason why this facility was given the working title Omarska Investigative Center for Prisoners of War. On the basis of the same decision, the facility was placed under the supervision of the police and the army. The police were thus entrusted with the task of providing direct physical security, while the army provided in-depth security in the form of two circles and by laying mines along the potential routes of escape by prisoners."[148]

Sexual violence was prevalent in Keraterm too. Witness H testified that she was raped multiple times in Keraterm by a number of perpetrators. After Keraterm she was transferred to the Omarska camp. Witness B testified that on one occasion in Keraterm she saw the men from Brdo lined up in two rows; the men in one row were standing naked from the waist down and the men in the other row were kneeling. It looked to her like "They were positioned in such a way as if engaged in intercourse."[149]

Manjača Camp

After the closing of the Prijedor camps, a number of the detainees, mostly the women, children, and others who were not of "security interest," were freed and deported to Karlovac (in Croatia). Those who were of interest to the Serb authorities were sent to the Manjača camp, a former army base on a mountain with the same name, some thirty-five kilometers south of Banja Luka. It served first as a POW camp during the war in Croatia in late 1991, but on May 15, 1992, it was reopened under the control of the 1st Krajina Corps (1 KK), by the orders of General Momir Talić. This camp was a regional one, containing detainees from all over the ARK. In September 1992, however, it was filled mostly with

---

147. See Prosecutor v. Stakić (Judgment), IT-97-24-T (ICTY), 70.
148. Prosecutor v. Sikirica et al., 46.
149. Prosecutor v. Sikirica et al., 71.

detainees from Prijedor. The commander of the camp was Colonel Božidar Popović. The warden and commander of the guards was Predrag Kovačević, aka Špaga. These were all military men from the 1 KK.[150] The number of detainees varied from 1,700 in June 1992 to 3,640 in August 1992. More than 95 percent of the detainees were Bosniaks.[151]

As one Bosniak from Banja Luka said, "What you saw at Manjača is a Class A camp compared with the others,"[152] The conditions in the camp were slightly better than in Prijedor, but the treatment was equally bad and even more dehumanizing. The detainees were kept confined in six large stables for livestock, where they slept on straw, blankets or in most cases on concrete. Food was served in an improvised canteen and was often insufficient.[153] There was no shower and no running water. The only water that detainees had access to was a nearby lake, which contained polluted water. The camp was surrounded by barbed wire and landmines to prevent escape. On the entrance was a sign *"LOGOR MANJAČA—ZABRANJEN ULAZ"* (Manjača Camp—Entrance Forbidden).

The detainees were frequently beaten, both en route to the camp and upon arrival. The first beatings were normally administered immediately upon arrival by military police, and detainees' valuables, if they had any left, were taken. During interrogations, both civilian and military police conducted beatings with batons, rifle butts, electric cables, etc. At least ten detainees died as a result of beatings, including Omer Filipović, a prominent Bosniak intellectual from Ključ.[154]

Anti-Muslim bigotry, intended to humiliate the detainees, was also present inside the camp. On one occasion "military policemen ordered the inmates to stand in a circle and raise their hands showing three fingers, after which they had to drop on the ground and say 'I am kissing this Serbian soil. I'm a Serb bastard. This is Serbian land.'"[155] On July 7, 1992, Sanski Most SJB organized the

---

150. Prosecutor v. Stanišić and Župljanin, IT-08-91 (ICTY), 59.

151. Prosecutor v. Sikirica et al., 61.

152. "Bosnia-Herzegovina; Thousands Held in Nazi-Style Camps; Corpses Pile Up in Open Pit as Disease Spreads Rapidly," in Roy Gutman, *A Witness to Genocide* (New York: Lisa Drew Book, 1993), 35.

153. Prosecutor v. Stanišić and Župljanin, IT-08-91 (ICTY), 63.

154. Prosecutor v. Stanišić and Župljanin, IT-08-91 (ICTY), 64. Former guards Željko Bulatović, Siniša Teodorević, and Zoran Gajić were convicted in the Banja Luka District Court of the murders of two Bosniak detainees and the beatings of several others. See "Izrečene kazne za zločine u logoru Manjača," *Voice of America*, May 29, 2006, https://ba.voanews.com/a/a-29-2006-05-29-voa10-85880 822/668185.html.

155. Prosecutor v. Stanišić and Župljanin, IT-08-91 (ICTY), 64.

PRIJEDOR 139

transfer of 560 prisoners from Sanski Most to Manjača. Some of the detainees were from the Betonirka detention camp in Sanski Most. They were locked into refrigerated trucks and by the time the truck arrived at Manjača, at least twenty persons inside the truck had suffocated.[156] On August 6, 1992, just a few days after the camp's existence was revealed by the world media, police gathered 1,300 detainees from the Omarska camp into fifteen buses and escorted them to Manjača.[157] When they arrived, Prijedor policemen and others, most probably military police, severely beat several selected men. Eight men, including a high-ranking member of the SDA—Dedo Crnalić—were beaten to death in front of the buses.[158] Tadeusz Mazowiecki, the special rapporteur of the United Nations Commission on Human Rights, tried to visit Manjača camp on the August 23, 1992, but he was denied access into the camp by Colonel Vukelić of the 1KK.[159] One witness, Adil Draganović, testified:

> I was given over to the military police who ran the camp with a group of other prisoners. The camp itself was run by the army but its security personnel also included police personnel. Police from Kljuc were particularly notorious for their cruelty in beating up prisoners, (. . .) all prisoners at the Manjača concentration camp had lost up to 30 kilo of their bodyweight because of malnourishment and regular abuse. At the Manjača stables, the prisoners were strictly prohibited from moving, and the only permitted activity was forced labor, which also included the construction of an Orthodox church."[160]

---

156. Prosecutor v. Stanišić and Župljanin, 65. Nikola Kovačević, aka Daniluško Kajtez, was convicted of this crime at the Court of Bosnia and Herzegovina. See "Kovačević: Potvrđena presuda na 12 godina," Detektor/BIRN, July 11, 2007, https://detektor.ba/2007/07/11/kovacevic-potvrdjena-presuda-na-12 -godina/.
157. Simo Drljača sent documentation about the detainees to the Manjača camp commander. See letter "To Chief of Security Services Center Banja Luka" signed by chief of the Public Security Station Prijedor Simo Drljača, dated August 23, 1992, no. 00633309 in Prosecutor v. Kvočka et al. (Judgment), IT-98-30/1-T (ICTY), Exhibit D01866.
158. Prosecutor v. Stanišić and Župljanin, IT-08-91 (ICTY), 66–68. The bodies of these detainees were exhumed from the Novo Groblje cemetery in Banja Luka.
159. Prosecutor v. Stanišić and Župljanin, 68.
160. Adil Draganović was a witness during Prosecutor v. Stanišić and Župljanin, IT-08-91 (ICTY). When he used the term "death camp" for Manjača, the defense council reacted and stated that that phrase should not be used. Draganović replied, "I am not a poet . . . I am just a witness of what I saw." He added that none of the detainees during the first months of their stay in the camp believed they would survive the daily beatings, maltreatment, and food shortages. "What was that than a plan for our destruction? I can accept that it was not as horrible as the Omarska or Keraterm camps, near Prijedor, because there people were indeed killed en masse and on a daily basis, but in my view, Manjača too was a death camp. See Velma Šarić, "Witness Describes Manjaca as Death Camp," Institute for War and Peace Reporting, December 6, 2009, https://iwpr.net/global-voices/witness-describ es-manjaca-death-camp.

Deportations

The expulsion of Bosniaks and Bosnian Croats from the Prijedor area was systematic and included deportations by buses in large numbers to Croatia or toward Bosnian government–controlled areas. On an uncertain date in late August 1992 Bosniaks and Bosnian Croats were deported by rail on cattle wagons toward Doboj in central Bosnia. It is estimated that at least two thousand civilians, mainly women and children, including entire families, were deported by rail on this occasion.[161] Local transport companies such as Autotransport Prijedor and the Ljubija mine used their buses for deportation and expulsion of non-Serbs from Prijedor. Autotransport Prijedor carried out deportations on behalf of the Crisis Committee throughout July 1992 to places like Trnopolje, Omarska, Keraterm, and Banja Luka. In the Stakić case, evidence was provided that "Autotransport Prijedor requested reimbursement to be granted by the Executive Committee for transports on behalf of the Crisis Staff during the month of July 1992 and that thirty-one buses ran a total of 1,300 kilometers to transport refugees."[162]

Such was the case after the attack on Čarakovo village. Those who were not killed on site were forced onto buses and transported to the Trnopolje camp. A number of inhabitants hid in the surrounding woods and surrendered a few days later. The Bosniak and Croat men from the group were gathered at the Žeger Bridge and stripped naked to the waist. A number of them were killed and their bodies thrown over the bridge into the Sana River, and the rest were placed on buses and transported away. The women and children were transported to the Trnopolje camp by Autotransport Prijedor buses and after a few days deported to Mt. Vlašić.[163] In June, at least 2,800 detainees from Trnopolje were deported by train from Trnopolje to Doboj, in overcrowded cattle wagons and in inhumane conditions. The wagons were brought to the Banja Luka train station, where they were kept until it was possible to continue on their way to Doboj. Ibrahim Krzović from Banja Luka, along with several other Bosniaks from the town, rushed to meet and try to help the refugees: "I saw four wagons, cattle wagons, at the station, (. . .) Skinny faces, big eyes, hands stretching through the small windows. We tried but we could not get close. We were

---

161. Prosecutor v. Radoslav Brđanin (Judgment), IT-99-36-T (ICTY), 35, 204–5.
162. See Prosecutor v. Stakić (Judgment), IT-97-24-T (ICTY), 189.
163. Prosecutor v. Radovan Karadžić (Judgment), IT-95-5/18-T (ICTY), 681.

blocked by the police. I heard one man say 'you can't imagine what's going on.' They were driven back and forward for four days to Doboj because they couldn't get across to Muslim territory."[164]

A Western diplomat in Belgrade was alerted to the fate of these civilians in Banja Luka. He telephoned the Banja Luka police and demanded they bring them food and water: "The police were polite, but said no, (. . .) I asked where the trains were going. They said Doboj. I said isn't it dangerous to send women and children to an area on the frontline. They said they can go home if they want, but we can't take any more refugees."[165] According to Trnopolje camp commander Slobodan Kuruzović, the local authorities in Prijedor were responsible for organizing transport of detainees from Trnopolje: "I asked the president of the executive community [*sic*] to provide transport, and the chief of the SUP to provide security for that transport. Some people took buses, some large lorries, they were escorted by the police."[166]

On an unknown date in the summer of 1992, the *Prijedor Chronicles* on TV Banja Luka aired a story on the possibilities of leaving Prijedor. Marko Đedanija from the Public Security Services in Prijedor provided details on which documents one would need in order to leave Prijedor. He stated that two kinds of individuals could not leave Prijedor: military conscripts (military-aged Serbs) and non-Serb persons of security interest. He also mentioned that there were three thousand citizens who want to leave Prijedor.[167] The ARK had already, in June 1992, formed an Agency for Population Movement and Exchange of Material Wealth for the ARK, and each municipality formed its own agency to deal with the resettlement of non-Serbs. In order for someone to leave Prijedor, a decision by the RS Ministry of Defense allowing eviction was needed.[168] The ARK agency organized biweekly convoys for deportation from the ARK, either toward Travnik or to Zagreb. People who wanted to leave had to buy a ticket.[169]

---

164. Ian Traynor, "How They Wiped Out Kozarac," *The Guardian*, October 17, 1992, 23.

165. Traynor, "How They Wiped Out Kozarac," 23.

166. See: Prosecutor v. Stakić (Judgment), IT-97-24-T (ICTY), 197.

167. Hronika Prijedora 6: Marko Djenadija (July 26, 2009), https://www.youtube.com/watch?v=6g5xzBG Cotk.

168. For example, Vasif Gutić received a decision on September 28, 1992. See Prosecutor v. Duško Tadić, IT-94-1-T (ICTY), Decision, no. 03/3-846-2, Gutić Vasif: Exhibit 297.

169. Prosecutor v. Radovan Karadžić (Judgment), IT-95-5/18-T (ICTY), 809–10.

Mass Graves

The entire region of Bosanska Krajina is filled with mass graves containing the remains of victims from the concentration camps in and around Prijedor. Victims from the Omarska camp can be found in mass graves in Tomašica, Jakarina kosa, Kevljani, Stari Kevljani, Lisac pit, and Hrastova glavica pit.[170] Victims from the Keraterm camp can also be found in Tomašica and also in Dizdarev potok, Stari Kevljani. Victims from the Trnopolje camp can be found in mass graves in Korićanske stijene, Trnopolje-Hrnići, Trnopolje-Matrići, Trnopolje-Redžići, and Trnopolje-Bešlagića mlin. Victims from the temporary detention facilities at the Ljubija football stadium and Miska Glava—a total of eighty-nine victims—were exhumed from mass graves at Redak and Redak I.[171] There are hundreds of other sites where remains of noncamp victims were found. The largest mass grave in Bosanska Krajina and most probably in the entire country is in Tomašica. On three different sites in Tomašica the remains of 469 people have been exhumed.[172] Jakarina kosa pit is a secondary mass grave, which means that some of the remains from Tomašica were removed and dumped in Jakarina kosa. The remains of 373 people were exhumed from this site. Other larger mass graves include Hrastova glavica, containing the remains of 126 people; Kevljani mass grave, containing the remains of 143 people; Stari Kevljani, which contained the remains of 456 people; and Korićanske stijene, which contained the remains of 114 people.[173]

One handwritten document gives us insight into the operations behind the concealment of the remains of victims in mass graves.[174] It shows a tabulated monthly overview of the usage of fuel by certain institutions. Two columns are very important: "ISTOČNA RUDIŠTA ZA SANACIJU" and "RUDNIK OMARSKA ZA SANACIJU I KRIZNI ŠTAB." Sanitation (*sanacija*) is a term

---

170. For example, Jozo Bozuk and Hrnić Dalija were beaten to death in Omarska and their remains were found in Kevljani. See Begić, "Genocid u Prijedoru," 90, 125, and Prosecutor v. Radovan Karadžić (Judgment), IT-95-5/18-T (ICTY), 709 (note 6065). The remains of Ekrem and Smail Alić as well as Sadeta Medunjanin were found in Lisac pit.

171. Begić, "Genocid u Prijedoru," 218.

172. VRS General Ratko Mladić was informed about the Tomašica mass grave and wrote in his diary that Drljača was proposing ways on how to get rid of several thousand bodies there. The bodies in the mass grave were those of civilians from Prijedor villages and from Omarska and Keraterm camps. See "Hundreds of 'Groups' in Tomasica Mass Graves," *Sense Agency*, June 24, 2015, http://archive. sensecentar.org/vijesti.php?aid=16644.

173. Begić, "Genocid u Prijedoru," 219–20.

174. Potrošena nafta od 23.5.1992–20.10.1992 po potrošačima (Used fuel May 23, 1992–October 20, 1992 by users), ICTY No. 00381755. Document in author's possession.

used to represent the removal of bodies. The hygienic context of the term used by the authorities is important to note. The term *istočna rudišta* refers to Eastern Mine Tomašica. RŽR "Ljubija" a.d. Prijedor (Ljubija iron ore mine) is composed of three mines: "Central Mine Ljubija," "Omarska," and "Eastern Mine Tomašica."[175] For less than five months (May 23 to October 20, 1992), for the purpose of *sanitation* in Tomašica, 1,183 liters of fuel were used and, for Omarska and the Crisis Committee, 5,507 liters. It can be assumed that the fuel was used to collect bodies and to dig and conceal mass graves, all of which points to the existence of a large and bureaucratic organization.

Destruction of Religious Buildings

As in other parts of Bosnia and Herzegovina, where Serb control was established, in mid-1992 all mosques and Catholic churches were destroyed or damaged.[176] The systematic destruction and the exact time period shows a pattern throughout the newly established Republika Srpska. The mosques were burned and looted by various different police and (para-)military units, but the physical destruction itself was conducted in most cases by the VRS. In and around Prijedor in 1992, all mosques and churches were destroyed. In late August 1992, the Roman Catholic church in Prijedor was planted with explosives and destroyed by VRS soldiers. The central mosque in Prijedor, the Čaršijska mosque, was burned down and demolished on May 30, 1992.[177] In Briševo, the VRS burned down the Roman Catholic church. The mosques in Kamičani, Ališići, Brezičani, Kevljani, Gomjenica, Čejreci, Gornja Puharska, and Rizvanovići, the Mutnik mosque in Kozarac, and the new mosque in Kevljani were completely destroyed. The mosques in Kozaruša and Gornji Jakupovići were badly damaged with explosives.[178]

---

175. Information stated in the "About Us" section. See "O nama," http://rzrljubija.com/osnovni_podaci.aspx.

176. Except for mosques in Banja Luka that were blown up in 1993. There are a handful of undamaged mosques such as the one in Mrkonjić Grad and in Umoljani village on Mt. Bjelašnica, but in total more than six hundred mosques and other Islamic buildings were leveled.

177. In the Karadžić case it was established who destroyed this mosque: "The individuals involved in setting fire to the mosque were Milenko Milić, a member of Milan Andžić's paramilitary group, as well as his commander, Momčilo Radanović, and Milorad Vokić, a police officer and personal bodyguard to Drljača." See Prosecutor v. Radovan Karadžić (Judgment), IT-95-5/18-T (ICTY), 655.

178. Prosecutor v. Radoslav Brđanin (Judgment), IT-99-36-T (ICTY), 237, and Prosecutor v. Radovan Karadžić (Judgment), IT-95-5/18-T (ICTY), 755.

Perpetrators

In the Brđanin case, in response to the defense's claims that the crimes had been committed by "uncontrollable elements" (i.e., random individuals out of control operating outside the law), the Trial Chamber stated in its judgment that "The impact of so-called uncontrolled elements was marginal. It is also satisfied beyond reasonable doubt that it was impossible to implement a systematic policy of this magnitude just by spontaneous action or by criminal actions by isolated radical groups (. . .) the actual methods used to implement the strategic plan were controlled and coordinated from a level higher than the respective municipalities, even though some municipalities distinguished themselves by taking certain initiatives."[179] Evidence has shown that local Serbs in Prijedor were already preparing for war as early as August 1991, when some four hundred Bosnian Serbs from Prijedor and surrounding towns were sent to Podgradci in Serb-controlled Croatia (Republika Srpska Krajina), where they were trained by instructors from Serbia under Captain Dragan Vasiljković, an infamous commander of a Croatian Serb paramilitary unit Knindže. Brđanin, Župljanin, and Drljača visited the training. This is clear evidence that the highest-ranking officials in the ARK, Prijedor, and Banja Luka were preparing and coordinating the military takeover of local municipalities in Krajina.[180] Regarding the attack and takeover of Prijedor, the ICTY established that the coup d'état started before May 19, 1992 (the date the JNA "retreated" from Bosnia and Herzegovina), but it was completed only after this date. Additionally, the attack on Kozarac on May 24, 1992, was "continued by the same JNA unit, restyled as a 1st KK unit and with the same officers in command."[181] As with Višegrad, the JNA withdrawal saw little change in reality.

Radmilo Zeljaja, the commander of the JNA 43rd Brigade, remained the commander of the same brigade, which was renamed VRS 343rd Brigade. Zeljaja spearheaded attacks on Bosniak villages and coordinated with Drljača and the SJB.[182] For example, the attack on Hambarine on May 23 included units of the "1st Krajina Corps such as the 6th Krajina Brigade and the 43rd Motorized Brigade, the Prijedor SJB, including the intervention squad, joined by members

---

179. Prosecutor v. Radoslav Brđanin (Judgment), IT-99-36-T (ICTY), 54.
180. Prosecutor v. Radovan Karadžić (Judgment), IT-95-5/18-T (ICTY), 647.
181. Prosecutor v. Radoslav Brđanin (Judgment), IT-99-36-T (ICTY), 65.
182. Prosecutor v. Radovan Karadžić (Judgment), IT-95-5/18-T (ICTY), 647.

PRIJEDOR 145

of Bosnian Serb paramilitary groups."[183] Whilst the rebadged JNA were key in providing physical threats and support, it was the Crisis Committees whom the ICTY defined as most crucial: "[T]he Crisis Staff, presided over by Dr. Stakić, was responsible for establishing the Omarska, Keraterm, and Trnopolje camps, and, as discussed before, that there was a coordinated cooperation between the Crisis Staff, later the War Presidency, and members of the police and the army in operating these camps."[184]

The guards of the Omarska camp—Miroslav Kvočka, Draglojub Prcać, Milojica "Krle" Kos, Mlađo "Krkan" Radić, and Zoran "Žiga" Žigić—belonged to the Omarska police station. Kvočka and Radić were professional policemen attached to the Omarska police station, Prcać was a retired policeman mobilized to serve there. Kos and Žigić were both civilians, a waiter and taxi driver respectively, who were mobilized to serve as reserve officers.[185] The Omarska camp was entirely run by the staff of the Omarska police station; the commander, deputy commander, and shift leaders of the camp were members of this station. The Public Security Station (SJB) in Prijedor was headed by Simo Drljača. The SJB was in the lower level of command in its regional Banja Luka Security Services Center (CSB).[186] The commander of the Police Station Department in Omarska was Željko Mejakić. As a result of this interacting jurisdiction, the interrogators at all the camps were a "mixed group consisting of national, public and military security investigators."[187] In June 1992, the Crisis Committee formed a police unit that consisted of civilians. It became known as the "Intervention Squad"(Interventni vod). The Intervention Squad was headed by Miroslav Paras and comprised two subsquads, one headed by Pero Čivčić and the other by Dragoljub Gligić. This squad was under the control of the military. The Intervention Squad was assigned the duties of:

> arresting and detaining individuals from Bosnian Muslim groups who were allegedly involved in the "attacks on Prijedor" from 30 May 1992, and "[normal-

---

183. Prosecutor v. Radovan Karadžić, 674.

184. Prosecutor v. Stakić (Judgment), IT-97-24-T (ICTY), 105. Dr. Stakić himself states that the "reception centers" were established by the civilian authorities in Prijedor: "These places such as Omarska, Keraterm, and Trnopolje were a necessity in a given moment and were formed according to a decision of the civilian authorities in Prijedor."

185. Prosecutor v. Kvočka et al. (Judgment), IT-98-30/1-T (ICTY), 2.

186. The head of the CSB was Stojan Župljanin, who was on trial at the ICTY for crimes committed throughout Bosnia and Herzegovina. See Prosecutor v. Župljanin and Stanišić, IT-08-91-T (ICTY), 137–39.

187. Prosecutor v. Kvočka et al. (Judgment), IT-98-30/1-T (ICTY), 11.

ising] life in Prijedor town and in the whole of the municipality." Furthermore, the intervention squad was ordered by its commanders to arrest certain Bosnian Muslims based on lists compiled by the commanders; these lists included prominent Bosnian Muslims, such as doctors, lawyers, professors, and religious leaders, and Bosnian Muslims linked to World War II through their predecessors.[188]

Unlike Višegrad, paramilitaries played a limited role in Prijedor. The crimes were committed by regular police and army units that did not allow paramilitaries to operate in the Prijedor region. In one document, Simo Drljača, chief of the Prijedor SJB, discusses paramilitary activity in Prijedor municipality and credits the ""synchronized activities of the Serbian army and police" with having, in large part, destroyed any paramilitary formations."[189] Mićo Stanišić, minister of the interior of Republika Srpska, and Stojan Župljanin, the chief of the Regional Security Services Center of Banja Luka and a member of the Crisis Staff of the Autonomous Region of Krajina (ARK) from May to July 1992, both knew about the existence of the camps. In July 1992, Stanišić sent Župljanin a letter stating that among the "many people, who are not interesting from the security aspect and can be treated as hostages" are a large number of captured Bosniaks in Prijedor. It further states that these *hostages* are "guarded by reserve and regular police forces."[190]

The VRS itself, with the exception of Manjača, had no role in the camps, but they did take part in the military operations against the Bosniaks and Croat villages, especially during the cleansing of the left side of the Sana River. The main brigade, which operated in the Prijedor region, was the 43rd Motorized Brigade. The commander of the 43rd Brigade was Colonel Arsić and all military and paramilitary units were under his control, according to a decision he issued on May 17, 1992.[191]

---

188. Prosecutor v. Radovan Karadžić (Judgment), IT-95-5/18-T (ICTY), 648.
189. Prosecutor v. Stakić (Judgment), IT-97-24-T (ICTY), 137.
190. Radoša Milutinović, "Army Responsible for Detention Camps," *Justice Report*, February 4, 2014, http://www.justice-report.com/en/articles/army-responsible-for-detention-camps.
191. Prosecutor v. Stakić (Judgment), IT-97-24-T (ICTY), 31.

PRIJEDOR 147

Crisis Committee and Concentration Camps

The Prijedor Crisis Committee played a large role in the ethnoreligious cleansing of non-Serbs from the Prijedor region. The Crisis Committee had a coordinating role regarding the security of the camps. They, however, not only had power over security issues but over a number of other significant questions. The Crisis Committee prohibited the releases of detainees, issuing guidelines on when and how a detainee could be released. Simo Drljača compiled a report that highlights the role of the Crisis Committee, stating that "it was in this kind of situation that the Crisis Staff of the municipality of Prijedor decided to use the premises of the Keraterm RO/work organization in Prijedor to accommodate captured persons under the supervision of the employees of the SJB and the military police of Prijedor."[192]

The Serb authorities were proud of their accomplishments and they often bragged about them. Srđo Srdić was the president of the Prijedor Red Cross and a delegate in the Republika Srpska Assembly. On one session in 1992 he stated, "We didn't ask you, or Mr. Karadzic, or Mr. Krajisnik, what we needed to do in Prijedor. Prijedor was the single 'green' municipality in the Bosnian Krajina, and had we listened to you, we would still be green today." He added, "We fixed them and firmly sent them packing where they belong."[193] When Srdić says "we" here, it is not known whether he was referring to the ARK or to Prijedor, since Prijedor had at that time been more part of the ARK than of the RS.

This speech, however, must not be used to free Karadžić or the ARK of any responsibility for crimes. The Prijedor Crisis Committee, as well as all other crisis committees, governed and worked with a large amount of autonomy, but with the knowledge, support, and coordination of higher political, military, and police authorities.

---

192. Prosecutor v. Stakić, 107.
193. Robert Donia, *Radovan Karadžić: Architect of the Bosnian Genocide* (Cambridge: Cambridge University Press, 2014), 203.

CHAPTER 5

Bijeljina

Introduction

Bijeljina was strategically important for the Serb political establishment. It is in the northeastern part of Bosnia and Herzegovina, near the border with Serbia. North of the town was the Sava River and to the east the Drina River. Thus Bijeljina sat across an important communication corridor between northeastern Bosnia and Herzegovina and Serbia, part of the "Posavina Corridor" that linked Krajina, western Slavonia, and the western part of Bosnia and Herzegovina with Serbia.[1] Securing it was number 2 on the Six Strategic Goals of the Serbian People from May 12, 1992. In addition Bijeljina was also strategically important for the implementation of strategic goals number 1 and 3.[2] During the January 1993 meeting of the Bosnian Serb Assembly, representatives said that there can be no Serbian state "without Podrinje [. . .] from Foča to Bijeljina."[3]

The preparations for Bijeljina's takeover started several months earlier, in late 1991. The proclamation of the Independent Autonomous Region of Northeastern Bosnia was made on November 19, 1991 (this was also known as the SAO Birač-Semberija). This included Bijeljina, Lopare, and Ugljevik. An article from *Javnost* dated September 28, 1991, states that "it will have a population of 200,000. It is also going to be a region of a vital importance, considering the fact that the grain-growing region of Semberija is going to be included in it."[4]

---

1. Prosecutor v. Radovan Karadžić (Judgment), IT-95-5/18-T (ICTY), 227.
2. Reynaud Theunens, "Radovan Karadžić and the SRBiH TO-VRS (1992–1995)," 18. See Theunens, "Radovan Karadžić," Exhibit P3033, 227.
3. Theunens, "Radovan Karadžić," 1073.
4. P. Simić, "Regionalizacija—volja naroda" (Regionalization—People's Will), *Javnost*, September 28, 1991, 2. See Prosecutor v. Radovan Karadžić (Judgment), IT-95-5/18-T (ICTY), Exhibit P06212.E.

In 1991, on the eve of the war, the Bijeljina municipality had a population of 96,988 people, out of which 57,389 (59.2 percent) were Serbs, 30,229 (31.2percent) were Bosniaks, and 492 (0.50 percent) were Croats.

A Bloody Eid

On April 1, 1992—the Muslim holiday of Eid—a joint mixed force of the Serb Territorial Defense, Arkan's paramilitary group the Tigers, Chetniks, and Serb police took part in the attack on Bijeljina, taking the town without any resistance.

Within days, the Tigers began terrorizing Bosniaks, murdering them in full view of the rest of the town. These murders in Bijeljina became well-known via the photographs taken by US photojournalist Ron Haviv, who was embedded with Arkan's Tigers.

A few days later, Bijeljina's local newspaper *SIM* published an official list of citizens killed in the "fighting." This list contained forty names, most of whom were Bosniaks and Albanians. In the first days of April, Jusuf Trbić, a journalist and director of Radio Bijeljina and local newspaper *Semberijske novine*, was arrested by Mirko Blagojević, whom he knew personally, and was taken to the headquarters of Arkan's Tigers. One of the most influential local Serb leaders was Ljubiša "Mauzer" Savić, commander of the Panthers military unit, who was working in close cooperation with the Crisis Committee and the local authorities. Trbić was sitting in Mauzer's office when a member of the Bosnian Serb presidency, Biljana Plavšić, called. Mauzer answered the phone and spoke to her saying, "Don't worry, we won't harm him. We know who we need to harm. We have been preparing this for months."[5] Others, however, were harmed. Bosniaks were rounded up for interrogation, and were often killed afterward. Dozens of bodies were left lying on the streets. It is estimated that at least forty-eight civilians (out of which forty-five were non-Serbs) were killed by Serb paramilitaries in the first days of April 1992.[6]

For Arkan, Operation Bijeljina was a publicity stunt that helped make him

---

5.   Faruk Sokolović, "Clouds over Bijeljina," IWPR/Mebius Film, April 20, 2012, https://www.youtube.com/watch?v=aIh3zgP_Y10.

6.   This is according to the Trial Chamber in Prosecutor v. Radovan Karadžić, IT-95-5/18-PT (ICTY), 236. Other sources put the number higher Emir Musli, "Bijeljinska i janjarska knjiga mrtvih" (Bijeljina: BKZ–Preporod, April 19, 2015), http://preporodbn.com/bijeljinska-i-janjarska-knjiga-mrtvih/.

150   TORTURE, HUMILIATE, KILL

into a Serb hero, fighting a righteous battle to defend Bosnian Serbs from Muslim radicals, Albanian gangs, and Croatian Ustaša. He gave several interviews to TV stations from Serbia, boasting of his unit's "achievements." Marko Pejić served as Arkan's deputy.

In its report, the JNA 17th Corps stated that the situation was out of control and that the party leaders were "incapable of ensuring peace and preventing the anarchical behavior of individuals and groups."[7] The next day, April 3, 1992, the report stated that even though the situation in Bijeljina had "calmed somewhat," there was still "general chaos, anarchy and panic in the town," with rumors that Bosnian Muslims were being slaughtered.[8] On April 4, 1992, a state commission composed of several high-ranking political and military officials, including Biljana Plavšić and Fikret Abdić, visited Bijeljina to assess the situation. The local authorities ordered the removal of bodies from the street prior to the delegates' arrival. Biljana Plavšić visited the Bijeljina Crisis Committee and thanked Arkan for saving the Bosnian Serbs. Their encounter, filled with hugs and kisses, was filmed and aired on TV channels.[9]

Being a minority, isolated and surrounded by Serb communities, Bosniaks around Bijeljina began to take drastic measures to survive. On April 6, 1992, a meeting was held in Janja, where the local Bosniak population was told that rumors about massacres of Bosniaks were false, after which they surrendered their weapons.[10] On April 16, 1992, Ugljevik SJB chief Vinko B. Lazić sent a telegram to Stanišić informing him that the Muslim population of Srednja Trnova, Glinje, Janjari, Atmačići, and Snježnica expressed loyalty to the SAO Semberija.[11] Soon after after Bijeljina was taken over, non-Serb employees were dismissed from municipal workplaces. Bosniaks working in the police were forced to pledge loyalty to the Bosnian Serb authorities and wear the Serb insignia on their uniforms. Those who had managerial positions in private firms were replaced by Serbs. Those who held nonmanagerial jobs were also threat-

---

7. Prosecutor v. Radovan Karadžić (Judgment), IT-95-5/18-T (ICTY), 234.
8. Prosecutor v. Radovan Karadžić, 236.
9. Prosecutor v. Radovan Karadžić, 239–40. While talking to a UNPROFOR official Plavšić said that Bijeljina was a "liberated" town.
10. Prosecutor v. Radovan Karadžić, 236. See testimony of witness Živan Filipović. Janja is a large, exclusively Bosniak village near Bijeljina.
11. Letter from the chief of SJB Ugljevik, Vinko B. Lazić, to the Ministry of Interior of the Serbian Republic of BiH to Minister Stanišić, no. 18-17/01-198/92, dated April 16, 1992. ICTY no. 0074-1374, Prosecutor v. Radovan Karadžić, IT-95-5/18 (ICTY), Exhibit P05490.E.

BIJELJINA 151

ened with losing them. There were a few exceptions, as when, for example, a school director, Lazar Manojlović, refused to expel his non-Serb employees.[12]

Bosniaks were harassed and their apartments were occupied by Serbs. They were told that they had to leave Bijeljina and find a new home somewhere else. Once again, Bosniaks became *homo sacer*, outside the law, outside the boundaries of morality, free to be treated however the perpetrators wanted. On June 15, 1992, Mauzer stated that should "the genocide against the Serbian people" in Bosnia and Herzegovina continue, all Bosniaks would lose their jobs and be expelled, adding that the least popular measure would be "to forcibly remove Muslims or something similar."[13] He further added, "I wish to say that we here in Bijeljina could very quickly and easily expel or mobilize Muslims, putting them in front lines to shoot at their brothers."[14] Lazar Manojlović testified about the Serb authority's policy on expelling Bosniaks: "First they said 10 percent of Bosniaks (should remain in Bijeljina). They came to me bragging about it. That figure was to include people who were over sixty years of age who would die by the time (the SDS) created the Serb state. Then they realized that that number was too large and in their next session they made the decision that only 2 percent could stay."[15]

In the chaos and the uncertainty, violence against Bosniaks increased. In June 1992, four Serb soldiers members of a VRS volunteer unit—Danilo Spasojević, Dragan Jović, Zoran Đurđević, and Alen Ristić—entered the house of Rama Avdić, took all his possessions, and raped his daughter Nizama Avdić and his daughter-in-law Hajreta Avdić. After killing Rama Avdić, they took the two girls and paraded them naked through town, bringing them to the Lejljenca village. There they were raped and sodomized again and then left on the roadside naked and barefoot.[16]

---

12. Manojlović received several awards after the war for his bravery.

13. Pero Simić, "Semberija lost for Alija's Islamic state," *List SAO Semberije i Majevice—SiM*, June 15, 1992, 4–5.

14. Simić, "Semberija lost for Alija's Islamic state," 4–5.

15. Faruk Sokolović, "Bijeljina: The Righteous Man," IWPR/Mebius Film, April 24, 2012, [3:30–3:45], https://www.youtube.com/watch?v=qIe0Ew5iJo0. Manojlović also stated, "I opposed the rule of Bishop Kačavenda who had come to Bijeljina before it all started and established the rule of terror." In Sokolović, "Bijeljina," [8:00–8:15].

16. The three were convicted in Belgrade while Danilo Spasojević was convicted in Bijeljina. For the judgment in Belgrade, see Prosecutor v. Jović et al. (Odeljenje za ratne zločine) br. K-Po2 br 7/2011 (Viši Sud u Beogradu, Republika Srbija), June 4, 2012, https://bit.ly/ProsvJovicJudgement.

152   TORTURE, HUMILIATE, KILL

On September 2, 1992, Karadžić visited Bijeljina, where he had a meeting with RS political and military leaders. On this occasion he stated that "[w]e are close to the goal and we must run across it [. . .] the Serbian people will either create their own state [. . .] or we will be squeezed into a small area." He also stated that there was "no political position as to how to proceed with Muslims who have declared loyalty," but that "we must have ethnic minorities in the state as well."[17]

It was General Ratko Mladić, however, who gave an order to establish a camp in Bijeljina to relieve the Birać brigade from guarding an estimated six hundred prisoners. Soon the Eastern Bosnia Corps Command issued an order for the selection of "locations and facilities to accommodate prisoners of war" in accordance with Mladić's order, and as a result the Batković camp was established.[18] Batković would be one of the longest operating camps during the war period.

Crisis Committee

SDS president Milan Novaković and Ljubiša "Mauzer" Savić were the Bijeljina Crisis Committee's leaders.[19] Novaković was impressed by the results of the Bosnian Serbs' massacres of Bosniaks in the nearby town Brčko and "announced on radio that the Jelisić 'factory' was the most productive at the time."[20, 21] The members of the committee were all prominent SDS figures. The Crisis Staff served as a "commanding body of defense and military forces" and provided logistical support to the JNA in Bijeljina.[22] The Bijeljina SDS branch had a close connection with the SDS Pale HQ and were regularly visited by Radovan Karadžić, Momčilo Krajišnik, and Biljana Plavšić.

---

17. Prosecutor v. Radovan Karadžić (Judgment), IT-95-5/18-T (ICTY), 1056.
18. Batković village is one of the rare cases where locals from the village asked the camp authorities to improve the conditions in the camp and to replace the guards with local people. Other villagers, however, used the opportunity to get free forced labor.
19. Other influential members of the SDS leadership included Dragomir Ljubojević, Marko Stanković, and Dragan Vuković. See Prosecutor v. Radovan Karadžić (Judgment), IT-95-5/18-T (ICTY), 227.
20. Novaković was referring to the Bosnian Serb–run Luka concentration camp in Brčko, where Goran Jelisić, a senior camp guard, gained notoriety for his brutality. See Radoša Milutinović, "UN Court Refuses to Free 'Serb Adolf,'" *Balkan Insight*, August 14, 2017, https://balkaninsight.com/2017/08/14/un-court-refuses-to-free-serb-adolf-08-14-2017/.
21. Prosecutor v. Radovan Karadžić (Judgment), IT-95-5/18-T (ICTY), 319.
22. Prosecutor v. Radovan Karadžić, 229–30.

Batković Camp

The camp was set up on an agricultural farm that had several large hangars. The official name of the camp was Ekonomija—Logor ratnih zarobljenika (LRZ), and it was located in the village of Batković. The name would later be changed to Sabirni Centar Batković. On June 6, 1992, VRS Eastern Bosnian Corps commander Dragutin Ilić ordered the establishment of the camp.[23] A commission of three VRS officers was formed to find a suitable location. The order stated that the camp location should be decided in consultation with the Bijeljina municipality authorities and that it needed to be outside of the town, have a toilet, and be fenced. Batković is 12 km north of Bijeljina, on the border with the Sava River and Serbia.

The military, the Eastern Bosnia Corps, was in control of the camp and it was under military jurisdiction, guarded by VRS reserve soldiers.[24] Momčilo Despot was appointed the camp's commander in June 1992, and he was replaced in August by Velibor Stojanović,[25] who was in turn succeeded by Đoko Pajić, and on August 31, 1994, Gojko Čekić was appointed the camp's final commandant. Petar Dmitrović was deputy commander of the garrison command in Bijeljina and detention camp manager in the period from September 4, 1992, to January 11, 1993. Đoko Pajić was detention camp manager from January 11, 1993, to June 6, 1994. Djordje Krstić was deputy manager of the detention camp in the period from 1993 to mid-1994, and Ljubisa Misić was commander of the Detention Camp Guard Squad in the period from June 5, 1992, to December 1, 1993.[26]

The camp had four guard posts: *Vaga* (weighing station); *Šator* (tent); *Kamen* (rock); and headquarters. An instruction was issued by Camp Commander Despot on the duties and obligations of guards.[27] This instruction also discussed circumstances wherein forced labor would be used. Despot ordered

---

23. Eastern Bosnia Corps Command, Confidential number. 11/2–683, dated June 17, 1992, "Treatment of prisoners of war, order," ICTY No. 06014174, Prosecutor v. Ratko Mladić, IT-09-92 (ICTY). Exhibit D3237
24. Prosecutor v. Radovan Karadžić (Judgment), IT-95-5/18-T (ICTY), 248.
25. Prosecutor v. Radovan Karadžić, 248.
26. Although Đorđe Krstić was indicted for war crimes, he was portrayed as a savior for facilitating the release of a detainee, Salih Hamzić. Tatjana Milovanović, "A Story about Đorđe and Salih," *Balkan Perspective*, January 6, 2016, 10, http://www.forumzfd.de/sites/default/files/downloads/Balkan.Perspectives_Eng.pdf.
27. "East Bosnia Corps Instruction No. 2/835-13 for the Work of the Warden of the Camp Sent to the Warden Command, July 2, 1992." See Prosecutor v. Radovan Karadžić, IT-95-5/18 (ICTY), Exhibit P02891 Prosecution.

154   TORTURE, HUMILIATE, KILL

that a list of all detainees be kept who could be used for maintenance and agricultural work.[28] That was followed by a detailed instruction of how the reception desk should function.[29] The highly bureaucratic paper trail shows the main difference between camps operated by the army and other actors, who did not leave much written evidence.

Batković soon became a regional camp, housing Bosniaks from places beyond Bijelina, and it served as both a transit and a labor camp.[30] Thousands of detainees passed through, brought from all over the self-proclaimed Serb Republic, and were kept there for differing periods of time. From there, many were transferred to other camps, exchanged, or deported after buying their freedom. These large numbers of detainees were from various municipalities: Kalesija, Brčko, Ključ, Lopare, Rogatica, Prijedor, Sanski Most, Sokolac, Ugljevik, Vlasenica, Živinice, and Zvornik.[31] Many detainees were transferred into Batković from other camps such as Manjača and Sušica. These transfers were conducted by the police rather than by the army. In late June 1992, approximately four hundred detainees from Sušica camp were transferred to Batković, and in late 1992 an estimated further five hundred detainees were transferred from Manjača camp.[32] Many detainees from Luka camp in Brčko were also transferred to Batković.[33] In mid-July 1992, the detainees from Čelopek camp in Zvornik were also transferred to Batković.[34] These transfers were conducted after those camps had been shut down. In July 1993, four hundred men from the camp were taken by bus to Lopare municipality and exchanged for Bosnian Serb civilians.

In November 1992, the Bosanski Šamac SJB chief, Stevan Todorović, in cooperation with the VRS, arranged for 180 detainees to be transferred to Batković.[35] Miroslav Tadić, the president of the Commission for Population

---

28. Prosecutor v. Radovan Karadžić (Judgment), IT-95-5/18-T (ICTY), 248.
29. "Command of S.C./Collection Center/'Ekonomija', Internal No. 2/835-12, Instruction on the work at the gate-house of SC 'Ekonomija' in the village of Batković," dated July 12, 1992, ICTY No. 0529-9074. See Prosecutor v. Radovan Karadžić, IT-95-5/18 (ICTY), Exhibit D03239.E.
30. Similar to the Nazi *Arbeitslager* or Soviet *gulags*.
31. Prosecutor v. Radovan Karadžić (Judgment), IT-95-5/18-T (ICTY), 249. When the group from Sušica camp was brought into Batković, 1,600 Bosniaks from various municipalities were in one hangar. See witness KDZ603 testimony. A group of 500 detainees was brought from Doboj to the Batković camp, where they spent a few nights after and then were transferred to Kula camp near Sarajevo. See Testimony of Muhamed H., "You Can't Forget. It's Impossible," *Justice Report*, April 19, 2006, http://www.justice-report.com/en/articles/for-the-record-you-can-t-forget-it-s-impossible.
32. Prosecutor v. Radovan Karadžić (Judgment), IT-95-5/18-T (ICTY), 249.
33. Prosecutor v. Radovan Karadžić, 312.
34. Prosecutor v. Radovan Karadžić, 533–43.
35. Prosecutor v. Simić et al. (Transcript: Witness Kemal Mehinović), IT-95-9-T (ICTY), May 6, 2002, 7380–77, http://www.icty.org/x/cases/simic/trans/en/020506IT.htm.

Exchange and a member of the Crisis Committee from Bosanski Šamac, visited Batković camp on at least one occasion. He came to exchange detainees from Bosanski Šamac. One detainee recalled:

> He came to the hangar in which we were detained at the camp, Batkovici. He had a list in his hands, and he was reading out names for exchange. At that time, my name was also on the list, and I personally saw how Mr. Sabah Seric explained and promised to give him money, and he gave him about 100 Deutschmarks in front of me. And after he went to the commander of the camp, to his office, he took off my name and put Mr. Sabah's name on the list.[36]

The length of time a detainee could spend in the camp might range from a few weeks to more than a year.

In early 1992, the detainees were divided into groups according to their municipality of origin. In this way the camp command kept track of each group. An unknown number of women, children, and the elderly, however, were kept in a separate hangar from the younger men. As detainees arrived at Batković camp, they were welcomed by being forced to pass through a cordon of soldiers who beat them with chains and batons and then escorted to the hangar.[37] They were told by the Serb officer in charge that they were "war prisoners" on Serb land and that they had no rights. The last group that was brought to Batković camp were Bosniaks from Karakaj and Srebrenica in July 1995.[38] Around 22 wounded Bosniak men were taken from the Bratunac Health Center to Batković.[39] A total of 171 Bosniak men from Srebrenica enclave were brought to Batković in July and were exchanged by December 1995.[40]

The camp authorities kept a record of detainees who were brought to Batković camp. It is by far the most detailed and organized record of any other

---

36. Prosecutor v. Simić et al.
37. "Upon arrival at Batković camp, detainees were beaten and their hair was shaved off. They were kept in the sunshine in the camp, which was closed off with five or six rows of barbed wired fences, sentry boxes, and observation points with machine guns." Prosecutor v. Stanišić and Župljanin, IT-08-91 (ICTY), 284.
38. Prosecutor v. Radovan Karadžić (Judgment), IT-95-5/18-T (ICTY), 250. On July 11 or 12, 1995, Milenko Todorović, the chief of security of the Eastern Bosnia Corps, received a telegram from Zdravko Tolimir that directed them to prepare accommodation at the Batković camp for approximately 1,000 to 1,200 Bosniaks who would arrive. These men, however, never arrived. For more detail see Prosecutor v. Radovan Karadžić, 2297.
39. List of Wounded Muslim Prisoners, dated July 18, 1995, handed over by 5th Military Police Battalion from Vlasenica to 3rd Battalion IBK, ICTY no. 01798523.
40. RS Ministry of Defense, List of Muslims Exchanged from the Batković SC, no. 8/1-08-77-4/02, dated March 12, 2002.

156 TORTURE, HUMILIATE, KILL

camp run by the Republika Srpska authorities: "Between 27 June 1992 and 22 December 1995, a total of 2,468 detainees were listed. Of these detainees, 28 were listed as having died, 2,002 were listed as having been exchanged, 406 were listed as having been released, 7 were listed as deported, 20 escaped or went missing, and 5 were remanded to another prison."[41] The actual number of detainees who passed through it as a transit camp, however, is surely larger.

The camp served as the base from which prisoner exchanges would occur. It was used as a transit camp from which detainees were transferred to other camps such as Kula (a Bosnian Serb run camp on the outskirts of Sarajevo) or were brought to Batković to be temporarily held until an exchange was agreed. For example, in June 1993 an agreement was made by HVO "Posavina" to exchange detainees from a HVO-held detention facility in Donja Mahala in Orašje and detainees from Batković. The detainees from Batković were a mixture of Bosniaks and Croats while the detainees from Donja Mahala were Serbs. The exchange took place in Dragalić on June 5, 1993, and was conducted between the VRS 1st Krajina Corps and the HVO "Posavina" Brigade.[42]

The VRS had the power to decide if someone should be confined in Batković or released. In one case, Dragomir Andan asked Colonel Ilić to release a Croat friend of his, which Ilić did. In another case, a military officer complained that a Husein Ćurtić, aka Apaka, insulted him on the street. Ćurtić was brought to Batković and murdered after a few days.[43]

The conditions in Batković were poor.[44] The detainees were forced to sleep on the concrete floor and the hangars were overcrowded. Detainees were, as Des Pres would state, reduced to infantile and childlike levels of behavior.[45] They were forbidden to sit with their legs crossed and were required to seek permission before using the toilet or getting water. They were also required to ask for permission to speak and ask the guards questions. Speaking to the guards was allowed by making the three-finger Serb nationalist salute, bowing

---

41. See Prosecutor v. Radovan Karadžić, IT-95-5/18 (ICTY), Exhibit no. P3213, 250, for the list of persons detained at the Batković camp.
42. "1st Krajina Corps, Commission for the Exchange of prisoners of war, Banja Luka, to the VRS /Army of Republika Srpska/ Main Staff—Commission to Colonel Zdravko Tolimir" No: 53/93, dated June 1, 1993, No. 89/94. In Prosecutor v. Simić et al., IT-95-9, Exhibit D13/3, https://bit.ly/ZdravkoTolimirCommision93.
43. Prosecutor v. Stanišić and Župljanin, IT-08-91 (ICTY), 282.
44. Although conditions in Batković were similar to those in Manjača, there were fewer beatings, fewer people called out at night, and better access to water.
45. Terrence Des Pres, *The Survivor: An Anatomy of Life in the Death Camps* (Oxford: Oxford University Press, 1980), 56.

BIJELJINA   157

their heads, and saying "Sir Serb soldier let me address you."[46] The toilet was a makeshift, ten-meter-long latrine that could be used only during the day. While walking through the camp, the detainees needed to bow their heads and keep their hands behind their back. Meals were infrequent—at best—"a slice of bread for breakfast, had some cooked food at lunch and boiled corn flour for dinner."[47]

The camp was organized in a military fashion. There were detainee representatives and also detainee guards—*kapos*—detainees who had privileges among the guards and beat other detainees. Two of these *kapos* were later convicted for war crimes: Fikret "Piklić" Smajlović and Džemal "Spajzer" Zahirović.[48]

The detainees were beaten on a regular basis. One of the first detainees to be beaten was Ejub Smajić: "Those were incredible injuries. The pain was so great that I could not lie down for a month. . . . I could only sit. Two of my ribs were broken due to the beating, so I could hardly breathe. The two of them died due to the beating. I survived somehow. I know that, because we were in the same room. I could see swellings and bruises all over their bodies and faces."[49]

Detainees would be beaten especially after Serb soldiers were killed on the frontline and the soldiers would take revenge on them all. In one instance, two detainees managed to escape from the camp. As a result, all other detainees were beaten.[50] One survivor recalled, "I know that one man, whose health was very bad, ran away from the detention camp by crawling underneath the wired fence, but they captured him in Batkovic village. When they brought him back, they ordered all of us to come out and beat him up badly. I noticed that the man was totally disoriented. I assumed that they did it in order to scare the rest of us, so we would not try to do the same."[51]

Detainee Šaban Mustafić was brought into the camp in one of the first groups: "They beat me up as soon as I arrived, but I didn't know anyone at that time. When I woke up, I thought I was dead, because I saw a thousand people

---

46. See Sakib Husrefović, "Witness Statement," ICTY, May 26–27, 1995, https://bit.ly/HusrefovicWitnessStatement.

47. Prosecutor v. Radovan Karadžić (Judgment), IT-95-5/18-T (ICTY), 250.

48. Another infamous *kapo* was Esad Bekrić, aka Beretka.

49. Boris Sekulić, "Constant Beating," *Justice Report*, March 8, 2013, http://www.justice-report.com/en/articles/news-constant-beating.

50. Prosecutor v. Radovan Karadžić (Judgment), IT-95-5/18-T (ICTY), 251–52. Similarly, on December 22, 1994, nine Bosniak men from Janja managed to escape from Batković, and for that all the other detainees were beaten. See Jusuf Trbić, *Gluho doba* (Sarajevo: BZK Preporod, 2004), 157.

51. Boris Sekulić, "Slapped without Reason," *Justice Report*, April 9, 2014, http://www.justice-report.com/en/articles/slapped-without-reason.

with their heads shaved, sitting there with their heads bowed." He also mentions the public torture of one man who was among the most targeted in the camp: "They used to hang Alija Konjanik until he fainted. Zoran Zaric and Gligor Begovic did that. They would pour water over him and hang him again."[52] In early 1993, several detainees were brought to the Bijeljina courthouse where they were put on trial for war crimes. One detainee, Kemal Mehinović, was sentenced to death for "killing Serb children."[53] There was a doctor in the camp but ill detainees were refused medical care. As a result, a number of them died. Detainees were also used as forced labor. The police would take them to factories while the army took them to the frontline, mostly to dig trenches or to be used as human shields.[54]

In other cases, local Serb farmers would take them as slaves to work on the fields. Several detainees died or were killed on the frontline while burying dead, clearing land mines, digging trenches etc.[55] At least twenty-two detainees were killed on the frontlines in Majevica.[56] This massacre prompted the UN Security Council to issue a public statement on April 8, 1993, reminding "all the parties" that they "must not compel detainees to do work of a military nature."[57] Another example of detainees being killed while performing slave labor was the killing of six Bosniak men from Janja, who were killed on the frontline in Tomanića kosa on May 13, 1993.[58]

In one case, in late 1994, more than a hundred Bosniak men from Janja were taken to Batković from where they took part in forced labor in Majevica, Batkovići, Vukšići, and Priboj mainly cutting wood. They were then taken to Mount Bjelašnica near Sarajevo, where they also performed labor, and then

---

52. Džana Brkanić, "Witnesses Describe Detainee Abuse at Batkovic Detention Camp," *Justice Report*, March 4, 2015, http://www.justice-report.com/en/articles/witnesses-describe-detainee-abuse-at-batkovic-detention-camp.
53. *Mehinovic v. Vuckovic*, Civil Action 1:98-cv-2470-MHS (N.D. Ga. May 2, 2002.), 13, https://casetext.com/case/mehinovic-v-vuckovic-3. See also "Record of Interview of Accused, Kemal Mehinović," dated January 19, 1993. See Prosecutor v. Simić et al., IT-95-9-T (ICTY), Exhibit P55.
54. Several worked at the local flour factory. See "Bosnia Herzegovina: Report from the Town of Bijeljina," Channel 4 News, March 17, 1993, Gaby Rado reporting, ITN BSP170393007, in András J. Riedlmayer, *Destruction of Cultural Heritage in Bosnia-Herzegovina, 1992–1996: A Post-war Survey of Selected Municipalities* (Cambridge, MA: 2002), 12, http://heritage.sensecentar.org/assets/sarajevo-national-library/sg-3-01-destruction-culturale-en.pdf.
55. Prosecutor v. Radovan Karadžić (Judgment), IT-95-5/18-T (ICTY), 253–54.
56. Musli, "Bijeljinska i Janjarska Knjiga."
57. Bertrand Ramcharan, *Human Rights and U.N. Peace Operations: Yugoslavia* (Leiden: Martinus Njihoff Publishers, 2001), 147.
58. Trbić, *Gluho doba*, 157.

were finally exchanged in Sarajevo in 1995.[59] Many of the detainees received certificates that they were on "obligatory work," which was signed by Major Vlado Simić.[60]

There was a group of selected detainees who were heavily targeted by the guards. This group was called "Extremists" or "Alija's Specialists."[61] They were treated the worst. One survivor recalled, "I don't know how those men survived at all. Their ears were like ashtrays. Their faces distorted. They would come back crawling."[62] Alija Gulašić, a construction worker from Bijeljina, was one of them. He spent three months in Batković camp before he was transferred to a camp in Doboj. He stated that they were beaten for "breakfast, lunch and dinner" using "chains, sticks, handles, axe handles." They tested all of that on us, and then eventually they would use stones, and I had to kneel to make it possible for them or easier for them to hit me with stones."[63] One of the aims of the perpetrators was to destroy the moral community and relationship of the Bosniak and Croat population. Sexual abuse was part of the degradation imposed by the guards:

"Q. And was there sexual activity that was forced on you? If so, in a sentence, tell us about that.
A. It's shame on them to force a man to sleep with a man.
Q. Was that done once or more than once?
A. More than once."[64]

The sexual abuse in Batković camp was part of Biljana Plavšić's indictment at the ICTY, to which she pleaded guilty.[65] Courts in Bosnia and Herzegovina have nevertheless given us still more detail about the abuses.

---

59. See judgment in Bego Hamzić v. Republika Srpska, no. 80 0 P 025505 10 P (Osnovni sud u Bijeljini), September 21, 2012.
60. Trbić, *Gluho doba*, 160.
61. "The detainees in this group were beaten at least three times a day, forced to beat each other, knocked over by fire hoses, and forced to have sexual intercourse with each other, often in front of other detainees. The guards were aware of these actions but did nothing but laugh. Some detainees suffered lasting harm which was both physical and psychological including post-traumatic stress disorder." See Prosecutor v. Radovan Karadžić (Judgment), IT-95-5/18-T (ICTY), 252–53.
62. Brkanić, "Witnesses Describe Detainee Abuse."
63. See testimony of witness Alija Gušalić in Prosecutor v. Vojislav Šešelj (Trial Transcript), IT-03-67-T (ICTY), March 4, 2009, 14283–92, http://www.icty.org/x/cases/seselj/trans/en/090304ED.htm.
64. Prosecutor v. Vojislav Šešelj, 14283–92.
65. Serge Brammertz and Michelle Jarvis, *Prosecuting Conflict-Related Sexual Violence at the ICTY* (Oxford: Oxford University Press, 2016).

In August 1992, a camp guard, Gligor Begović, forced N.M. and Mirsad Kuralić to put their penises into each other's mouth, after which he shoved the barrel of an automatic rifle up Kuralić's rectum. Later he repeated this action to N.M. and M.Š. and to Kuralić and A.B.; A.H. and B.M.; and A.H. and Alija Gušalić.[66] Begović also personally beat and tortured N.M. and Ejub Smajić. Together with other guards, Begović kicked and beat Zulfo Hadžiomerović, Ferid Zečević, and Husein Ćurtić until they died. On one occasion he ordered the *kapo* Džemal "Spajzer" Zahirović to hit Mirsad Buljugić with an axe in his chest. In July 1992, he and other guards took out detainee Husein Halilović and placed a gun into his mouth, saying, "Let's play Russian roulette."[67]

Executions

The mortality rate in Batković camp was lower than in other camps since it was primarily a transit camp. There were, however, several executions in the camp throughout its existence. One Bosniak intellectual was brought out by ten guards and killed after being beaten. Two elderly men, including Zulfo Hadžiomerović, were beaten to death. On another occasion Ferid Zečević and another man were taken out by a guard and killed. Ekrem Ćudić from Brčko was severely beaten and forced to work. According to a witness, he slapped a guard and took his rifle and was then shot and killed by other guards.[68] One of the most brutal murders occurred on an unknown day in 1993; two detainees from Ključ, Fuad Islamagić and Fadil Šabanović, who had previously been held in Manjača camp, were on forced labor in Vanek's mill (*Vanekov mlin*), from where they were taken out by Bosnian Serb soldiers and beheaded.[69]

---

66. Tužilaštvo BiH v. Gligor Begović (First Instance Judgment), S 1 1 K 009588 12 Kri (Sud Bosne i Hercegovine), December 11, 2015, 5 and 8, http://www.sudbih.gov.ba/predmet/3328/show.
67. Tužilaštvo BiH v. Gligor Begović, 9.
68. "Tfsrol: Severe Human Rights Abuses in B-H: Eye-Witness Describes Torture/Executions in Luka And Batkovic Camps, Names Perpetrators," *Wikileaks* (February 28, 1994), accessed May 6, 2017, https://wikileaks.org/plusd/cables/94ZAGREB827_a.html.
69. This story was confirmed by several sources but no direct witnesses. See Trbić, *Gluho doba*, and Boris Sekulić, "Witness Heard about Mistreatment and Murders," *Justice Report*, December 5, 2014,http://www.justice-report.com/en/articles/witness-heard-about-mistreatment-and-murders.

Camp "Discovery"

Several days after the Omarska and Trnopolje camps in Prijedor were discovered by journalists, two American journalists tried to find the Batković camp. They were turned away by soldiers at a checkpoint. The local Serb leader, Vojo, told the journalists, "We don't have prisons. I have no reason to lie to you."[70] After more than a week of pressure, however, access to the camp was allowed. Their guide was a top camp official, Major Jovica Savić. American journalist Peter Maass wrote about what he saw: "More than 1,500 Slavic Muslims are crammed into two fetid livestock sheds here, crouching silently amid the stench of filth and fear in a prison camp that Serb security forces swore did not exist. Under the gaze of armed Serb guards, the prisoners shuffle one by one to a lunch of bread and bean soup, their heads bowed low, their hands clasped behind their backs as though pinned by invisible handcuffs."[71]

Walking with their heads bowed low and hands behind their backs was a rule imposed by VRS-held camps such as Manjača and Batković. This rule was not used in other camps and detention facilities. When Maass asked Savić why were people walking around the camp in this way, Savić replied. "It is a custom among Bosnian people."[72]

ICRC Visits

The ICRC visited the Batković camp several times. The first time was in late August or early September 1992. Every time an ICRC visit was announced, the women and children detainees would be hidden in a nearby forest. The group of around ten "extremists" were hidden in a part of the camp known as the Čardak. Other detainees were instructed to lie:

> . . . and tell the ICRC representatives that conditions were fine, that food was good, that they were provided with cigarettes, and had not been beaten. Anyone who did not say what they were instructed to say was beaten severely. While the

---

70. Vojo was most probably Vojkan Đurković. See Peter Maass, "The Search for a Secret Prison Camp," *Washington Post*, August 13, 1992, https://bit.ly/MaassSearchSecretPrisonCamp.
71. Maass, "The Search for a Secret Prison Camp."
72. Peter Maass, "Illusory Serb Prison Camp Materializes," *Washington Post*, August 27, 1992, https://bit.ly/MaassSerbCamp.

162   TORTURE, HUMILIATE, KILL

ICRC provided the detainees with supplies, such as blankets, soap, shoes, gloves and cigarettes, the soldiers would take anything they wanted once the ICRC left the camp. However, the conditions at Batković did improve after the ICRC began to visit the facility.[73]

The last ICRC visit was on December 4, 1995, after which the last detainees were exchanged.[74]

The Batković facility was disbanded in January 1996. Camp commander Col. Gojko Čekić wrote a report on January 11 identifying the material-technical resources the camp had and that it was returning to the army. This included four military beds, 600 blankets, 130 mattresses, 60 metal plates, 70 spoons, etc. The lack of necessities sufficient for a camp containing several thousand prisoners gives some insight into how the conditions in the camp had been.[75]

Besides the ICRC, the Batković camp was visited by a delegation led by US congressman Frank Wolf on September 1, 1992: "There are approximately 1,280 ethnic Muslim men from northeastern Bosnia that are being held at Batkovic. There's gross overcrowding. There is hygienic and medical facilities that are clearly inadequate. The prisoners appeared thin, but not emaciated. There were no signs of gross physical abuse of prisoners. Congressman Wolf and his party were not permitted to speak privately to the detainees."[76]

The ICTY, in addition to the Batković camp, also identified six other detention centers in Bijeljina: the Bijeljina agricultural school, KP Dom Bijeljina, the Bijeljina SUP, the Bijeljina sugar factory, a fortified castle, and the "4th of July" public utilities building. The slaughterhouse in Bijeljina was used as "Mauzer's private jail," where at least five Bosniaks were confined in a refrigerated room.[77] In a report on paramilitaries dated August 8, 1992, Davidović states that Mauzer

---

73. Prosecutor v. Radovan Karadžić (Judgment), IT-95-5/18-T (ICTY), 256.
74. Document of the Main Staff of the Army of Republika Srpska, Number: 06/20–437, dated December 1, 1995, signed by General Manojlović. ICTY no. 04258226. See Prosecutor v. Ratko Mladić, IT-09-92 (ICTY), Exhibit D03242.E.
75. Collection Center Batković, Report on the closing of the Collection Centre and hand over of MTS / material and technical equipment, Confidential number: 2/2999–131, dated January 11, 1996, ICTY no. 0529-9092. Camp commander Gojko Čekić in his statement to the ICTY claims that they had 4,310 blankets and 315 mattresses. He also denied that there was any sexual abuse, stating that the camp guards are "people with families, hosts, older people with children and they would never do such acts." See Izjava svjedoka—Gojko Čekić, dated March 31, 2013. Prosecutor v. Ratko Mladić, IT-09-92 (ICTY), D03238.E.
76. Richard Boucher, "State Department News Briefing," September 8, 1992, https://www.c-span.org/video/?32050-1/state-department-news-briefing.
77. Prosecutor v. Momčilo Krajišnik (Judgment), IT-00-39-T (ICTY), September 27, 2006, 116, https://www.icty.org/x/cases/krajisnik/tjug/en/kra-jud060927e.pdf.

organized "a private prison in the new abattoir to which Muslims were brought to be abused and tortured while a part of the premises were used to store war booty (freight and passenger vehicles, technical goods, foodstuffs and other stolen in war operations)."[78]

"Voluntary" Removal

Bijeljina is one of the rare cases in Bosnia and Herzegovina where Bosniaks were not quickly and brutally expelled. Many managed to leave but they were given clear threats as to what would happen to them if they were to return. In one interview, Mauzer stated that Bosnian Muslims who left "will not come back and I would advise them not to."[79] The Serb authorities in Bijeljina opted rather for a quiet, slow-motion cleansing process. This was done by raising the level of fear among Bosniaks. In August 1992, there were at least seventeen thousand Bosniaks who remained in Bijeljina and around twelve thousand in Janja. In comparison to other towns in Serb-held Bosnia and Herzegovina, this was a relatively high number of Bosniaks. Most of these Bosniaks, however, decided to stay in Serb-held Bijeljina and live there as long as possible for several reasons. First, getting out of Bijeljina was difficult. Bosniaks trying to get out of the town were turned back because of their identity, their Muslim names. Second, a significant number of Bosniaks or Muslims opted to remain loyal to the new authorities and in return keep their lives and property. A number of them even joined the VRS. Others decided to change their names and even converted to Orthodox Christianity. A number of Bosniak children continued attending schools, in most cases adopting Serb names so as to not have problems with other children or teachers.

Milorad Davidović was a former inspector in the Yugoslav federal SUP.[80] In spring 1992 he was sent by the authorities in Belgrade to help establish the MUP RS. As a result he had several meetings with high-ranking officials in the RS including Karadžić, Mladić, Stanišić, and others. At the ICTY, he was one of the

---

78. "Report on the engagement of SMUP Police Brigade members to provide expert assistance to the Serbian Republic of Bosnia and Herzegovina MUP," August 8, 1992, ICTY no. 1D19-0069, 7. See Prosecutor v. Stanišić and Župljanin, IT-08-91 (ICTY), Exhibit 1D00646.E.

79. Prosecutor v. Radovan Karadžić (Judgment), IT-95-5/18-T (ICTY), 259.

80. Davidović used to work and live in Bijeljina, working for the police, and later became an official in Yugoslav SUP. In 1992, he was sent to help establish the MUP RS and later to help dissolve paramilitary units.

164   TORTURE, HUMILIATE, KILL

rare insiders who testified in the trials. Regarding Bijeljina, he gave some valuable information. He stated that several days after he arrived in 1992, a plan was discussed for the "ethnic cleansing" of Muslims who remained in Bijeljina and Zvornik. This plan was discussed by Mauzer, members of the SDS, and the Crisis Committee. Mićo Stanišić was also informed about the plan. The Crisis Committee developed a plan that differed from other crisis committees' plans to cleanse Bosniaks and Bosnian Croats from the municipalities. It would cover three phases:

> In the first phase, scheduled to start in September or October 1992, there would be a division of the city and the creation of an atmosphere of fear to convince the Bosnian Muslims to leave. In the second phase, Bosnian Muslims who refused to respond to the call for mobilization would be fired from their positions, and would have their services cut and would be required to report for work obligations, including on the frontlines. In the third phase, wealthy and intellectual Bosnian Muslims were to be targeted for humiliation by assigning them to menial tasks such as sweeping the streets."[81]

Milorad Davidović also testified that "he saw Bosnian Serb officials compile a list of Bosnian Muslim names for 'cleansing'. . . . and that a list of wealthy Bosnian Muslims that were to be robbed and killed was found with Arkan's and Mauzer's men."[82] Dragomir Ljubojević, the president of the Municipal Assembly and SDS leader, was responsible for drawing up the lists while Vojkan Đurković was responsible for implementation.[83] Soon afterwards, in September 1992, Duško Malović's special police unit, the "Snowflakes" (Pahuljice), began a campaign of intimidation against Bosniaks who stayed in Bijeljina. Twenty-two Bosniak civilians from the Sarajlić, Malagić, and Sejmenović families were massacred by the Snowflakes. Their bodies were thrown into the Drina River and later exhumed in Sremska Mitrovica and Šabac in Serbia.[84] Once again, this served as a powerful warning to all Bosniaks to comply. Those who did not accept mobilization or work obligations were rounded up and taken to the Batković camp or were deported. This resulted in a large number of Bosniaks

---

81. Prosecutor v. Radovan Karadžić (Judgment), IT-95-5/18-T (ICTY), 260.
82. Prosecutor v. Radovan Karadžić.
83. Karadžić would later personally promote Vojkan Đurković to the rank of major and award him a medal at a ceremony in Bijeljina in 1994.
84. Musli, "Bijeljinska i Janjarska Knjiga."

BIJELJINA 165

leaving Bijeljina. Đurković became the main go-to person if somebody wanted to leave Bijeljina,[85] and he organized, with friends from Serbian MUP, the transportation of people to third countries. In one instance, Đurković expelled a Bosniak who was in good relations with senior SDS members and who had helped establish a VRS unit composed of Bosniaks. Đurković was arrested because of this, but he was quickly released after he showed them documents authorizing him to expel all Bosniaks from Bijeljina. The authorization was apparently signed by Momčilo Krajišnik.[86] Đurković made a fee list for people who wanted to leave Bijeljina or the Batković camp. He would decide per case how much freedom cost would cost. On average it was one thousand deutschmarks per male and around two hundred for women and children.[87] At one point, after expelling 100 to 150 Bosniaks, he bragged about collecting 150,000 to 200,000 deutschmarks. In a BBC report he claimed that he was a "social worker" and that he should receive the "Nobel prize."[88] In some cases, even those loyal to the Serbs were deported.[89]

The expulsion of Bosniaks lasted from September 1992 to September 1994. The 1994 expulsions received a lot of media attention, so much so that Karadžić wrote a letter to ICRC head Andreas Khun stating that they are "not conducting ethnic cleansing" and that he recognizes "that a problem exists" and he will sort the issue.[90] By the time the Dayton Accords were signed, around 500 to 1,000 Bosniaks still remained in Bijeljina.[91] These were those most loyal to the Serb republic, most of whom were members of the VRS Third Semberija Bri-

---

85. Đurković institutionalized this with a program called "State Commission for the Free Transfer of Civilian Population." See Jonathan S. Landay, "Bosnian Serbs Expel Non-Serbs From the North," *Christian Science Monitor*, September 7, 1994, https://www.csmonitor.com/1994/0907/07011.html.

86. Prosecutor v. Momčilo Krajišnik (Transcript: Witness Milorad Davidović), IT-00-39-T (ICTY), June 10, 2005, 14243–32, http://www.icty.org/x/cases/krajisnik/trans/en/050610IT.htm. Certain evidence shows that Đurković was splitting the money he took from Bosniaks with Krajišnik and Karadžić. See "'Typhoon' from Republika Srpska," *Sense Agency*, July 1, 2011, http://archive.sensecentar.org/vijesti.php?aid=12951.

87. Chuck Sudetić, "Serbs Drive 800 More Muslims From Homes," *New York Times*, September 5, 1994, 5, http://www.nytimes.com/1994/09/05/world/serbs-drive-800-more-muslims-from-homes.html. See also Prosecutor v. Stanišić and Župljanin, IT-08-91 (ICTY), 280.

88. "Nobody Expelled Muslims and They Shelled Themselves", *Sense Agency*, March 6, 2013, http://archive.sensecentar.org/vijesti.php?aid=14730.

89. See for example the case of Sead Čanić's family from Janja. "Kako živi porodica Bošnjaka koji je poginuo za Republiku Srpsku", *RTVBN*, December 23, 2013, https://www.rtvbn.com/22046/kako-zivi-porodica-bosnjaka-koji-je-poginuo-za-srpsku. .

90. Letter from Radovan Karadžić to Dr Andreas Kuhn, dated September 5, 1994, ICTY No. R0116337. See Prosecutor v. Radovan Karadžić, IT-95-5/18 (ICTY), Exhibit D01431.

91. Prosecutor v. Radovan Karadžić (Judgment), IT-95-5/18-T (ICTY), 263–64.

gade, which was even commanded by a Muslim, Pašaga Halilović.[92] This brigade consisted of Muslims from Bijeljina and Janja. Karadžić, in an interview in July 1995, stated that Muslims in Bijeljina were safe and that there "is some intimidation by terrorist elements, by extreme Serbs who have lost everything in central Bosnia. But the authorities protect our citizens, regardless of whether they are Muslims or Croats. Therefore, what is happening is not ethnic cleansing, but ethnic displacement, people who want to leave."[93]

Religious Conversion and Name Changing

Bijeljina is also specific for another example of identity loss, the forceful conversion of Muslims to Orthodox Christianity. There is not a lot of information about these cases except for a few news reports, and these conversions were not a part of the ICTY's investigations. Most of the conversions were conducted in 1993 and 1994 by those who were still living in Bijeljina. These were civilians who pledged loyalty to the new Serb republic and did not want to or could not leave. According to one source—at least three hundred Muslims changed their names and twenty-eight were baptized. Captain Milorad Javić from the VRS stated in 1994, "We try not to let too many people do it. . . . There are some newer officers here in town and they may not know who really is a Muslim. We don't want people to be able to infiltrate our organizations because they've changed their name. But then again, if we are sure someone is a 'loyal' Muslim, we have no objections."[94] The conversion and name changing was seen as the last chance to keep their property and not be "ethnically cleansed" from Bijeljina. As one journalist noticed, "In the latest twist in the game of survival played by Slavic Muslims trapped in enemy territory, hundreds are changing their names, divesting themselves of their heritage in a joyless attempt to avoid being 'ethnically cleansed'—forcibly driven out—by Bosnian Serbs. Those who drop their Muslim names can travel and for the time being have secured some protection for their homes and businesses."[95] Although some of the local lead-

---

92. For more information see the testimony of Alija Gušalić in Prosecutor v. Slobodan Milošević (Trial Transcript, B-071), IT-02-54 (ICTY), April 1, 2003, 18268–82, https://www.icty.org/x/cases/slobodan_milosevic/trans/en/030401ED.htm.
93. Prosecutor v. Radovan Karadžić (Judgment), IT-95-5/18-T, 1265.
94. Barbara Demick, "Name Change Can Save Life," *Calgary Herald*, January 3, 1994, A1.
95. John Pomfret, "Muslims Try 'Name Cleansing' to Survive in Serb-Held Bosnia," *Washington Post*, December 21, 1993, https://bit.ly/PomfretWaPoMuslimsTryNameCleansing .

ers approved the conversion, saying that Muslims were "returning to their roots," others, such as Rev. Nedeljko Pajić, the city's parish priest, had a much more rational explanation, stating that most of the people who changed their names were traders and businessmen who had something to lose. Changing their religion was a form of survival.[96]

Destruction of Mosques

All mosques in Bijeljina were destroyed or damaged in 1993. The Atik mosque in the center of Bijeljina was destroyed between March 13 and 15, 1993.[97] The final bulldozing of the mosque's remains was secretly filmed by British journalists.[98] The mosques in Atmačić, Srednja Trnova, and Krpić mosque were also destroyed while the Janjari mosque was damaged and vandalized.

Perpetrators

The VRS operative group of the Eastern Bosnia Corps had its headquarters in Bijeljina. The corps commander in May 1992 was Colonel Nikola Denčić, but by June 7, 1992, he had been replaced by Colonel Dragutin Ilić. Bijeljina was also the center of the CSB for SAO Semberija.[99] It was home to the sector of the National Security Service and a detachment of the Special Police Brigade (SP3). With regard to the Batković camp, it was a VRS-controlled concentration camp, assisted by MUP RS, who provided the external security. This was a common practice in several VRS-run camps such as Manjača, Sušica, etc.[100] The entire

---

96. Pomfret, "Muslims Try 'Name Cleansing' to Survive in Serb-Held Bosnia."
97. Video of destruction can be seen in this report: Bosnia Herzegovina: Report from the town of Bijeljina, Channel 4 News, March 17, 1993, Gaby Rado reporting, ITN BSP170393007. See also Prosecutor v. Milošević, IT-02-54-T (ICTY), Exhibit P488 Tab 2: ITN TV video footage of Bijeljina of March 17, 1993. "The removal of the remains of destroyed buildings (usually on the grounds of 'public safety') was typically carried out by contractors authorized by the local authorities, or in the case of the mosques in Bijeljina, by bulldozers of the Bosnian Serb Army (VRS)." See Helen Walasek, *Bosnia and the Destruction of Cultural Heritage* (London: Ashgate Publishing, Ltd, 2015), 37.
98. Jusuf Džafić, "Atik džamija u Bijeljini," BZK—Preporod Bijeljina, August 14, 2014, http://preporodbn.com/atik-dzamija-u-bijeljini/; Mirko Mlakar, "Vreme: Bijeljina Dynamiters; The Night the Minarets Fell," *Transitions Online*, March 22, 1993, https://tol.org/client/article/15027.html.
99. Prosecutor v. Radovan Karadžić (Judgment), IT-95-5/18-T (ICTY), 83.
100. Prosecutor v. Ratko Mladić (Prosecution Pretrial Brief), IT-09-92-PT (ICTY), February 24, 2012, 34, https://www.icty.org/x/cases/mladic/custom3/en/120224a.pdf.

168   TORTURE, HUMILIATE, KILL

operation that brought the detainees into the camp and to cleanse the territory of non-Serbs was a joint RS civilian authority/VRS/MUP RS operation, however, that needed help from every sector.

Ratko Mladić, as the head of VRS, was directly involved with the camp on several occasions. As mentioned at the beginning of the chapter, he called for its creation, and on another occasion he asked Karadžić what to do with 134 "able-bodied" Croats in the Batković and Kula camps.[101] According to some sources, Arkan's Tigers, the paramilitary group that terrorized the town at the beginning of the war, were controlled and subordinated to the Serbian MUP.[102] They were also referred to as the Serb Volunteer Guard. Arkan was the commander and was the deputy commander of the Tigers.

Arkan's Tigers, as well as other units from Serbia, were invited by SDS authorities. Biljana Plavšić, at the 22nd session of the RS Assembly in November 1992, said that she had sent letters to many people including Arkan and others willing to fight for the "Serbian cause."[103] In 1995, Karadžić attended an event in Bijeljina and inspected the Tigers, stating, "I am deeply thankful and I congratulate you, and I hope that we will meet again in peace and you will always have a place in the heart of those who you have defended." Arkan responded by saying that "we are ready if you call us and that we will be back to defend our ancient homeland, to defend our women and children, to defend the Serbian territory and our Orthodox religion."[104] Mauzer's Panthers were a paramilitary formation numbering roughly one thousand men that operated in Bijeljina, Zvornik, and Brčko.[105] They were referred to as the Serbian National Guard. Savić was a member of the SDS and the Bijeljina Crisis Committee.[106] The unit was composed of members of the SDS from Bijeljina, most of whom had been trained by Arkan in Serbia. In June 1992, they were integrated into the Eastern Bosnian Corps.[107] Mauzer was initially commander of the SAO Sem-

---

101. Prosecutor v. Ratko Mladić, 49.
102. According to witness Milorad Davidović. See Prosecutor v. Radovan Karadžić (Judgment), IT-95-5/18-T (ICTY), 89.
103. Prosecutor v. Radovan Karadžić, 231–32.
104. Prosecutor v. Radovan Karadžić, 1221.
105. Another witness, Dragomir Ljubojević, claims "that Mauzer's Panthers was a unit of the VRS and 'never a party army' and consisted of people from all areas including from Bijeljina itself and it was not formed by the SDS but by the staff of the TO of the municipality." See Prosecutor v. Radovan Karadžić, 90.
106. According to a report by Zdravko Tolimir from 1992, the SNG was formed as an "army of Bijeljina" and operated on behalf of the Crisis Committee. See Prosecutor v. Stanišić and Župljanin, IT-08-91 (ICTY), 277.
107. Prosecutor v. Radovan Karadžić (Judgment), IT-95-5/18-T (ICTY), 89–90.

berija TO and operated with the support of the Bijeljina municipal authori-ties.[108] In June he was appointed assistant chief of security intelligence affairs within the Eastern Bosnian Corps.[109]

Mirko Blagojević was president of the Serbian Radical Party (SRS) and headed a paramilitary unit called the Chetniks, which was part of the larger SRS movement headed by Serb radical politician Vojislav Šešelj. This unit had around fifty members. The chief of the Bijeljina SJB reported regularly to Mićo Stanišić on the situation in the municipality.[110] All paramilitary and other organized armed groups were tolerated by the Bosnian Serb authorities, providing they kept in line with the Crisis Committee. They operated with impunity and in coordination with the SJB. All groups that were not aligned with the Crisis Committee or the SDS, however, were told to leave. Only after these groups started attacking local Bosnian Serbs did the authorities start insisting on real control over them. In May 1992 the Presidency of the Bijeljina Assembly imposed a ban on armed units that arrived in the municipality without invitation by the legal authorities.[111]

---

108. Prosecutor v. Radovan Karadžić, 233.
109. Prosecutor v. Stanišić and Župljanin, IT-08-91 (ICTY), 277.
110. Prosecutor v. Radovan Karadžić (Judgment), IT-95-5/18-T (ICTY), 229–30.
111. Prosecutor v. Radovan Karadžić, 242–43.

CHAPTER 6

Bileća

Introduction

The small town of Bileća is in eastern Herzegovina, in the southeast corner of Bosnia and Herzegovina, bordering Montenegro, surrounded on the south by Trebinje and on the north by Gacko. In 1991, the town had a population of 13,284, of which 1,947 (14.65 percent) were Bosniaks. Bosnian Serbs numbered 10,628 (80 percent), while Bosnian Croats numbered 39 (0.29 percent), and the rest (448, or 3.37 percent) were "others."

In the kingdom of Yugoslavia, a concentration camp was formed in Bileća in 1939 to incarcerate communist activists, mainly from Belgrade University.[1] The camp was established in the old Austro-Hungarian military barracks built there in the previous century.[2] One of its most famous prisoners was future Partisan official Moše Pijade.[3] During World War II, the region of eastern Herzegovina was the scene of mass atrocities committed against the Bosniak population by the Četnik forces and also against the Serb population by the Ustaša forces.[4] One of the worst massacres was committed in 1941, when several hun-

---

1. Radoje Pajović, "O Studentskom Pokretu Beogradskog Univerziteta (1934–1941)," *Matica* 60/61 (2014/2015): 183, http://www.maticacrnogorska.me/files/60/07%20radoje%20pajovic.pdf.
2. The Austro-Hungarians built a military barracks on the location of an older Ottoman military barracks.
3. Moše Pijade was born in 1890 in Belgrade in a Jewish family. He worked as an art teacher before joining the Communist Party, because of which he ended up in Bileća camp in 1940. During World War II, he was a senior Partisan official. He later on became a high-ranking Yugoslav official until his death in 1957.
4. The sole survivor of this massacre was Hadžera Ćatović-Bijedić. None of this, however, was allowed to be mentioned during the Yugoslav period.

BILEĆA   171

dred Bosniak civilians were massacred and their bodies thrown into the Čavkarica pit.[5] After World War II, the Yugoslav army established their military barracks on the existing location and it was officially named the Moše Pijada Military Barracks. These military barracks were used for the training of reserve army officers throughout the communist era. Thus the site already had a long tradition of incarceration by the time the war broke out.

The first prisoners to be brought to Bileća were from the Dubrovnik region, captured during the JNA attack on Croatia in late 1991.[6] Several hundred prisoners were kept at this camp, where they were severely beaten and tortured, until late May 1992.[7]

On May 27, 1991, "the Assembly of the Union of Municipalities of East and Old Herzegovina" was constituted in Trebinje. This included municipalities from eastern Herzegovina: Trebinje, Gacko, Bileća, Nevesinje, Ljubinje, Kalinovik, Čajnice, and Rudo. An assembly was established and Bozidar Vučurović from Trebinje was elected president of the "Union," while Milorad Vujović from Bileća and Duško Kornjača from Čajnice were appointed vice presidents.[8] Tensions mounted still further when in late 1991 the SDS began handing out weapons to local Serbs. In January 1992, the local Bosnian Serb policemen stopped wearing the communist-style five-pointed star on their caps, indicating a further step in their separation. Then on September 12, 1992, the Serb Autonomous Area of Herzegovina was proclaimed, which included "Bileća, Cajnice, Gacko, Kalinovik, Ljubinje, Nevesinje, Rudo, Trebinje and Foca, as well as of the municipalities from this region with a Serb majority, seated in Trebinje."[9] This did not prove to be such a surprise, however, as from late September 1991, the SAO Herzegovina was already considered a separate, autonomous region. For example, a new report was published in *Javnost* about the

---

5. Tahir Pervan, *Čavkarica—vrata pakla* (Sarajevo: Zonex ex libris, 2006).
6. "Testimony by Marko Knežić," ICTY, September 17, 2003 http://www.icty.org/en/content/marko-kne%C5%BEi%C4%87. An American citizen who was serving in the Croatian army was held in a camp near Bileća witnessed the torture and death of one prisoner. United Nations Security Council, "Final Report of the United Nations Commission of Experts Established pursuant to Security Council Resolution 780 (1992)," Annex VIII: Prison Camps, l, May 27, 1994, 67, https://bit.ly/FinalRepUNExRepAnnexVIII.
7. See the judgment against Branko Ljubišić, former security commander of the POW camp in Bileća; see Tužilac v. Branko Ljubišić, K.16/00-134, (Prvostupanjska presuda, Županijski sud u Dubrovniku), September 8, 2001.
8. Smail Čekić, *The Aggression against the Republic of Bosnia and Herzegovina* (Sarajevo: Institute for the Research of Crimes against Humanity and International Law, 2005), 550.
9. Branka Magaš and Ivo Žanić, *The War in Croatia and Bosnia-Herzegovina, 1991–1995* (London: Frank Cass Publishers, 2001), 153; Čekić, *The Aggression*, 561.

172   TORTURE, HUMILIATE, KILL

establishment of a Srpska narodna čitaonica (Serbian National Reading Room), and the article ends by stating that "this meeting is expected to be the start of a truthful and fruitful cooperation between Nikšić and Bileća, Montenegro and SAO Herzegovina, respectively."[10] After the Croatian War ended with a ceasefire in January 1992, the JNA Rijeka Corps, commanded by Momčilo Perišić, was moved to Bileća. This corps was used to form the operational group of Trebinje-Bileća.

The Takeover of Bileća

With Bosniaks a clear minority in Bileća and the SDS already in power, it was not difficult for the Bosnian Serbs to take control of the municipality. The takeover of the Bileća municipality occurred in June 1992 and was conducted as a joint operation with multiple actors: the JNA, paramilitaries, and police units.[11] There was no resistance in the town, and the event passed peacefully. The peaceful nature of the takeover belies the sense of terror and fear that accompanied it however, all of which was aimed at intimidating the non-Serb population of the town. These armed units, after roaming through Bileća, went on toward Stolac.

The president of the municipality was Milorad Vujović while the head of the SJB was Goran Vujović. In May 1992, soon after the VRS was formed, Colonel Tihomir Kundačina, a former JNA officer, started to train newly mobilized Bosnian Serb recruits in the town.[12] The barracks were renamed "Bileća fighters" (*Bilećki borci*).

Bosniaks were restricted from leaving the town. In March 1992, the deputy police commander, Miomir Milošević, announced that the uniforms of the

---

10. "Uskoro Srpska narodna čitaonica," *Javnost*, September 21, 1991, 2. See Prosecutor v. Radovan Karadžić, IT-95-5/18 (ICTY), Exhibit P06212.E.

11. Prosecutor v. Momčilo Krajišnik (Judgment), IT-00-39-T (ICTY), 224–25. In several cases it is mentioned that paramilitary groups took an active role in the detention and terrorizing of Bileća's Bosniaks and Croats. In a CSB Trebinje report, however, it is stated that there were registered activities of these groups in Bileća and Trebinje and that "with the adequate steps, above all policemen from these SJBs quite successfully and in continuity prevented and disabled their aims." See Security Services Centre Trebinje, Information on activities of the members of so-called paramilitary formations on the territory of Serbian Autonomous Region of Herzegovina, Number: 01-172/92, dated August 4, 1992, ICTY no. 00741280. See Prosecutor v. Stanišić and Župljanin, IT-08-91 (ICTY), Exhibit P00161.E.

12. Colonel Tihomir Kundačina's statement in "Istorija Bilećke kasarne—II dio," *Radio Televizija Republike Srpske*, April 25, 2017 [30:00–30:30], https://www.youtube.com/watch?v=qZB30PUz_jw.

BILEĆA 173

Serb police would be worn. This was following a decision of the RS leadership to separate the Bosnia and Herzegovina police and form a Serb police force.[13] In late May, the Croatian POWs from the Dubrovnik region were transferred from the Moše Pijada Military Barracks to Morinj camp near Kotor in Montenegro.[14] A few weeks later, the first Bosniaks of Bileća were arrested and taken to the camp inside the military barracks. Other Bosniaks were detained in the Bileća police station (SJB Bileća), the Bileća prison, and the municipal youth house (Đački Dom).[15] Bosniaks were expelled from their workplaces and forbidden to travel without special permission from the Serb authorities. Ramiz Pervan, who had worked for years as the vice commander of the Territorial Defense and General People's Protection force in Bileća was relieved from his position because he refused to participate in the JNA attack on Dubrovnik in September 1991. He was assigned to a desk job until February 1992, when he was sent home and told not to return. The Bileća police commander, Miroslav Duka, ordered him to report to the police by telephone twice a day. He was arrested on June 11, 1992.[16] A few days after his arrest, the Pervan family's neighbors and longtime friends came to their house armed and evicted them without allowing them to take any of their possessions. Another Bosniak, Junuz Murguz, had a similar fate. He worked at the Energoinvest TMO-Bileća factory. In 1991, during the war in Croatia, he ignored the mobilization call and on February 18, 1992, he was fired from his job on the basis of his refusal.[17]

Within the SJB, a "special unit" or an "intervention squad" was formed, known as the Bileća volunteers (*Bilećki dobrovoljci*). It was composed of active and reserve members of the SJB, and their commander was Miroslav Duka. The purpose of this unit was, in cooperation with JNA, to take part in the "cleansing" operations of Bosniaks in Bileća. Similar units were set up in nearby towns.[18] Special unit *Bilećki dobrovoljci* was formed in April 1992 and the most high-ranking Bosnian Serb officials knew about its existence. On April 23, 1992, a telephone conversation was held between Momčilo Mandić, the deputy min-

---

13. Prosecutor v. Stanišić and Župljanin, IT-08-91 (ICTY), 293.
14. The Croatian POWs were exchanged in August 1992.
15. Prosecutor v. Momčilo Krajišnik (Judgment), IT-00-39-T (ICTY), 225–26.
16. Canada (Minister of Citizenship and Immigration) v. Rogan, 396 F.T.R. 47 (FC), August 18, 2011, 27, https://www.cbc.ca/bc/news/bc-110818-branko-rogan-federal-court-decision.pdf.
17. Prosecutor v. Stanišić and Župljanin, IT-08-91 (ICTY), 294.
18. Prosecutor v. Stanišić and Župljanin, 294. See also Tošić Čedo i Vojin Vuković, "Report on repeated monitoring of the implementation of the implementation of the order of the Ministry of Internal Affairs of the Serb Republic BiH, strictly confidential Number 10–17/92," dated August 10, 1992, ICTY no. 06492096, Exhibit 1D00649.E.

174   TORTURE, HUMILIATE, KILL

ister of interior of the Republic of Bosnia and Herzegovina and later RS minister of justice, and Zorica Sarenac, the former administrative legal advisor in MUP Mostar, who later on transferred to Trebinje to take part in the establishment of CSB Trebinje. During this conversation about personnel problems in Trebinje police, Mandić and Zorica mentioned Duka in their conversation, stating that he should be appointed commander of the special unit, adding, "I know that he's an exceptional chap."[19]

In early June 1992, a high-level SDS meeting was held in Bileća and attended by Karadžić, Mladić, and Plavšić.[20] During the meeting, Karadžić stated that all Bosniaks who met the "Serbian criteria" were to be arrested, that is, all people who were considered a security threat. On June 10, a number of local Serbs protested in front of the municipality building chanting "Kill the Muslims." That same day, military units entered Bileća from Gacko and started shooting at and terrorizing the town. Bosniaks were arrested by members of the regular and reserve police. Colonel Grubac, commander of the Herzegovina Corps, reported on June 11 to the VRS Main Staff that an action to seize illegal weapons had been concluded.[21] Historian Christian A. Nielsen, in his expert report on Bileća, cited this VRS report:

> According to this report, "on 10 June 1992, the organs of SUP [i.e. SJB] Bileća carried out an action of confiscation of weaponry from persons who possess them illegally. On this occasion, a large number of persons were detained, of whom 41 were placed in the Barracks." The report went on to criticize the authorities in Bileća for not adhering to a previously reached agreement by which the military would hold "approximately 15 persons for 48 hours." If no further appropriate instructions were received from the local authorities, the detainees would be removed from the barracks. The report concluded that "the manner of carrying out this action has had a negative effect on the largest part of the inhabitants of Bileća, above all on interethnic relations.[22]

---

19. Intercepted telephone conversation held on 23 April 1992 between Momcilo Mandic and Traparic, and between Momcilo Mandic and Zorica, 23 April 1992, Prosecutor v. Karadžić, (IT-95-5/18), Exhibit no. P05701.E.
20. Prosecutor v. Stanišić and Župljanin, IT-08-91 (ICTY), 295.
21. Prosecutor v. Stanišić and Župljanin, 295.
22. Christian Axboe Nielsen, "Expert's Report: Report on the Events in Bileća Municipality, Bosnia Herzegovina, From November 1990 Until the End of 1992, With a Focus on the Role of Police and Reserve Police in Those Events," Crimes Against Humanity and War Crimes Section of the Department of Justice (Canada: May 2009), 22.

As the arrests started, Bosniak families were expelled from their homes, which were then taken over by local Serbs or by Serb refugees from Mostar, Stolac, and Čapljina. Other houses were just burned to the ground. Bosniak civilians, women, and children were deported by buses to Montenegro. The deportations were organized by the local Serb authorities in cooperation with the police.[23] According to a report by the Trebinje CSB, the "massive moving of Muslims" from Gacko, Nevesinje, Bileća, and Ljubinja was caused by the disarmament of "extreme Muslims."[24] The report also mentions an interesting fact: "In Trebinje 700 Muslims responded to mobilization or after arrest were sent to the front, and their families stay in their place of residence." This relatively high number of Bosniaks who stayed behind and were members of VRS was rare in eastern Herzegovina.[25]

Bileća, along with other towns in the region—Nevesinje, Gacko, Kalinovik—experienced a brutal campaign of mass atrocities. In these towns, cooperation with the perpetrators did not exist. Trebinje is important, however, as was the seat of the CSB for the region. The attacks on and detention of Bosniaks in Bileća should be viewed in a regional context, not as an isolated case but as part of a larger plan, of which the Trebinje CSB was the heart:

> The element of a widespread attack clearly arises from the fact that the critical events took place in the wider area of eastern Herzegovina where numerous crimes were perpetrated, resulting in a huge number of direct and indirect victims, while the element of being systematic reflects in an almost identical manner of carrying out the attack in each of the four municipalities, that is, according to pre-established and routine pattern, starting from the municipality of Gacko and continuing in Bileća, Nevesinje, and Kalinovik.[26]

---

23. Prosecutor v. Stanišić and Župljanin, IT-08-91 (ICTY), 296.

24. "Assessment of the political and security situation in the territory of Trebinje CSB," dated August 19, 1992, 3, P162, ICTY No. 00749651. See Prosecutor v. Stanišić and Župljanin, IT-08-91 (ICTY), Exhibit P00162.E.

25. This is similar to the case of some parts of Bijeljina. There might be two possible reasons for this: first, a prearranged deal between the local Bosniak and Serb leaders and second, many believed that if they cooperated and served in the VRS, their property and lives would not be endangered. As in Bijeljina, however, the situation changed dramatically for them, and in January 1993 they left Trebinje en masse. See also Helsinki Watch/HRW, *War Crimes in Bosnia and Herzegovina, Volume II* (New York: 1993), 382–91.

26. Tužilaštvo Bosne i Hercegovine v. Krsto Savić (First Instance Verdict), X-KR-07/400 (Sud Bosne i Hercegovine), March 24, 2009, 40–41, http://www.sudbih.gov.ba/predmet/2526/show.

176 TORTURE, HUMILIATE, KILL

The crimes committed in Bileća were not as brutal as those in Gacko or Nevesinje, but the preplanned detention and collective traumatization was still executed in the most successful way.[27] Even though the population of Bosniaks in Bileća was less significant, it was still larger than what the Bosnian Serb leadership wanted.

Moše Pijade Military Barracks

The detention centers in Bileća served as place of short-term incarceration for Bosniak and Croat civilians.[28] Often, after being confined in Bileća, the detainees would be transferred to other camps or exchanged. As will be shown in the following detailed accounts, the Bileća detention centers were also used for incarceration of Bosniaks from Kalinovik, Gacko, Nevesinje, Foča, and Trebinje. For this purpose, four detention camps were established in Bileća, with the Moše Pijade Military Barracks being the largest.

The Moše Pijade Military Barracks, also known as the Reservist Officers' School, was used as a concentration camp to incarcerate a few hundred detainees during the period from June to December 1992.[29] Under the control of the VRS 7th Battalion of the military police, detainees were brought from the town and surrounding villages and also from other concentration camps and detention facilities. Moše Pijade Military Barracks was an old JNA military base and had a fortified structure including a concrete wall around it. The base was under the control of the VRS, who used parts of it as the concentration camp, while the rest of the base was used to train soldiers and officers of the VRS. Detainees were interrogated, beaten, and tortured regularly. Detainee A-1 stated, "They mistreated and hit us every day as if there was a schedule, an agenda for it. Whoever was able to approach the room would enter it."[30]

On June 11, 1992, around sixty Bosniak and Croat men were detained throughout Bileća and brought to Moše Pijade Military Barracks. Ramiz Per-

---

27. "[L]oss of employment, the Muslim of Bileća also faced restrictions on their travel and the destruction or confiscation of their homes." See Canada v. Rogan, 396 F.T.R. 47 (FC), 100.
28. The CSB Trebinje would send captured civilians to this camp from Nevesinje and Gacko. See Savić, Appeals Judgment, p. 8–10. Tužilaštvo BiH v Krsto Savić (Second Instance Verdict), X-KRŽ-07/400 (Sud Bosne i Hercegovine), April 11, 2011, 8–10. http://www.sudbih.gov.ba/predmet/2526/show.
29. The interesting history of this military base is explained in the introduction of this chapter.
30. Marija Taušan, "Ex-Prisoner Recalls Regular Beatings in Bileca," *Detektor*, August 16, 2016, http://detektor.ba/en/ex-prisoner-recalls-regular-beatings-in-bileca/.

BILEĆA   177

van was one of the men arrested that day. At the barracks he encountered a Serb he knew, Deputy Lieutenant Branko Šegrt. Pervan asked Šegrt why he had been arrested, and Šegrt "probably felt embarrassed at that moment because we were friends. . . . He didn't look into my eyes. He turned his head and he said; 'You are arrested only because you are a Muslim.'"[31]

Detainees were interrogated about political activities and arms possession. Torture using electric shocks was a favorite method. In one instance, a Croat detainee from Stolac, Marinko Pažin, recalled, "A soldier comes and orders us to keep our heads down and arms behind our backs. They hit you twice, three times and you fall. They electrocuted us—[with] electric batons and they used fists and kicked us."[32] He also added that on one occasion "he was once taken to another room where he saw a naked woman and that he was ordered to rape her. After refusing, he was beaten. Later he learned the woman was mentally ill." One detainee, Bajro Miljanović, recalled how his brother was denied medical care and not given water and sugar although he was a diabetic, soon after which he was killed.[33]

In mid-June, around thirty Bosniak and Croat men were brought from Sjeverni logor military barracks in Mostar. As they arrived in Bileća, they were beaten with bats. They were later beaten with electric batons. One detainee, Mile Azinović, was forced to swallow salt. He was given an injection into his chest and placed in solitary confinement.[34] On 16 July 1992 another group of Bosniak men was transferred from Nevesinje. As they arrived in Bileća that night, they were met in front of the military barracks by shouting, armed men. The beatings started immediately, a kind of welcome for the newcomers. They were then placed up against the wall—hands up and legs spread—and beaten still further. One detainee counted fifty strikes to his head.[35]

A group of Bosniak detainees from Gacko were also held in this camp. The group of around 140 Bosniak men were transferred from two detention facilities in Gacko, the SJB, and Samački hotel. When they arrived they were forced to walk between two rows of guards who beat them with batons and sticks. The

---

31. Canada v. Rogan, 396 F.T.R. 47 (FC), 31.
32. "Witness Recalls Electric Shock Torture in Bileca," *Detektor*, May 24, 2016, https://detektor.ba/2016/05/24/witness-recalls-electric-shock-torture-in-bileca/?lang=en.
33. Albina Sorguč, "Bošnjak i ostali: Optuženi Mavrak najviše tukao," *Detektor*, September 9, 2017, http://detektor.ba/bosnjak-i-ostali-optuzeni-mavrak-najvise-tukao/.
34. Džana Brkanić, "Bošnjak i ostali: Strah i trepet za zatvorenike," *Detektor*, September 5, 2017, http://detektor.ba/bosnjak-i-ostali-strah-i-trepet-za-zatvorenike/.
35. Brkanić, "Bošnjak i ostali: Strah i trepet za zatvorenike."

Gacko group was placed into the basement of the military barracks, where some 200 detainees were already being kept. They were not allowed to use the toilet nor were they given food for the next three days. The beatings and torture continued for days. At least four detainees from Gacko were killed inside the camp.

In June 1992, around fifty Bosniak men were transferred from Miladin Radojević school in Kalinovik to the Moše Pijade barracks, where they were confined and mistreated. After spending twenty days in Bileća they were returned to Kalinovik, where they spent the night in the aforementioned school. Finally they were transferred to KPD Foča, where most of the men were killed.[36] This concentration camp was visited on at least one occasion by Serb authorities including Goran Vujović, the Bileća police chief, and Milorad Vučerević, president of SAO Herzegovina.[37] At one point in late July 1992, the Gacko police authorities wrote to the VRS Herzegovina Corps, asking that the detainees from Gacko not be released because it would have a "very negative repercussion in the population, and we cannot foresee the consequences of it."[38] One report noted the arrival of a Belgrade TV crew to the camp:

> On August 10, the prisoners were taken upstairs for an interview conducted by Radivoje Gutic from the Bosnian Serbian News Agency (SRNA) and FNU Vulacic from Belgrade Television, in the presence of Red Cross officials. Days prior to this interview, the prisoners were allowed for the first time to take a shower and shave. After the interview was over, the prisoners were taken to the interrogation and torture room and were tortured for telling the truth about the conditions and treatment received at the camp. These tortures continued until August 18 when 378 prisoners from the camp were exchanged in Stolac, Bosnia."[39]

---

36. Tužilaštvo Bosne i Hercegovine v. Ratko Bundalo i dr. (First Instance Judgment), X-KR-07/419 (Sud Bosne i Hercegovine), December 21, 2009, 2, http://www.sudbih.gov.ba/predmet/3593/show.
37. Prosecutor v. Momčilo Krajišnik (Judgment), IT-00-39-T (ICTY), 225.
38. Nielsen, "Expert's Report: Report on the Events in Bileća," 23.
39. "(Eighth Report of War Crimes in the Former Yugoslavia) Supplemental United States Submission of Information to The United Nations Security Council in Accordance with Paragraph 5 of Resolution 771 (1992) and Paragraph 1 of Resolution 780 (1992)," June 16, 1993, https://phdn.org/archives/ www.ess.uwe.ac.uk/documents/sdrpt8a.htm. This was around seventy square meters in area.

SJB Bileća

The police station (SJB) was in the center of town. The building was "approximately 30 feet by 25 or 26 feet, or some 750 to 780 square feet in area."[40] It was divided into a number of rooms, which were divided by a corridor. Detainees were confined in several of these rooms, while the rest were used for storage and other purposes. In one of the rooms, nineteen detainees were kept in a room that was a mere three by four meters. A group of other detainees were kept in a coal bin and had to lay down wooden boards over it to try and sleep. On June 10, six Bosniak men were arrested near the village of Rebići by two armed Serb soldiers who took them to the SJB in Bileća. In the SJB, there were already fifteen other Bosniak detainees. One detainee, A-1, was arrested in his village of Đeće, where Miroslav Duka forced him to burn his house and property, after which he was taken to SJB. Over the next seven days, there were between thirty and forty men detained in two rooms. They were beaten and threatened on a daily basis. They were not fed, but a few times their wives were allowed to bring them food. After seven days, some of the detainees were transferred to the Đački dom detention facility. One of the detainees—Ferhat Avdić—was beaten to death by four Serb policemen.[41]

With time, the SJB became overcrowded, holding an estimated 150 detainees. Due to the lack of space, the detainees slept "in a head-to-toe line in the rooms available to them, including the corridor."[42] There were no beds, mattresses, blankets, or pillows in this detention facility. The only things they could use were those things provided by their families. There was no bathing facilities and there was only one toilet, "a latrine-style squat toilet and a sink." The detainees were not allowed to change clothes, so for several months after they were confined most of them wore the same clothes they had been arrested in. They were not given any soap, shampoo, toothpaste, or any other hygienic products. The detainees were not allowed to leave the SJB, which was particularly difficult during the summer when temperatures rose to 40C, which made the overcrowded conditions unbearable for the detainees in the SJB.[43]

On June 10, 1992, several dozen Bosniak men were arrested in the village of

---

40. Canada v. Rogan, 396 F.T.R. 47 (FC), 38.
41. Tužilaštvo BiH v. Goran Vujović i dr. (First Instance Judgment), S1 1 K 014293 13 KrI (Sud Bosne i Herzegovine), July 8, 2016, 9, http://www.sudbih.gov.ba/predmet/3198/show.
42. Canada v. Rogan, 396 F.T.R. 47 (FC), 39.
43. Canada v. Rogan, 39–40.

Orahovice and brought to SJB. There Duka ordered one detainee, Ismet Bajramović, to make a list of men from his village who were in hiding and their location. Almost the entire group was interrogated and beaten and confined at SJB for several days and then transferred to another camp.[44] One detainee was transferred from Đački dom to SJB:

"The first night when I was brought there, my hands were tied with barbed wire, I was kicked with feet, hands and iron bars. They broke my arm and leg. I had concussion." He was then assigned to clean the toilet, in a particularly degrading and dehumanizing manner: "They forced me to clean that hole with bare hands and then to lick it."[45]

Sadik Mujačić recalled the beating he received:

One day, at around 3 or 4, a prisoner named Murguz came and said, 'Zeljko Ilic sends his greetings. He said he would come to visit you tonight,' . . . They beat me in the corridor. They broke my left arm, damaged my jaw and a nerve in my left eye. Zeljko Ilic took me out [of the cell]. They beat me in the corridor between the prison cells. Ilic kicked me with his boot and broke my arm.[46]

Mesud Bajramović testified about the interrogations:

At around 1 a.m., policeman Nedjeljko Delić told me to accompany him to the guardroom. He and Milenko Stajić questioned me about the places I'd been hiding. They asked me the same questions about my cousins and neighbors . . . At around 4 a.m., Stajic took a knife, grabbed me by my ear, and said, "Tell me or I'll cut your ear off." After that everybody started hitting me, mostly on my head. . . . They took me to an isolation cell. At 6 a.m. Stevanovic came again and took me to the guardroom. Stajic asked me the same questions again. Stevanovic took a hand bomb from a closet and stuffed it into my mouth. I pulled the grenade with my hand. Then he [Stevanović] hit me on the nape of my neck with it, making a cut on my head.[47]

---

44. Tužilaštvo Bosne i Hercegovine v. Krsto Savić (First Instance Verdict), X-KR-07/400, 48.
45. Albina Sorguč, "The Wall of Silence about Crimes in Bileca," *Detektor*, November 20, 2014, https://detektor.ba/2014/11/20/the-wall-of-silence-about-crimes-in-bileca/?lang=en.
46. Albina Sorguč, "Witness Describes Prisoner Abuse at Bileca Detention Facilities," *Detektor*, April 7, 2015, https://detektor.ba/2015/04/07/witness-describes-prisoner-abuse-at-bileca-detention-facilities/?lang=en.
47. Jasmina Đikoli, "Prosecution Witness Describes Prisoner Abuse in Bileca," *Detektor*, March 3, 2015, https://detektor.ba/2015/03/03/prosecution-witness-describes-prisoner-abuse-in-bileca/?lang=en.

In most cases in Bileća, the perpetrators knew their victims. Nedžad Bajramović was offered a ticket to freedom from his former physical education teacher: "Duka told me that I would only be released if I signed a document, which confirmed that he had treated me correctly and that I had waived [the rights to] my movable and immovable assets. . . . I highly respected Duka as a professor. We had a correct relationship."[48] Similarly, Munib Ovčina, a former professor and politician, was targeted. His former student Radomir Bojović entered the room where detainees were kept and said, "Let the professor come out." He was beaten by four policemen, including Duka. Besides Ovčina, two other detainees were also kept in the room. Duka then played a videotape and said, "Look at what Alija's fundamentalists do to Serbs; this is what we will do to you," and he cursed their Turk mothers. He then started interrogating and beating Ovčina, asking him about political decision from before the war. He asked him why the memorial to Vladimir Gaćinović had been moved;[49] why had the elementary school been named Džemal Bijedić;[50] why had his son left the JNA? Ovčina fell unconscious due to the beatings.

After fifteen days of detention, Edin Bajramović was selected and taken out by his former friend, Veso Šakotić, and brought to Duka's office. There he was interrogated and beaten. Duka told him that he would break his nose so that he would have something to remember him by.[51] Velija Mandžo was brought from Đački dom to the SJB for interrogation: "He hit me on my head with an armrest that looked like a herringbone, a hard object. I took my handkerchief in order to stop the blood, but he took it away from me. The bearded guy told me to put my hands on the table. Then the same guy who hit me on my head began hitting me on my fingers. The bearded guy told me to get up. He hit me on my stomach with his fist, so I felt like losing air."[52]

On June 10, 1992, a group of Bosniak men from Seliste village were arrested and brought to the SJB and then to Đački dom. One of the party, Enver Avdić, recalled, "A group of men arrested us. I did not know any of them. Some were

---

48. Emina Dizdarević, "Witness Describes Prisoner Beatings and Torture in Bileca," *Detektor*, March 31, 2015, https://detektor.ba/2015/03/31/witness-describes-prisoner-beatings-and-torture-in-bileca/?lang=en.

49. Vladimir Gaćinović was a Bileća-born Serb activist and member of the Mlada Bosna terror organization that operated against the Austro-Hungarian Empire.

50. Džemal Bijedić was the prime minister of the Socialist Federal Republic of Yugoslavia from 1971 to 1977.

51. Tužilaštvo BiH v. Goran Vujović i dr. (First Instance Judgment), S1 1 K 014293 13 KrI, 140.

52. Albina Sorguč, "Beaten Up in Police Station," *Detektor*, December 23, 2014, https://detektor.ba/2014/12/23/beaten-up-in-police-station/?lang=en.

dressed in plain military uniforms, others in camouflage uniforms, while two or three men had police uniforms. They took us out, one by one, during the first evening. I do not know whether it was an examination or brutal torture." Mehmed Murguz was brutally beaten that day: "Duka was talking to us, but this man interrupted him. Duka kicked him on his head. There were injuries. Later on Murguz was transferred with me to the dormitory."[53] Asim Đapo was beaten several times, usually during interrogation: "They just called on me and said that they wanted to interrogate me. . . . The room was darkened by blankets [blankets were hung over the windows]. I knew something was going to happen. I saw Miroslav Duka there. He had a gun on the table, and a baton, and he wrapped his head with a cloth. . . . I heard that he was the deputy commander or commander."[54] Unlike other camps, detainees from SJB who were badly injured due to the beatings were on a few occasions taken to the Bileća hospital for treatment. This was a rare case, but these detainees might have been important enough to be kept alive for information and especially for prisoner exchange.[55] The SJB also had a isolation cell in which specially selected detainees were placed. Detainee A-1 was one of them: "I had nothing, so help me God. Not even a bed or blanket. The room surface was 90 x 180."[56]

He also added an important note regarding Goran Vujović that suggested he had the motivation to commit mass atrocity: "Songs like 'From Trebinje to Bileca everybody will be christened, even if it is against their will' were sung. He did, so help me God, publicly say that Muslims had nothing to do in Bileca and that the land belonged to Serbs."[57] Statements from detainees on arms possessions were taken by Slavko Vučinić. He stated that "No criminal actions were present in the statements I took" and that he did not notice any signs of beatings on the detainees.[58]

---

53. Albina Sorguč, "Visible Injuries on Detainees," *Detektor*, January 20, 2015, https://detektor. ba/2015/01/20/visible-injuries-on-detainees/?lang=en.
54. Albina Sorguč, "Witness Describes Detainee Beatings at Bileca Police Station," *Detektor*, March 10, 2015, https://detektor.ba/2015/03/10/witness-describes-detainee-beatings-at-bileca-police-station/ ?lang=en.
55. Tužilaštvo BiH v. Goran Vujović i dr. (First Instance Judgment), S1 1 K 014293 13 KrI, 142.
56. Džana Brkanić, "Bosniaks Left Bileca," *Detektor*, November 4, 2014 https://detektor.ba/2014/11/04/ bosniaks-left-bileca/?lang=en.
57. Brkanić, "Bosniaks Left Bileca."
58. Albina Sorguč, "Witnesses Took Statements from Bosniak Prisoners in Bileca," *Detektor*, August 25, 2015, https://detektor.ba/2015/08/25/witnesses-took-statements-from-bosniak-prisoners-in-bileca/ ?lang=en.

Đački Dom

The Old Student Dormitory (Đački dom) was an older building comprising "five rooms, one corridor, and one toilet that had to be shared by all the prisoners."[59] There were at least eighty Bosniak detainees incarcerated inside these rooms. As one detainee recalled, "We slept on concrete floors. We only had some blankets. There were many of us . . . I didn't go out for four months, except once, when I got sick."[60] The rooms they were kept in were extremely overcrowded. One detainee, Kemal Hadžić, described his sleeping space as being "approximately 16–18 inches wide."[61] The detainees were not provided with food or water by the camp guards, but their families were allowed to bring them food once a day. Furthermore, Đački dom had only one toilet available to the detainees, a single urinal and a latrine-style toilet. It was very hot inside the building and opening the windows was prohibited. The detainees were not allowed to take a bath for the entire period they were there. Thus the "close proximity of numerous unwashed bodies added to the oppressive atmosphere."[62]

The guards were members of the reserve police force and were replaced by regular policemen in mid-July 1992. Once again, as with all the other camps, the detainees were beaten on a daily basis. On August 10, nine detainees were brought from the SJB; they were unrecognizable due to the beating inflicted on them. Detainee A-5 testified that one day when Mujo Babović returned he had been so badly beaten his face was unrecognizable. Asim Ćatović, aka 'Malovilo'was incarcerated along with his son in Đački dom. Ramiz Pervan testified how a guard, Branko Rogan, abused Asim Ćatović on multiple occasions. Pervan observed how Rogan came up to Đački dom and called out Ćatović and took him to the nearby SJB building, after which "for the next hour, we are listening to [Mr. Catovic] scream."[63] Pervan further stated:

> According to Mr. Pervan, Mr. Rogan then asked Mr. Catovic's son "Did you hear how I killed your father?" Mr. Pervan says that the son was afraid to say anything other than "Yes." Mr. Rogan then told Mr. Catovic's son that "As long

---

59. Prosecutor v. Stanišić and Župljanin, IT-08-91 (ICTY), 297.
60. Denis Džidić, "Prosecution Witnesses Say Police Commander Beat Detainee in Bileca," *Detektor*, February 10, 2015, https://detektor.ba/2015/02/10/prosecution-witnesses-say-police-commander-beat-detainee-in-bileca/?lang=en.
61. Canada v. Rogan, 396 F.T.R. 47 (FC), 41.
62. Canada v. Rogan, 43.
63. Canada v. Rogan, 54. Rogan was a member of the Bileća reserve police force.

184 TORTURE, HUMILIATE, KILL

as I am a guard, this is going to happen. This is always going to happen to him."[64]

This abuse and beating of Ćatović was carried on several times. Each time, he was returned black and bruised. On September 1, 1992, guards caught detainee ST028 trying to smuggle pages of his diary through his wife. One guard, Neđo Kuljić, took him to a room and rigged the detainee with two electric cables attached to his extremities. He then administered electric shocks using wires from a field telephone, which made the detainee lose consciousness. Kuljić revived him and gave him electric shocks two more times. Kuljić threatened him and said that next time he would "strip the skin off him" and that he wanted to "slaughter" him but had been ordered not to.[65] The practice of giving electric shocks was a favorite torture technique, used not only by Kuljić but also by two other guards—Mišo Ilić and Radomir Denda—who tortured ten other detainees using this method. The wires were attached to the detainee's genitals, earlobes, and nipples. This method of torture was used from June until December 1992.[66] A-1 described the electric shocks:

> One was turning the device, and Željko Ilić was there and he told the other man to switch to number two and in that way the electricity was stronger, and I then lost conscious, the wires were strapped above both my hands [i.e.,] my fists, it lasted for 5 to 6 minutes, after which Ilić said to switch to number 2 and then I lost consciousness. I woke up after two days when one Jovo gave me some water.[67]

A-1 also added that "In most cases I was examined by Duka. He would first hit me and say 'Do not let your blood drip down to the floor.'"[68] Ismet Bajramović had a similar experience. The perpetrator told him "to stretch my hand, I stretched and he tied them to wire pliers and switch the electricity, through my body, he is sitting down, but you cannot sit because you are afraid, your body is

---

64. Canada v. Rogan, 54.
65. Prosecutor v. Stanišić and Župljanin, IT-08-91 (ICTY), 299.
66. Tužilaštvo BiH v. Goran Vujović i dr. (First Instance Judgment), S1 1 K 014293 13 KrI, 8. In the case of Vujović et al., it was established that at least seven detainees were tortured with electric shocks.
67. Tužilaštvo BiH v. Goran Vujović i dr, 119.
68. Selma Učanbarlić, "Connected to Electricity, Beaten, Mistreated," Detektor, October 28, 2014, https://detektor.ba/2014/10/28/connected-to-electricity-beaten-mistreated/?lang=en.

shaking. He tied me by the ears and sexual organs."[69] One detainee recalled when speaking of a survivor of this torture: "When he came back, he was practically out of his mind. He was just lying for two or three days. He was practically dead."[70]

On one occasion, several gas canisters were thrown in the corridor and three rooms. The perpetrators shouted, "Damn Turks, we will slaughter you." The gas caused the detainees to "gasp, choke, vomit, and have severely irritated eyes. The next day, a detainee named Sajto Bajramović was urinating blood and having fits."[71] On October 5, 1992, a number of detainees were released and expelled from Bileća while thirty-eight others were transferred to the detention facility behind the SJB. Before the groups were released they were forced to sign a form stating that they were leaving voluntarily and could decide where they were to be deported: Serbia, Montenegro, or some other country. They also had an option to stay in Bileća. Two detainees who decided to stay in Bileća were beaten during the night until they changed their minds.[72]

Stari Zatvor Detention Center

In June 1992, a building behind the Bileća SJB known as Stari zatvor (Old prison) was transformed into a detention center. This building was built and used by the Austro-Hungarians as a prison. The center was guarded by regular and reserve policemen, and its commander was Željko Ilić, a regular policeman. There were at least ninety detainees in this center. An estimated fourteen and twenty detainees were kept in a cell 3.5 by 3.5 meters in size. They shared a toilet and sink and slept on wooden planks. Munib Čamo described his circumstances: "The conditions were horrible. We endured a huge amount of humiliation. We slept on a concrete floor. I had three fingers of space for myself. They took people away in the evening. They connected them to electricity."[73] Like other detention facilities in this town, the detainees were not given food.

---

69. Tužilaštvo BiH v. Goran Vujović i dr. (First Instance Judgment), S1 1 K 014293 13 KrI, 121.
70. Amer Jahić, "Bosnian Serb Policemen Accused of Torture in Bileca," *Detektor*, October 21, 2014, https://detektor.ba/2014/10/21/bosnian-serb-policemen-accused-of-torture-in-bileca/?lang=en.
71. Prosecutor v. Stanišić and Župljanin, IT-08-91 (ICTY), 299.
72. Prosecutor v. Stanišić and Župljanin, 300.
73. Jasmina Đikoli, "Former Prisoner Describes Abuse in Bileca Detention Camps," *Detektor*, May 12, 2015, https://detektor.ba/2015/05/12/former-prisoner-describes-abuse-in-bileca-detention-camps/?lang=en.

186 TORTURE, HUMILIATE, KILL

This building was used as an annex to the SJB. The detainees from this building were taken to the SJB for interrogation and beatings. On one occasion, similar to Đački dom, gas canisters were thrown into the detention facility, causing serious physical and mental harm to the detainees.[74] At one point a detainee, Ferhat Avdić, was called out and brought to the SJB, where he was severely beaten by Miroslav Duka and other policemen. Avdić was brought back and thrown into the detention facility, where he died. His body was taken to the hospital and the doctor there pronounced death due to natural causes. Nezir Đapo recalled the conditions inside the detention facility: "It was a real prison. It had three small rooms and a corridor. Many people were held in it, about 80, but the number kept changing. There wasn't enough room. I couldn't enter one of the cells, so I stayed on the concrete floor in the corridor."[75] On one occasion, Duka and other policemen threw in smoke bombs and started shooting through the window into the cell: "Somebody had a blanket, which was set on fire by the tear gas bomb. Later on they started shooting at us. Some people were wounded. A bullet pierced through my brother-in-law's hand. This was horrible."[76] Ramiz Pervan also witnessed the gas attack:

He fired at the window where I was [standing]. We [Pervan and the other prisoners] hid and the bullets began to ricochet. Then he took tear gas and threw it into the room. Then he fired again. Then the choking started. I ran out of the room and a bullet hit me, but it only grazed the skin. I threw myself into a storage room and hid. After a while, I heard Duka and Zeljko Ilic coming, I recognized their voices. Zeljko said, 'Let's burn the warehouse.' Duka didn't answer. Then the fire bomb was heard as well as the flames, but the cistern quickly extinguished it."[77]

The first group from this detention facility was released on October 4 and the second group on December 17, 1992.[78]

---

74. Prosecutor v. Stanišić and Župljanin, IT-08-91 (ICTY), 301.
75. Denis Džidić, "Witness Describes Inhumane Conditions and Abuse at Bileca Detention Facility," *Detektor*, April 21, 2015, https://detektor.ba/2015/04/21/witness-describes-inhumane-conditions-and-abuse-at-bileca-detention-facility/?lang=en.
76. Džidić, "Witness Describes Inhumane Conditions."
77. Denis Džidić, "Former Prisoner Describes Abuse at Hands of Duka," *Detektor*, June 30, 2015, https://detektor.ba/2015/06/30/former-prisoner-describes-abuse-at-hands-of-duka/?lang=en.
78. Prosecutor v. Stanišić and Župljanin, IT-08-91 (ICTY), 301.

Visits by ICRC and CSCE

The detention facilities were visited by the ICRC and by a CSCE delegation. The ICRC visited Đacki dom on August 18, 1992. Before the visit, nine badly beaten detainees were transferred to the hospital to be kept there so that the Red Cross would not see them.[79] They visited the SJB on the same day. One CSCE mission visited Đacki dom in September 1992. In their report, the CSCE mission mentions that there were seventy-four detainees in the Đacki dom in September 1992. All the detainees except for one were Bosniaks from Bileća and surrounding villages. The report continues: "The facility is overcrowded, there are reports about mistreatment and one prisoner appeared severely injured."[80] One of the detainees who spoke to the delegation was later beaten and a pistol was placed in his mouth.[81]

RS Government Report

Shortly after the Prijedor concentration camps were exposed to the world, causing public outrage, the RS government decided to *officially* look into the matter. The RS Ministry of Justice was instructed to set up a commission and produce a report on detention centers throughout RS and including SAO Herzegovina. The commission was established in August 1992 and was led by Slobodan Avlijaš from the Ministry of Justice and Goran Sarić from MUP RS.[82] The report noted that two "collective centers/camps" existed in Bileća, "one in the Barracks, the other in the town of Bileća on the premises of SJB Bileća and the old Students' Home." It also stated that 140 Bosniaks were detained in the SJB:

> These are persons from the territory of the municipality of Bileća who were isolated for security reasons, because the possibility of reprisal existed. These persons are detained in relatively good quarters. The berths are on the floor,

---

79. Prosecutor v. Stanišić and Župljanin, 297.
80. Report of CSCE Mission to Inspect Places of Detention in Bosnia–Hercegovina, August 29–September 4, 1992, 59. See Prosecutor v. Radoslav Brđanin (Judgment), IT-99-36-T (ICTY), Exhibit P1617/S217b, https://bit.ly/ProsvBrdaninExP1617.
81. Prosecutor v. Stanišić and Župljanin, IT-08-91 (ICTY), 299.
82. The commission was set up as a response to the "discovery" of Prijedor camps by Western journalists and international public pressure as a reaction to the reports.

188   TORTURE, HUMILIATE, KILL

[they have] joint sanitary facilities and it is light and ventilated enough. The isolated persons are fed by the families who visit them daily. We have spent some time in conversation with the aforementioned persons. Several questions have been posed to them. None of them has had any objections to the conduct of the employees who guard them. We note that there are 10 persons over 60 years of age in this group. We have suggested to the chief of the SJB that it is necessary to release them.[83]

Destruction of Mosques

The emperor's mosque in Bileća was dynamited in 1992, destroying the roof and minaret. The Orthodox Church right across it remained intact. The Avdić mosque in Plana was also completely destroyed with explosives in June 1992.[84]

Perpetrators

The establishment of concentration camps and detention facilities in Bileća was a joint VRS and MUP RS effort. The SJB and Đački dom were in control of the MUP, while the Moše Pijada Military Barracks were under VRS control. The head of the SJB was Goran Vujović, while Miroslav Duka was the commander of the police station.[85] The SJB had twenty-four employees, while the "special unit" was composed of twenty members.[86] The number of reserve policemen, however, was crucial: 219 members.[87] Nielsen in his report states, "The use of SJB Bileća as a place of detention and mistreatment of detainees could not have transpired without the direct knowledge and, at a minimum, tacit approval of

---

83. Nielsen, "Expert's Report: Report on the Events in Bileća," 24.
84. András J. Riedlmayer, "From the Ashes: The Past and Future of Bosnia's Cultural Heritage," in *Islam and Bosnia: Conflict Resolution and Foreign Policy in Multi-Ethnic States*, ed. Maya Shatzmiller (Montreal: McGill-Queens University Press, 2002), 98–135.
85. "Spisak radnika za isplatu LD za mjesec maj 1992. godine," ICTY no. 02971881. See Prosecutor v. Stanišić and Župljanin, IT-08-91 (ICTY), Exhibit P00308. In this document, Vujović is listed as "Načelnik" while Duka is "Komandir SM." SM stands for "Stanica Milicije" or police station.
86. See "Spisak radnika specijalne jedinice za isplatu LD za mjesec april 1992. godine," ICTY no. F120-1962. See Prosecutor v. Stanišić and Župljanin, IT-08-91 (ICTY), Exhibit P00305.
87. See: "Spisak rezervnog sastava milicije SJB Bileća, koji su angažovani u mjesecu julu 1992. godine," ICTY no. F120-2743. See Prosecutor v. Stanišić and Župljanin, IT-08-91 (ICTY), Exhibit P00311.

the chief and commander of SJB Bileća. This would also have been known to both active and reserve police officers employed in SJB Bileća."[88] The SJB Bileća was subordinated to the regional Trebinje CSB. Krsto Savić was the head of the Trebinje CSB and at the same time chief of the office of the minister of the interior of SAO Herzegovina until July 13, 1992, when it ceased to exist. The CSB played a large role in the planned campaign against Bosniaks civilians in the region.

In one report, Savić noted that fifty-five policemen were taking part in guarding "collection centers-camps" and that one of these "collection centers" was located in the SJB and Đački dom.[89] This means that the SJB, Stari zatvor, and Đački dom were all under the control of the police authorities, that is, Goran Vujović and Krsto Savić, while the Moše Pijade Military Barracks were under VRS control. The coordination and synchronized actions of the VRS and MUP were visible:

> It clearly follows from the testimony of a large number of witnesses who have been examined that everything had been organized by and synchronized between the army and the police. In their testimony, the witnesses have unequivocally and categorically confirmed that the non-Serbs from Nevesinje and Gacko were detained by the police and then, under police escort, transported to the Bileća camp that was under the military jurisdiction; some of the witnesses were returned to the police.[90]

Krsto Savić is considered one of the masterminds in Herzegovina of the plan to establish a state for solely Serbs, "Greater Serbia." As stated in the judgment delivered by the Court of Bosnia and Herzegovina, Savić, as

> a participant in a joint criminal enterprise undertaken by Mićo Stanišić, minister of the interior of the Serb Republic of Bosnia and Herzegovina, Radovan Grubač, commander of the Herzegovina Corps, Novica Gušić, commander of the Nevesinje Brigade, Vojin Popović, chief of the Gacko Public Security Station ("SJB"), Gojko Stajić, chief of the Nevesinje SJB, Boško Govedarica, chief of the Kalinovik SJB, and Goran Vujović, chief of the Bileća SJB, and other promi-

---

88. Nielsen, "Expert's Report: Report on the Events in Bileća," 21.
89. Tužilaštvo Bosne i Hercegovine v. Krsto Savić (First Instance Verdict), X-KR-07/400 (Sud Bosne i Hercegovine), March 24, 2009, 90.
90. Tužilaštvo Bosne i Hercegovine v. Krsto Savić, 21.

nent members of municipal leaderships of these municipalities, he acted with a discriminatory intent and the common purpose to implement the common policy designed by the Strategic Goals of the Serb People adopted on 12 May 1992 at the Assembly of the Serb R BiH, and thus conduct persecution of Bosniak and Croat civilians on ethnic and religious grounds, given that the first strategic goal the "separation from the other two national communities—separation of states" also meant a permanent removal of a fairly large number of non-Serbs from the territory of the designed state of Bosnian Serbs; with a view to implementing this purpose he planned and ordered the persecution of Bosniak and Croat population in the municipalities of Gacko, Bileća, Nevesinje and Kalinovik.[91]

---

91. Tužilaštvo Bosne i Hercegovine v. Krsto Savić, 5.

CHAPTER 7

Conclusions

Demographic Changes

Over the previous chapters, it has been clearly demonstrated that the Bosnian Serb concentration camp system sat at the heart of a genocidal campaign to rid its newly seized territory of Bosniaks and Croats. As previously explained, the concentration camps were an integral part of the cleansing campaign. The extent of the Bosnian Serbs' success in destroying and stealing Bosniak property; murder; the psychological destruction of the Bosniak 'family of mind' through rape, torture, and macabre ritual is made starkly clear in the demographic changes recorded in Višegrad, Prijedor, Bijeljina, and Bileća.

During the war, Bosniak civilians suffered a high mortality rate across RS as a result of being deliberately targeted for murder. The most famous example of this is the genocide in Srebrenica in July 1995. This book has shown, however, that the genocide of Bosniaks did not begin and end with Srebrenica. It was an ongoing program, spread across the whole territory, that ran from 1992 until 1995. Physical elimination, long and incorrectly understood to be the only component of genocide, was not the key aim of the Bosnian Serbs. Rather it was the psychological destruction of the Bosniaks that they sought along with the physical removal, either by deportation or by murder, and the destruction of all signs of Bosniak culture from their new para-state.

Just how successful were Bosnian Serbs? Statistics show that they were devastatingly successful. Comparing the prewar and postwar population census is the most simple and accurate way to understand this success. The last prewar census was conducted in 1991 and provides accurate data on the ethnic composition of municipalities in Bosnia and Herzegovina. The first postwar census was conducted much later, in 2013. While not completely inaccurate, results of this census should be taken with caution since it does not represent the true demographic profile. Because of an energetic campaign urging Bosniaks in the diaspora to register in their prewar homes as a way to increase the influence of the remaining Bosniaks politician in the RS, the data gathered shows a higher number of Bosniaks in these areas is higher than were really there. Nevertheless, the 2013 results still show that there were many fewer Bosniaks registered and living in RS than in 1991.

For this research, however, other credible sources were used, such as the OSCE voter registration in 1997 and the extensive research on this topic done by Ewa Tabeau, an ICTY expert, who testified on multiple occasions at trials for high-ranking war criminals. Her expert reports were also incredibly useful.

In the following, results from the 1991, 1997, and 2013 censuses will be given according to each town, and results of an RS population survey are also given. According to the census from 1991, Višegrad had a population of 21,199, of which Bosniaks were 13,471 (63.54 percent) and Serbs 6,743 (31.80 percent). During the 1997 general elections, the OSCE voter registration recorded a total of 9,241 Serbs and 3 Bosniaks.[1] According to the census from 2013, Višegrad had a population of 9,338 (87.5 percent) Serbs and 1,043 (9.8 percent) Bosniaks.[2] The RS authorities' figures put the number of Bosniaks at 895.[3] The 1997 voter registrations show that the Serb authorities in Višegrad were very successful in cleansing the town of Bosniaks. The number of Bosniak returnees to Višegrad has risen, but they still remain a small and insignificant minority.

Prijedor, according to the 1991 census, had a total of 112,543 inhabitants, of which 49,351 where Bosniaks, 47,581 were Serbs, 6,459 were Yugoslavs, 6,316 were Croats, and 2,836 were "others." In a 1993 survey the Republika Srpska authorities stated that 42,000 Muslims "moved out," while a 1995 survey stated that there were 3,600 Muslims residing in the Prijedor municipality, less than 5 percent.[4] According to the 1997 OSCE data, there were 397 Bosniak Muslim registered voters in Prijedor, less than 2 percent of the total. According to the

---

1. Ewa Tabeau et al., "Ethnic Composition, Internally Displaced Persons and Refugee from 47 Municipalities of Bosnia and Herzegovina, 1991 to 1997," February 3, 2009, 31. Prosecutor v. Radovan Karadžić, IT-95-5/18 (ICTY), Exhibit P04994.B
2. Federalni zavod za statistiku, "Popis 2013," http://www.statistika.ba/?show=8#link1.
3. Republički zavod za statistiku: Republika Srpska, "Rezultati Popisa 2013, Gradovi, opštine, naseljena mjesta," http://rzs.rs.ba/front/article/2369/.
4. Tabeau, "Ethnic Composition," 23.

CONCLUSIONS   193

2013 census, Prijedor had 55,895 (62.5 percent) Serbs, 29,034 (32.5 percent) Bosniaks, and 1,762 (2.0 percent) Croats. The RS authorities' figure put the number of Bosniaks at 22,303, a few thousand less than the state agency's figures. The number of Bosniaks in Prijedor is significantly higher than in other parts of the country. These figures mainly represent the area around the town of Kozarac and the west side of Sana River, locations where return of Bosniaks has been largest.

In 1991, the Bijeljina municipality had a population of 96,988 people, of which 57,389 (59.2 percent) were Serbs and 30,229 (31.2 percent) were Bosniaks. As stated in this chapter, the Serb authorities in Bijeljina had a different policy toward its Bosniak population. The policy of cleansing was not *as brutal* as it was in other municipalities. Bijeljina is also one of the rare places where there was still a *large* Bosniak population in 1997. Some of these Bosniaks pledged loyalty to RS and stayed in Bijeljina, a not insignificant number of them serving the VRS. According to the 2013 census, Bijeljina had a significant minority of Bosniaks (more than 10 percent).

In 1991, Bileća had a population of 13,284, of which 1,947 (14.65 percent) were Bosniaks and 10,628 (80 percent) were Serbs. Bileća is today an exclusively Serb town with an insignificant Bosniak population. According to the 2013 census, Bileća had a population of 10,807, of which 10,646 (98.5 percent) were Serbs and a total of 26 (0.2 percent) were Bosniaks.[5] The RS authorities' statistics are identical. These results show only a glimpse of the reality, however, which is far worse. These statistics results do not go far enough in representing the reality on the ground. In fact, the number of Muslims living in RS in 1997 was less than 4,000,[6] a fraction of the RS population, mere fragments of the rich communities that had existed there before. The lingering, invisible effects of the camps live on in the lives of the survivors, their families, and their communities.

The returnee process, guaranteed and protected under Annex 7 of the Dayton Accords, was to some extent successful in some parts of the country, and a few Bosniaks have returned permanently, most notably to Srebrenica and the Prijedor regions. Other returnee communities are considered "weekend returnees" (*vikendaši*) or "summer returnees" (*ljetni povratnici*), people who have changed their prewar home into a weekend cottage while their permanent

---

5. Federalni zavod za statistiku, "Popis 2013."
6. United States Committee for Refugees and Immigrants, "U.S. Committee for Refugees World Refugee Survey 1998—Bosnia and Herzegovina," accessed January 1, 2021, https://www.refworld.org/docid/3ae6a8ab10.html.

home is in the predominantly Bosniak and Bosnian Croat entity known as the Federation of Bosnia and Herzegovina (FBiH) Most are registered as living in RS out of spite, or for certain benefits. In Kozarac near Prijedor, where the cleansing process was most gruesome, many former residents rebuilt their homes to spite those who expelled them. These houses are known as "houses of spite" (*inat kuće*).

A counterargument that can be made against this presentation of demographic changes is that it does not prove the results of the cleansing projects. Demographic changes, after all, occur in each and every war, and also for other reasons. But the research in the towns shows that the Bosniak and Croat communities were decimated. One conclusion that can be drawn from this is that the larger the Bosniak population, the more intense and brutal the cleansing campaign was. Another connected conclusion is that the more intense the cleansing process was and the more brutal the crimes were, the fewer number of Bosniaks and Croats opted to return to their prewar homes, and vice versa.

Camp Comparisons and Similarities

The Bosnian Serb camps resembled the first Nazi regime camps set up in 1933, set up in makeshift, temporary locations. The RS authorities picked existing facilities and converted them into camps. Public institutions such as schools and fire stations were transformed into concentration camps. Schools were popular due to their central position in towns, with large sports halls and a fenced ground making them more convenient. Their purpose and function was changed from an educational institution into a killing site and collective traumatization center.

These facilities were used for the two types of detention facility that emerged in the Bosnia and Herzegovina context: concentration/detention camps and detention facilities. The main difference between the two is in the command structure: the camps had a clear separation of power while the detention facilities did not. Camps such as Omarska, Manjača, or Batković had a clear command structure, documentation related to the establishment of the camps, and other elements related to the functioning of an ad hoc institution. They were also formed to last longer. Detention facilities were existing institutions that were temporarily converted into detention sites. They had no clear command structure and were usually run by an existing armed entity such as the police,

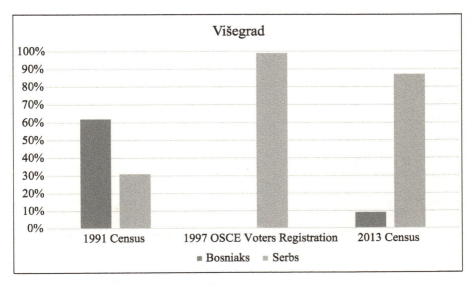

Figure 2. Ethnic Composition of Višegrad 1991–2013.

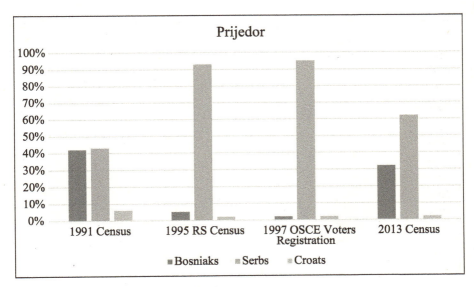

Figure 3. Ethnic Composition of Prijedor 1991–2013.

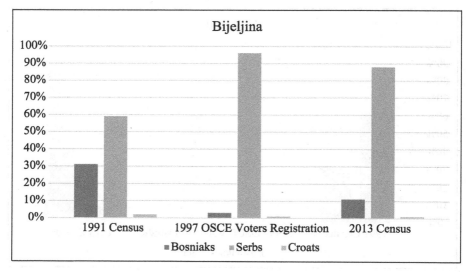

Figure 4. Ethnic Composition of Bijeljina 1991–2013.

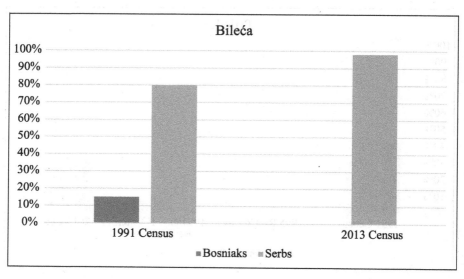

Figure 5. Ethnic Composition of Bileća 1991–2013.

CONCLUSIONS 197

military, or paramilitary group. The SJB in Bileća or the fire station in Višegrad are examples of detention facilities. There are no decisions recorded that established such facilities, nor was there a clear command structure assigned to them. A third category is locations run by private citizens holding their own private prisoners; these can be categorized as private prisons, a term already used by certain media outlets.

As can be seen throughout the previous chapters, a range of practices were devised in each location to collectively traumatize non-Serbs. The camps were organized in such a way as to permanently inflict severe psychological, transgenerational trauma, thus they were indeed an integral part of the entire cleansing project.

The events that took place in Višegrad are an example of one the most brutal campaigns of ethnoreligious cleansing. The municipality was not part of any Serb autonomous regions, since it had a larger Bosniak population. The genocidal campaign of ethnic cleansing was quick and extreme, expelling the Bosniak population over the course of two and a half months.

Looking closely at the detention sites in Višegrad, a difference between them can be seen. There were several smaller detention camps in which the Bosniaks were incarcerated. These camps were small and not well-organized. There was no clear command structure nor are any documents available showing their establishment or chain of command. Unlike the rest of the Bosnian Serb camps, they were not divided by gender except for one camp: Vilina Vlas, which was solely used for raping women and girls. A specific aspect of this traumatization were the public theatrical executions. The Hasan Veletovac School is a textbook example of collective traumatization. One incident, a brutal murder, was remembered by everybody incarcerated inside the school. On the night of June 28, 1992, an elderly man, Ibro Šabanović, was taken out of the school hall and his throat was slit. Then his severed head was thrown among the detained people.

This event has an important meaning. First, St. Vitus Day or Vidovdan, is an important day in the Serb Orthodox calendar. On this date in 1389, the Battle of Kosovo occurred, in which the Serbian Army was defeated by the Ottomans. As Steven Mock states, "at each commemoration, priests and politicians would exhort the people to avenge Kosovo by unifying the divided territory of Serbia." Second, the ceremonial and public execution had was intended to demonstrate power. In this case, the public decapitation of Ibro Šabanović not only had the purpose of showing the power of the new law in town, but also to collectively traumatize the Bosniak detainees. Former detainees remember to this day the severed head being tossed into the hall where the detainees were kept.

Prijedor is an example of the most well-planned and coordinated camp system in Serb-held territories. Unlike Višegrad, Prijedor had three main camps: Omarska, Keraterm, and Trnopolje. These were three large, well-organized camps that incarcerated large numbers of non-Serbs. They had a clear authority and chain of command. Omarska and Keraterm were camps where males were kept, while Trnopolje was a mixed camp largely made up of women and children. Another specific element related to Prijedor is the direct relation between camps and mass graves, which is highly important and shows that the crimes were coordinated with multiple actors.

Similar to Višegrad and the beheading of Ibro Šabanović, another atrocity that is inscribed into the collective memory of detainees was committed in Prijedor: the burning alive of detainees in Omarska camp for St. Peter's Day or Petrovdan on July 12, 1992. This was another crime with an ethnoreligious element. A huge bonfire composed mostly of tires was set ablaze in front of the infamous white house in Omarska camp. On this occasion, the guards selected a number of detainees and beat them with sticks, knives, and batons while forcing them to walk around the burning fire. They were then burned alive. The ceremonial and public murder of these detainees is important to underline. This ceremony had three actors: the perpetrators (the guards), the victims, and, most importantly, the audience. The effect on the audience was what mattered and it forever traumatized them: "I remember that, and I'll remember it for the rest of my life, the cries of women who were outside or in the first room. I'll never forget their cries and screams. Then I smelt the stench of burning meat."

While Prijedor and Višegrad rank high on the scale of camp brutality, the camps in the other two towns in Bijeljina and Bileća were not as lethal as those in Omarska or Keraterm. Not to understate the suffering of detainees in Bijeljina and Bileća compared to Omarska or Vilina Vlas, the camps in Bileća and Bijeljina were slightly less brutal places. The Batković camp in Bijeljina, for example, had a different purpose from the other camps. A military-run camp, it was used as place of detention, transit, and labor. It had mainly male detainees, although in the early stages it incarcerated a large number of women and children cleansed from surrounding villages. Bijeljina, until 1994, still had a Bosniak minority living in the town. The local authorities used different methods of cleansing their territory, such as involuntary religious conversions. Bijeljina is actually an example of a blitzkrieg cleansing operation in which the collective traumatization was the April 1 attack by Arkan's Tigers. Also, Bijeljina is one of the locations in Republika Srpska where there was a significant cooperation of the ghettoized Bosniaks and the authorities, in the sense that Bosniaks who stayed behind pledged loyalty to RS and some were even mobilized to fight in the VRS. Also, as Manojlović stated, the Crisis Committee in 1992 decided to let 10 percent of Bosniaks to live in Bijeljina. In 1994 this was lowered to 2 percent and it corresponds to the 1997 OSCE voter registration figures.

Bileća differs from other towns since the main targeted group within the camps was non-Serb males. The female members of the group were either able to live under curfew or were already deported. The mortality rate of camp detainees in Bileća was low, but the brutality of guards was much higher than in Batković, for example. Detainees were kept in camps in Bileća for a longer time period than in Višegrad. Also, Bileća was geographically isolated, which made it more difficult for foreign journalists or observers to visit. This of course allowed the guards and local authorities to do what they wanted. Also, the camps in Bileća were divided into three locations with their own guards and a smaller number of detainees, which made it possible for the guards to focus on each and every detainee. They were not caught up in the masses of detainees like in Omarska or Trnopolje. Thus guards in Bileća came up with new methods of torture and started using electric shocks and tear gas. In addition to this, unlike other cases, Bileća was majority Bosnian Serb, with Serbs making up 80 percent of the population.

The main distinction between the camps is the source of authority, who established the camps. The division is made between the camps formed by MUP RS and those formed by the VRS. The difference between the police or army is important since the military-operated camps were better organized, less brutal, and had more paper trails. Camps such as Manjača, the Moše Pijada Military Barracks, or the Batković camps show a better-organized and clear command structure. The MUP-run camps such as Omarska, SJB Bileća, Đački dom, or SJB Višegrad were poorly organized and more brutal. Except for Omarska, the other locations had no clear command structure or camp commandant. The main conclusion when comparing the MUP- and VRS-run camps is that the MUP camps were more brutal, with more torture and sexual abuse. This is further supported by the facts laid out in the previous chapters, which show that the largest number of convicted direct perpetrators of atrocities committed within the camps were active or reserve police officers.

Another distinction between the camps is that the scope of people detained differed throughout municipalities, ranging from widespread incarceration of almost the entire population, such as in the case of Prijedor, to detention of only males, such as in the case of Bileća. This can be explained by the size of the non-Serb populations in these municipalities: In Prijedor, the Bosniaks and Croats made up a majority of the population, while in Bileća they were a small minority. The perpetrators perceived the targeted group as a larger threat if they were larger in size.

Patterns of Genocide: Ethnic Cleansing and Collective Trauma

Michael Mann states that homogeneous nation-states in Europe "mostly resulted from cleansing of relatively mild types."[7] The establishment of RS, however, is an example of a religiously legitimized, violent, severe, genocidal form of ethnic cleansing. While Bosnian Serbs did not succeed in establishing the unification of Republika Srpska and the Republic of Serbia, they did succeed in fulfilling the key elements of the "Six Strategic Goals of the Serbian People" in establishing de facto "state borders separating the Serbian people from the other two ethnic communities." The cleansing process, which rested partially on murder but most heavily on the collective traumatization in camps, was successful in essentially fulfilling the plans set out in May 1992. The RS remains in Bosnia and Herzegovina, and it remains almost empty of Bosniaks.

In order to ethnically cleanse the territory, the Bosnian Serbs created the camps to be places of collective trauma. The primary aspects of the collective traumatization in these camps was torture, sexual abuse, humiliation, and killings. These were key crimes undertaken in order to inflict pain on a large mass of people. Since the crimes were committed and organized by members of the local community, the victims knew the perpetrators, making the crimes much more personal.

This collective traumatization was perfected by the Bosnian Serb perpetrators as the purpose for their concentration camps. The perpetrators were able, in a short time, to collectively traumatize a large population of Bosniaks and Croats to such an extent that they would leave the RS broken, never having the

---

7. Michael Mann, *The Dark Side of Democracy: Explaining Ethnic Cleansing* (Cambridge: Cambridge University Press, 2005), 61.

CONCLUSIONS   201

will to return to their homes. In this way, RS was successful in establishing a new Bosnian Serb homogeneous nation-state, founded on genocide, at the end of the twentieth century.

While there are variations in the various camps' establishment and management, when examining their operational behavior, patterns emerge that point to a certain unity of purpose vis-à-vis Bosniaks.

The first commonality was the separation of families and then genders. This was the first initial shock intended by the perpetrators. In most cases, the men were kept in separate camps or compartments from the women. Omarska and Keraterm were for male detainees while Trnopolje was for mainly women and children.

A second pattern that emerged was torture and humiliation. Across the camp system, beatings, murders, and rapes were conducted by various camps' guards and even more by visitors: opportunistic perpetrators, individuals, ordinary citizens, civilians, members of police and military units who entered camps to sadistically beat or kill. In Omarska, just like in Uzamnica, anyone could enter and beat detainees. Perpetrators showed up to take revenge or to settle scores from the past. In the case of the Batković camp, local Serb farmers took advantage of free forced labor, using detainees to work on their farms.

Beatings with different weapons and instruments were a regular occurrence in all the camps. Detainees in Omarska, Batković, and Uzamnica were forced to sing Serb nationalist songs and raise the three-finger salute. Norman M. Naimark noted that "ethnic cleansing is not just about attack, violence and expulsion; in almost every case it also includes punishment. Those who are driven off are punished for their existence, for the very need to expel them."[8] Detainees went through a variety of disciplinary methods, mainly humiliation and beatings. The *hygienic abuse* was most remembered by detainees. They were not allowed to bathe; use of the toilet was limited; they wore the same clothes in which they were brought into the camp, where some stayed for months. Such circumstances made the detainees feel dehumanized. They were forced to adopt to "childlike behavior"; adults had to ask for permission to use the toilet. Another author, Basić, noticed how humiliation rituals were intended to morally exhaust, leading to "a shift in an inmate's moral career."[9] A clear example of this is the Crisis Committee decision in Bijeljina: "in the third phase, wealthy

---

8.   Quoted in Edward Weisband, *The Macabresque* (New York: Oxford University Press, 2017), 330.
9.   Goran Basic, "Concentration Camp Rituals: Narratives of Former Bosnian Detainees," *Humanity and Society* 41, no. 1 (December 23, 2015): 73–94, https://doi.org/10.1177/0160597615621593.

and intellectual Bosnian Muslims were to be targeted for humiliation by assigning them to menial tasks such as sweeping the streets."

Rape and sexual abuse are other patterns that emerge. Women in camps like Omarska, Trnopolje, the Višegrad fire station, and Vilina Vlas were raped and sexually abused by the perpetrators. It was not just a show of force or power but rather also a sort of punishment. Keith Doubt states in his book that the role of sexual abuse and rape is to sever the foundations of a community's care and trust among each other; "such bonds are what hold communities and families together. The premeditated and methodic use of rape to attack and destroy the foundations of family is evil."[10]

The rape and sexual abuse of males, a topic that is still taboo in Bosnia's society as well as in academia, was also deliberately inflicted with the intent to destroy both the individual men and the family foundation. There were two parts to this atrocity: the forcing of detainees to commit sexual acts on each other and the sexual abuse and rape of detainees by the perpetrators themselves.

Weisband calls the camps in Bosnia "shame-camps." He states that collective violence perpetrated by the Serbs far exceeded the presumed requirements of ethnic cleansing and that it was in done in a *particular way*: "Serb forces adopted distinct tendencies to congregate Bosniak men together, to congregate Bosniak women together, each into demarcated and separated geographical areas, the former primarily for purposes of brutal beating and eventual murder, the latter primarily for purposes of mass rape."[11] Punishment was a key segment of the cleansing process. It was not enough just to expel the targeted group but rather the aim was to punish them permanently.

The brutality and sadistic conduct of perpetrators that emerges so powerfully in the survivors' court testimonies was to be found in all camps. Often the crimes had an ethnoreligious connotation and motivation. A clear example is the ceremonial theatrical murder of several detainees for Petrovdan (St. Peter's Day) in Omarska, which was viewed as a sacred act by the perpetrators. Micheal Sells makes a brilliant explanation of the relation between religion, mythology, and genocide. Bosniaks, as Slavic Muslims, were regarded as enemies because they were considered "betrayers of the faith" or Christ-killers, people who

---

10. Keith Doubt, "Scapegoating and the Simulation of Mechanical Solidarity in Former Yugoslavia: 'Ethnic Cleansing' and the Serbian Orthodox Church," *Humanity & Society* 31, no. 1 (2007), 37. https://doi.org/10.1177/016059760703100105.

11. Weisband, *The Macabresque*, 338.

betrayed Christianity and converted to Islam.[12] For this historical sin they needed to be punished. The labels imposed on the victims and detainees by the perpetrators fit this explanation: *turci* (Turks) or *balija* (a derogatory term for Bosnian Muslims). The use of these labels was common not only by the direct perpetrators but also by the Bosnian Serb political, military, and police structure. This shows that there was an overall mainstream ideology backed by popular support that believed that the atrocities committed were justified and necessary.

Another pattern is the destruction of Bosniak cultural religious heritage in all of the towns mentioned. With the Bosniaks either dead, corralled into camps waiting to die, or "cleansed" from the land already, the Bosnian Serbs set about removing all physical signs of their ever having existed. This pattern was common everywhere the Bosnian Serbs occupied.

Macro- and Micro-Level Perpetrators

One of the strongest commonalities lies in the fact that the bodies behind the establishment, filling, and running of the camps, in all four towns, were the municipal Crisis Committees, who acted as the meso-level authorities who coordinated the establishment and functioning of the camps. In Prijedor, the Crisis Committee made the decision to establish the Omarska and Keraterm camps. In Bijeljina, the Crisis Committee liaised with the VRS in establishment of the Batković camp, setting up a commission to find the most suitable location for the camp. They were also responsible for filling it with Bosniaks. In the cases of Višegrad and Bileća, the Crisis Committee documentation is unavailable since it was lost in the late 1990s after the ICTY started its investigations. The establishment of most of these camps had a legal basis, or a legal document issued by a quasi-legal body. The subsequent detention of large masses of people, however, did not have any legal basis.

These crimes were planned and executed by the municipal Crisis Committees, who were all subordinate to Karadžić, who was responsible for the setting of the overall targets laid out within the Six Strategic Goals. Because of this, the extent and nature of the crimes committed were not identical, but the patterns were. The extent of brutality and murder visited on the targeted group was con-

---

12. Michael A. Sells, *The Bridge Betrayed* (Berkeley: University of California Press, 1999), 37.

nected with several factors: (a) The percentage of the population of Bosniaks in the municipality was significant. If the population was half or a majority Bosniak, the crimes were larger and more brutal than in the case of a municipality with a Bosniak minority. This is visible in eastern Bosnia and the Krajina region, where Bosniaks were a majority. (b) The municipalities located in regions related to the Six Strategic Goals of the Serb People had a higher rate of crimes committed. This is most evident in the Drina River valley in relation to the Third Strategic Goal of "Eliminating Drina as the border between Serb people." The Six Strategic Goals, along with the RS political and military directives that followed, were crucial in defining the situation on the terrain. The conquering of geographical and territorial aims defined by the Six Strategic Goals resulted in greater atrocities than those that were not. (c) The personality of the Serb authorities was important. In some cases, the Serb authorities opted for a less brutal campaign with the aim of achieving the same results. This is evident in cases such as Bileća and Bijeljina.

In a majority of cases, the perpetrators were *ordinary men*. They were from the local communities and they knew the victims and they were known to the victims. By looking at the formal membership of the perpetrators in these chapters, it can be determined that most of the perpetrators were members either of the regular police force or the reserve police force (i.e., MUP RS). This is an important connection because it shows that the perpetrators were members of a fundamental institution with a clear command structure.

In other words, this means that even though there was not a unified level and degree of murder and brutality, the policy of ethnic cleansing via the infliction of collective trauma existed, but its implementation varied to a small extent. The execution of the ethnoreligious cleansing coordinated between the micro and meso level and was improvised by local governments, thus the actions differed in certain areas.

Postwar Reality and Camp Memory

The 1995 Dayton Peace Accords constituted Bosnia and Herzegovina into two entities: the Federation of Bosnia and Herzegovina and Republika Srpska. The borders of these entities were drawn up more or less along front lines. All the towns presented in the previous chapters are today in the entity Republika Srpska, which is almost exclusively populated by Bosnian Serbs. Since a majority of the perpetrators were from local communities, they remained in their communities and established their narrative about the war. The existence of camps in Prijedor, Višegrad, Bijeljina, and Bileća is denied and ignored. Euphemisms such as transit centers or refugee camps are used by the Bosnian Serb political and academic establishment. Thus no memorials are allowed to be built on these sites.

While conducting research, I visited Prijedor and Višegrad to see the state of the campsites today. Almost all locations where the camps and facilities operated today are still standing and functioning for a different purpose. These detention sites, such as schools, police stations, and factories, were used as detention sites only temporarily, and after the need for them was over, their predetention function returned: schools, police stations, factories still function today at the same site. The Hasan Veletovac School is still standing and functioning as a school, but its name has been changed (Veletovac was a Bosniak communist Partisan fighter in World War II) to Vuk Karadžić after a famous Serb linguist. While standing in the playground of the Hasan Veletovac School, I asked a local contact there where the local Serb children went to school in 1992. His reply was "Hasan Veletovac." It then hit me that the school had been used as a camp for only three months and then reopened as a school again in September when the new school year started. This made me realize the extent of the bystander effect in the local population; the school was located inside the town, surrounded by houses, and the perpetrators were locals. Everybody knew what was going on inside the school and yet parents sent their children to be educated in a site where a month earlier people had been murdered, raped, beheaded, and traumatized. The Hasan Veletovac School is a perfect example of the lack of confrontation with the past by RS authorities and the local population.

In Prijedor, the Omarska camp returned to its prewar function. It is a mine owned partially by a UK steel company, and the Prijedor municipality has denied attempts to set up a memorial for the victims. In Trnopolje, on the site of the camp, a memorial for fallen Serb soldiers was built and still stands today, while repeated attempts by victim groups were refused by the municipality. The Keraterm camp returned to its prewar function as a ceramics factory and is the only former camp that has some sort of memorial, a small plaque with a neutral text placed in the premises of the parking lot of the Keraterm. The premises of the Manjača camp was turned into a farm by the Banja Luka municipality and the current authorities allow commemorations to take place, but not a memorial.

In Višegrad, the former rape camp, hotel Vilina Vlas is today still being used as a hotel, and the municipality has not allowed the building of any memorial. The elementary school Hamid Beširović, which carried the name of a World War II Muslim Partisan fighter, was renamed after Vuk Karadžić, a Serb linguist. It still operates as a school today and all attempts to place a memorial have been denied. The fire station is still being used by the local fire department. The Uzamnica military compound is used by the armed forces of Bosnia and Herzegovina and no memorial or entry is allowed. In the entire municipality, there is not a single memorial to the various camps that were set up.

In Bijelina, the former Batković camp has been privatized and is used as a farm. The current owner allows for commemorations to take place but no memorial. In Bileća, the police station serves the same purpose. The building of Đački dom was privatized while the military base Moše Pijada, named after a World War II Jewish Partisan, was renamed Bilećki borci (Bileća fighters). There are no known attempts to try and memorialize these locations.

The collective trauma endured by the Bosniak and Croat population was so severe almost none of them ever expressed any desire to return to their former hometowns. Their physical and mental traumas remain, and they are long-lasting and numerous. During one trial related to a rape victim from a Višegrad camp, a neuropsychiatrist was called to testify as to her diagnosis of the victim. She stated that the victim was "very tense and upset. She was anxious and couldn't sit still," adding that the diagnosis was posttraumatic stress disorder and hypertension.[13] A 2010 study on concentration camp survivors conducted at the psychiatric clinic in Sarajevo showed that a majority of the studied patients suffered from PTSD, while smaller numbers suffered from depression, anxiety disorders, personality disorders, panic attacks, and drug and alcohol abuse.[14] This kind of mental state and trauma was discussed during the 1960s after Holocaust survivors' treatment and research naming it the "concentration camp syndrome."[15] The survivors understandably tend to stay away from anything which resembles or reminds them of the wartime events and camp expe-

---

13. Emina Dizdarević, "Neuropsychiatrist Describes Trauma of Victim in Kovacevic Trial," *Detektor*, July 6, 2015, https://detektor.ba/2015/07/06/neuropsychiatrist-describes-trauma-of-victim-in-kova cevic-trial/?lang=en.

14. Ifeta Licanin, "PTSD and Other Psychiatric Disorders among Concentration Camp Survivors in Bosnia and Herzegovina," *European Psychiatry* 25, no. 1 (2010): 1629, https://doi.org/10.1016/S0924-9338(10)71608-4.

15. Herbert Bower, "The Concentration Camp Syndrome," *Australian & New Zealand Journal of Psychiatry* 28, no. 3 (September 1, 1994): 391–97, https://doi.org/10.3109/00048679409075864.

rience. An additional characteristic of the enduring trauma is the sheer level of betrayal felt by the survivors over the fact that the majority of the atrocities were committed by local, ordinary men, their neighbours and colleagues, who knew very well those they were killing.

As I started researching the camps in Prijedor, I contacted a local friend and survivor Sudbin Musić and asked him about the first signs of something wrong that he noticed in 1992. He replied that in May 1992 he was in high school, and school ended early that year and their grades were being concluded by their class teacher, a Serb. When he finished concluding their grades, he closed the grade book and said, "See you next school year, who survives" (*Vidimo se naredne skolske godine, ali ko preživi*). The teacher soon went on to become a member of the VRS. This moment, he said, highlighted perfectly the atmosphere in Prijedor on the eve of war. The perpetrators knew what was going to happen, and they knew their victims. In this case, a teacher, an educator, turned into a perpetrator overnight. Musić would survive a massacre in his village of Čarakovo and end up in Trnopolje camp in summer 1992, barely making it alive. The trauma and loss he and his family endured, however, is haunting him to this day.

The current state of camp survivors is quite poor, especially among victims of rape and sexual abuse. First, there are other multiple traumas endured by people who were not in camps, such as war veterans, siege survivors, genocide survivors, etc., which thus does not place camp survivors in any privileged position. Second, the state of awareness about mental health and treatment is low and in some cases even taboo. The best conditions for former camp survivors have been in Scandinavian countries and Australia, where they were able to get proper medical care and benefits because of their camp experiences. Additionally, the camp survivors are organized along ethnic lines, forming three separate umbrella organizations made up of smaller survivor organizations. All three umbrella organizations are used as an instrument of manipulation in everyday politics. Several years ago, former Bosniak detainees started suing RS for damages and pain inflicted during their detention in camps. Several thousand lawsuits were filed, which led the RS authorities to intentionally conduct decades-long, complex trials that ended up being dismissed on various judicial levels by RS courts. Additionally, the courts started to routinely order former camp detainees to pay for judicial fees as high as five thousand euros. Most of the victims could not pay these fees and ended up having parts of their property impounded by court orders. A minority of cases, filed right after the war, were won by the former detainees, who received a symbolic reparation of approximately 4.5 euros per day spent in the camps.

In the past few years there have been attempts by former detainee organizations to pass a state-level law on wartime victims of torture. This new law, which would regulate rights of former detainees, was opposed by Bosnian Serb legislators, who insisted that this new law discriminated against Serb victims. Rather, a new law on torture in RS was proposed that was aimed at minimizing rights for the returnee Bosniak and Croat population. Once again, camp detainees became the center of political manipulation and clashes, with no end in sight. It is clear that overall there still is institutional-level discrimination and favoring along ethnic lines aimed at strengthening political power in this highly polarized society.

Domestically, the collective memory of camps is slowly being revived and engaged with throughout Bosniak society. In 2009, a documentary called "The XX Century Man" was aired in Sarajevo. It told the story of a eighty-six-year-old man, a Bosniak from Banja Luka, who in his lifetime was incarcerated in three camps by three different regimes: in Mathausen by the Nazis in 1942; in Goli Otok by the communists in 1949, and in Mali logor by the Bosnian Serb Army in 1995. He ended up in each camp because of different beliefs and convictions or because he was labeled as an enemy by whoever found him to be inconvenient at that time,but the camps and punishments remained similar. A vital step would be to continue on from this and see the publication of more research into camps, and especially the collection and publication of more survivor testimonies.

Placing the Bosnian Serb Concentration Camps in Their Global Context

One of the purposes of this book is to place the Bosnian Serb camp system in its rightful place alongside those described in the earlier chapters. They clearly fit within Dan Stone's definition of camps, and they share many of the same features as other camp systems mentioned: death, rape, terror, starvation, beating, psychological destruction, usage of *kapos*, etc.

Originally, concentration camps were created to ensure the isolation of insurgents and their families or suspected enemies from the general populace; to carry out enforced labor; to correct politically deviant behavior; and finally, to become part of the industrialization of death in the Nazi camps. As with each and every concentration camp system the world has known, the Bosnian Serb camps have their own peculiarities that reflect the aims of the perpetrators. Studying them will prove fruitful to genocide scholars in a number of ways.

Isolation was not the aim of the Bosnian Serb camp system in Bosnia and Herzegovina. Indeed, some of the facilities were in the hearts of the towns (Bileća and the various Višegrad detention centers). Enforced labor was used in some cases but did not constitute a major feature of the camps. Political correction is out of the question because there were no re-education or correctional aspects of these camps. Lastly, these were not death camps since—although brutal murders, executions, and death occurred in the camps—it was not the main aim of the perpetrators.

Three elements of camps in Bosnia and Herzegovina stand out among other examples in history: brutal torture, rape, and sexual abuse designed to inflict maximum trauma; the presence of local perpetrators, and finally, the presence of mass graves.

Torture—an amusement of the perpetrators inflicted upon the incarcerated—was a regular activity. Sexual abuse and rape of women, girls, and men was conducted intentionally with the aim of destroying the family foundations of the patriarchal Bosniak and Croat families. Acts of spectacular violence were used to psychologically destroy inmates, to break their humanity and connection to reality and to other humans.

Next, most of the crimes committed were personal, and intimately so; the identity of the perpetrator was very often known to the victim and vice versa. The camps themselves were formed within the community, inside the town, visible to the public. Finally, the bodies of those who were murdered or executed were dumped into hidden mass graves with the aim of concealing the crimes committed. The bodies were mainly dumped into primary mass graves, but in the case of Prijedor, for example, the Tomašica mass grave was dug up and the remains removed to at least two secondary mass graves in other locations.

In conclusion, two key points may be derived from the experience of the Serb-run camp system in Bosnia and Herzegovina. First, the Bosnian Serb authorities used detention camps and facilities as a widespread and systematic tool in their ethnoreligious genocidal cleansing of the territories they seized. The fact that in four geographically different locations a similar pattern of organized collective violence has been proved leads us to conclude that camps and facilities were a tool. They were established around the same time with the same or similar features, by similar structures, planned from one document, all linked under one figure. All of this indicates that the camps were at the heart of an ethnic cleansing campaign of genocide.

Lastly, the role and functioning of state institutions show that each genocide, each camp system in history, is unique. The most disheartening point, however, is that perpetrators learn from each other, as Radislav Brđanin clearly remarked: "If Hitler, Stalin, and Churchill could have working camps so can we. Oh come on, we are in a war after all."[16]

---

16. Prosecutor v. Radoslav Brđanin (Judgment), IT-99-36-T (ICTY), 201.

Figure 6. The playground and school building in Trnopolje near Prijedor, used as a camp in 1992. (Courtesy of Pawel Starzec.)

Figure 7. The ceramic tile factory Keraterm near Prijedor, used as a camp in 1992. (Courtesy of Pawel Starzec.)

Figure 8. The main building and the infamous white house at Omarska mine near Prijedor, used as a camp in 1992. (Courtesy of Pawel Starzec.)

Figure 9. The Vilina Vlas spa in Višegrad, used as a rape camp for Bosniak women and girls by Serb forces in 1992. (Courtesy of Pawel Starzec.)

Figure 10. The police station in Višegrad, used as a detention facility for Bosniak civilians in 1992. (Courtesy of Pawel Starzec.)

Figure 11. The fire station in Višegrad, used as a detention facility for Bosniak civilians in 1992. (Courtesy of Pawel Starzec.)

Figure 12. The Hasan Veletovac School in Višegrad, used as a detention facility for Bosniak civilians in 1992. (Courtesy of Pawel Starzec.)

Figure 13. The Batković farm near Bijeljina, site of the concentration camp for Bosniaks and Bosnian Croats by Serb authorities during the entire 1992–95 war. (Courtesy of Pawel Starzec.)

Figure 14. The police station in Bileća, used as a detention facility for Bosniak civilians in 1992. (Courtesy of Sadmir Mustafić.)

Figure 15. The student dormitory in Bileća, used as a detention facility for Bosniak civilians in 1992. (Courtesy of Sadmir Mustafić.)

Figure 16. The Moše Pijada Military Barracks, used as a detention camp for Bosniak civilians in 1992. (Courtesy of Sadmir Mustafić.)

Figure 17. The old prison in Bileća, used as a detention camp for Bosniak civilians in 1992. (Courtesy of Sadmir Mustafić.)

References

1st Krajina Corps, Commission for the Exchange of Prisoners of War, Banja Luka. "To the VRS /Army of Republika Srpska/ Main Staff—Commission to Colonel Zdravko Tolimir." No: 53/93, dated June 1, 1993, No. 89/94. In Prosecutor v. Simić et al, IT-95-9, Exhibit no. D13/3. https://bit.ly/ZdravkoTolimirCommision93.

Ahmetašević, Nidžara, Nerma Jelačić, and Selma Boračić. "Visegrad Rape Victims Say Their Cries Go Unheard." *Balkan Insight*, December 10, 2007. https://balkaninsight.com/2007/12/10/visegrad-rape-victims-say-their-cries-go-unheard/.

Allen, Beverly. *Rape Warfare: The Hidden Genocide in Bosnia-Herzegovina and Croatia.* Minneapolis: University of Minnesota Press, 1996.

Amnesty International. "Amnesty International Special Report: Indonesia 1965 Documents." Accessed on January 20, 2016. http://www.indonesia1965.org/wordpress/.

Amnesty International. "Bosnia-Herzegovina: The 'Disappeared.' Himzo Demir—Head-Teacher: 'Disappeared' from Višegrad." December 3, 2001. http://www.amnesty.org/en/library/info/EUR63/016/2001/en.

Anušić, A. "Migrants—With the State's Mediation," *Glas*, July 18, 1992.

Applebaum, Anne. *Gulag: A History.* New York: Anchor Books, 2003.

"Approval for visit of the International Committee to the detention camps at Manjača, Trnopolje, Omarska and Prijedor." Dated August 3, 1992. See ICTY no. 01029866, Prosecutor v. Radoslav Brđanin (Judgment), IT-99-36-T (ICTY), Exhibit no. P405.

Arendt, Hannah, and Jerome Kohn. *Essays in Understanding, 1930–1954.* New York: Schocken Books, 2005.

"Assessment of the Political and Security Situation in the Territory of Trebinje CSB." Dated August 19, 1992. P162, ICTY No. 00749651. Prosecutor v. Stanišić & Župljanin, IT-08-91 (ICTY), Exhibit no. P00162. E.

Ataria, Yochai. "Becoming Nonhuman: The Case Study of the Gulag." *Genealogy* 3, no 2 (2019): 1–3, https://doi.org/10.3390/genealogy3020027.

Augustyn, Adam. "South African War." In *Encyclopaedia Britannica*, last modified October 4, 2020. http://www.britannica.com/event/South-African-War.

218 REFERENCES

Australian War Memorial. "Australia and the Boer War 1899–1902," Accessed January 18, 2016. https://www.awm.gov.au/atwar/boer/.

Banac, Ivo. *With Stalin against Tito: Cominformist Splits in Yugoslav Communism*. Ithaca, NY: Cornell University Press, 1988.

Bandura, Albert, Bill Underwood, and Michael E. Fromson. "Disinhibition of Aggression Through Diffusion of Responsibility and Dehumanization of Victims." *Journal of Research in Personality* 9, no. 4 (1975): 253–69. https://doi.org/10.1016/0092-6566 (75)90001-X.

Barnes, Steven A. *Death and Redemption: The Gulag and the Shaping of Soviet Society* (E-Book). Princeton NJ: Princeton University Press, 2011.

Bar-Tal, Daniel, and Phillip L. Hammack. Conflict, Delegitimization, and Violence. In *The Oxford Handbook Of Intergroup Conflict*, edited by Linda Tropp, 29–52. New York: Oxford University Press, 2012.

Basic, Goran. "Concentration Camp Rituals: Narratives of Former Bosnian Detainees." *Humanity and Society* 41, no. 1 (December 23, 2015): 73–94. https://doi.org/10.1177 /0160597615621593.

Battiata, Mary. 1992. "Slayings in Bosnia Confirmed." *Washington Post*, September 27, 1992. https://www.washingtonpost.com/archive/politics/1992/09/28/slayings-in-bo snia-confirmed/c29f87fb-b1f5-4cff-b727-bf2113a418e0/?utm_term=.142e8588 3310.

Bećirević, Edina. *Genocide on the Drina River*. New Haven, CT: Yale University Press, 2014.

Begić, Mujo. "Genocid u Prijedoru—Svjedočenja." In *Hrvatski memorijalno-dokumentacijski centar Domovinskog rata u Zagrebu* (HMDCDR), Sarajevo/Zagreb: Institut za istraživanje zločina protiv čovječnosti i međunarodnog prava Univerziteta u Sarajevu, 2015.

Bego Hamzić v. Republika Srpska, No. 80 0 P 025505 10 P (Osnovni sud u Bijeljini). September 21, 2012.

Bergholz, Max. 2016. *Violence as a Generative Force: Identity, Nationalism, and Memory in a Balkan Community*. Ithaca, NY: Cornell University Press.

Bernstein, Nina. "Private Prisoners: Small-Group Detention Believed Common in Bosnia." *Newsday*, September 7, 1992.

Bettelheim, Bruno. *The Informed Heart*. New York: Avon, 1971.

BIRN Balkans. "TV Justice Magazine I Episode 24: Crimes on the River Drina Bank." February 18, 2013. https://www.youtube.com/watch?v=a631z7x2Elw.

BIRN BiH. "Krsmanovic: Covered in Bruises Due to Beating." *Detektor*, September 19, 2012. https://detektor.ba/2012/09/19/krsmanovic-covered-in-bruises-due-to-beatin g/?lang=en.

Blum, Rony, Gregory H. Stanton, Shira Sagi, and Elihu D. Richter. "'Ethnic Cleansing' Bleaches the Atrocities of Genocide," *European Journal of Public Health* 18, no. 2 (April 2008): 204–209. https://doi.org/10.1093/eurpub/ckm011.

"Bosnia Herzegovina: Report from the town of Bijeljina." Channel 4 News, March 17, 1993, Gaby Rado reporting. ITN, ICTY No. BSP170393007.

Boucher, Richard. "State Department News Briefing." September 8, 1992, https://www.c-span.org/video/?32050-1/state-department-news-briefing.

Bower, Herbert. "The Concentration Camp Syndrome." *Australian & New Zealand Journal of Psychiatry* 28, no. 3 (September 1, 1994): 391–97. https://doi.org/10.3109/0004 8679409075864.

Brammertz, Serge and Jarvis, Michelle J. *Prosecuting Conflict-Related Sexual Violence at the ICTY.* Oxford: Oxford University Press. 2016.

Bridgman, Jon M. *The Revolt of the Hereros.* Berkeley: University of California Press, 1981.

Brkanić, Džana. "Bošnjak i ostali: Strah i trepet za zatvorenike." *Detektor*, September 5, 2017. http://detektor.ba/bosnjak-i-ostali-strah-i-trepet-za-zatvorenike/.

Brkanić, Džana. "Bosniaks Left Bileca." *Detektor*, November 4, 2014. https://detektor.ba/2014/11/04/bosniaks-left-bileca/?lang=en.

Brkanić, Džana. "Witnesses Describe Detainee Abuse at Batkovic Detention Camp." *Justice Rreport*, 2015. http://www.justice-report.com/en/articles/witnesses-describe-detainee-abuse-at-batkovic-detention-camp.

Brooks, Geraldine. "The Book of Exodus." *New Yorker*, November 26, 2007. https://www.newyorker.com/magazine/2007/12/03/the-book-of-exodus.

Brosveen, Emily. 2010. "World War II Internment Camps." In *The Handbook of Texas Online.* Texas State Historical Association (TSHA). *Tshaonline.org.* http://www.tshaonline.org/handbook/online/articles/quwby.

Browning, Christopher. *Ordinary Men: Reserve Police Battalion 101 and the Final Solution in Poland.* New York: Harper Perennial, 1998.

Browning, Christopher. "Sajmiste as a European Site of Holocaust Remembrance." *Filozofija i drustvo* 23, no. 4 (2012): 99–105. National Library of Serbia. https://doi.org/10.2298/fid1204099b.

"Buković kod Benkovca, govor dr. Jovana Raškovića 17.8.1990., Osnivačka skupština SDS-a," *Zivstepa*, March 8, 2010, https://www.youtube.com/watch?v=LhkaQdzhm8s.

Buljugić, Mirna. "Indictee in 'Vilina Vlas' with Lukic's Team." *Detektor*, May 28, 2013. https://detektor.ba/2013/05/28/indictee-in-%C2%93vilina-vlas%C2%94-with-lukic%C2%92s-team/?lang=en.

Butcher, Thomas M. "A 'Synchronized Attack': On Raphael Lemkin's Holistic Conception of Genocide." *Journal of Genocide Research* 15, no. 3 (September 2013): 253–271. https://doi.org/10.1080/14623528.2013.821221.

Byford, Jovan. "The Semlin Judenlager in Belgrade: A Contested Memory." The Holocaust and United Nations Outreach Programme, accessed July 1, 2016. http://www.un.org/en/holocaustremembrance/docs/paper20.shtml.

Byrne, Jeffrey James. *Mecca of Revolution: Algeria, Decolonization, and the Third World Order.* New York: Oxford University Press, 2016.

Campbell, Bradley. *The Geometry of Genocide: A Study in Pure Sociology.* Charlottesville: University of Virginia Press, 2005.

Campbell, David. "Atrocity, Memory, Photography: Imaging the Concentration Camps of Bosnia—The Case of ITN Versus Living Marxism, Part 2." *Journal of Human Rights* 1, no. 2 (2002): 143–72. https://doi.org/10.1080/14754830210125656.

Canada (Minister of Citizenship and Immigration) v. Rogan, 396 F.T.R. 47 (FC), August 18, 2011, 27. https://www.cbc.ca/bc/news/bc-110818-branko-rogan-federal-court-de cision.pdf.

Caplan, Richard. *Europe and the Recognition of New States in Yugoslavia.* Cambridge: Cambridge University Press, 2005.

Chandler, David. *Voices from S-21: Terror and History in Pol Pot's Secret Prison.* Berkeley: University of California Press, 1999.

Čekić, Smail. *The Aggression against the Republic of Bosnia and Herzegovina.* Sarajevo: Institute for the Research of Crimes Against Humanity and International Law, 2005.

Certificate issued by the Command of the 1st Višegrad Light Infantry Brigade. International Criminal Tribunal for the former Yugoslavia (ICTY) No.: 0422-4603-EDT/ draft translation. https://bit.ly/LukaDragicevicCert1992.

Cigar, Norman L. *Genocide in Bosnia.* College Station: Texas A&M University Press. 1995.

Clough, Marshall S. *Mau Mau Memoirs; History, Memory, Politics.* Boulder, CO: Lynne Rienner Publishers, 1998.

Cockrell, Cathy. 2010. "How Japanese Americans Preserved Traditions behind Barbed Wire." *Berkeley News,* June 10, 2010. http://news.berkeley.edu/2010/06/10/muram oto/.

Cohen, Roger. "Cross vs. Crescent: The Battle Lines Are Being Redrawn in Bosnia along Old Religious Scars." *New York Times,* September 17, 1992. https://bit.ly/NYTCrossv Crescent.

Collection Centre Batković. Report on the Closing of the Collection Center and Hand Over of MTS/Material and Technical Equipment." Confidential number: 2/2999–131, dated January 11, 1996, ICTY No. 0529-9092.

"Command of S.C./Collection Centre/ 'Ekonomija,' Internal No. 2/835-12, Instruction on the work at the gate-house of SC 'Ekonomija' in the village of Batković." Dated July 12, 1992, ICTY no. 0529-9074. See Prosecutor v. Radovan Karadžić, IT-95-5/18 (ICTY), Exhibit no. D03239.E.

Committee for Collecting Data on Crimes Committed Against Humanity and International Law. "The Situation in the Municipality of Višegrad Prior to The Outbreak of War and Crimes Committed Against Serbs during The War." Belgrade: October, 1996. http://www.slobodan-milosevic.org/documents/reports/8-a.htm.

Commission for the inspection of the municipalities and the Prijedor, Bosanski Novi and Sanski Most SJB /Public Security Stations/. "Report Concerning the Situation as Found and Questions Relating to Prisoners, Collection Centers, Resettlement and the Role of the SJB in Connection with These Activities." August 14, 1992. International Criminal Tribunal for the former Yugoslavia (ICTY) No. B0032527.

"Cygool: Human Rights Abuses in Bosnia—Hercegovina [*sic*]—Cases of X., F.B., and A.V.;—The Personnel Structure at Omarska Camp." *Wikileaks*, October 16, 1992. Accessed May 6, 2017. https://wikileaks.org/plusd/cables/92ZAGREB2038_a.html.

Demick, Barbara. 1994. "Name Change Can Save Life." *Calgary Herald*, January 3, 1994, A1.

"Defense Counsel Karadzic Defends His Client Karadzic." *Sense Agency*, January 11, 2011. http://archive.sensecentar.org/vijesti.php?aid=13331.

Des Pres, Terrence. *The Survivor: An Anatomy of Life in the Death Camps.* Oxford: Oxford University Press, 1980.

Đikoli, Jasmina. "Former Prisoner Describes Abuse in Bileca Detention Camps." *Detektor*, May 12, 2015. https://detektor.ba/2015/05/12/former-prisoner-describes-abuse-in-bileca-detention-camps/?lang=en.

Đikoli, Jasmina. "Prosecution Witness Describes Prisoner Abuse in Bileca." *Detektor*, March 3, 2015. https://detektor.ba/2015/03/03/prosecution-witness-describes-prisoner-abuse-in-bileca/?lang=en.

Discovering Anzacs. "Index to Album of Identification Photographs of Enemy Aliens (Civilian and Prisoner of War) Interned at Liverpool Camp, NSW During World War I—A to L." Accessed January 24, 2016, 25, https://discoveringanzacs.naa.gov.au/browse/records/457761/25.

Dizdarević, Emina. "Witness Describes Prisoner Beatings and Torture in Bileca." *Detektor*, March 31, 2015. https://detektor.ba/2015/03/31/witness-describes-prisoner-beatings-and-torture-in-bileca/?lang=en.

Dizdarević, Emina. "Neuropsychiatrist Describes Trauma of Victim in Kovacevic Trial." *Detektor*, July 6, 2015. https://detektor.ba/2015/07/06/neuropsychiatrist-describes-trauma-of-victim-in-kovacevic-trial/?lang=en.

Donia, Robert. *Radovan Karadžić: Architect of the Bosnian Genocide.* Cambridge: Cambridge University Press, 2014.

Doubt, Keith. "Scapegoating and the Simulation of Mechanical Solidarity in Former Yugoslavia: 'Ethnic Cleansing' and the Serbian Orthodox Church." *Humanity & Society* 31, no. 1 (2007), 65–82. https://doi.org/10.1177/016059760703100105.

Drinnon, Richard. *Keeper of Concentration Camps.* Berkeley: University of California Press, 1989.

Državni zavod za statistiku Republike Bosne i Hercegovine. "Popis stanovništva, domaćinstava, stanova i poljoprivrednih gazdinstava 1991. godine, Nacionalni sastav stanovništva—Rezultati za Republiku po opštinama i naseljenim mjestima 1991. Godine." Sarajevo, decembar 1993. godine, statistički bilten broj 234. https://bit.ly/ResultsBiHPopSurv1991.

Džafić, Jusuf. "Atik džamija u Bijeljini." *BZK—Preporod Bijeljina*, 2014. http://preporodbn.com/atik-dzamija-u-bijeljini/.

Džidić, Denis. "Former Prisoner Describes Abuse at Hands of Duka." *Detektor*, June 30, 2015. https://detektor.ba/2015/06/30/former-prisoner-describes-abuse-at-hands-of-duka/?lang=en.

Džidić, Denis. "Prosecution Witnesses Say Police Commander Beat Detainee in Bileca." *Detektor*, February 10, 2015. https://detektor.ba/2015/02/10/prosecution-witnesses-say-police-commander-beat-detainee-in-bileca/?lang=en.

Džidić, Denis. "Witness Describes Inhumane Conditions and Abuse at Bileca Detention Facility." *Detektor*, April 21, 2015. https://detektor.ba/2015/04/21/witness-describes-inhumane-conditions-and-abuse-at-bileca-detention-facility/?lang=en.

"(Eighth Report of War Crimes in the Former Yugoslavia) Supplemental United States Submission of Information to The United Nations Security Council in Accordance with Paragraph 5 of Resolution 771 (1992) and Paragraph 1 of Resolution 780 (1992)." June 16, 1993. https://phdn.org/archives/www.ess.uwe.ac.uk/documents/sdrpt8a.htm.

Elkins, Caroline. 2006. *Imperial Reckoning: The Untold Story of Britain's Gulag in Kenya*. New York: Henry Holt and Co.

Erichsen, C. W. *"The Angel of Death has Descended Violently among Them": Concentration Camps and Prisoners-of-War in Namibia, 1904–08*. Leiden: African Studies Centre, 2005.

Erjavec, Dragana. "Policeman 'Raped Male Prisoners.'" *Detektor*, April 3, 2013. https://detektor.ba/2013/04/03/policeman-raped-male-prisoners/?lang=en.

Ethnographic Museum in Belgrade. "Bulletin of the Ethnographic Museum, Vol. 2." https://etnografskimuzej.rs/en/o-muzeju/izdavastvo/periodika/gem-2/.

Federalni zavod za statistiku. "Popis 2013." http://www.statistika.ba/?show=8#link1.

Feierstein, Daniel. *Genocide as Social Practice: Reorganizing Society under the Nazis and Argentina's Military Juntas*. Translated by Douglas Andrew Town. New Brunswick, NJ: Rutgers University Press, 2014.

Finkel, Evgeny, and Scott Straus. 2012. "Macro, Meso, and Micro Research on Genocide: Gains, Shortcomings, and Future Areas of Inquiry." *Genocide Studies and Prevention* 7 (1): 56–67. Johns Hopkins University Press. https://doi.org/10.1353/gsp.2012.0008.

Federalni zavod za statistiku (Yugoslav Federal Bureau of Statistics). "Popis stanovništva 1991." 1991 Census of B&H, now available at Bosna i Hercegovina Federalni zavod za statistiku—The Bosnian and Herzegovinan Federal Bureau of Statistics). http://fzs.ba/index.php/popis-stanovnistva/popis-stanovnistva-1991-i-stariji/.

"First Report on the War Crimes in the Former Yugoslavia: Submission of Information to the United Nations Security Council in Accordance With Paragraph 5 of Resolution 771 (1992)." September 22, 1992. Accessed March 3, 2016. https://www.phdn.org/archives/www.ess.uwe.ac.uk/documents/sdrpt1.htm.

Fond za humanitarno pravo. "Transkripcija i redaktura transkripta—Tužilac protiv Mitra Vasiljevića (Predmet IT-98–32-A)." December 15, 2005. https://bit.ly/TranscriptMitVasiljevic.

"The Forgotten Women of the 'War in the East.'" *BBC*, October 19, 2014. http://www.bbc.com/news/magazine-29665232.

REFERENCES   223

Fournet, Caroline. *The Crime of Destruction and the Law of Genocide*, Farnham, UK: Ashgate, 2007.

"*Genocid u Prijedoru—Brezicani -pravoslavna crkva i genocid*", Genocid92,October 19, 2007, https://www.youtube.com/watch?v=777wlJsV498.

"Germany Returns Namibian Skulls." *BBC News*, September 30, 2011. Accessed January 18, 2016. http://www.bbc.com/news/world-europe-15127992.

"Glavni štab Vojske Republike Srpske, Broj: 06/20-437," dated December 1, 1995, signed by general Manojlović. ICTY No. 04258226.

Gow, James. *The Serbian Project and Its Adversaries: A Strategy of War Crimes*. London: Hurst Publishers, 2003.

"Grupa koja je učestvovala u napadu na Prijedor 30.5.1992," II-98-35/1-T, ICTY, No. 2657.

Gutman, Roy. "Bosnia-Herzegovina; Thousands Held in Nazi-Style Camps; Corpses Pile Up in Open Pit as Disease Spreads Rapidly." *Newsday–Ottawa Citizen*, 1992.

Gutman, Roy. "Bosnia-Herzegovina; Thousands Held in Nazi-Style Camps; Corpses Pile Up in Open Pit as Disease Spreads Rapidly." In *Roy Gutman, A Witness to Genocide*. New York: Lisa Drew Book, 1993.

Gutman, Roy. "Serbs Have Slain Over 1,000 in 2 Bosnia Camps, Ex-Prisoners Say." *Los Angeles Times*, August 2, 1992. https://www.latimes.com/archives/la-xpm-1992-08 -02-mn-5646-story.html.

Goeschel, Christian, and Nikolaus Wachsman. *The Nazi Concentration Camps, 1933– 1939: A Documentary History*. Lincoln: University of Nebraska Press, 2012.

Hack, Karl. "Detention, Deportation and Resettlement: British Counterinsurgency and Malaya's Rural Chinese, 1948–60." *Journal of Imperial and Commonwealth History* 43, no. 4 (2015): 611–40. https://doi.org/10.1080/03086534.2015.1083218.

Hagan, John, and Todd Haugh. *Forging a Convention for Crimes against Humanity*. New York: Cambridge University Press, 2011.

Hayden, Robert M. *From Yugoslavia to the Western Balkans: Studies of a European Disunion, 1991–2011*. Leiden: Brill, 2013.

Helsinki Watch/HRW. *War Crimes in Bosnia and Herzegovina, Volume II*. New York: 1993.

Hilberg, Raul. *The Destruction of the European Jews*. New Haven, CT: Yale University Press. 2003.

Hinton, Alexander Laban. "Critical Genocide Studies." *Genocide Studies and Prevention* 7, no. 1 (2012): 4–15. https://scholarcommons.usf.edu/cgi/viewcontent.cgi?article=1 044&context=gsp.

Human Rights Watch. "Genocide in Iraq: The Anfal Campaign Against the Kurds," 1993. https://www.hrw.org/reports/1993/iraqanfal/.

Human Rights Watch. "If the Dead Could Speak: Mass Deaths and Torture in Syria's Detention Facilities." December 16, 2015. Accessed January 20, 2016. https:// bit.ly/HRWIfdeadcouldspeak .

"Hundreds of 'Groups' in Tomasica Mass Grave." *Sense Agency*, June 24, 2015. http:// www.sense-agency.com/icty/hundreds-of-%E2%80%98groups%E2%80%99-in-to masica-mass-graves.29.html?news_id=16644.

224 REFERENCES

Hukanović, Rezak. "The Evil of Omarska." *New Republic*, February 12, 1996.

Hukanović, Rezak. *The Tenth Circle of Hell*. New York: Basic Books, 1996.

Huseinović, Avdo. "*Bloody Višegrad on the Drina, Pravda Bosna*, May 21, 2015. https://www.youtube.com/watch?v=-oJW0HGwNKg&ab_channel=PravdaBosna.

Husejnović, Merima. 2009. "A Month in the Hands of Milan Lukic." *BIRN*, November 6, 2009. http://www.justice-report.com/en/articles/for-the-record-a-month-in-the-hands-of-milan-lukic.

"Hronika Prijedora 6: Marko Djenadija,"*Genocid92*,July 26, 2009. https://www.youtube.com/watch?v=6g5xzBGCotk.

Ingrao, Charles W. *Confronting the Yugoslav Controversies: A Scholars' Initiative*. West Layafette, IN, Purdue University Press. 2013.

Intercepted telephone conversation held on 23 April 1992 between Momcilo Mandic and Traparic, and between Momcilo Mandic and Zorica, 23 April 1992, Prosecutor v. Karadžić, (IT-95-5/18), Exhibit no. P05701.E.

International School for Holocaust Studies—Yad Vashem. "Concentration Camps." Accessed January 19, 2016. http://www.yadvashem.org/odot_pdf/Microsoft%20Word%20-%205925.pdf.

Irvin-Erickson, Douglas. "Genocide, the 'Family of Mind' and the Romantic Signature of Raphael Lemkin." *Journal of Genocide Research* 15, no. 3 (2013): 273–96. https://doi.org/10.1080/14623528.2013.821222.

Irvin-Erickson, Douglas. *Raphael Lemkin and the Concept of Genocide*. Pittsburgh: University of Pennsylvania Press, 2016.

Irwin, Rachel. "Survivor Tells of Bosniak 'Volunteers' Selected for Death." *Institute for War and Peace Reporting*, February 22, 2013. https://iwpr.net/global-voices/survivor-tells-bosniak-volunteers-selected-death.

"Istorija Bilećke kasarne—II dio," *Radio Televizija Republike Srpske*, April 25, 2017, [30:00–30:30], https://www.youtube.com/watch?v=qZB30PUz_jw.

Ivanović, Stanoje. *The Creation and Changes of the Internal Borders of Yugoslavia*. Belgrade: Ministry of Information of the Republic of Serbia, 1991.

"Izrečene kazne za zločine u logoru Manjača." *Voice of America*, 29 May 2006. https://ba.voanews.com/a/a-29-2006-05-29-voa10-85880822/668185.html.

"Izvještaj o rasformiranju Sabirnog Centra i predaja MTS." Pov.broj:2/2999-131 dated January 11,1996, ICTY No. 0529-9092.

"Izvještaj o zatečenom stanju i pitanjima u vezi sa zarobljenicima, sabirnim centrima, iseljavanju i ulozi SJB u vezi ovim aktivnostima." ICTY No. B0032527.

"Izvod iz zapisnika izbora i popune mjesnog odbora srpske demokratske stranke Koazarac." dated May 20, 1992, and Odluka no. 05-010/93 dated May 10, 1993.

Jacobson, Mandy, and Karmen Jelincic. *Calling the Ghosts*. Croatia/USA: Bowery Productions, 1996. https://www.imdb.com/title/tt0115805/.

Jahić, Amer. "Bosnia Upholds Convictions for Prijedor Mosque Killings." *Detektor*, February 16, 2015. https://detektor.ba/2015/02/16/bosnia-upholds-convictions-for-prijedor-mosque-killings/?lang=en.

REFERENCES   225

Jahić, Amer. "Bosnian Serb Policemen Accused of Torture in Bileca." *Detektor*, October 21, 2014. https://detektor.ba/2014/10/21/bosnian-serb-policemen-accused-of-tortu re-in-bileca/?lang=en.

Jahić, Amer. "Tasic Was not Responsible for Convoy." *Detektor*, October 22, 2013. https:// detektor.ba/2013/10/22/tasic-was-not-responsible-for-convoy/?lang=en.

Jahić, Amer. "Witnesses Recall Visegrad Bosniak Convoys." *Detektor*, March 11, 2014. http://detektor.ba/en/witnesses-recall-visegrad-bosniak-convoys/.

Japanese American Relocation Digital Archive. "Essay: Relocation and Incarceration of Japanese Americans During World War II," Calisphere/University of California, accessed February 3, 2016. https://calisphere.org/exhibitions/essay/8/relocation/.

Kaiser, Andree. "Prisoners in the Manjaca Camp, Bosnia and Herzegovina." Agencja Fotograficzna Caro / Alamy Stock Photo (Manjaca, Republika Srpska, Bosnia and Herzegovina, July 6, 1992). https://bit.ly/AlamyManjacaCamp

"Kako živi porodica Bošnjaka koji je poginuo za Republiku Srpsku." *RTVBN*, December 23, 2013. https://www.rtvbn.com/22046/kako-zivi-porodica-bosnjaka-koji-je-pogin uo-za-srpsku.

Karačić, Darko, "Od promoviranja zajedništva do kreiranja podjela." In Darko Karačić, Tamara Banjeglav, and Nataša Govedarica, *Re:vizija prošlosti: politike sjećanja u Bosni i Hercegovini, Hrvatskoj i Srbiji od 1990. godine*. Sarajevo: ACIPS/ Fondacije Friedrich Ebert, 2012.

Karčić, Hikmet. *An Appeal for Truth*. Sarajevo: Fondacija Konrad Adenauer e. V., 2013.

Karčić, Hikmet. "Blueprint for Genocide: The Destruction of Muslims In Eastern Bosnia." *Open Democracy*. May 11, 2018. https://bit.ly/BlueprintGenKarcic.

Karčić, Hikmet. *Derviš M. Korkut: A Biography*. Sarajevo: El Kalem, 2020.

Karčić, Hikmet. "Uncovering the Truth: The Lake Perućac Exhumations in Eastern Bosnia." *Journal of Muslim Minority Studies* 37, no. 1 (March 2017): 114–28. https://doi .org/10.1080/13602004.2017.1294374.

Keane, Fergal. "Grim History of Bosnia's 'Rape Hotel.'" *BBC*, April 8, 2016. https://www .bbc.com/news/av/world-europe-35992642.

Killing Fields Museum of Cambodia. "S-21 Prison and Choeung Ek Killing Fields: Facing Death." Accessed on January 20, 2016. http://www.killingfieldsmuseum.com /s21-victims.html.

Kljun, Ibrahim. *Hronika genocida nad Bošnjacima Višegrada*. Zenica: Centar za istraživanje zločina i zločina nad Bošnjacima, 1996.

"KOMANDA ISTOČNO-BOSANSKOG KORPUSA." Pov.br.11/2–683 dated June 17, 1992. ICTY No. 06014174.

Kotek, Joel. "Concentration Camps." In *Encyclopedia of Genocide and Crimes against Humanity*, edited by Dinah Shelton, 196–200. Detroit: Thomson/Gale, 2005.

"Kovačević: Potvrđena presuda na 12 godina," *Detektor / BIRN*, July 11, 2007, https://det ektor.ba/2007/07/11/kovacevic-potvrdjena-presuda-na-12-godina/.

"Kovacevic: 12-Year Sentence Confirmed: Justice Report." *Justice-report.com*. 11 July, 2007. http://www.justice-report.com/en/articles/kovacevic-12-year-sentence-confirmed.

Kowner, Rotem. "The Japanese Internment of Jews in Wartime Indonesia and its Causes." *Indonesia and the Malay World* 38, no. 112 (October 2010): 349–71. https://doi.org/10.1080/13639811.2010.513846.

Kulišić, Špiro, and Petar Ž. Petrović. *Srpski mitološki rečnik.* Beograd: Etnografski Institut SANU, 1998.

Kurspahić, Kemal. *Prime Time Crime.* Washington, DC: United States Institute of Peace Press, 2003.

Landay, Jonathan S. "Bosnian Serbs Expel Non-Serbs From the North." *Christian Science Monitor,* September 7, 1994. https://www.csmonitor.com/1994/0907/07011.html.

Lange, Matthew. *Comparative Historical Methods* (E-book version). Newbury Park, CA: Sage Publications, 2013.

Leslie, Ann. "Rape as an Instrument of War?" *Daily Mail,* January 25, 1993.

Letter of the Chief of SJB Ugljevik Vinko B. Lazić to the Ministry of Interior of the Serbian Republic of BiH to Minister Stanišić, No. 18-17/01-198/92, dated April 16, 1992. ICTY No. 0074-1374. Prosecutor v. Radovan Karadžić, IT-95-5/18 (ICTY), Exhibit no. P05490.E.

Licanin, Ifeta. "PTSD and Other Psychiatric Disorders among Concentration Camp Survivors in Bosnia and Herzegovina." *European Psychiatry* 25, no. 1 (2010): 1629. https://doi.org/10.1016/S0924-9338(10)71608-4.

List of employees for the payment of salary for the month of May 1992. ICTY no. 02971881.

"List of Persons from the Brdo Area Who Participated in Procuring Weapons and Preparing the Genocide against the Serbian People," dated June 2, 1992. ICTY No. 00635454. Prosecutor v. Stakić, IT-97-24 (ICTY), Exhibit no. D257A.

List of persons detained at Batković camp, ICTY Exhibit no. P3213.

List of those who supposedly possessed arms, see II-98-30/1-T, no. 2643.

List of wounded Muslim prisoners, dated July 18, 1995, handed over by 5th Military Police Battalion from Vlasenica to 3rd Battalion IBK, ICTY no. 01798523 M, R. 2012.

Maass, Peter. "Illusory Serb Prison Camp Materializes." *Washington Post,* August 27, 1992. https://bit.ly/MaassSerbCamp.

Maass, Peter. *Love Thy Neighbor.* New York: Vintage, 1997.

Maass, Peter. "The Rapes in Bosnia: A Muslim Schoolgirl's Account." *Washington Post,* December 27, 1992. https://bit.ly/MaassWaPoRapesinBosnia.

Maass, Peter. "The Search for a Secret Prison Camp." *Washington Post,* August 13, 1992. https://bit.ly/MaassSearchSecretPrisonCamp.

MacDonald, David B. *Balkan Holocausts? Serbian and Croatian Victim-Centred Propaganda and the War in Yugoslavia.* Manchester: Manchester University Press, 2002.

Madley, Benjamin. *An American Genocide: The United States and the California Indian Catastrophe, 1846–1873.* New Haven, CT: Yale University Press, 2016.

Magaš, Branka, and Ivo Žanić. *The War in Croatia and Bosnia-Herzegovina, 1991–1995.* London: Frank Cass Publishers. 2001.

REFERENCES   227

Makšić, Adis. *Ethnic Mobilization, Violence, and the Politics of Affect: The Serb Democratic Party and the Bosnian War*. London: Palgrave Macmillan, 2017.

Maksić, Adis. "Priming the Nation for War: An Analysis of Organizational Origins And Discursive Machinations of the Serb Democratic Party in Pre-War Bosnia-Herzegovina, 1990–1992." *Journal of Muslim Minority Affairs* 35, no. 3 (August 2015): 334–43. doi:10.1080/13602004.2015.1073959.

Mann, Michael. *The Dark Side of Democracy: Explaining Ethnic Cleansing*. Cambridge: Cambridge University Press, 2005.

Markov, Ivan. "Otmica u Sjeverinu." *B92* (2002). https://www.b92.net/specijal/sjeverin/foto.php.

Marković, Ante. ICTY testimony, 2003. https://bit.ly/ICTYAnteMTest.

Medić, Jasmin. *Genocid u Prijedoru*. Cazin: Grafis d.o.o., 2013.

Medić, Jasmin. "'Kozarski vjesnik' u službi zločina." *Godišnjak Bošnjačke zajednice kulture: Preporod* 1 (2016).

Mesić, Stjepan. ICTY testimony, 2002. https://bit.ly/ICTYStipeMTest.

Megargee, Geoffrey P., ed. *The United States Holocaust Memorial Museum Encyclopedia of Camps and Ghettos,* Vol. I, 140–41. Washington, DC: United States Holocaust Memorial Museum, 2009.

Mehinovic v. Vuckovic, Civil Action 1:98-cv-2470-MHS (N.D. Ga. May 2, 2002), 13. https://casetext.com/case/mehinovic-v-vuckovic-3.

Milošević, Slobodan. "St. Vitus Day Speech." https://bit.ly/SlobMilStVDay.

Milovanović, Tatjana. "A Story about Đorđe and Salih." *Balkan Perspective*, no. 2 (January 6, 2016,): 10. https://www.forumzfd.de/system/files/document/Balkan.Perspectives_EN_2.pdf.

Milutinović, Radoša. "Army Responsible for Detention Camps." *Justice Report*, 2014. http://www.justice-report.com/en/articles/army-responsible-for-detention-camps.

Milutinović, Radoša. "UN Court Refuses to Free 'Serb Adolf.'" *Balkan Insight*, August 14, 2017. https://balkaninsight.com/2017/08/14/un-court-refuses-to-free-serb-adolf-08-14-2017/.

Mishra, Pramod Kumar. *Human Rights Reporting*. Delhi: Isha Books. 2006.

"Mladic: Big Crimes in Small Village." *Detektor/BIRN*, September 6, 2012. https://detektor.ba/2012/09/06/mladic-big-crimes-in-small-village/?lang=en.

"Mladic: Bosniak ex MP Talks About Omarska Camp: Justice Report." *Justice Report*, 2012. http://www.justice-report.com/en/articles/mladic-bosniak-ex-mp-talks-about-omarska-camp.

"Mladic: Bosniak ex MP Talks About Omarska Camp." *Detektor/BIRN*, October 2, 2012. http://www.justice-report.com/en/articles/mladic-bosniak-ex-mp-talks-about-omarska-camp.

"Mladic's Witness: Serbs are Genetically Stronger, Better, Handsomer and Smarter." 2018. *Sense Agency*. http://www.sense-agency.com/icty/mladic%E2%80%99s-witness-serbs-are-genetically-stronger-better-handsomer-and-smarter.29.html?news_id=15996.

228 REFERENCES

Mlakar, Mirko. "Vreme: Bijeljina Dynamiters; The Night the Minarets Fell." *Transitions Online*, March 22, 1993. https://tol.org/client/article/15027.html.

Mock, Steven. *Symbols of Defeat in the Construction of National Identity*. Cambridge: Cambridge University Press, 2012.

Møller, Bjørn. *Refugees, Prisoners and Camps: A Functional Analysis of the Phenomenon of Encampment*. Basingstoke: Palgrave Macmillan, 2015.

Mulaosmanović, Admir. "Islam and Muslims in Greater Serbian Ideology: The Origins of an Antagonism and the Misuse of the Past." *Journal of Muslim Minority Affairs* 39, no. 3 (September 2019): 300–16. https://doi.org/10.1080/13602004.2019.1652408.

Musli, Emir. 2015. "Bijeljinska i janjarska knjiga mrtvih." *BZK–Preporod Bijeljina*, April 19, 2015. http://preporodbn.com/bijeljinska-i-janjarska-knjiga-mrtvih/.

"Na 'mozganje' kod Karadžića." *Sense Agency*, 31 March, 2006. https://arhiva.sensecentar.org/vijesti.php?aid=163.

Nielsen. Christian Axboe. "The Bosnian Serb Ministry of Internal Affairs: Genesis, Performance and Command and Control, 1990–1992." United Nations International Criminal Tribunal for the Former Yugoslavia. Research report prepared for the case of Krajišnik (IT-00-39), updated for Mićo Stanišić (IT-04-79). May 19, 2011.

Nielsen, Christian Axboe. "Expert's Report: Report on the Events in Bileća Municipality, Bosnia Herzegovina, from November 1990 Until the End of 1992, with a Focus on the Role of Police and Reserve Police in Those Events." Crimes against Humanity and War Crimes Section of the Department of Justice. Canada: May 2009.

"Nobody Expelled Muslims and They Shelled Themselves." *Sense-agency.com*, March 6, 2013. https://archive.sensecentar.org/vijesti.php?aid=14730.

Obradović, Goran. "Bosnian Serb Soldiers Jailed for Prijedor Murders." *Detektor/BIRN*, December 8, 2014. https://detektor.ba/2014/12/08/bosnian-serb-soldiers-jailed-for-prijedor-murders/?lang=en.

Obradović, Goran. "Tadic Sentenced to Five Years for Killing a Detained." *Detektor/BIRN*, July 5, 2013. https://detektor.ba/2013/07/05/tadic-sentenced-to-five-years-for-killing-a-detained/?lang=en.

O'Kane, Maggie. "UN Condemns Serb 'Policy' of Rape." *Guardian Weekly*, December, 27, 1992, 8.

Okun, Herbert. ICTY testimony. 2003. https://bit.ly/ICTYHerbOTest.

Opotow, Susan, Janet Gerson, and Sarah Woodside. "From Moral Exclusion to Moral Inclusion: Theory for Teaching Peace." *Theory Into Practice* 44, no. 4 (2005): 303–18. https://doi.org/10.1207/s15430421tip4404_4.

Ostler, Jeffrey. "Genocide and American Indian History." In *Oxford Research Encyclopedia of American History*. https://bit.ly/GenocideAmericanHist.

Ostler, Jeffrey. *Surviving Genocide: Native Nations and the United States from the American Revolution to Bleeding Kansas*. New Haven, CT: Yale University Press, 2019.

Pajović, Radoje. "O Studentskom Pokretu Beogradskog Univerziteta (1934–1941)." *Matica*, 60/61 (2014/ 2015): 183. http://www.maticacrnogorska.me/files/60/07%20radoje%20pajovic.pdf.

REFERENCES   229

Parry, Marc. "Uncovering the Brutal Truth About the British empire." *The Guardian*, August 18, 2016. https://www.theguardian.com/news/2016/aug/18/uncovering-tru th-british-empire-caroline-elkins-mau-mau.

Percy, Norman. *Yugoslavia: Death of a Nation*. DVD. United Kingdom: BBC2, 1995.

Pervan, Tahir. *Čavkarica—vrata pakla*. Sarajevo: Zonex ex libris, 2006.

Pervanić, Kemal. *The Killing Days*. Blake, 1999.

Petrović, Petar Ž. "Lila, olalija i srodni običaji." *Bulletin of the Ethnographic Museum*, 2. Belgrade: Ethnographic Museum, 1927. https://etnografskimuzej.rs/en/o-muzeju/iz davastvo/periodika/gem-2/.

Petrović, Vladimir, "Etnicizacija čišćenja u reći i nedelu: Represija i njena naučna legiti- mizacija." *Hereticus*, no. 1 (2007): 11.

Pitzer, Andrea. *One Long Night*. Boston: Little, Brown and Company, 2017.

Pomfret, John. 1993. "Muslims Try 'Name Cleansing' to Survive in Serb-Held Bosnia." *Washington Post*, December 21, 1993. https://bit.ly/PomfretWaPoMuslimsTryName Cleansing.

Potrošna nafta od 23.5.1992–20.10.1992 po potrošačima (Used fuel, May 23, 1992–October 20, 1992 by users), ICTY no. 00381755.

Prosecutor v. Darko Mrđa (Sentencing Judgment), IT-02-59-S, International Criminal Tribunal for the former Yugoslavia (ICTY), March 31, 2004.

Prosecutor v. Đorđević (Trial Judgement), IT-05-87/1, International Criminal Tribunal for the former Yugoslavia (ICTY), February 25, 2014.

Prosecutor v. Duško Sikirica, Damir Došen, Dragan Kolundžija (Sentencing Judgment), IT-95-8-S, International Criminal Tribunal for the former Yugoslavia (ICTY), November 13, 2001.

Prosecutor v. Duško Tadić, IT-94-1-T (ICTY), Decision, No. 03/3-846-2, Gutić Vasif: Exhibit no. 297.

Prosecutor v. Duško Tadić aka "Dule" (Opinion and Judgment), IT-94-1-T, International Criminal Tribunal for the former Yugoslavia (ICTY), May 7, 1997. https://www.icty .org/x/cases/tadic/tjug/en/tad-tsj70507JT2-e.pdf.

Prosecutor v. Jadranko Prlić, Bruno Stojić, Slobodan Praljak, Milivoj Petković, Valentin Corić, Berislav Pušić (Prosecutor v. Prlić et al.) (Judgment, Volume III), IT-04-74-A, International Criminal Tribunal for the former Yugoslavia (ICTY), November 29, 2017. https://bit.ly/ICTYPrlic171129.

Prosecutor v. Jović et al. (Odeljenje za ratne zločine) br. K-Po2 br 7/2011 (Viši Sud u Beogradu, Republika Srbija), June 4, 2012. https://bit.ly/ProsvJovicJudgement.

Prosecutor v. Jovica Stanišić and Franko Simatović, IT-03--69 (ICTY), Witness state- ment by Milomir Kovačević given to the International Criminal Tribunal for the former Yugoslavia (ICTY) on April 29, 2003.

Prosecutor v. Mićo Stanišić and Stojan Župljanin (Judgment, Volume 2), IT-08-91-T, International Criminal Tribunal for the former Yugoslavia (ICTY), March 27, 2013. https://www.icty.org/x/cases/zupljanin_stanisicm/tjug/en/130327-2.pdf.

Prosecutor v. Milan Lukić and Sredoje Lukić (Judgment), IT-98-32/1-T, International

Criminal Tribunal for the former Yugoslavia (ICTY), July 20, 2009. https://www.ic ty.org/x/cases/milan_lukic_sredoje_lukic/tjug/en/090720_j.pdf.

Prosecutor v. Milomir Stakić (Judgment), IT-97-24-T, International Criminal Tribunal for the former Yugoslavia (ICTY), July 31, 2003. https://www.icty.org/x/cases/stakic /tjug/en/stak-tj030731e.pdf.

Prosecutor v. Miroslav Kvočka et al (Judgment), IT-98-30/1-T, International Criminal Tribunal for the former Yugoslavia (ICTY), November 2, 2001. https://www.icty.org /x/cases/kvocka/tjug/en/kvo-tj011002e.pdf.

Prosecutor v. Mitar Vasiljević (Judgment), IT-98-32-T, International Criminal Tribunal for the former Yugoslavia (ICTY), November 29, 2002. https://www.icty.org/x/cases /vasiljevic/tjug/en/vas021129.pdf.

Prosecutor v. Mitar Vasiljević (VG022 Witness Statement), IT-98-32-T, International Criminal Tribunal for the former Yugoslavia (ICTY), September 10, 2001. https:// www.icty.org/x/cases/vasiljevic/trans/en/010910ED.htm.

Prosecutor v. Momčilo Krajišnik (Judgment), IT-00-39-T (ICTY), September 27, 2006, 116, https://www.icty.org/x/cases/krajisnik/tjug/en/kra-jud060927e.pdf.

Prosecutor v. Radoslav Brđanin (Judgment), IT-99-36-T, International Criminal Tribunal for the former Yugoslavia (ICTY), September 1, 2004. http://www.icty.org/x/cas es/brdanin/tjug/en/brd-tj040901e.pdf.

Prosecutor v. Radovan Karadžić ("Prosecution's Submission Pursuant to Rule 65 ter (E) (i)-(iii)"), IT-95-5/18-PT, International Criminal Tribunal for the former Yugoslavia (ICTY), May 18, 2009. https://bit.ly/ICTYKaradzic090518.

Prosecutor v. Radovan Karadžić (Judgment), IT-95-5/18-T, International Criminal Tribunal for the former Yugoslavia (ICTY), March 24, 2016.https://bit.ly/ICTYKaradz ic160324 .

Prosecutor v. Ratko Mladić (Judgment, Vol. 4), IT-09-92-T, (ICTY), November 22, 2017, https://www.icty.org/x/cases/mladic/tjug/en/171122-4of5_1.pdf.

Prosecutor v. Stakić (Statement by Minka Čehajić), IT-97-24-T, International Criminal Tribunal for the former Yugoslavia (ICTY), May 14, 15 and 16, 2002. https://www.ic ty.org/x/cases/stakic/trans/en/020514IT.htm.

Prosecutor v. Stakić (Transcript), IT-97-24-T, International Criminal Tribunal for the former Yugoslavia (ICTY), June 26, 2002. http://www.icty.org/x/cases/stakic/trans /en/020626ED.htm.

Prosecutor v. Stakić, (Transcript, Witness Testimony by Nusret Sivac) IT-97-24-T, International Criminal Tribunal for the former Yugoslavia (ICTY), July 31, 2002. http:// www.icty.org/x/cases/stakic/trans/en/020731ED.htm.

Prosecutor v. Vlastimir Đorđević (Judgment, Vol. 1), IT-05-87/1-T, International Criminal Tribunal for the former Yugoslavia (ICTY), February 23, 2011. https://www.icty .org/x/cases/djordjevic/tjug/en/110223_djordjevic_judgt_en.pdf.

Prosecutor v. Vojislav Šešelj (Trial Transcript), IT-03-67-T (ICTY), March 4, 2009, 14283–92, http://www.icty.org/x/cases/seselj/trans/en/090304ED.htm.

REFERENCES   231

Prosecutor v. Željko Lelek (Second Instance Judgment), X-KRŽ-06/202 (Sud Bosne i Hercegovine), January 12, 2009. http://www.sudbih.gov.ba/predmet/2445/show.

"Radoslav Brdjanin's Off-Color Jokes." *Sense Agency*, October 31, 2011. http://archive.sen secentar.org/vijesti.php?aid=13325.

Ramcharan, Bertrand G. *Human Rights and U.N. Peace Operations: Yugoslavia.* Leiden: M. Nijhoff Publishers, 2001.

Raxhimi, Altin, Michael Montgomery, and Vladimir Karaj. "KLA Ran Torture Camps in Albania." *Balkan Insight BIRN*. April 9, 2009, http://www.balkaninsight.com/en/art icle/kla-ran-torture-camps-in-albania.

Read, Peter and Marivic Wyndham. "Putting Site Back into Trauma Studies: A Study of Five Detention and Torture Centres in Santiago, Chile." *Life Writing* 5, no. 1 (June 2008): 79–96. https://doi.org/10.1080/14484520801902365.

Record of Interview with the Accused Milan Lukić, Kio. no. 118/92. October 30, 1992. International Criminal Tribunal for the former Yugoslavia (ICTY) Evidence, no. 0644-6149-0644-6154-ET/Translation. https://bit.ly/MilanLukicInt30Oct1992.

"Record of Interview of Accused, Kemal Mehinović," January 19, 1993, Prosecutor v. Simić et al., (ICTY) IT-95-9-T, Exhibit no. P55.

Redžić, Enver. *Bosnia and Herzegovina in the Second World War.* London: Routledge. 2005.

"Report of CSCE Mission to Inspect Places of Detention in Bosnia–Hercegovina, August 29–September 4, 1992," 59. See Prosecutor v. Radoslav Brđanin (Judgment), IT-99-36-T (ICTY), Exhibit no. P1617/S217b. https://bit.ly/ProsvBrdaninExP1617.

"Report of the Chilean National Commission on Truth and Reconciliation Notre Dame." South Bend, IN: University of Notre Dame Press, 1993. Accessed on January 19, 2016. https://bit.ly/ChileanTruthandRecon.

Republički zavod za statistiku: Republika Srpska. "Rezultati Popisa 2013, Gradovi, opštine, naseljena mjesta." http://rzs.rs.ba/front/article/2369/.

Riedlmayer, András J. *Destruction of Cultural Heritage in Bosnia and Herzegovina 1992–1995, A Post-war Survey of Selected Municipalities.* Cambridge, MA: 2002. https://bit .ly/DestructionCultHeritageBH.

Riedlmayer, András J. "From the Ashes: The Past and Future of Bosnia's Cultural Heritage." In *Islam and Bosnia: Conflict Resolution and Foreign Policy in Multi-Ethnic States*, edited by Maya Shatzmiller, 98–135. Montreal: McGill-Queens University Press, 2002.

Rieff, David. *Slaughterhouse: Bosnia and the Failure of the West.* New York: Vintage, 1995.

"Rođen po drugi put." *Sense Agency*. 26 September, 2008 https://arhiva.sensecentar.org /vijesti.php?aid=5604

Rosenbaum, Alan S, and Israel W. Charny. *Is The Holocaust Unique?* Boulder, CO: Westview Press, 2009.

RS Ministry of Defense. "List of Muslims Exchanged from the Batković SC." No. 8/1-08-77-4/02 dated March 12, 2002.

RS Ministry of Interior Srbinje Public Security Centre. "List of participation in war of all v/o /conscripts/ who had wartime assignments in the SJB /Public Security Station/ in the period from 4 August 1991 to 30 June 1996." June 7, 1999, number: 15-5/-010239/99, ICTY no.: 06345001, Exhibit no. 2D00060.E. https://bit.ly/RSMUPListC onscripts1991-96.

S, A. "Koricanske stijene: Standing in Line for Shooting." *Justice Report*, 2010.

Sanyal, Debarati. *Memory and Complicity: Migrations of Holocaust Remembrance.* New York: Fordham University Press, 2015.

Šarić, Velma. "Bosnian Serb Power Grab Was Pre-Planned." *Institute for War and Peace Reporting*, June 3, 2011. https://iwpr.net/global-voices/bosnian-serb-power-grab -was-pre-planned.

Šarić, Velma. "UK Reporter Recalls Visegrad Offensive." *Institute for War and Peace Reporting*, May 24, 2010. https://iwpr.net/global-voices/uk-reporter-recalls-visegr ad-offensive.

Šarić, Velma. "Witness Describes Manjaca as Death Camp." *Institute for War and Peace Reporting*, December 6, 2009. https://iwpr.net/global-voices/witness-describes-ma njaca-death-camp.

Sarkin-Hughes, Jeremy. *Germany's Genocide of the Herero: Kaiser Wilhelm II, His General, His Settlers, His Soldiers.* Rochester, NY: James Currey, 2011.

Security Services Center Trebinje. "Information on Activities of the Members of So-Called Paramilitary Formations on the Territory of Serbian Autonomous Region of Herzegovina." Number: 01-172/92, dated August 4, 1992, ICTY no. 00741280.

Sekulić, Boris. "Constant Beating." *Justice Report*, 2013. http://www.justice-report.com /en/articles/news-constant-beating.

Sekulić, Boris. "Slapped Without Reason." *Justice Report*, 2014. http://www.justice-repo rt.com/en/articles/slapped-without-reason.

Sekulić, Boris. "Witness Heard about Mistreatment and Murders." *Justice Report*, 2014. http://www.justice-report.com/en/articles/witness-heard-about-mistreatment-and -murders.

Sells, Michael A. *The Bridge Betrayed.* Berkeley: University of California Press, 1999.

Sells, Michael. "Crosses of Blood: Sacred Space, Religion, and Violence in Bosnia-Hercegovina." *Sociology of Religion* 64, no. 3, Special Issue (Autumn 2003): 309–31. https://doi.org/10.2307/3712487.

Shatzmiller, Maya, ed. *Islam and Bosnia: Conflict Resolution and Foreign Policy in Multi-Ethnic States.* Montreal: McGill-Queen's University Press, 2002.

Shaw, Martin. *What Is Genocide?* Cambridge: Polity Press, 2015.

Sokolović, Faruk. "Clouds over Bijeljina," *Institute for War and Peace Reporting/Mebius Film*, April 20, 2012. https://www.youtube.com/watch?v=aIh3zgP_Y10.

Sokolović, Faruk. "Bijeljina: The Righteous Man," *Institute for War and Peace Reporting/ Mebius Film*, April 24, 2012, [3:30–3:45], https://www.youtube.com/watch?v=qIe0E w5iJo0.

REFERENCES   233

Shields, Jacqueline. "Concentration Camps: The Sonderkommando." Jewish Virtual Library. http://www.jewishvirtuallibrary.org/the-sonderkommando.

Sherwell, Philip. "Ratko Mladic Arrest: The Balkan Beasts Are No More." *The Telegraph*, May 26, 2011. https://bit.ly/SherwellTelegraphMladicarrest.

Silber, Laura, and Allan Little. *The Death of Yugoslavia*. New York: Penguin Books, 1997.

Simić, P. "Regionalizacija—volja naroda" (Regionalisation—People's Will), *Javnost*, September 28, 1991.

Simić, Pero. "Semberija izgubljena za Alijinu državu (Semberija Lost for Alija's State)." *List SAO Semberije i Majevice—SiM*. 1992.

Sirkin, Micol. "Expanding the Crime of Genocide to Include Ethnic Cleansing: A Return to Established Principles in Light of Contemporary Interpretations." *Seattle University Law Review* 33 (2010): 489–526. https://digitalcommons.law.seattleu.edu/cgi/viewcontent.cgi?article=1984&context=sulr.

Sivac, Nusret. *Kolika je u Prijedoru čaršija: zapisi za nezaborav*. Sarajevo: Bonik, 1995.

Smith, Iain R., and Andreas Stucki. "The Colonial Development of Concentration Camps (1868–1902)." *The Journal of Imperial and Commonwealth History* 39, no. 3 (September 2011): 417–37. https://doi.org/10.1080/03086534.2011.598746.

Solzhenitsyn Aleksandr. *The Gulag Archipelago 1918–1956*, vol. 1. Translated by Thomas P. Whitney. New York: Harper & Row, 1975.

Sorguč, Albina. "Beaten Up in Police Station." *Detektor*, December 23, 2014. https://detektor.ba/2014/12/23/beaten-up-in-police-station/?lang=en.

Sorguč, Albina. "Brutal Beating in Uzamnica." *Detektor*, January 14, 2015. https://detektor.ba/2015/01/14/brutal-beating-in-uzamnica/?lang=en.

Sorguč, Albina. "Bošnjak i ostali: Optuženi Mavrak najviše tukao." *Detektor*, September 9, 2017. http://detektor.ba/bosnjak-i-ostali-optuzeni-mavrak-najvise-tukao/.

Sorguč, Albina. "Prisoner Recalls Visegrad Police Station Abuse." *Detektor*, April 9, 2013. http://detektor.ba/en/prisoner-recalls-visegrad-police-station-abuse/.

Sorguč, Albina. "Visible Injuries on Detainees." *Detektor*, January 20, 2015. https://detektor.ba/2015/01/20/visible-injuries-on-detainees/?lang=en.

Sorguč, Albina. "The Wall of Silence About Crimes in Bileca." *Detektor*, November 20, 2014. https://detektor.ba/2014/11/20/the-wall-of-silence-about-crimes-in-bileca/?lang=en.

Sorguč, Albina. "Witness Describes Detainee Beatings at Bileca Police Station." *Detektor*, March 10, 2015. https://detektor.ba/2015/03/10/witness-describes-detainee-beatings-at-bileca-police-station/?lang=en.

Sorguč, Albina. "Witness Describes Prisoner Abuse at Bileca Detention Facilities." *Detektor*, April 7, 2015. https://detektor.ba/2015/04/07/witness-describes-prisoner-abuse-at-bileca-detention-facilities/?lang=en.

Sorguč, Albina. "Witnesses Took Statements from Bosniak Prisoners in Bileca." *Detektor*, August 25, 2015. https://detektor.ba/2015/08/25/witnesses-took-statements-from-bosniak-prisoners-in-bileca/?lang=en.

234 REFERENCES

Spisak pripadnika rezervnog sastava milicije u avgustu 1992.(zaposleni), ICTY no. P000–4269.

Spisak pripadnika rezervnog sastava milicije za naknadu LD Maj 1992, ICTY no. P0004473.

Spisak radnika specijalne jedinice za isplatu LD za mjesec april 1992. godine, ICTY no. F120–1962.

Spisak radnika za isplatu LD za mjesec maj 1992. godine, ICTY no. 02971881.

Spisak rezervnog sastava milicije SJB Bileća koji su angažovani u mjesecu julu 1992. godine, ICTY no. F120—2743.

Srebrenica, Šaćir. "Žrtve agresije na Bosnu i Hercegovinu." *Zbornik radova: Genocid nad Bošnjacima 1992–95* (Sarajevo: Okrugli sto, 2012).

Stewart, Phil. "China Putting Minority Muslims in 'Concentration Camps,' U.S. Says." *Reuters*, May 4, 2019. https://bit.ly/ChinaMuslimCamps.

Stiglmayer, Alexandra, Marion Faber, and Roy Gutman. *Mass Rape: The War against Women in Bosnia-Herzegovina.* Lincoln: University of Nebraska Press. 1994.

Stone, Dan. *Concentration Camps: A Short History.* New York: Oxford University Press, 2017.

Stover, Eric. *Medicine under Siege in the Former Yugoslavia, 1991–1995.* Boston: Physicians for Human Rights. 1996.

Straus, Scott. "The Promise and Limits of Comparison: The Holocaust and the 1994 Genocide in Rwanda." In *Is the Holocaust Unique? Perspectives on Comparative Genocide,* edited by Alan S. Rosenbaum, 245–57. Boulder CO: Westview Press, 1997.

"Strpci Victims' Relatives 'Heard about Abductions via Media.'" *BIRN BiH,* May 16, 2016. http://www.justice-report.com/en/articles/strpci-victims-relatives-heard-about-ab ductions-via-media#sthash.PdWBMsxb.dpuf.

Subotić, Jelena *Yellow Star, Red Star: Holocaust Remembrance after Communism.* Ithaca, NY: Cornell University Press, 2019.

Sudetić, Chuck. 1994. "Serbs Drive 800 More Muslims From Homes." *New York Times,* September 5, 1994. https://www.nytimes.com/1994/09/05/world/serbs-drive-800 -more-muslims-from-homes.html.

Suljagić, Emir. "*Ethnic Cleansing: Politics, Policy, Violence (Serb Ethnic Cleansing campaign in former Yugoslavia)*", PhD thesis, Universität Hamburg, 2009.

Tabeau, Ewa, et al. "Ethnic Composition, Internally Displaced Persons and Refugee from 47 Municipalities of Bosnia and Herzegovina, 1991 to 1997." February 3, 2009, Prosecutor v. Radovan Karadžić, IT-95-5/18 (ICTY), Exhibit no. P04994.B.

Taušan, Marija. "Defence Witnesses Speak about Abusers in Uzamnica." *Detektor,* August 20, 2013. https://detektor.ba/2013/08/20/defence-witnesses-speak-about-ab users-in-uzamnica/?lang=en.

Taušan, Marija. "Ex-Prisoner Recalls Regular Beatings in Bileca." *Detektor,* August 16, 2016. http://detektor.ba/en/ex-prisoner-recalls-regular-beatings-in-bileca/.

Taušan, Marija. "Prosecution Calls for Long-Term Imprisonment for Krsmanovic."

REFERENCES   235

Detektor (BIRN), May 19, 2015. https://detektor.ba/2015/05/19/prosecution-calls-for-long-term-imprisonment-for-krsmanovic/?lang=en.

Taylor, Alan. 2012. "20 Years Since the Bosnian War." *The Atlantic*, April 13, 2012. http://www.theatlantic.com/photo/2012/04/20-years-since-the-bosnian-war/100278/#img14.

"Testimony by Marko Knežić," ICTY, September 17, 2003. http://www.icty.org/en/content/marko-kne%C5%BEi%C4%87.

"Tfsrol: Severe Human Rights Abuses In B-H: Eye-Witness Describes Torture/Executions in Luka And Batkovic Camps, Names Perpetrators," February 28, 1994. https://wikileaks.org/plusd/cables/94ZAGREB827_a.html.

"The 'Wailing Wall' in Prijedor." *Sense Agency*, 2011. https://archive.sensecentar.org/vijesti.php?aid=13231.

Theunens, Reynaud, "Radovan Karadžić and the SRBiH TO-VRS (1992–1995)." ICTY no. 0704-6234, July 11, 2011.

Tošić Čedo i Vojin Vuković. "Report on repeated monitoring of the implementation of the implementation of the order of the Ministry of internal affairs of the Serb Republic BiH, strictly confidential Number 10–17/92," dated August 10, 1992, ICTY no. 06492096, Exhibit no. 1D00649.E.

Totten, Samuel, and Paul R. Bartrop. *Dictionary of Genocide*. Westport, CT: Greenwood Press, 2008.

Totten, Samuel, William Parsons, and Israel Charny. *Century of Genocide: Critical Essays and Eyewitness Accounts*. London: Psychology Press, 2004.

TPOS. http://www.tranzicijska-pravda.org/.

Transcript of conversation. SUBJECT: The conversation held on April 23, 1992 between Momčilo MANDIĆ and TRAPARIĆ, and between Momčilo MANDIĆ and Zorica. Internal number: CD-52-20-5/03/026. Prosecutor v. Radovan Karadžić, IT-95-5/18 (ICTY), Exhibit no. P05701.E.

Traynor, Ian. "How They Wiped Out Kozarac; An Area of Northern Bosnia Abandoned by International Monitors Became the Target of a Bloody Serb Operation to Decimate the Muslim Majority and Exterminate Its Leaders." *The Guardian*, October 17, 1992, 23.

Trbić, Jusuf. 2004. *Gluho doba*. Sarajevo: BZK Preporod.

Tužilac protiv Branko Ljubišić, K.16/00–134, Prvostupanjska presuda, Županijski sud u Dubrovniku, September 8, 2001.

Tužilaštvo BiH v. Boban Šimšić (First Instance Verdict), X-KR-04/05 (Sud Bosne i Hercegovine), July 11, 2006. http://www.sudbih.gov.ba/predmet/2417/show.

Tužilaštvo BiH v. Boban Šimšić (Appeals Chamber Verdict), X-KRŽ-05/04 (Sud Bosne i Hercegovine), August 7, 2007. http://www.sudbih.gov.ba/predmet/2417/show.

Tužilaštvo BiH v. Babić Zoran i dr., S1-1-K-003472-12 Kžk (Sud Bosne i Hercegovine, 2009), http://www.sudbih.gov.ba/predmet/2574/show.

Tužilaštvo BiH v. Čivčić Petar i dr., X-KR-09/772 (Sud Bosne i Hercegovine, 2009), http://www.sudbih.gov.ba/predmet/2621/show.

236 REFERENCES

Tužilaštvo BiH v. Dragomir Soldat i dr., (Dragomir Soldat et al), S1 1 K 011967 14 Krž (Sud Bosne i Hercegovine, 2015). http://www.sudbih.gov.ba/predmet/3048/show.

Tužilaštvo BiH v. Dušan Milunić i dr. (Dušan Milunić et al), S1 1 K 017538 15 KrI (Sud Bosne i Hercegovine, 2018). http://www.sudbih.gov.ba/predmet/3403/show.

Tužilaštvo BiH v. Gligor Begović (First Instance Judgment), S 1 1 K 009588 12 Kri (Sud Bosne i Hercegovine), December 11, 2015, 5 and 8. http://www.sudbih.gov.ba/predm et/3328/show.

Tužilaštvo BiH v. Goran Vujović i dr. (First Instance Judgment), S1 1 K 014293 13 KrI (Sud Bosne i Herzegovine), July 8, 2016. http://www.sudbih.gov.ba/predmet/3198/show.

Tužilaštvo BiH v. Krsto Savić (First Instance Verdict), X-KR-07/400 (Sud Bosne i Hercegovine), March 24, 2009. http://www.sudbih.gov.ba/predmet/2526/show.

Tužilaštvo BiH v Krsto Savić (Second Instance Verdict), X-KRŽ-07/400 (Sud Bosne i Hercegovine), April 11, 2011, 8-10. http://www.sudbih.gov.ba/predmet/2526/show

Tužilaštvo BiH v. Momir Savić (First Instance Judgment), X-KR-07/478 (Sud Bosne i Hercegovine), July 3, 2009. http://www.sudbih.gov.ba/predmet/2528/show.

Tužilaštvo BiH v. Momir Savić (Second Instance Judgment), X-KRŽ-07/478 (Sud Bosne i Hecegovine), February 19, 2010. http://www.sudbih.gov.ba/predmet/2528/show.

Tužilaštvo BiH v. Nenad Tanasković (First Instance Judgment), X-KR/06/165 (Sud Bosne i Hercegovine), August 24, 2007. http://www.sudbih.gov.ba/predmet/2443 /show.

Tužilaštvo KS v. Novo Rajak (Trial Judgment), K-53/04 (Kantonalni sud u Sarajevu), November 27, 2006.

Tužilaštvo BiH v. Oliver Krsmanović (First Instance Judgment), S 1 1 K 006028 11 Kri (Sud Bosne i Herzegovine), August 31, 2015. http://sudbih.gov.ba/predmet/2867 /show.

Tužilaštvo BiH v. Petar Kovačević (First Instance Verdict), S 1 1 K 014093 14 Kri (Sud Bosne i Hercegovine), November 2, 2015. http://www.sudbih.gov.ba/predmet/3286 /show.

Tužilaštvo BiH v. Predrag Milisavljević et al. (First Instance Verdict), S1 1 K 0011128 12 Krl (Sud Bosne i Hercegovine), October 28, 2014. http://www.sudbih.gov.ba/predm et/3013/show.

Tužilaštvo BiH v. Ratko Bundalo i dr. (First Instance Judgment), X-KR-07/419 (Sud Bosne i Hercegovine), December 21, 2009. http://www.sudbih.gov.ba/predmet/3593 /show.

Tužilaštvo BiH v. Slobodan Taranjac et al., S1 1 K 024175 17 Kri (Sud Bosne i Hercegovine). http://www.sudbih.gov.ba/predmet/3625/show.

Tužilaštvo BiH v. Vitomir Racković (First Instance Verdict), S1 1 K 014365 14 Kri (Sud Bosne i Hercegovine), May 11, 2015. http://www.sudbih.gov.ba/predmet/3175/show.

Tužilaštvo BiH v. Željko Lelek (First Instance Verdict), X-KR/06/202 (Sud Bosne i Hercegovine), May 23, 2008. http://www.sudbih.gov.ba/predmet/2445/show.

Tužilaštvo BiH v. Željko Mejakić i dr. (Mejakić et al), (Verdict), X-KR/06/200 (Sud Bosne i Hercegovine), May 30, 2008. https://bit.ly/ProsvMejakicVerdict.

REFERENCES 237

"'Typhoon' from Republika Srpska." *Sense Agency*, July 1, 2011, http://archive.sensecentar
.org/vijesti.php?aid=12951.

Učanbarlić, Selma. "Connected to Electricity, Beaten, Mistreated." *Detektor*, October 28,
2014. https://detektor.ba/2014/10/28/connected-to-electricity-beaten-mistreated/
?lang=en.

United Nations Office on Genocide Prevention and the Responsibility to Protect. "Definitions: Ethnic Cleansing." Accessed November 13, 2020. https://www.un.org/en/ge
nocideprevention/ethnic-cleansing.shtml.

United Nations Security Council. "Final Report of the United Nations Commission of
Experts Established Pursuant to Security Council Resolution 780 (1992)." Annex
VIII: Prison Camps, l, May 27, 1994, 67. https://bit.ly/FinalRepUNExRepAnnexVIII.

United States Committee for Refugees and Immigrants. "U.S. Committee for Refugees
World Refugee Survey 1998—Bosnia and Herzegovina." Accessed January 1, 2021.
https://www.refworld.org/docid/3ae6a8ab10.html.

United States Holocaust Memorial Museum. "Auschwitz." https://www.ushmm.org/wlc
/en/article.php?ModuleId=10005189.

United States Holocaust Memorial Museum. "Concentration Camps: 1933–1939." http://
www.ushmm.org/wlc/en/article.php?ModuleId=10005263.

United States Holocaust Memorial Museum. "Concentration Camps: 1939–1942."
Accessed January 19, 2016. http://www.ushmm.org/wlc/en/article.php?ModuleId=1
0005474.

United States Holocaust Memorial Museum. "An Early Concentration Camp (Photograph)." In Concentration Camps: 1933–1939. Accessed January 7, 2016. https://www
.ushmm.org/wlc/en/media_ph.php?ModuleId=10005263&MediaId=775.

United States Holocaust Memorial Museum. "Persecution of Roma (Gypsies) In Prewar Germany: 1933–1939." https://www.ushmm.org/wlc/en/article.php?ModuleId=
10005482.

United States Holocaust Memorial Museum. "Killing Centres: In Depth" In *Holocaust
Encyclopedia*. Accessed January 5, 2020. https://encyclopedia.ushmm.org/content/en
/article/introduction-to-the-holocaust.

Uskoro Srpska narodna čitaonica." *Javnost*, September 21, 1991, 2.

"Višegradska brigada branila i odbranila srpski narod." *Glas Srpske*, May 26, 2012.
https://www.glassrpske.com/lat/drustvo/panorama/visegradska-brigada-branila
-i-odbranila-srpski-narod/80241.

Vukušić, Iva. "Serbian Paramilitaries in the Breakup of Yugoslavia." PhD dissertation,
Utrecht University, 2020.

Vulliamy, Ed. "'Neutrality' and the Absence of Reckoning: A Journalist's Account." *Journal of International Affairs* 52, no. 2 (Spring 1999): 603–20. Accessed December 20,
2020. http://www.jstor.org/stable/24358055.

Vulliamy, Ed. *Seasons in Hell*. New York: St. Martin's Press. 1994.

Wachsmann, Nikolaus. *KL: A History of the Nazi Concentration Camps*. New York: Farrar, Straus and Giroux, 2015.

238   REFERENCES

"The Wailing Wall in Prijedor." *Sense Agency*, August 28, 2011. http://archive.sensecentar
.org/vijesti.php?aid=13231.

Walasek, Helen. *Bosnia and the Destruction of Cultural Heritage*. London: Ashgate Publishing, Ltd, 2015.

Weisband, Edward. *The Macabresque*. New York: Oxford University Press, 2017.

Weine, Stevan M. *When History Is a Nightmare: Lives and Memories of Ethnic Cleansing in Bosnia-Herzegovina*. New Brunswick, NJ: Rutgers University Press, 1999.

"Witness Recalls Electric Shock Torture in Bileca." *Detektor*, May 24, 2016. https://detek
tor.ba/2016/05/24/witness-recalls-electric-shock-torture-in-bileca/?lang=en.

Witness statement by Sakib Husrefović, ICTY, dated 26–27.5.1995https://bit.ly/Husrefov
icWitnessStatement.

Witness statement by witness VG-32 given to the International Criminal Tribunal for the former Yugoslavia (ICTY) on September 4, 2008. https://www.icty.org/x/cases
/milan_lukic_sredoje_lukic/trans/en/080904ED.htm.

Witness statement by witness VG-042 given to the International Criminal Tribunal for the former Yugoslavia (ICTY) on October 27, 2008. https://www.icty.org/x/cases/mi
lan_lukic_sredoje_lukic/trans/en/081027ED.htm.

Wiesel, Elie. *Night*. London: Penguin Books Limited, 2012.

Wunsch Gaarmann, Margit V. *The War in Our Background: The Bosnia and Kosovo War Through The Lenses of the German Print Media*. Berlin: Neofelis Verlag, 2015.

"You Can't Forget. It's Impossible." *Justice Report*, April 19, 2006. http://www.justice-rep
ort.com/en/articles/for-the-record-you-can-t-forget-it-s-impossible.

Name Index

A (witness), 90
A.B. (witness), 160
Abdić, Fikret, 69, 150
Agić, Emin, 91n67
Agić, Meho, 91n67
Aguinaldo, Emilio, 48
A.H. (victim-witness), 91n68, 160
Ahmetagić, Naila, 84n34, 85
Ahmetspahić, Amela, 84n32
Ahmetspahić, Jasmina, 106
Alić, Ekrem, 142n170
Alić, Fikret, 71
Alić, Smail, 142n170
Aljić, Meho, 83
Allen, Beverly, 70–71
Andan, Dragomir, 156
Andrić, Duško, 90
Andrić, Ivo, 75, 75n1, 75n3
Andžić, Milan, 143n177
Arendt, Hannah, 36
Arkan. See Ražnatović, Željko
Arsić, Vladimir, 113, 118, 146
A.V. (witness), 123
Avdić, Enver, 181–182
Avdić, Ferhat, 179, 186
Avdić, Hajreta, 151
Avdić, Nizama, 151
Avdić, Juso, 98
Avdić, Rama, 151
Avdić, Rasim, 98
Avlijaš, Slobodan, 187
Azinović, Mile, 177

Babović, Mujo, 183
Bajić, Mizra, 98

Bajramović, Edin 181
Bajramović, Hasena, 85n40
Bajramović, Ismet, 184–185
Bajramović, Mehmed, 85n40
Bajramović, Mesud, 180
Bajramović, Nedžad, 181
Bajramović, Sajto, 185
Baltić, Asmir, 124
Bandura, Albert, 42
Barnes, Steven, 34
Bar-Tal, Daniel, 42
Basić, Goran, 201
Bečirević, Ćamil, 96
Bečirević, Edina, 104n127
Bečirević, Igbala, 89
Bečirević, Meho, 96
Beglerbegović, Ibraham, 113
Begović, Gligor, 158, 160
Bera, Vojin, 117n43
Berberović, Adem, 96–97, 98, 98n103
Bernstein, Nina, 99–100
Beširević, Mugbila, 130
Bettelheim, Bruno, 37–38
Bijedić, Džemal, 181, 181n50
Blagojević, Mirko, 149, 169
B.M. (victim), 160
Boban, Mate, 25
Bojović, Radomir, 181
Boras, Franjo, 25
Bozuk, Jozo, 142n170
Brđanin, Radoslav, 29, 73, 113–114, 117, 125, 144, 210
Briggs, Harold, 62
Browning, Christopher, 7, 65
Budimir, Slavko, 110n16

240 NAME INDEX

Bulatović, Huso, 91n67
Bulatović, Ismet, 84
Bulatović, Željko, 138n154
Buljugić, Mirsad, 160
Burazerović, Faruk, 125
Butcher, Thomas, 32
Butrick, Daniel, 35

C (witness), 90
Čamo, Munib, 185
Campbell, David, 71–72
Carrington, Peter (Lord), 24
Ćatović, Asim "Malorilo", 183–184
Ćatović-Bijedić, Hadžera, 170n4
Ćehajić, Minka, 125n88
Ćehajić, Muhamed, 107, 112, 112n23, 125,
    125n88
Čekić, Gojko, 153, 162, 162n75
Chomsky, Noam, 71
Churchill, Winston, 114, 210
Cigar, Norman, 40
Cigelj, Jadranka, 129
Čivčić, Pero, 145
Clough, Marshall S., 45n63, 62
Cohen, Roger, 21
Comrade Duch, 64
Cornaton, Michel, 63
Crnalić, Dedo, 112, 139
Ćudić, Ekrem, 160
Čukojević, Muhamed, 93
Ćuprija, Anes, 98n103
Ćuprija, Mustafa, 96
Ćurtić, Husein "Apaka," 156, 160
Cutileiro, José, 24

D (witness), 90
Dalija, Hrnić, 142n170
Đapo, Asim, 182
Đapo, Nezir, 186
Dautović, Edina, 126n91, 130
Davidović, Milorad, 162–163, 163–164, 163n80
Đedanija, Marko, 141
Dedić, Ahil, 123, 123n80
Deichmann, Thomas, 71
Delić, Nedjeljko, 180
Demir, Himzo, 80, 81–82
Denčić, Nikola, 167
Denda, Radimir, 184
Đerić, Branko, 112n24

Derviševic, Nurko, 97, 98
Des Pres, Terrence, 38, 156
Despot, Momčilo, 153–154
Didović, Osman, 117n46
Dimač, Pero, 119
Dizdarević, Behija, 99n111
Dizdarević, Duda, 114n103
Dmitrović, Petar, 153
Đogo, Gojko, 20
Dolovac, Kemal, 93
Dolovac, Suvad, 92, 93
Došen, Damir, 135
Doubt, Keith, 40, 202
Draganović, Adil, 139, 139n160
Dragić, Milovan, 110n16
Dragičević, Luka, 21, 102–103, 103n125,
    104n129
Dragović, Mustafa, 99n111
Drljača, Simo, 110, 110n16, 112, 122, 130–131,
    133n127, 137, 139n157, 142n172, 143n177, 144,
    145, 146, 147
Duka, Miroslav, 179
Dukić, Živko, 115
Duraković, Nijaz, 111
Duratović, Smail, 127
Đurđević, Zoran, 151
Đurišić, Đure, 96
Đurković, Vojkan (Vojo), 161, 161n70, 164,
    164n83, 165, 165n85, 165n86
Džaferović, Dževad "Cipa," 97
Džaferović, Enes, 97
Džaferović, Enver, 92
Džafić, Zajko, 94
Džambasović, Asim, 76–77
Džananović, Esad, 100

Eicke, Theodor, 55
Eisenhower, Dwight David (General), 60
Ekmečić, Milorad, 22
Elkins, Caroline, 62
Emina S. (survivor of Vilina Vlas spa hotel
    dentention center), 89

Feierstein, Daniel, 31–32, 31n3, 36
Ferdinand, Franz (Archduke), 39
Fetahagić, Mustafa, 53n96
Filipović, Omer, 138
Fischer, Eugen, 53, 53n94
Foucault, Michel, 86

NAME INDEX 241

Fournet, Caroline, 43
Fustar, Dušan, 135

Gacić, Pero, 97
Gaćinović, Vladimir, 181, 181n49
Gaj, Petrov, 123
Gajić, Zoran, 138n154
Gavrilović, Drago, 102
Gligić, Dragoljub, 145
Gluščević, Hasan, 91n67
Gluščević, Hasib, 91n67
Gluščević, Mujo, 91n67
Govedarica, Boško, 189
Grubač, Radovan, 174, 189
Grynszpan, Herschel, 56
Gulašić, Alija, 159, 160
Gušić, Novica, 189
Gutić, Radivoje, 178
Gutman, Roy, 67, 131, 132

H (witness), 128, 129, 137
Hadžalić, Riza, 126
Hadžić, Hajra, 126n91, 130
Hadžić, Kemal, 183
Hadžiomerović, Zulfo, 160
Hafizović, Alma, 85
Hajra [prisoner in the Prijedor camp], 38
Halilović, Hanka, 83
Halilović, Husein, 160
Halilović, Pašaga, 166
Haljković, Suljo, 77
H.M. (victim), 96
Hammack, Phillip L., 42
Hamzić, Salih, 153
Harambašić, Fikret, 128–129
Haviv, Ron, 149
Hayden, Robert M., 6, 72–73
Hess, Rudolf, 56–57
Himmler, Heinrich, 55, 56, 57
Hitler, Adolf, 2, 54, 55, 113–114, 210
Hodžić, Dželal, 91n67
Hodžić, Dževad, 91n67
Hodžić, Jasmin , 95, 106
Hodžić, Latifa, 84
Hodžić, Sead, 91n67
Hodžić, Ševko, 81n22
Hukanović, Rezak, 38, 73, 123
Hurem, Razija "Šuhra," 85, 86
Hurem, Senada, 85, 86

Husović, Izet, 100, 101, 101n117

Ibišević, Esad, 88
Icić, Hase, 127
Ilić, Dragutin, 153, 156, 167
Ilić, Jovan, 14–15
Ilić, Mišo, 184
Ilić, Željko, 180, 184, 185, 186
Imamagić, Muharem, 97
Inđić, Boban, 97n98, 103n125
Inđić, Petko, 103n125
Irvin-Erickson, Douglas, 32, 33
Isić, Fatima, 97, 99, 99n111
Islamagić, Fuad, 160
Izetbegović, Alija, 22, 76n5

Javić, Milorad, 166
Jelačić, Fadil, 93
Jelisić, Goran, 152n20
Jović, Dragan, 151
Jovičić, Mico, 103n25
J.T. (witness), 94

Kačavenda, Vasilije (Bishop), 151n15
Kahriman, Abdullah "Dule," 100, 101
Kaiser, Andre, 131
Kalinić, Dragan, 29
Karadžić, Luka, 20
Karadžić, Radovan, 12, 17, 18, 18n21, 19–20, 22,
    25, 26, 27–28, 27n54, 28n28, 31, 76n5,
    101n120, 105, 128, 132, 147, 152, 163, 164n83,
    165, 166, 168, 174, 203
Karadzić, Vuk, 39, 205, 206
Karadžić-Zelem, Ljiljana, 101n120
Karagić, Nermin, 120
K.B. (witness), 110n15
Keljmendi, Aziz, 11
Kešmer, Hamed, 91n67, 95
Kešmer, Ibrahim, 91n67
Kešmer, Said, 95
Khun, Andreas, 165
Kitchener, Horatio Herbert (Field Marshal),
    50
Knežić, Marko, 171n6
Kolundžija, Dragan, 135
Konjanik, Alija, 158
Korkut, Derviš, 44
Kornjača, Duško, 171
Kos, Milojica "Krle", 145

242 NAME INDEX

Kovačević, Milan, 110n16, 112
Kovačević, Milomir "Kole," 78, 78n12, 81, 81n21
Kovačević, Nikola, 139n156
Kovačević, Predrag ("Špaga"), 138
Kozić Adem, 91n67
Krajišnik, Momčilo, 18, 19, 22, 25, 28, 28n58, 147, 152, 165, 165n86
Krsmanović, Oliver, 89, 103n25
Krstić, Djorde, 153
Krstić, Đorđe, 73, 153n26
Krzović, Ibrahim, 140
Kulelija, Zineta, 90
Kuljić, Neđo, 184
Kundačina, Tihomir, 172
Kuprešanin, Vojo, 18, 125, 128
Kuralić, Mirsad, 160
Kurspahić, Kemal, 10
Kurspahić, Osman, 92
Kuruzović, Slobodan, 110n16, 123, 141
Kustura, Islam, 87n51, 96, 97
Kustura, Zijad, 92
Kvočka, Miroslav, 145

Lazar Hrebeljanović (Prince), 11–12, 13
Lazić, Vinko B., 150
Lelek, Željko, 80, 89–90, 103
Lemkin, Raphael, 30, 31, 32–33, 33n12, 34, 36, 47
Lukić, Milan, 1, 81, 81n22, 84, 85, 86, 87, 88–89, 90, 97, 97n98, 99n106, 103–104, 104n129, 106
Lukić, Sredoje, 88, 89, 103, 104–105
Ljubišić, Branko, 171n7
Ljubojević, Dragomir, 152n19, 164, 168n105

Maass, Peter, 68, 89, 161
MacDonald, David B., 15, 40
Madley, Benjamin, 35–36
Maharero, Samuel, 51
Mahmuljin, Osman, 115
Mahmuljin, Velida, 130
Maidan, Rashid, 62n137
Makšić, Adis, 43
Maksimović, Mićo, 103
Malagić (family), 164
Maletić, Ranko, 118
Malović, Duško, 164
Mameledžija, Mirsad, 98

Mamuzo, Cigo, 123
Mandić, Boško, 110n16
Mandić, Momčilo, 79, 173–174, 174n19
Maksimović, Mićo, 103
Mandžo, Velija, 181
Mann, Michael, 19n22, 200
Manojlović, Lazar, 151, 151n12, 151n15, 199
Manuel de Céspedes, Carlos, 48
Marković, Brano, 100, 100n12
Marshall, Penny, 2, 71, 132
Maručić, Jozo, 125
Mayhew, Barnabas, 120
Mazowiecki, Tadeusz, 131, 139
McLeod, Charles, 120
Medić, Jasmin, 112n23
Medina (step-daughter of Hasena Bajramović), 85n40
Medunjanin, Anes, 127
Medunjanin, Bećir, 115, 127
Medunjanin, Sadeta, 115, 126n91, 127, 130, 142n170
Mehinović, Kemal, 158
Mejakić, Željko, 123, 130, 145
Melkić, Ahmet, 23n40
Menzilović, Ismet, 88
Menzilović, Mehmed, 88
Mersiha (survivor of Vilina Vlas spa hotel), 89
M.H. (witness), 90
Mijic, Ranko, 117n43
Milanković, Veljko, 108–109, 109n7
Milić, Milenko, 143n177
Miljanović, Bajro, 177
Milosavljević, Radovan, 89
Milošević, Slobodan, 11–13, 16, 24, 25, 39, 66, 101
Milošević, Miomir, 172–173
Mirković, Nenad, 92–93
Misić, Ljubiša, 153
Mišković, Simo, 109
Mladić, Ratko, 7, 28, 28n58, 29, 31, 142n172, 152, 163, 168, 174
Mlinarević, Ramo, 100
M.M. (victim), 96
Mock, Steven, 86, 197
Møller, Bjørn, 36
M.Š. (victim), 160
Mučovski, Rešad, 92
Muharemović, Hasena, 99n111
Muharemović, Nermina, 99n111

NAME INDEX   243

Muharemović, Nusreta, 99n111
Muharemović, Sena, 98n103
Mujačić, Sadik, 180
Mujadžić, Mirsad, 114, 114n32
Mujo (a detainee in the Omarska camp), 124
Muratagić, Šaban, 98–99, 98n103
Murguz, Junuz, 173
Murguz, Mehmed, 180, 182
Murtić, Abid, 92
Murtić, Bajro, 88
Murtić, Ibro, 88
Murtić, Ševal, 79
Murtić, Zineta, 85
Musić, Adem, 120
Musić, Sudbin, 120n65, 207
Mustafić, Šaban, 157
Mutić, Mile, 114
Mutić, Rade, 114

Nasić, Irfan, 121n72
Nedić, Milan, 65
N.M. (victim), 160
Novaković, Milan, 12, 152n29
Nuhanović, Amira (Dada), 85
Nuhanović, Avdija, 91n67

Ojdanić, Dragoljub, 77–78
Opotow, Susan, 42
Ostojić, Velibor, 13
Ovčina, Munib, 181

Pajić, Đoko, 153
Pajić, Nedeljko, 167
Pantelić, Miloš, 93
Paras, Miroslav, 145
Pandurević, Vinko102
Pavelić, Ante, 65
Pažin, Marinko, 177
Perišić, Momčilo, 172
Perišić, Risto, 79, 82, 100, 103
Pervan, Ramiz, 173, 177, 183–184, 186
Pervanić, Kemal, 38
Petrović, Vladimir, 39
Pidić, Hakija, 131
Pinochet, Augusto, 63
Pitzer, Andrea, 46–47, 49, 53
Pjevo, Sead, 95
Plavšić, Biljana, 21, 149, 150, 150n9, 152, 159, 168, 174

Poljo, Fatima, 84n34
Poljo, Šemso, 84
Poluga, Novak, 103n125
Poluga, Obrad, 103n125
Popović, Božidar, 138
Popović, Goran, 97
Popović, Vojin, 189
Prcać, Dragoljub, 145

Racković, Vitomir, 103
Radić, Mlađo "Krkan," 123, 130, 145
Radić, Predrag, 125
Rajak, Novo, 93, 103
Rajković, Zdenka, 125
Ramić, [First Name Unknown], 85
Rašković, Jovan, 12, 43 108
Ražnatović ("Arkan"), Željko, 24
Riedlmayer, András J., 44
Rieff, David, 44–45, 68–69
Ristić, Alen, 151
Ristić, Radojica, 103n125
Roberts, Frederick (Lord), 50
Rodic, Jugoslav, 117n
Rogan, Branko, 183–184, 183n63
Roosevelt, Franklin D., 59
Roosevelt, Theodore, 49
Rosenberg, Alfred, 44

Šabanović, Azmir, 84
Šabanović, Fadil, 160
Šabanović, Fata, 85
Šabanović, Ibro, 1, 85, 86, 197, 198
Šabanović, Murat, 78n13
Šabanović, Mustafa, 91n67
Šabanović, Salko, 100
Saddam Hussein, 63
Sadiković, Esad, 23n40, 112, 125
Šakotić, Veso, 181
Salić, Bekto, 96
Sarajlić (family), 164
Sarajlić, Mehmedalija, 38, 126, 134
Sarenac, Zorica, 174, 174n19
Sarić, Goran, 187
Sarić, Silvije, 125
Savanović, Dragan, 112, 118, 118n53
Savić, Jovica, 161, 168
Savić, Krsto, 189–190
Savić, Ljubiša "Mauzer," 149, 152
Savić, Momir, 87, 103

NAME INDEX

Šegrt, Branko, 177
Sejdić, Ahmet, 98
Sejdić, Fahrija, 98
Sejmenović (family), 164
Sejmenović, Mevludin, 128, 164
Šekarić, Dragan, 97n98, 103, 103n125
Selimbegović, Mirsad, 96
Sells, Michael A., 13, 42–43, 75n3, 202–203
Seric, Sabah, 155
S.H. (victim), 85
Shaw, Martin, 82
Sherwell, Philip, 78–79
Sibalo, Mustafa, 95
Sikirica, Duško, 135, 135n138
Sikora, Željko ("Monster Doctor), 114–115
Simić, Branko, 25
Simić, Vlado, 159
Šimšić, Boban, 84, 86, 87, 91n65, 103
Šišić, Bajro, 98
Sivac, Nusret, 119, 120n63, 131n117
Sivac, Nusreta, 113, 129, 132
Sivac, Sejad, 128n105
Škondric, Vaso, 117n43
Smajić, Ejub, 154, 160
Smajić, Eniz, 84
Smajić, Kemal, 95
Smajić, Medo, 81, 81n23
Smajić, Nezir, 98
Smajić, Sadija, 98n102
Smajić, Sadika, 81, 81n23
Smajić, Sumbula, 98
Smajlović, Fikret "Piklić", 157
Softić, Meho, 91n67
Softić, Samir, 91n67
Sokolović, Mehmed-paša, 75, 75n2
Solzhenitsyn, Alexandr, 34
Spahić, Ferid, 102n123
Spasojević, Danilo, 151, 151n16
Spasojević, Mićo, 98n103
Srdić, Srđo, 147
Stajić, Gojko, 189
Stajić, Milenko, 180
Stakić, Milomir, 107, 109, 110n16, 111, 112, 125, 145, 145n184
Stalin, Josef, 61, 114, 120
Stambolić, Ivan, 11
Stanišić, Mićo, 25–26, 104–105, 146, 150, 163–164, 169, 189
Stanković, Marko, 152n19

Starhonić, Enes, 95
Stevanović [Perpetrator], 180
Stiven (Serb police officer), 121n72
Stojanović, Velibor, 153
Stone, Dan, 46–47
Subašić, Suvad, 92
Subašić, Zijad, 78
Sućeska, Salko, 91n67
Suljagić, Emir, 69–70
Šušnjar, Milivoje, 90, 90n63

Tabeau, Ewa, 182
Tadić, Dušan, 128–129
Tadić, Duško, 129n109
Tadić, Milorad, 128n105
Tadić, Miroslav, 154–155
Talić, Momir, 118, 125, 132n121, 137
Tanasković, Nenad, 92, 103
Teodorević, Siniša, 138n154
Timotić, Milan, 95
Tito, Josip Broz, 10, 76
Todorović, Milenko, 155n38
Todorović, Nebojša, 97
Todorović, Stevan, 154
Tolimir, Zdravko, 155n38, 168n106
Tomić, Dobro, 103
Tomić, Dragan, 103
Traparić [perpetrator], 174n19
Traver, Ranko, 110n16
Traynor, Ian, 77–78
Trbić, Jusuf, 24n43, 149
Treanor, Patrick, 17–18
Trifković, Slavko, 93
Trnjanin, Fehim, 115
Trnjanin, Suad, 115
Tuđman, Franjo, 12, 16, 19, 108
Tufekčić, Junuz, 92–93
Tvrtković, Safet, 92, 93

Uljarević (Dr.), 82n25
Užičanin, Mula, 85

Valentino, Benjamin, 19n22
Vasilijević, Mitar, 90n63
Vasiljković, Dragan, 109n7, 144
Velić, Šerif, 126n93
Veselinović, Sveto, 20
VG-025 (ICTY witness), 97
VG-042 (ICTY witness), 81n22

NAME INDEX 245

VG-063 (ICTY witness), 85
VG-094 (ICTY witness), 88
VG-22 (witness to Visegrad negotiations), 79
VG-32 (ICTY witness), 82n25
VG-131 (ICTY witness), 89
Vilić, Husein, 91n67
Vlahović, Veselin "Batko", 25
Vojinović, Miloš, 116
Vokić, Milorad, 143n177
Vokić, Radovan, 130
Vom Rath, Ernst, 56
Von Trotha, Lothar, 51–52, 52n87
Vučerević, Milorad, 178
Vučinić, Slavko, 182
Vučurović, Božidar, 171, 172
Vujić, Radoslav, 125
Vujović, Goran, 172, 178, 182, 188, 188n85, 189–190
Vujović, Milorad, 171
Vukelić, Milutin, 139
Vuković, Dragan, 152n19
Vuković, Slobodan, 89
Vulliamy, Ed, 2, 67–68, 71, 132

Wachsmann, Nikolaus, 58
Walasak, Helen, 44
Waruhiu (Mau Mau Senior Chief), 61
Weine, Stevan, 38
Weisband, Edward, 36–37, 202
Wiesel, Elie, 37
Wolf, Frank, 162
Wyler y Nicolau, Valeriano, 48, 48n75

Zahirović, Džemal "Špajzer," 157, 160
Zarić, Zoran, 158
Zečević, Ferid, 160
Zejnilović, Safet, 82, 82n25, 82n26
Zeljala, Radmilo, 113, 117n46, 118, 144
Žigić, Zoran "Žiga," 145
Zukić, Behija, 81, 81n22, 81n23
Zukić, Džemo, 81, 81n22
Zukić, Fadil, 92
Zukić, Fatma, 92
Zulanović, Ahmo, 94
Zulfikarpašić, Adil, 16
Žunić, Nezir, 92, 93
Župljanin, Stojan, 104, 116, 125, 134n131, 144, 145n186, 146

Trial Judgments Index

Canada (Minister of Citizenship and Immigration) v. Rogan, 173n16, 176n27, 177n31, 179n40, 179n42, 179n43, 183n61, 183n62, 183n63, 184n64

Prosecutor v. Darko Mrđa (Sentencing Judgment), 134n128

Prosecutor v. Đorđević (Trial Judgment), 66n156

Prosecutor v. Dusko Sikirica, Damir Dosen, Dragan Kolundzija (Sentencing Judgment), 135n136, 135n137, 135n138, 135n139, 135n140, 136n141, 136n145, 136n146, 137n148, 137n149, 138n151

Prosecutor v. Duško Tadić (Decision), 141n168

Prosecutor v. Duško Tadić aka "Dule" (Opinion and Judgment),124n82, 124n823, 124n84, 129n107, 129n109, 141n168

Prosecutor v. Jadranko Prlić, Bruno Stojić, Slobodan Praljak, Milivoj Petković, Valentin Corić, Berislav Pušić (Prosecutor v. Prlić et al.) (Judgment, Volume III), 19n24

Prosecutor v. Jović et al., 151n16

Prosecutor v. Mićo Stanišić & Stojan Župljanin (Judgment, Volume 2), 25n47, 25n48, 29n66, 105n130, 145n186

Prosecutor v. Milan Lukić and Sredoje Lukić (Judgment), 81n22, 82n25, 83n28, 83n29

Prosecutor v. Milomir Stakić (Judgment), 109n9, 109n10

Prosecutor v. Miroslav Kvočka et al. (Judgment), 119n59

Prosecutor v. Mitar Vasiljević (Judgment), 76n6

Prosecutor v. Mitar Vasiljević (VG022 Witness statement), 77n9, 77n10, 79n16

Prosecutor v. Momčilo Krajišnik (Judgment), 162n77, 172n11, 173n15, 178n37

Prosecutor v. Radoslav Brđanin (Judgment), 108n4, 108n6, 109n8, 109n11, 114n31, 116n39, 116n40, 116n41, 117n44, 117n45, 117n47, 118n52, 125n87, 125n90, 126n98, 130n115, 132n121, 133n125, 134n129, 134n130, 136n144, 140n161, 143n178, 144n179, 144n181, 187n80, 210n16

Prosecutor v. Radovan Karadžić (Judgment), 19n21, 22n38, 23n41, 27n53, 27n54, 28n56, 28n57, 28n58, 28n60, 29n61, 28n62, 29n63, 29n64, 29n65, 79n17, 79n18, 105n31, 113n29, 113n30, 116n42, 118n51, 119n62, 121n69, 121n70, 125n86, 127n103, 129n110, 133n127, 136n143, 140n163, 141n169, 142n170, 143n177, 143n178, 144n180, 144n182, 145n183, 146n188, 148n1, 148n4, 149n6, 150n7, 150n8, 150n9, 150n10, 150n11, 152n17, 152n19, 152n21, 152n22, 153n24, 153n25, 153n27, 154n28, 154n29, 154n31, 154n32, 154n33, 154n34, 155n38, 156n41, 157n47, 157n50, 158n55, 159n61, 162n73, 163n79, 164n81, 164n82, 165n90, 165n91, 166n93, 167n99, 168n102, 168n103, 168n104, 168n105, 168n107, 169n108, 169n110, 169n111, 172n10, 102n1

Prosecutor v. Ratko Mladić (Judgment, Volume 4), 28n59, 153n23, 162n74, 162n75

Prosecutor v. Vlastimir Đorđević (Judgment, Volume 1), 66n156

Prosecutor v. Vojislav Šešelj (Trial Transcript), 159n63, 159n64

248   TRIAL JUDGMENTS INDEX

Prosecutor v. Željko Lelek (Second Instance Judgment), 106n133

Tužilac v. Branko Ljubišić, 171n7

Tužilaštvo BiH v. Babić Zoran i dr., 134n131

Tužilaštvo BiH v. Boban Šimšić (Appeals Chamber Verdict), 85n40, 85n41, 86n44

Tužilaštvo BiH v. Boban Šimšić (First Instance Verdict), 83n31, 84n32, 84n36, 85n37, 91n65, 91n66, 91n67

Tužilaštvo BiH v. Čivčić Petar i dr., 134n131

Tužilaštvo BiH v. Gligor Begović (First Instance Judgment), 160n66, 160n67

Tužilaštvo BiH v. Goran Vujović i dr. (First Instance Judgment), 179n41, 181n51, 182n55, 184n66, 184n67, 185n69

Tužilaštvo BiH v. Momir Savić (First Instance Judgment), 87n49, 87n50, 87n52

Tužilaštvo BiH v. Nenad Tanasković (First Instance Judgment), 93n75, 96n92, 96n93

Tužilaštvo BiH v. Oliver Krsmanović (First Instance Judgment), 92n73

Tužilaštvo BiH v. Predrag Milisavljević et al. (First Instance Verdict), 102n123

Tužilaštvo BiH v. Slobodan Taranjac et al., 120n65

Tužilaštvo BiH v. Vitomir Racković (First Instance Verdict), 100n113, 100n114, 100n115

Tužilaštvo BiH v. Željko Lelek (First Instance Verdict), 90n60, 90n61, 92n71

Tužilaštvo Bosne i Hercegovine v. Dragomir Soldat i dr., (Dragomir Soldat et al.), 119n56

Tužilaštvo Bosne i Hercegovine v. Dušan Milunić i dr. (Dušan Milunić et al.), 119n57

Tužilaštvo Bosne i Hercegovine v. Krsto Savić (First Instance Verdict), 175n26, 180n44, 189n89, 189n90, 190n91

Tužilaštvo Bosne i Hercegovine v. Petar Kovačević, (First Instance Verdict), 97n97, 99n107, 99n108, 99n109

Tužilaštvo Bosne i Hercegovine v. Ratko Bundalo i dr. (First Instance Judgment), 178n36

Tužilaštvo Bosne i Hercegovine v. Željko Mejakić i dr. (Mejakić et al.), (Verdict), 124n81, 126n91, 126n92, 126n95, 126n96, 126n100, 127n103, 127n104, 130n112, 130n113

Tužilaštvo KS v. Novo Rajak (Trial Judgment), 93n76, 93n77, 93n78, 93n79, 93n80, 95n85, 95n86, 95n87

Subject Index

ABiH Višegrad Brigade, 98
Agency for Population Movement and Exchange of Material Wealth (Agencija za preseljenje stanovništva i razmjenu materijalnih dobara), 116, 117
Algerian genocide, 33–34, 36
Alija's Specialists, 159. *See also* extremists
Ališići mosque, 143
Anfal Campaign (Iraq, 1988), 63
ARK (Autonomna Regija Krajina/Autonomous Region Krajina), 17, 18, 108–109, 110, 112, 113, 116–117, 125, 137, 141, 144, 146, 147; *Official Gazette*, 116
Arkan's Tigers, 24, 149, 168, 199
Assembly of the Bosnian Serb People of Prijedor Municipality, 109, 110, 110n16, 108
Assembly of the Serb Democratic Party, 108
Assembly of the Serb People, 27, 109n9
Assembly of the Serb R BiH, 109, 190
Assembly of the Union of Municipalities of East and Old Herzegovina, 171
Association of Bosanska Krajina Municipalities (Zajednica opština bosanske Krajine, ZOBK). *See* ZOBK
Atik mosque (Bijeljina), 167
Atmačići (village), 160
Atmačići mosque (Bijelina), 167
Autonomous Region of Romanija, 17
Autotransport Prijedor, 140
Avdić Mosque (Plana), 188
Avengers (Osvetnici), 87, 88, 90, 103, 104

Bajina Bašta (town), 98
Bajina Bašta Hydroelectric Dam, 98n99, 106

Banja Luka, 27, 29, 29n66, 108n5, 114, 122n75, 125, 128, 130, 131, 134, 137, 138,140, 141, 144, 205, 208; Banja Luka TV, 114, 141; District Court, 138n154; *Glas* (daily newspaper), 116; mosques, 143n176; Novo Groblje cemetery, 39n158; prison, 125n88; Security Services Center, 26, 120, 130–131, 133n127, 139n157, 145, 146; Serb Democratic Party (SDS) branch, 16–17
Barimo (village), 83, 106
Barimo religious school (*maktab*), 105
Batković (village), 152n18
Batković camp, 153–160; conditions, 156–157, 156n44; executions, 160; hangars, 153, 154n31, 155, 156; headquarters, 153; International Committee on the Red Cross visits to, 161–163; Kamen (rock), 153; Kapos, 157; mortality rate, 160; Šator (tent), 153; Vaga (weighing station), 153. *See also* Bijeljina (Autonomous Region Romanija-Birač)
Battle of Kosovo (June 1389), 11–12, 197
Battle of Waterberg (August 1904), 51
Belgrade, 14, 16, 20, 39, 65, 66, 70, 109, 141, 151n16, 163, 170n3; Belgrade TV, 178
Belgrade Initiative, 16
Belgrade University, 14, 170
Benkovac (JNA military camp), 108, 118
Bigotry, anti-Muslim, 21, 21n34, 138–139
Bijeljina (Autonomous Region Romanija-Birač), 7, 148–169; agricultural school (detention center), 162; Assembly, 169; bloody Eid in, 149–152; census, 9; crisis committee, 12, 152, 164, 168, 168n106, 169; ethnic composition 1991–2013, *196*; forced

249

250 SUBJECT INDEX

Bijeljina (*continued*)
  labor, 153, 158; fortified castle (detention center), 162; "4th of July" public utilities building (detention center in Bijeljina), 162; KP Dom Bijeljina (detention center), 162; "Mauzer's private jail" (slaughterhouse) (detention center), 162; name changing, 166–167; religious conversions, 166–167; sugar factory (detention center), 162; SUP (Secretariat for Internal Affairs) (detention center), 162. *See also* Batković camp
Bileća (Autonomous Region Herzegovina), 170–190; emperor's mosque, 105, 188; ethnic composition 1991–2013, *196*; municipal youth house (Đački Dom) 183–185; perpetrators, 188–190; prison, 173; SJB (Public Security Station), 179–182; SJB Bileća (police station), 173, 174, 179–182, 187, 188–189, 199; takeover of, 172–176; volunteers (*Bilećki dobrovoljci*), 173
"Bileća fighters" (*Bilećki borci*), 172
Bišćani (area), 118, 118n55, 136
Bleiburg Massacre, 13
Bosanska Jagodina (village), 102
Bosanska Krajina (municipality), 16, 65, 108, 108n5, 109, 122n74, 128
Bosanska Krupa (municipality), 108n6, 127
Bosanski Brod, 24
Bosanski Petrovac transit camp (1941), 65
Bosanski Šamac, 154, 155; crisis committee, 154, 155
Bosansko Grahovo (municipality), 108n5
Bosnia and Herzegovina: attack on, 23–25; democracy and division, 13–16; ethnic relations in, 10–29; parallel state institutions, 16–19; postwar reality, 204–208; previous research on concentration camps, 67–74; referendum on independence, 18–19, 23, 109n9, 129n110
Bosniak Patriotic League, 77, 78
Bosniaks, as subhuman, 21; as descendants of Ustaša, 21, 22–23; elites, 81–82; as portrayed as an existential threat, 20–21
Bosnian Croats (HDZ), 12, 13, 16, 25 30, 101, 115, 117, 140, 164, 170
Bosnian Serb Army (VRS). *See* VRS Vojska Republike Srpske (Army of Republika Srpska)
Bosnian Serbian News Agency (SRNA), 178

Bosnian Serb Police Force (MUP RS), 25–27
Božići (village), 113n26
Bratunac Health Center, 155
Brčko (village), 24, 73, 152, 154, 160, 168
Brezičani (village), 118; mosque, 143
"Bridging the Gap," 73
Briggs Plan (1950), 62

Čajetina (village), 78
Čajnice (village), 82n25, 171
Calling the Ghosts (1996 documentary), 129
"camps de regroupement" (Algeria, 1959–1961), 162
Čapljina (village), 175
Čarakovo (village in Prijedor), 44, 119, 140, 207; mosque, 119n60
Čavkarica pit, 171
Čejreci (village), 143; mosque, 143
Čelinac (municipality), 108
Čelopek camp, 154
censuses, 9; Bileća, 193; Bosnia Herzegovina, 15–16, 191–192; Prijedor, 107; 192–193; Višegrad, 76, 192
Center for Democracy and Transitional Justice, 73
Central Committee of the League of Communists of Serbia, 11
Chetniks (Četniks), 13, 78, 81n22, 86, 149, 169, 170
Chetnik songs, 86
"Christoslavic" views, 42–43
collective traumatization, 30–74; 200–203. *See also* trauma
Commission for Population Exchange, 154–155
Committee for Collecting Data on Crimes Committed Against Humanity and International Law, 101
Community Center Dobrun, 99–100
Community of Municipalities of Bosanka Krajina (Zajednica Opština Bosanske Krajine, ZOBK). *See* ZOBK
concentration camps: brutality, 31, 68, 152n 20, 198, 198; characteristics of according to Stone, 47; collective memory of, 208, comparisons and similarities, 194–200, 201; crisis committees role in establishing, 121, 203; definitions, 45–47, 69; historical background, 47–66; Holocaust and Republika

SUBJECT INDEX 251

Srpska systems compared, 72; place within their global context, 208–210; postwar memories, 204–208; Prijedor, 147; Prijedor Crisis Committee and, 147; previous research on in Bosnia and Herzegovina, 67–74; similarities between Soviet camps and British camps in Kenya, 45n63; Višegrad, 105–106
Concentration Camps: A Short History (Stone), 46
conversions, religious, in Bijeljina, 166–167
Court of Bosnia and Herzegovina, 4, 39, 86n44, 89, 91n65, 94, 139n156
"Creation of Changes of the of the Internal Borders of Yugoslavia, The" (booklet), 14
crisis committees (Krizni štab), 7; Bijeljina, 152, 164, 203; Bileća, 203; central role in cleansing process, 18, 121, 164, 203; Ljubija, 120; Prijedor, 112–114, 145, 147, 203; tasks of, 112n24; Višegrad, 203
Crnčići: mass grave, 102
Crni Vrh (village), 93
Croatia, 10, 15, 16, 17, 24, 27, 29, 70; concentration camps, 65; ethnic cleansing and, 9; JNA attack on, 171; tensions between Serbia and, 12, 15
Crystal City, Texas (American relocation camp site), 60
CSB Centar službe bezbjednosti (Security Services Center/Services), 25, 26, 116, 117n44, 172n11, 175n23; Banja Luka, 130–131, 133n127, 145, 145n186; Trebinje, 174, 175, 176n28, 189; Trebinje Report, 172
CSCE (Conference on Security and Co-operation in Europe): visits to Bileća, 187
cultural genocide, 10–11, 43
Cvetković-Maček Agreement (1939), 16, 25, 64–65

Đački Dom detention facility (Bileća), 9, 179, 180, 181, 183–185, 186, 187, 188, 189, 199, 206
Dayton Accords, 165, 193, 204
death camps (*logori smrti*), 6, 30, 33, 43, 58, 209
Đeće (village), 179
"Decision on the Organization and Work of the Prijedor Municipal Crisis Staff," 112, 112n25

dehumanization, 20–23, 42, 45; of Bosniak Muslims, 42–43
delegitimization, 42
demographic changes, 9, 191–194
denial, 2, 72–73
deportations, 101; massacres during, 102; from Prijedor, 140–141; as "voluntary" removal from Bijeljina, 163–166
Desaparecidos, Los (the disappeared ones) (Chile), 63
Detention Camp Guard Squad, 153
detention camps, 194, 209, Bileća, 176; Chile, 63; temporary, 121; Višegard, 197
disappearances, enforced, 100–101
Doboj (Serb region), 26, 140, 141, 154n31, 159
Dobrun (village), 77, 78, 95, 97; mosque, 105. *See also* Community Center Dobrun
Donja Lijeska (village), 93, 100
Donja Mahala (village), 156
Donje Podrinje (region), 3
Donji Dubovik(village), 102
Donji Vakuf (municipality), 108n5
Dretelj camp, 68n161
Drina Valley, 24, 105
Drinsko (village), 87, 101; mosque, 105
Dubrovnik, 76, 171, 173
Dubrovnik Municipal Court, 4

Eastern Bosnia Corps Command, 152, 153, 155n38, 167
Eastern Herzegovina, 7, 15, 170, 175
Ekonomija—Logor ratnih zarobljenika (LRZ). *See* Batković camp
electric shocks, 97, 177, 184, 184n66, 199
elitocide, 23n40
emperor's mosque: Bileća 108; Višegrad, 105
Endlösung der Judenfrage, 32,58
Energoinvest TMO- Bileća factory, 173
ethnically clean (etnički čisto), 39, 166, 200
ethnic cleansing ("etničko čišćenje"), 45, 69, 72, 115, 164, 165, 166, as a form of genocide, 8, 39–43, 47, 197, 200–204, 210
ethnoreligious cleansing, 5, 6, 9, 28, 112, 116, 147
European Commission Monitoring Mission (ECMM), 120
execution sites (Nazi German), 57
Executive Order 9066, 59

252   SUBJECT INDEX

exhumations, 13, 106; at Lake Perućac, 78n14, 87n53, 98n101, 101n117; at Slap, 98n101
expulsion: of Bosniaks, 47, 104n127, 118140, 165, 201
"extremists," 5, 18, 80, 114, 119n59, 159, 161. *See also* Alija's Specialists

Federal Yugoslavia, 15, 109n9
Federation of Bosnia and Herzegovina (FBiH), 4, 194, 204
"Final Solution of the Jewish Question," 57
First Serbian Uprising against the Ottoman Turks 1804, 11
FNU Vulačić (Belgrade Television), 178
Foča, 24, 28, 28n56, 73, 76, 78, 78n14, 148, 171, 176. *See also* KDP Foča camp, 6, 70, 95, 95n86, 178
forced labor, 52, 61, 64, 152n18, 208, 209; Batkovic camp, 201; Bijeljina, 153, 158; Majevica, 158; Manjača camp, 139; Uzamnica camp, 97; Vanek's mill, 160

Gacko (municipality), 170, 171, 174,175, 176, 176n28, 177–178, 190; Public Security Station, 189
Garavi Sokak (Sooty Alley), 103, 104
gas canisters, 185, 186
gazije (heroes (Turkish)), 117n48
genocide: definition, 41; ethnic cleansing as, 39–43, 200–203; societal reorganization, 31; trauma as, 30–37; UN Genocide Convention (1948), 30, 31, 34, 41
Gestapo, 55
Glamoč (municipality), 108n5, 116
Glas (Banja Luka based daily newspaper), 116
Glinje (village), 150
Gomjenica mosque, 143
Goražde (town), 79, 80, 82n25, 96, 97, 100
Gornja Lijesko (village), 91
Gornja Puharska mosque, 143
Gornje, 3, 102
Gornji Jakupovići mosque, 143
Gostilja (village), 84, 98
Graz, Austria, 25
Grbavica (area of Sarajevo), 24, 25
"Greater Serbia," 8, 12, 189
Grebak (village), 100
"Green Transversal," 21

Guantanamo Bay, 64
Gulag, 34–35, 38, 45, 61, 62, 154

Hambarine (village), 114n32, 117, 118, 136, 144
Hamid Beširović school, 206
Hamzići (village), 96
Hasan Veletovac Elementary School, 1, 3, 6, 8, 83–88, 91, 97, 101, 107, 205, 214(figure 12)
HDZ Hrvatska demokratska zajednica (Croatian Democratic Union), 12, 13, 14, 19, 26, 122, 125
Herceg-Bosna, 19, 19n24
Hereros, 51–52
historical comparative research, 4–5
Holiday Inn (Sarajevo), 17
Holijaci (Bosniak village), 96, 100, 105
Holijaci religious school (*maktab*), 105
homo sacer (outside the law), 151
"houses of spite" (*inat kuće*), 194
Human Rights Watch, 64
humiliation, 5, 6, 45, 72, 89, 164, 200, 201–202, Keraterm, 136; as recorded in survivor testimony, 37–39; Stari Zatvor Detention Center, 185
HVO Hrvatsko vijeće obrane (Croatian Defense Council), 44, 69, 156
HVO "Posavina" Brigade, 156
hygienic abuse, 162, 179, 201

ICTY (International Criminal Tribunal for the former Yugoslavia), 4, 24, 31, 39, 78, 81n22, 82n25, 90n63, 101, 104, 124, 129, 144, 145, 145n186, 159, 162, 162n75, 163–164, 166, 192, 203; Outreach Department, 73
il Kal grande (Sarajevo Sephardi synagogue), 43
Independent Autonomous Region of Northeastern Bosnia. *See* SAO Birač-Semberija
Independent State of Croatia (Nezavisna Država Hrvatska—NDH), 65
Independent Television News (ITN), 71
"Instruction for Organization and Activity of Organs for the Serb People in Bosnia and Herzegovina in Extraordinary Circumstances," 17
"Instruction for the work of the municipal Crisis Staffs of the Serbian People," 112n24
International Committee on the Red Cross (ICRC): visits to Bileća, 187

SUBJECT INDEX 253

"Intervention Squad" (Interventi vod), 133–134, 144, 145–146, 173
internment, 51: defined, 4; during World War I, 53–54; Cambodia, 64; China, 64; Serbia, 65; of Japanese Americans, 59–60; of Native Americans, 35
Išerić brdo, 102
"Islamic Arc," 21
Islamophobia, 21–22
istočna rudišta (Eastern Mine Tomašica), 142, 143

Jadovno camp, 65
Janja (Bosniak village), 150, 150n10, 157n50, 158, 163, 165n89, 166
Janjari (village), 150; mosque, 167
Jasenovac camp, 65
Javnost, 148, 171–172
Jelisić 'factory', 152
JNA (Jugoslovenska narodna armija/Yugoslav People's Army), 11, 14, 24, 29, 44, 76, 77–79, 80–81, 92, 95, 102, 103, 110, 111, 112n24, 118, 121, 144–144, 150, 152, 171, 172, 173, 176, 181; Benkovac military camp, 118; 43rd Brigade, 144; Prijedor barracks, 121; Rijeka Corps, 172; Second Military District headquarters, 29; 17th Corps, 150; Uzamnica military barracks, 95; Užice Corps (Visegradska brigade Vojske Republic Srpske), 77, 102

Kabernik (Bosniak village), 96, 100
Kalesija (municipality), 54
Kalinovik (municipality), 171, 175, 176, 178, 190; Public Security Station (SJB), 189
Kamičani (Bosniak village), 122, 136; mosque, 143
kapos, 57, 157, 208
Karađorđevo, Serbia, 16
KDP Foča camp, 6, 70, 95, 95n86, 178
Keraterm camp, 8, 37, 73, 115, 119, 120, 121, 121n69, 125n88, 130, 132, 135–137, 135n138, 139n160, 140, 142, 142n172, 145, 145n184, 147, 198, 201, 203, 205, 211; conditions, 135, 136n142; sexual abuse, 137
Kevljani: mass grave, 125, 127, 142, 142n170; mosque, 143
Khmer Rouge (Cambodia), 64
Killing Days, The (Pervanić), 38
killings, 5, 44, 92, 118, 200

KL: A History of the Nazi Concentration Camps (Wachsmann), 58
Kladanj, 101
Ključ (municipality), 108n5, 138, 139, 154, 160
Knindže (Croatian Serb paramilitary unit), 144
Konzentrationslager, 52, 54
Kozarac (Bosniak village), 115, 117, 117n46, 123, 129, 129n109, 130, 132, 143, 144, 193
Kozaruša mosque, 143
Kosovo Liberation Army (KLA), 66
Kotor Varoš (village), 108n5, 134; mosque (site of massacre in Hanifići), 44
Kozarski vijesnik (Radio-Television Prijedor), 109, 110, 114, 115, 117–118, 122n75
KP Dom Bijeljina (detention center), 162
Kragujevac (village), 91
Krajina. *See* Prijedor (Autonomous Region of Krajina); ARK (Autonomna Regija Krajina/ Autonomous Region Krajina)
Kristallnacht, 43, 56
Krpić mosque (Bijelina), 167
Kruščica (village), 65
Kula camp, 154n31, 168
Kupres (munincipality), 24, 108n5
Kurds, 63

Laktaši (municipality), 108
Lamovita (municipality), 113
Lapušnik (detention facility), 66
Lebensraum (living space), 5, 54
Lejljenca (village), 151
"Lim Bridge," 87
Lisbon Agreement (1982), 24
"List of participation in war of all v/o conscripts who had wartime assignments in the in the SJB/Public Security Station in the period from 4 August to 30 June 1996," 103n126
Living Marxism (magazine), 71
Ljubija: crisis committee, 120; football stadium (temporary detention center), 120, 121, 121n71, 121n72, 142; iron ore mines, 140, 143; mass grave, 120; VRS 6th Battalion, 120
Ljubinje (municipality), 171
Lopare, 148, 154
Love Thy Neighbor: A Story of War (Maass), 68
Luka concentration camp, 152n19, 154

SUBJECT INDEX

Macedonia, 28, 86, 101
Majevica, (mountain range), 158; forced labor, 158
Manjača camp, 67, 122, 122n74, 131, 132n121, 133n127, 137–139, 139n159, 139n160, 146, 154, 156n44, 160, 161, 167, 194, 199, 205
"Mapping of Detention Camps in Bosnia and Herzegovina, 1992–95" (project), 3–4, 73
"March on the Drina" (Serb patriotic song), 28n56
Marzhan camp (Roma camp), 54
massacres, 8, 9, 22, 23, 24, 29, 35, 49, 66, 67, 152, 170; Bleiburg, 13; Čarakovo, 119n60, 207; denial of, 73, 150; during deportations, 102; genocidal, 41; ; Korićanske stijene, 134n131; Majevica, 158; Omarska, 123; Prijedor, 119, 136; Višegard, 83
mass graves, 8, 9, 105–106; 120, 126, 130, 134, 136, 143–144; Barimo, 106; Chile, 63; concealment of the remains of victims, 142–143; concentration camps, 105–106, 198; Dizdarev potok, 142; Drina River, 106; Hrastova glavica pit, 125, 142; Jakarina kosa, 142; Kameničko točilo, 106; Kevljani, 125, 126, 142, 142n70; Korićanske stijene, 142; Kurtalići, 106; Lisac pit, 142, 142n70; Prijedor, 105, 142–143, 209; Redak, 120n67; Redak I, 120n67; ; "Sanitation" (sanacija), 142–143; Slap, 106; Srebrenica, 105; Stari Kevljani, 142; Tomašica, 142, 142n172; Trnopolje-Bešlagića mlin, 142; Trnopolje-Hrnići, 142; Trnopolje-Marići, 142; Trnopolje-Redžić, 142; Višegrad (Lake Perućac), 106
Mataruško Brdo (area), 118
Mau Mau Uprising (Kenya (1952–1960), 61–62
Mauzer's Panthers, 168, 168n105
Međeđa (village), 87
medical experiments, 53, 57
Mehmed-pasa Sokolović Bridge, 75, 78, 83, 84
Menzilovići (village), 88
Miladin Radojević school, 178
Miska Glava (village), 120, 121n71, 142
Miska Glava Dom (temporary detention camp), 121, 121n71
Mlada Bosna (terror organization), 181n49
"Modus Operandi of Municipalities in the Conditions that Republican Organs Cease to Function" (SDS position paper), 14

Mokra Gora (village), 102
Montenegro, 14, 15, 28, 28n6, 70, 77, 170, 172, 173, 175, 185
mortality rate, 6, 45, 191; Batović camp, 160; during the Spanish-Cuba war (1868–71), 48; Uzamnica camp, 97
Moše Pijade Military Barracks, 9, 176–179, 189
mosques, destruction of. See religious and cultural heritage, destruction of
Mostar, 68n161, 174, 175, 177
Mount Bjelašnica, 158
Mount Kozara, 23n40, 108
Mrkonjić Grad, 108n5; mosque, 143n176
mujahedin (derogatory term for non-Serb), 114
MUP (Ministarstvo unutarnjih poslova—Ministry of Interior): reserve police force, 25–27, 103, 104, 204; RS, 24, 29, 82, 83, 163, 163n80, 167, 168, 187, 188, 199
MUP Mostar, 174
Mušići (village), 88
Muslim Uighurs, 64
Mutnik mosque, 143

name changing: Bijeljina, 166–167
National Security Service, 167
Native American genocide, 35–36, 54
Native American reservations, 49
Nazi concentration camps: Auschwitz (1940), 33, 47, 56, 58, 65, 68, 72, 73; Belzec, 46, 57; Buchenwald (1937), 2, 55, 56; Chelmno, 57; Dachau (1933), 55, 57; extermination camps, 57; Flossenbürg (1938), 55; function of, 56; Gross-Rosen (1940), 57; Gusen (1939), 57; labor camps, 57; Majdanek (1943), 57; Mauthausen (1938), 56; Natzweiler (1940), 57; Neuengamme (1940), 57; prisoner of war camps, 57; Ravensbrück (1939), 56; Sachsenhausen (1936), 55; Sobibor, 46, 57; Stutthof (1942), 57; transit camps, 57; Treblinka, 46, 57, 73
Neretva River, 27
Neretva Valley, 77
Nevesinje (municipality), 171, 175, 176, 176n28, 177, 189, 190; Public Security Station (SJB), 189
Nevesinje Brigade, 189
Nikšić (city in Montenegro), 172
1936 Olympic Games, 54, 55

SUBJECT INDEX 255

NKVD (Soviet secret police), 61
Nohra (Thuringia) (village), 54
Nuremberg Race Laws of 1935, 53n94, 55

Ochstumsand camp, 54
Odžak (village), 91
Okolište (village), 79, 95, 97
Olovo (town), 86n47, 91n101, 102
Olympic Games, 54, 55
Omarska camp, 115, 118, 122–132, 136, 137, 139, 142, 145, 212; burning alive of detainees, 198; conditions, 124, 126, 129, 132; hangars, 122, 124, 124n82, 126, 128, 129; ICTY and, 73; postwar function, 205; red house (*crvena kuća*), 124; white house (*bijela kuća*), 124, 126, 127, 128n105
Omarska Investigative Center for Prisoners of War, 137
Omeragići (village), 84
One Long Night: A Global History of Concentration Camps (Pitzer), 46
Operation Bijeljina, 149–150
Orahovci (Bosniak village), 96, mosque, 105
Orahovci Elementary School, 8, 96, 100
Orahovice (village), 179–180
"Organic nationalism," 19n22
Organization of Islamic Countries, 22
Osojnica (Bosniak village), 93, 96
othering of Bosniaks, 40, 43
"Otmica u Sjeverinu" (documentary), 90n62

Paklenik pit, 102
Palančište, 113n26
paramilitary groups, 23, 24, 84, 104n127, 105, 143n177, 145, 146, 163, 172n11, 197. *See also* Arkin's Tigers, Avengers, Chetniks, Mauzer's Panthers, Wolves of Vučjak, White Eagles
Partisan camp (Foča), 6
Partisan Veterans Association (SUBNOR), 23n40
People's Republic of China, 64
perpetrators: aims, 159; Bileća, 188–190; Bijeljina, 167–169; brutality and sadistic conduct of, 202–203; meso- and micro-level, 7–8, 203–204
Prijedor, 144–146; Višegrad, 102–105
"person under control" (PUC), 64

Petrodavnsko lilanje (feast of St. Peter's Day), 27
Philippines: United States "humanitarian" intervention (December 1899), 48–49
Pjevo, 95
Podgradci, 144
Popular Army Camp Tikrit (Iraq), 63
Popular Army Camp Topzawa (Iraq), 63
"Posavina Corridor," 3, 148
Poturice (derogative term), 21, 21n32
"preventive detention" (*Vorbeugungshaft*), 55
Priboj (town), 78, 158
Prijedor (Autonomous Region of Krajina), 107–147; crisis committee, 112–114; ethnic composition 1991–2013, 195; killing days, 115–122; media, 114–115; Municipal Board of the SDS, 109, 110; Municipal Executive Committee, 112n24, 112n25; Municipal People's Defense, 112n25; Municipal Secretariat for Town Planning, Housing, Utilities and Legal Property Affairs, 112–113n25; Municipal Territorial Defense, 112n25; Public Security Station, 110, 110n16, 112n25, 116n43, 130, 133n127, 139n157, 141–145
Prijedor Center, 113
Prijedor Chronicles (Prijedorska hronika), 114, 141
Prijedor SJB Building (temporary detention camp), 121
Prijepolje (town), 78
Prnjavor (municipality), 108n5, 109
"protective detention" (*Schutzhaft*), 55
PTSD, 159n161, 206, rape as a reason for, 206
Public Security Stations. *See* SJB (Služba javne bezbjednosti/Public Security Station)
Public Utilities Company, 110
Puharska mosque, 143

Radio Bijeljina, 149
Radio Prijedor, 111, 113, 114, 117n46
Radmilovo (formally Kozarac), 118
Rakovćani (village), 119, 136
rape, 32, 35, 40, 61; at exclusive women's detention camps, 3; genocidal, 70–71; Hasan Veletovac School, 205; Keraterm, 137; of males, 92, 202; mass, 70, 202; means to inflict maximum trauma, 209; as a modus operandi within camps, 70, 208; Omarska camp, 126, 128; psychological

256 SUBJECT INDEX

rape (*continued*)
    destruction through, 191, 202; PTSD due to,
    206; as a tool for ethnic cleansing, 41; sur-
    vivors, 207; survivor testimony, 85, 129–130,
    137, 177; Trnopolje camp, 133; Vatrogasni
    dom (fire station), 91–94; Vilina Vlas Hotel,
    88–90, 90n61, 106, *206*, 212; by the VRS
    volunteer unit, 151. *See also* sexual abuse
Rape Warfare: The Hidden Genocide in Bosnia
    Herzegovina and Croatia (Allen), 70
Rebić (village), 179
(re)concentrados, 48
reburials: importance, 13
re-education camps, 45, 61, 209
religious and cultural heritage, destruction of,
    43–45, 203; Bijeljina, 167; Prijedor, 143;
    Višegrad, 105
"Reports from Prijedor, Bosanski Novi, and
    Sanski Most SJBs regarding the current sit-
    uation of detainees, detention centers and
    refugees and the role of SJBs in relation to
    these," 116
Republic of Serbia Krajina, 24
Republika Srpska (RS): Government Report,
    187–188; Ministry of Defense, 111, 141; Min-
    istry of Information, 14; Ministry of Inte-
    rior Srbinje Public Security Centre, 103n116
"repurchase-your-child" tactic, 84
Reserve Police Forces of the RS Ministry of
    the Interior, 87, 103, 110
Reservist Officers' School. *See* Moše Pijade
    Military Barracks
River Drina, 9, 27, 28, 28n56, 75n1, 81, 81n22,
    83, 84, 84n36, 87, 90, 91, 95, 98, 98n99, 100,
    101, 105–106, 148, 164, 204
Rizvanovići (village), 119; mosque, 143
Rogatica (municipality), 20, 95, 105, 154
Rudo (municipality), 171
RŽR "Ljubija" a.d. Prijedor (Ljubija iron ore
    mine), 143

SA (Sturmabteilungen, Storm Troopers), 55
Sabirni Centar Batković. *See* Batković camp
Samački hotel, 177
Sana River, 118, 140, 146, 193
Sanski Most (municipality), 108n5, 116,
    116n43, 117, 130, 138–139, 154
SAO Birač-Semberija, 24, 148
SAO Herzegovina, 171, 172, 178, 187, 189

SAO Semberija, 150, 167, 168–169
SAO Srpska autonomna oblast (Serbian
    Autonomous Regions), 7, 172n11
Sarajevo Haggadah, 43–44
Sava River, 148, 153
Savez logoraša BiH (association of former
    camp detainees), 69; Center for Research
    and Documentation, 69
SDA (Stranka demokratske akcije/Party of
    Democratic Action), 13, 14, 19, 26, 43, 76,
    76n5, 79, 80, 107, 111, 112, 114, 122, 128, 139
SDB (Služba državne bezbjednosti/State Secu-
    rity Service), 26
SDS (Srpska demokratska stranka/Serb Dem-
    ocratic Party), 12, 14, 17, 19, 26, 82, 108n4,
    112, 113, 125, 151, 152n19, 164, 165, 168, 171,
    172; attacks on villages around Prijedor, 114;
    Banja Luka branch, 16; Bijeljina branch, 152,
    168; cooperation with JNA, 77; crisis com-
    mittees, 18, 79, 103, 112, 152, 164; Deputies
    Club, 18n11; elections, 76, 76n5, 107, 109;
    Glavni Odbor (General Committee),
    79n118; "Islamic threat," 43; Kozarac,
    129n109; meeting at the Holiday Inn in
    Sarajevo (December 20, 1991), 17, 18; meet-
    ing in Bileća (June 1992), 174; militias, 23;
    negotiations with JNA and SDA, 76; orga-
    nized exhumations of Serb genocide vic-
    tims from World War II, 13; Pale HQ, 152;
    Prijedor, 110; Prijedor Municipal Board,
    119, 110; Rogatica, 20
Seasons in Hell (Vulliamy), 67
šehiti (martyrs (Turkish)), 117n48
Selište (village), 181
Semberijske *novine* (newspaper), 149
Serb Autonomous Region of Birač-Semberija,
    17
Serbia and Croatia, tension between, 12, 15
Serbian Academy of Arts and Sciences
    (SANU), 10
Serbian Autonomous District of Herzegovina,
    26
Serbian Autonomous District of Northern
    Bosnia, 26
Serbian Autonomous District of Semberija, 7,
    26, 148, 150, 167
Serbian Ministry of Interior, 78
Serbian Orthodox Church, 1, 13, 40, 86, 118,
    127

SUBJECT INDEX 257

Serbian Republic Army Main Staff, 118
Serb Radical Party (SRS), 169
Serb Republic of Bosnia and Herzegovina, 18, 23, 189
Serb Territorial Defense, 149
Serb Volunteer Guard, 168
Šešelj's Chetniks. *See* Chetniks
sexual abuse, 5, 6, 70, 85, 90n61, 94, 98–99, 128, 129, 130, 159, 162n75, 199, 200. *See also* rape
"shame-camps," 202
Shark Island (Haifischinsel) concentration camp (Lüderitz), 53
Sijerčić Tomb, 105
Šipovo (municipality), 108n5
Six Strategic Goals of the Serbian People, 8, 27–29, 28n58, 29, 47, 148, 190, 200, 203–204
SJB (Služba javne bezbjednosti/Public Security Station), 25, 26–27, 110n16, 117n44, 120, 188; Bijeljina, 169, 172; Bileća, 172n11; 173, 174, 177, 179–182, 183, 185, 186, 187, 188–189, 197, 199; Bosanski Novi, 116, 117, 116n43; Bosanski šamać, 154; Gacko, 189; Kalinovik, 189; Nevesinje, 189; Prijedor, 110, 112n25, 116, 117, 116n4, 121n69, 122, 130, 133n127, 133, 139n157, 144, 145, 146, 147; Sanski Most, 116, 117, 116n43, 138–139; Stari Zatvor, 189; Trebinje, 172n11; Uglevik, 150, 150n11; Višegrad, 80, 82, 92, 93, 103n126, 199
"SJB/Public Security Station in the period from 4 August 1991 to 30 June 1996," (document), 103n126
Sjeverin (village), 90, 104
Sjeverni logor military barracks (Mostar), 177
Skender Vakuf (municipality), 108n5, 134
Slap (village): exhumations, 98n101, 100; mass grave, 106
slave labor, 45, 52, 99, 158
Smrijeće (village), 102
SNG (Srpska nacionalna garda/Serbian National Guard), 168, 168n106
Snježnica (village), 150
"Snowflakes" (Pahuljice), 164
Socialist Democratic Party, 11
"Socialist Republic of Bosnia and Herzegovina State Security Service (SRBiH MUP SDB) Rulebook on Wartime Organization," 26
Socialist Republic of Yugoslavia, 11

sofa (stone wall bridge balcony), 83
Sokolac (municipality), 154
Sonderkommandos, 58
South African War (Boer War) (1899–1902), 49–51
Spanish-Cuban Ten Year's War (1868–78), 48–49
Special Police Brigade (SPB), 167
Srbac (municipality), 108n5
Srbinje (formerly Foča), 22
Srebrenica (UN Safe Area), 2, 5, 31, 105, 155; genocide in, 73, 191
Srednja Trnova (Bijelina), 150; mosque, 167
Sremska Mitrovica (city): mass grave, 164
Srpska narodna čitaonica (Serbian National Reading Room), 172
SRS (Srpska radikalna stranka/Serbian Radical Party), 169
SS (Schutzstaffel), 55, 56, 57, 58, 59
St. Peter's Day (Petrovdan), 127, 198, 202
St. Vitus Day (Vidovdan), 1, 197
"Stara Hercegovina" (SDS Regional Council), 76
Stari Grad (town), 116
Stari Zatvor Detention Center, 185–186
Staro Sajmište internment camp (Serbia), 65–66
"State Commission for the Free Transfer of Civilian Population," 165n85
Stolac (town), 172, 175, 177, 178
summer returnees (*ljetni povratnici*), 193–194
SUP (Sekreterijat unutrašnjih poslova/Secretariat for Internal Affairs), 141, 162, 163, 163n80, 174
"Surviving All Therapies" ("Preživio sve terapije") (article), 115
Survivor: An Anatomy of Life in the Death Camps (Des Pres), 38
survivors: current state of, 207–208; state law recognizing, 208. *See also* testimonies
survivor testimony: humiliation and trauma, 37–38
Sušica camp, 154, 154n31, 167

tamić (TAM—*Tovarna avtomobilov Maribor*, Truck Company), 126, 126n99
tear gas, 136, 186, 199
Tenth Circle of Hell, The (Hukanović), 38, 73

258 SUBJECT INDEX

Territorial Defense and General People's Protection, 16n14, 37, 38, 39, 67
testimonies: false, 100–101; survivor, 4, 37–38, 131, 202, 208
Titov Drvar (municipality), 108n5
Tjideng camp (Jakarta, Indonesia), 69
Tomanića kosa (mountainous ridge), 15
TO (Teritorijalna odbrana/Territorial Defense), 25, 77, 110, 110n16, 111, 112n24, 117, 149, 168n105, 111; Bileća, 173; Omarska, 125; Prijedor, 112n25; SAO Semberija, 168–169; Višegrad, 168–169
Transitional Justice (NGO), 73
Transitional Justice, Accountability and Remembrance in B&H (TJAR in BiH), 73
trauma: destructive power of, 33–34. *See also* collective traumatization
Travnik (town/municipality), 133, 134, 141
Treaty of Vereeniging (1902), 51
Trebinje (municipality), 26, 170, 171, 172, 174, 175, 176, 182
Trnopolje camp, 2, 3, 6, 67, 132–134; 133n127, 140, 141, 142, 145, 161, 207; playground and school building, *211*
Tukovi (suburb of Bosnia and Herzegovina), 113n26, 133

Ugljevik (village), 148, 154; Public Security Station (SJB), 150, 150n11
Umoljani (village), 143; mosque, 143n176
United Nations (UN), 131
United Nations General Assembly (UNGA), 40
United Nations Genocide Convention (1948), 30, 31, 34, 41
United Nations High Commissioner for Refugees (UNHCR), 125
United Nations Security Council (UNSC), 81, 158; Resolution 752, 81
Upper Podrinje (region), 7
Ustaše (Croatian fascist and ultranationalist organization), 43
Uvac River, 95
Uzamnica camp, 79, 92, 93, 95–99, 100

Vancouver Federal Court in Canada, 4
Vanek's mill (Vanekov Mlin), 160
Večernje Novosti (newspaper), 10

Velatovo (village), 102
victimhood myth, 12, 13
Vilina Vlas Hotel, 8, 88–90, 90n61, 90n63, 106, 197, 198, 202, 206, *212*
Višegrad, 75–106; attack from Serbia, 76–81; ethnic composition 1991–2013, *195*; hydroelectric dam, 78, 78n13, 95, 98n99, 106; mass graves, 105–106; police station, 92–95, *213*; Public Security Station (SJB), 80, 82, 92, 93, 103n126; secondary school, 80; spa, 8, 88; Ušće Sports Center, 80; Vatrogasni dom (fire station), 91, 197, 202, 206, *213*
Višegrad Tactical Group (Taktička grupa Višegrad), 102
Vlada narodnog spasa (Government of National Salvation) (Nazi puppet regime, 1941), 65
Vlahovići (village), 84
Vlasenica (village), 24, 105, 154, 155n39
Vocational Training Internment Camps (Xinjiang, China), 64
Volkdeutsche, 39
VRS (Vojska Republike Srpske/Army of Republika Srpska; 1, 7, 29, 44, 69, 81, 83, 84, 87, 89, 90, 91, 92, 95, 96, 97, 98, 99, 100, 102, 103, 104, 104n129, 105, 117, 118, 119n60, 131n117, 142n172, 143, 146, 153, 154, 156, 161, 163, 165, 166, 167, 167n97, 168, 168n105, 172, 175; Eastern Bosnian Corps, 153; 5th Kozara Brigade, 119; 5th Military Police Battalion (Vlasenica), 155n39; 1st Krajina Corps (1 KK), 118, 132n121, 137, 139, 156; 43rd Motorized Brigade, 144, 146; 4th Company of the Višegrad Brigade, 103; Goražde Brigade, 103; Herzegovina Corps, 178; Main Staff, 174; Prijedor Brigade, 118; 7th Battalion, 176; 6th Krajina Brigade, 119, 144; 6th Ljubija Battalion of the 43rd Brigade, 120; 343rd Brigade, 144; 3rd Battalion IBK, 155n39; 3rd Company of the Višegrad Brigade, 87, 103; 3rd Semberija Brigade, 165–166; Višegrad Brigade87, 102 volunteer unit, 151
Vukovar (village), 76
Vukšići (village using forced labor), 158

"War Presidency" (Prijedor Crisis Committee), 113, 113n27, 145

SUBJECT INDEX 259

War Relocation Authority (WRA), 59
"Weekend returnees" (*vikendaši*), 193–195
Weimar, 2, 54, 56, 59
When History Is a Nightmare (Weine), 38
white camps vs. black camps, 50–51
White Eagles (Beli orlovi), 78, 103, 104
Witness to Genocide (Gutman), 67
"Wolves of Vučjak" (*Vukovi s Vučjaka*), 108–109
World War I, 28n56, 53 53n96, 54
World War II, 8, 13, 16 22, 23, 23n40, 44, 56, 59, 59n122, 60, 64–65, 108, 146, 170, 170n3, 171, 205, 206

Yugoslav Federal SUP, 163, 163n80

Žagre (village), 102, 119n57
Zagreb, 14, 16, 21, 141
Zapadna Bosna (militia), 69
Žarko Zgonjanin Barracks, 121n69
Zecovi (village), 119
Žeger Bridge, 140
Žepa (UN enclave), 84, 94, 95, 96, 100
Živinice (municipality), 154
Žlijeb (village) 84, 91, 91n65; mosque, 105
ZOBK (Zajednica opština Bosanske Krajine/ Community [Association] of Bosanska Krajina Municipalities), 16–17, 108
Zvornik (village), 24, 105, 154, 164, 168
Zvornik Brigade (Zvornička brigada Vojske RS), 102
Župa (village), 86, 102